6TH EDITION

REAL ESTATE Exam GUIDE

Designed for ASI Sales and Broker Exams

William H. Pivar

Dearborn™

Real Estate Education

While a great deal of care has been taken to provide accurate and current information, the ideas, suggestions, general principles, and conclusions presented in this text are subject to local, state and federal laws and regulations, court cases, and any revisions of same. The reader is thus urged to consult legal counsel regarding any points of law—this publication should not be used as a substitute for competent legal advice.

Publisher: Diana Faulhaber
Development Editor: Anne Huston
Managing Editor: Ronald J. Liszkowski
Art and Design Manager: Lucy Jenkins

Published by Real Estate Education Company®,
a division of Dearborn Financial Publishing, Inc.®
155 North Wacker Drive
Chicago, IL 60606-1719
(312) 836-4400
http://www.REcampus.com

Printed in the United States of America.

10   9   8   7   6   5

Library of Congress Cataloging-in-Publication Data

Pivar, William H.
    Real estate exam guide : designed for ASI sales and broker exams /
William H. Pivar. — 6th ed.
        p.   cm.
    Includes index.
    ISBN 0-7931-3655-5
    1. Real estate agents—Licenses—United States—Examinations,
questions, etc.   2. Real estate business—Licenses—United States—
Examinations, questions, etc.   3. Real property—United States—
Examinations, questions, etc.   I. Title.
HD278.P58   2000
333.33'076—dc21   00-032331

Contents

Foreword

In compiling this study guide for the salesperson and broker examinations administered by Assessment Systems, Inc. (ASI), we have tried to provide the necessary information to candidates prior to their taking the ASI examination. Note, however, that ASI is not responsible for the content of this book. The structure of this book follows the content outline that was put together by ASI and has been accepted by various jurisdictions for use in their licensure process. ASI is a testing service and as such is responsible for the structure of testing programs.

This guide was written for salesperson and broker examinations in all of the ASI exam states. If your class instructor does not cover all the material in this guide, it may be because some material or terminology is not covered in your state examination. Keep in mind, however, that you can never know too much, especially when preparing for a career in which you will aid buyers and sellers in making some of their most important life decisions.

Because the intent of this study guide is to provide helpful information to candidates preparing for the examination, we hope you find this sixth edition to be of value. We wish you success on the examination and in your career.

—The Editors

> If you have any questions relating to the text as well as suggestions for future editions, you can contact the author at pivarfish@webtv.net.
>
> William H. Pivar

Acknowledgments

My very special thanks to the following individuals for their assistance with the sixth edition of *Real Estate Exam Guide*: Ron Baker, Alamo Real Estate Institute, San Antonio, Texas; Thomas Battle, Real Estate Certification Program, Bloomington, Indiana; Kenneth Beer, Beer School of Real Estate, Milford, Indiana; Stephanie Blackburn, Jones College, Denver, Colorado; Darryl Bradshaw, Mykut Real Estate School, Lynwood, Washingon; Richard Clemmer, D&D School of Real Estate, Johnson City, Tennessee; Kay Knox Crawford, Continual Learning Institute, Nashville, Tennessee; Michael C. Glazer, Ivy Tech State College, Indianapolis, Indiana; Katharine Hale, Arizona School of Real Estate and Business, Scottsdale; Kent Keahey, Broadway School of Real Estate, Hot Springs, Arkansas; Peggy McConnochie, Alaska Coastal Homes, Inc., Juneau, Alaska; John Morgan, Morgan Testing Services, Waterford, Connecticut; Jerry Passon, North Central Institute, Clarksville, Tennessee; Janice Price, Partners Real Estate School, Highland, Indiana; Larry Rickard, Realty School of Kansas, Wichita, Kansas; Phyllis Rudnick, Annex Real Estate School, Quincy, Massachusetts; Joan Sheppard, Sheppard & Associates, Anchorage, Alaska; Marie Spodek, Professional Real Estate Services, David City, Nebraska; Arnold Stringham, Stringham Real Estate School, Salt Lake City, Utah; Ruth Vella, Omega Real Estate School, Wilmington, Delaware; and Jerry Wooten, Tucker School of Real Estate, Indianapolis, Indiana.

—William H. Pivar
Real Estate Exam Guide

The ASI Examination

ABOUT THE EXAMINATION

The ASI real estate examination was developed by the staff of Assessment Systems, Inc. (ASI), in conjunction with national examination committees. ASI, an independent testing company, administers the exam under contract with state licensing authorities.

The examination is not designed to be a test of language ability, reading, or test-taking skill. Its purpose is to identify candidates who have sufficient skills and knowledge to serve the interests of the public, and to lead those who are lacking in these skills to further study. The material you will be tested on was selected for use after analyzing numerous responses from real estate salespeople and brokers as to the scope of tasks required by their profession and the knowledge and skills needed to perform these tasks.

Bear in mind that the purpose of a licensing exam is not to disqualify applicants but to protect the public. This is done by requiring real estate salespeople and brokers to have the knowledge necessary to meet their professional obligations.

ASI's examination is divided into two parts: Part One covers general topics and Part Two covers state laws. All questions are of the four-answer multiple-choice variety. The examination contains 110 questions that count for salesperson candidates (80 general knowledge and 30 state-specific) and 120 questions that count for broker candidates (80 general knowledge and 40 state-specific).

You will have a greater total number of questions on your examination because pretest questions will be included. Pretest questions are given to evaluate performance levels that help to determine whether the questions are appropriate for future examinations. These questions will not appear to be different from the other questions and they will not count toward your examination score; however, they will not be identified as pretest questions.

Your state licensing agency will provide you with a "Real Estate Assessment for Licensure Candidate Guide" (or Handbook) that sets forth the content outline for your state portion of the examination. It is recommended that you use state manuals to study for the state section of your examination. These manuals contain specific state laws and may be available from your state licensing agency.

The following is the general-content outline for the general portion of your ASI examination. This book is arranged to follow this outline as closely as possible.

General Content Outline

The general portion of the real estate exam will be in accordance with the content outline below, which contains five areas to be covered.

For educational purposes, we have arranged the content of this exam guide into eight chapters, including one on mathematics, plus a collection of review examinations. This guide covers every topic presented in the following ASI outline.

ASI General Real Estate Examination Content Outline for Both Sales and Broker Examinations

The exams have 80 scored questions and 5 pretest questions.
Approximately 10 percent of the scored questions will involve mathematical computations.

I. Real Property Characteristics, Definitions, Ownership, Restrictions, and Transfer (20% - 16 questions)

    A.   Definitions, Descriptions, and Ways To Hold Title
        1.   Elements of Real and Personal Property
        2.   Property Description and Legal Description
        3.   Estates in Real Property
        4.   Forms, Rights, Interests, and Obligations of Ownership
    B.   Land Use Controls and Restrictions
        1.   Public (e.g., Zoning, Taxation, Police Power)
        2.   Private (e.g., Liens, Encumbrances, Recording and Priorities, Subdivision/Association Rules)
    C.   Transfer/Alienation of Title to Real Property
        1.   Voluntary and Involuntary
        2.   Deeds, Warranties, and Defects in Title

II. Assessing and Explaining Property Valuation and the Appraisal Process (15% - 12 Questions)

    A.   Principles, Types, and Estimates of Property Value
    B.   Influences on Property Value
    C.   Approaches to Property Valuation and Investment Analysis

III. Contracts, Agency Relationships with Buyers and Sellers, and Federal Requirements (25% - 20 Questions)

    A.   Contract Elements, Types (e.g., Valid, Enforceable), and Terminology
    B.   Agency Employment Contracts, Listing and Buyer Agency Agreements, and Required Elements
    C.   Purchase/Sales Contracts and Contingencies
    D.   General Agency Relationships and Fiduciary Responsibilities
    E.   Property Conditions and Disclosures (e.g., Property, Environmental)
    F.   Procedures and Laws Governing Real Estate Activities (e.g., Federal Fair Housing Act, Americans with Disabilities Act, Antitrust, Marketing Controls)

IV. Financing the Transaction and Settlement (25% - 20 Questions)

    A.   Financing Components
        1.   Financing Instruments (e.g., Notes, Mortgages, Contract for Deed, Deed of Trust)

    2.   Sources (e.g., Primary and Secondary Mortgage Markets, Seller Financing)

    3.   Types of Loans

    4.   Financing Concepts and Terminology

  B.   Lender Requirements and Obligations

  C.   Settlement Procedures

  D.   Settlement Documents (e.g., Title Review, RESPA)

  E.   Financing Costs, Property Taxation, Proration Calculations, and Other Closing Costs

V.   Leases, Rents, and Property Management (15% - 12 Questions)

  A.   Types and Elements of Leasehold Estates, Leases, Lease Clauses, and Rental Agreements

  B.   Lessor and Lessee Rights, Responsibilities, and Recourse

  C.   Management Contracts and Obligations of Parties

Candidates have from three and one-half to four hours to take the test, depending on the particular state. Test scores are based on the number of questions answered correctly. The passing score for each state is established by the state real estate agency based on standards of competence that it deems appropriate for licensure.

Questions are based on topics that real estate salespeople or brokers actually deal with in the course of their work. Questions appear at the end of each chapter.

Key words such as MOST, BEST, or MOST LIKELY will be CAPITALIZED. While ASI avoids using negative questions in the general portion of the examination, negative questions using terms such as EXCEPT or LEAST LIKELY might be used in the state-specific portion of your examination, so you should be prepared to see them. The possibility of inclusion of a negative question reinforces the need for careful reading.

The examination may contain case-study questions in which a block of information is given, followed by two or three related questions. However, questions stand alone and are not based on preceding answers. Thus, one wrong answer does not affect the score on another question.

Questions are carefully reviewed to make certain there are no clues to the answer that could aid a candidate who doesn't know the material. Each question is either a clear and straightforward statement that calls for one of four answers, or it is an incomplete statement (stem) to be completed with the correct answer.

Each question has one right answer that will be clear to those candidates prepared for the examination. Wrong answers are often distracters that either tend to confuse or seem plausible to someone who does not fully understand what is sought. These wrong answers are likely to come from any of the following:

- Common misconceptions
- Common errors (a math answer resulting from a common computation error is likely to agree with one of the distracters)
- A carefully worded but incorrect statement that will appear plausible to an uninformed candidate
- Statements that, although true, are not really relevant to the question

The exam takes a positive approach to achieve fair measurement of a candidate's knowledge and skills. Therefore, do not fear your examination but treat it as an opportunity to demonstrate the knowledge and skills you have acquired to serve others as a real estate salesperson or broker.

HOW TO STUDY

Any career decision requires preparation, and preparing for a career in real estate takes time and dedication. Although your motivation to spend the time necessary must come from within, a few simple suggestions can make the hours you spend more productive.

1. Study on a Daily Basis if Possible You will retain much more information if you study over many days than if you try to cram everything into a few marathon sessions. Set aside particular blocks of time for study; early mornings are preferred because you are more likely to be at your mental peak for the day. Try to avoid study periods after heavy meals or in too warm a study area, as a nap could take precedence over concentration.

2. Find a Quiet Place While some people have no problem studying in the midst of chaos, most students do best with as few distractions as possible. Such students should utilize the quietest room in their home for study purposes. Studying near televisions, next to the phone, or even outdoors can be extremely difficult.

3. Break up Your Study Time With pressures of work and family, most people don't have large blocks of time to study. Therefore, be opportunistic by taking advantage of short available time periods, even as short as 10 minutes. Actually, it is easier to concentrate over a short period than over a long period. If you do have large blocks of time available for studying, break up your study time into blocks no longer than 45 minutes and take a break by doing some other activity for 10 to 15 minutes. A short walk is an excellent way to refresh yourself and aid concentration.

4. Use Good Study Techniques

Scan Before you study each section, spend no more than five minutes scanning the material. A general understanding of what you will study helps your retention. Look for unfamiliar terms in your scanning process. Check the definitions in the text material or glossary.

Read and Paraphrase After reading each paragraph, stop, close your eyes, and ask yourself what you read. By putting the material into your own words mentally (or verbally if your study area permits it), your likelihood of retaining the information increases dramatically. By forcing yourself to paraphrase the material, you avoid the likelihood of giving too light a treatment to any one area.

Reread and Paraphrase A second reading should involve paraphrasing more than one paragraph (for example, whole topic areas).

5. Take the Test After the second reading, take the quiz at the end of the chapter as if it were an actual examination. If possible, schedule a single block of time for this purpose.

When taking the examinations in this book, use the examination techniques described later in this chapter. Mastering proper exam techniques can mean the extra points that make the difference between passing and failing.

Don't write on the examinations in this book. Use a separate answer sheet. If you mark the examination answers in the book, you will not gain the maximum benefit from a review. You will see the answer and not analyze each question and the answer choices.

On your answer sheet you should place a "c" next to those answers you are certain of and a "?" next to those you are uncertain of. By doing so, checking the answers is more likely to be a learning experience than just a simple evaluation.

6. Check Your Results After taking each test, check your answers. Don't limit your evaluation to those questions you answered incorrectly. Understanding *why* an answer is correct is more important than the fact that it is correct. Pay particular attention to wrong answers that you were certain of. For all wrong answers, ask yourself why you were drawn to that answer and how you will relate to the same material in the future. You don't want that same wrong answer to seem correct in the future.

7. Study before Class Complete your study of a subject before it is covered in class. Immediately before class, spend another few minutes quickly scanning the material so it is fresh in your mind.

By coming to class already understanding the topic, you get the greatest possible benefit from your instructor. That is, instead of trying to learn basic facts in class, you can use classroom time as it is meant to be used—asking questions, clarifying difficult points, and learning about changes as well as material specific to your state.

8. Mark Your Book Highlighting key areas in the text will help you recall and review particularly important points. Too much special emphasis, though, defeats the purpose of making a few points stand out.

Notes on your instructor's comments are best written in the margins. This way, you have one integrated text to study.

9. Know the Vocabulary Using a 3″ × 5″ card, write each word you have trouble with on one side, and write its definition(s) on the other side. Whenever you have a few minutes free during the day, review your cards. When you feel you have mastered a term, discard that card.

10. Review All Material While preparing for the ASI examination, it is a good practice to review on a weekly basis the material you have covered up to that point. This will result in greater review time for material you learned first. This way, you will compensate for the effect of time loss on your memory process. In preparing for your examination, don't limit your review to the material you feel you are weak in or to topics you think the exam will emphasize. For a comprehensive review, a good starting point is the review examinations at the end of this book, followed by the text material. Your review should include several readings of the glossary at the end of this book, a process that will be of great help in tying all the material together. Retake the examination in each section as well as the review examinations. These practice examinations are especially beneficial. Of course, the same level of study must be applied to information unique to your state.

Don't Become Discouraged Because of the sheer volume of new material, some students use their confusion as an excuse to drop out. Realize that confusion is normal for the first few weeks (sometimes months) of study; as you progress, things will come together slowly. Students often are well into the review process before they realize they are no longer confused. Whenever you feel you will never "get it," think of everyone you know in real estate. The reason they succeeded is not because they are smarter than you but because they refused to quit.

PERTINENT STATE INFORMATION

At the end of each chapter, we have presented a number of questions under the heading "Your Pertinent State Information." These questions allow you to consider state-specific information that may be covered on the state portion of your licensing examination.

You may wish to mark the margins of this book with notes on material for your specific state, because not every question is applicable in every state. If you are using this book in a classroom setting, your instructor will likely point out state-specific material of importance, as well as which questions you may disregard.

LICENSING REQUIREMENTS

Your state statutes set forth the requirements for licensing as real estate salespersons and brokers. They might include minimum education and age requirements (18) as well as taking and passing a real estate examination.

In addition to state requirements, the Federal Personal Responsibility and Work Opportunity Act requires that license applicants provide proof of their legal right to be in the United States. The act denies public benefits, which includes professional licensing, to illegal immigrants. The act applies to both original licensing and license renewals.

SITTING FOR THE EXAMINATION

Mental Preparation

Know where you will take your ASI examination and where you will park. Allow time to cover unexpected traffic delays. If you rush to the examination site with worries about being on time, you will likely be in an agitated frame of mind. This can have a negative effect on your examination performance.

It is natural to be nervous before an examination. Even though you understand nervousness can detract from your test-taking ability, remaining calm isn't easy. Even the candidate who appears relaxed has a few butterflies. You can help yourself by avoiding preexam socializing with other candidates. Nervousness breeds nervousness, and talking with a group of agitated people is not the way to relax.

Some students who encounter an early difficult question become frustrated, which can have a negative effect on the remainder of their performance. You must keep in mind that one question, no matter how difficult, will not by itself be the difference between success and failure. Everyone taking the examination will have similar problems with a number of questions. If this were not the case, it wouldn't be much of a test.

Immediately before taking your ASI examination, you can help yourself to relax by doing a short breathing exercise, taking ten deep breaths while counting to five for each of them. You will find this forced activity has a calming effect. Once you begin the exam, most of your initial apprehension will disappear.

You will take your real estate exam using a state-of-the-art portable unit with a touch screen that shows each question and records your answer. This is a user-friendly device, even for those who have had no computer experience. You will find the device very easy to operate. The device allows for a paperless examination, eliminates any possibility of grading error, increases exam security and lets each applicant take a different but equivalent examination. With the device, you can keep track of time and soon after completion of the exam, know whether you achieved a passing score. You can go forward or backward to review questions and/or change answers.

Tools

You are allowed to bring a simple electronic calculator. It cannot have an alphabet keyboard or be otherwise programmable. It also cannot make an audible tone. Make certain your calculator has fresh batteries, or you may find yourself doing long division with a pencil or, worse yet, working with false readings. Don't use a solar calculator because the light may be insufficient for sustained use. On the day before your examination, test your calculator with simple addition, subtraction, multiplication, and division problems. A malfunctioning calculator is not grounds for challenging exam results or getting an extension of the time limit. Even a perfect calculator is of no use if you can't operate it correctly. If you borrow one or buy a new one for the exam, be certain you understand fully how that model functions.

Listen

Pay attention to the instructions. Cheating will result in your immediate dismissal from the examination room and notification to the state licensing agency. Attempting to copy questions or remove exam material constitutes cheating.

Read

Read each question carefully to be sure you understand what is asked. Don't mentally change the wording or assume the question means something other than it says. If a question makes an assumption, accept it as true; students often read more into a question than is asked. Each question (stem) should be read carefully, and the answer should apply to *that* question. A correct statement that answers the wrong question is still a wrong answer.

If there is a negative term such as EXCEPT or LEAST LIKELY in the state-specific portion of your examination, be especially careful so that you understand what is being asked for.

Answer

Read every answer before giving your computer answer or marking your answer sheet. If you are not certain of the answer, eliminate what you believe to be the wrong answers and take a guess from the others. An informed candidate should be able to eliminate at least one answer, possibly two; an uninformed candidate will find all four answers very plausible. When you have two answers that appear to be right, you should look at the answers in a reverse light. Look for something wrong with one of the answers. The thing that makes it wrong could be in the stem or in the answer. ASI takes great effort to ensure that three of the four answers are wrong.

Words should be interpreted using their common meaning unless a word has a special meaning in regard to real estate, in which case the real estate meaning should be used.

You may find questions that go beyond what you have studied. These questions are intended to test your judgment utilizing what you have learned. They are not intended to be tricky.

Just as in real-life situations, questions may present facts or figures that are not necessary to answer the questions. If careful reading of a question indicates that information given is not relevant to the answer, ignore it.

Because your testing device will tell you if you have left any question unanswered, it is suggested that you commit yourself to at least two passes through the test.

On the first pass do the easy questions first, that is, material you are familiar with where the correct answer is obvious to you. When you are finished with the first pass, you will feel good about yourself and you will be ready for the second pass.

There are three types of questions you should press "next screen" for and pass up for the second pass. They are

1. questions you absolutely don't know,
2. lengthy questions that fill up practically the whole screen, and
3. math questions. Even if you are great in math, math questions are time consumers.

Ideally, when you have completed your first pass, you will feel that you have answered the majority of the questions correctly and you need to answer only a few more right to be on your way with a real estate license. Best of all, you have a lot of time to finish.

Go to the summary page on your answering device, press "Review unanswered" and the questions left unanswered will come up one after the other. Now finish the examination.

Your electronic testing device will show the time remaining, but time shouldn't be a problem unless you really get hung up on a math question. If this is the case, leave it until you have answered the rest of the questions.

Math Questions

Before you work out a mathematics question, make a mental estimate of the answer. If your computed answer differs significantly, there's a good chance you made an error in computation. Just because your computed answer agrees exactly with an answer choice does not mean it is correct. Wrong answers are the results of common mistakes, such as reversing dividend and divisor; failing to carry the mathematics to the final step; failing to convert inches to feet, square feet to square yards, cubic feet to cubic yards, and the like; and misplacing a decimal point.

Use Your Time

Remember, you have three and one-half to four hours to complete the examination (depending on your state). Don't rush to leave when you are finished. Take time to review the questions and answers. Staying longer can mean more points for you.

Start from the beginning, and go through the entire examination.

Use every minute of the time allotted, even if you finish early and are certain you passed with flying colors. Reread the questions, asking yourself what is really being asked, then check your answers.

You will likely discover you answered several questions based on the way you thought the question should read and not on what was actually asked. Misreading questions does not excuse a wrong answer.

Changing Answers

Never change an answer for change's sake. Your first decision is usually the best. However, if you discover that you misread a question or a later question jogs your memory so that you now understand what is sought, change the answer.

Clues

If a question or an answer includes a word that is not familiar to you, it might help you to keep in mind that words ending in "or" are givers, such as **grantor** (one who makes a grant) and **donor** (one who makes a gift). Words ending in "ee" describe receivers, such as **grantee** and **donee.**

Calculations

For calculations on the examination, unless otherwise indicated you should

- round off math answers to the nearest whole number.
- assume there are 5,280 feet in a mile and 43,560 square feet in an acre.
- base prorations on the time scale indicated in the question, which will state if there are assumed to be 360 or 365 days in a year as well as who is responsible for the date of closing. (Use the actual days in a month for prorating unless the question indicates otherwise.)

Real Property and Ownership

PROPERTY

All property is divided into two categories: real property and personal property.

Elements of Real Property

Real property includes land and the benefits that transfer or go with the land, such as buildings, fences, trees, water rights, mineral rights, air rights, easements, etc. The rights, benefits, and improvements that go with the land are known as **appurtenances**. In most states, mobile homes on permanent foundations are regarded as real property.

Bundle of Rights

The beneficial rights to use, exclude others, lease, encumber, transfer, and inherit are ownership rights referred to as the *bundle of rights.*

Elements of Personal Property

Also known as **chattels,** personal property is any property that is not real property. Personal property is considered movable, whereas real property is regarded as immovable. Mobile homes on wheels are usually regarded as personal property. Naturally growing plants, perennial crops and trees *(fructus naturales)* are classified as real property, but cultivated annual crops *(fructus industriales)* are considered personal property.

Chattels Real   Real estate interests less than fee ownership, such as tenant leasehold interests and mortgages, are known by the seemingly contradictory term *chattels real* but are personal property.

FIXTURES

Fixtures are items that were once personal property but have become so affixed to the real property that they have become part of it. Fixtures are transferred with and are taxed as real estate.

Tests of Fixture

Courts require that at least one of the following four tests be met to determine that an item is a fixture.

1. **Agreement**   A written agreement of the parties as to whether an item is a fixture and shall remain with the real estate or shall be regarded as personal property will govern the character of the property between the parties.

2. **Intent**   If there is no agreement, courts determine the intention of the parties. Intent is considered the most important test of a fixture when there isn't an agreement. Did the parties intend that property would become part of the real estate? It can be difficult to prove intent.

3. **Attachment or Method of Annexation**   Can the item be removed without causing major damage to the real property? Is the method of attachment of a permanent nature?

4. **Adaptability**   Adaptability is a legal rather than a physical attachment. If an item is reasonably necessary for the normal use of the property, it probably is a fixture, even though it is not attached.

Relationship of Parties   If the other tests are inconclusive, the law generally favors the buyer in a buyer-seller relationship or the tenant in a landlord-tenant relationship.

Trade Fixtures   Fixtures installed by a tenant for the purpose of conducting a business or trade ordinarily remain personal property and can be removed by the tenant any time prior to expiration of the lease. The tenant is liable for any damage caused by the removal.

Emblements   Cultivated annual crops are personal property. Unless otherwise agreed, a tenant has the right to enter the property after expiration of the lease to harvest those crops that were the fruits of his or her labor.

METHODS OF PROPERTY DESCRIPTIONS

> **Note:** Concentrate on the method(s) of land description used in your state.

There are three methods of legally describing real property: lot, block, and tract; metes and bounds; and government survey. Street addresses and tax-assessor descriptions, while sufficient for some purposes, are considered informal descriptions and are not legal descriptions.

1. Lot, Block, and Tract

State and/or local subdivision law requires recording of a subdivision map. This legal description uses the parcel's designation on the recorded map as well as recording information. For example:

> Lot 17, Block 4 of Atlantic Heights Third Addition recorded on pages 814–815 in Volume 36 of the official records of the County of Oceanside.

2. Metes and Bounds

Also called **measurements** and **directions,** this is the oldest method of describing property; it was used extensively in the original 13 states. The metes-and-bounds method shows the boundaries of a parcel by measuring from point to point. The measuring points in a metes-and-bounds description are known as **monuments.** Trees, rocks, and rivers are examples of natural monuments, whereas iron stakes, fences, and roads are examples of artificial monuments. In the case of a difference between stated distances and actual monuments, the actual monuments would prevail. Metes-and-bounds descriptions are given in a clockwise manner, starting at the **point of beginning (POB)** and ending at the POB. Angles in a metes-and-bounds description are measured in degrees (°), minutes (') and seconds (") from a north-south line. The size of a metes-and-bounds parcel may be described as "____ acres MOL." The abbreviation MOL stands for "more or less" and indicates the acreage is not guaranteed to be exact. If a description fails to end at the point of beginning, it is defective because the property is not encircled.

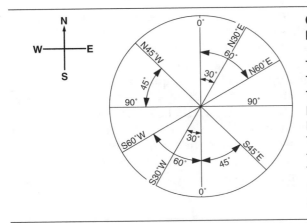

Circle Demonstrating Angles in a Metes-and-Bounds Description

There are 360° in a circle.
There are 180° in a half-circle.
There are 90° in a quarter-circle (right angle).
Each degree is divided into 60 minutes.
Each minute is divided into 60 seconds (").
The point of beginning is at the intersection of the two lines (or the center of the circle).
The "bearing" of a course is described by measuring easterly or westerly from the north and south lines.

In cases where the boundary is in dispute, the parties can agree to a boundary line (doctrine of agreed boundaries). The agreed boundary would be binding on future owners.

3. Government (Rectangular) Survey

Most U.S. land is laid out in a rectangular pattern by government survey. (If your state uses the government survey method, pay close attention to the following material. If not, read it, but concentrate more on your own state's method[s] of land description.) The government survey method measures land from the intersections of principal surveying lines. Lines going east and west are called **base lines;** those going north and south are called **meridians.** From the intersection of base lines and meridians, land is measured in **townships.** Townships are 6 miles square and contain 36 square miles.

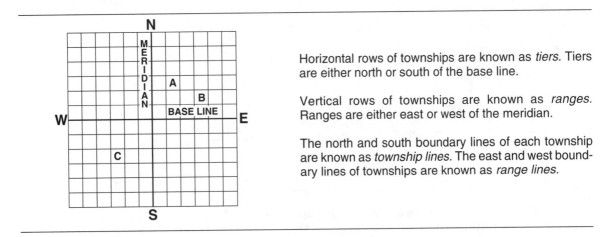

Horizontal rows of townships are known as *tiers*. Tiers are either north or south of the base line.

Vertical rows of townships are known as *ranges*. Ranges are either east or west of the meridian.

The north and south boundary lines of each township are known as *township lines*. The east and west boundary lines of townships are known as *range lines*.

The township marked *A* in the illustration is three tiers north of the base line and two ranges east of the meridian line. Therefore, it would be designated Tier 3 North, Range 2 East, or T3N,

R2E. To have a complete legal description, reference also must be made to the specific base line and meridian.

Township *B* is two tiers above or north of the base line and four ranges east of the meridian, thus is designated Tier 2 North, Range 4 East, or T2N, R4E, with reference to the appropriate base line and meridian.

Township *C* is three tiers south of the base line and three ranges west of the meridian and is described as T3S, R3W, with reference to the appropriate base line and meridian.

Correction Lines   Correction lines are surveyors' lines that compensate for the curvature of the earth. North-south lines run every 24 miles east and west of the principal meridian and are called **guide meridians,** and east-west lines run every 24 miles north or south of the base line and are called **standard parallels.** The 24-mile-square (24-mile-by-24 mile) parcels resulting from the correction lines or parallels are known as **government checks** or **quadrangles.**

Because of the curvature of the earth, adjustments are made in sections on the north and west boundaries of a township. Eleven sections of a township could be so affected.

Because of lakes and rivers, some quarter sections will have less than 160 acres. Such quarter sections are designated as **government lots** and would be identified by a lot number.

Each township is six miles square and contains 36 sections. Each **section** is one mile square and contains 640 acres. Sections in a township are always numbered as shown in the diagram below.

SECTIONS IN A TOWNSHIP

			N			
6	5	4	3	2	1
7	8	9	10	11	12
18	17	16	15	14	13
19	20	21	22	23	24
30	29	28	27	26	25
31	32	33	34	35	36

W ... E ... S

Adjoining this township are other townships, so east of Section 24 would be Section 19 of the adjoining township. In the same way, south of Section 33 would be Section 4 of another township.

Note that the numbering starts in the upper right-hand corner (NE) and continues in a zigzag pattern.

Land normally is described by its location within a specific section.

NW ¼

Since a section contains 640 acres, the NW¼ contains 160 acres.

Legal descriptions are not always as simple as finding a ¼ section. Suppose the description is the S½ of the NW¼ of the SE¼ of section 27, T8N, R17W, SBBL&M (San Bernardino base line and meridian). We first find the township by counting 8 north from the base line and 17 west from the meridian. We find the section by the numbering, as previously explained.

We can find the size of a parcel by simply going backward, using its description alone.

S ½ 20 acres since it is ½ of 40 acres.	←—*of*—	NW ¼ 40 acres since it is ¼ of 160 acres.	←—*of*—	SE ¼ 160 acres since it is ¼ of a section.

In finding the location of the S½ of NW¼ of SE¼, we look at our description and go *backward*. First, we find the SE¼. Because it is ¼ of a section, it contains 160 acres (¼ of 640). Second, we find the NW¼ of it, which gives us a 40-acre parcel (¼ of 160). Third, we find the S½ of it, which gives us a 20-acre parcel (½ of 40).

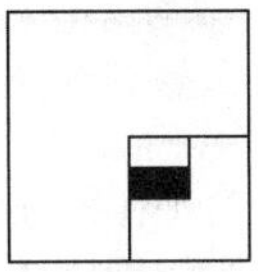

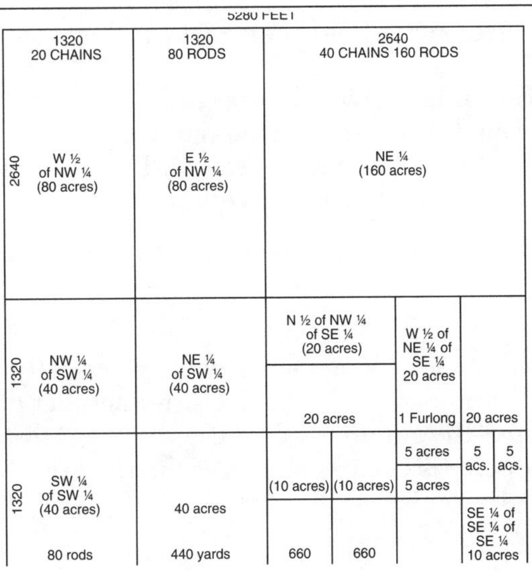

Legal descriptions of parcels of land within a section.

Know these measurements:

- One township = 6 miles square (36 square miles)
- One section = 640 acres
- One mile = 5,280 feet
- One acre = 43,560 square feet

To help you understand the size of an acre, a square acre is approximately 208.7 feet square.

Benchmarks are permanent markers that have been set by the U.S. Geological Survey. They indicate elevation above sea level. (The datum or datum plain is a horizontal plane from which elevation is measured. It is used by surveyors.)

Topographical lines are lines on a map that indicate contour of the land. Lines set close together mean the surface has a slope; lines set far apart indicate relatively level land.

ESTATES IN REAL PROPERTY

An estate is the degree or nature of the ownership interest a person has in real property.

Freehold Estates

Freehold estates are estates for an indefinite period of time. Fee simple and life estates are the two basic types of freehold estates. Freehold estates are considered real property.

Fee Simple or Fee Simple Absolute Estates

Fee simple is the highest ownership possible in real property. All other estates have a lesser interest than fee simple.

Fee simple is characterized by three features:

1. It has no time limitation.
2. It is freely transferable.
3. It may be inherited.

Fee Simple on Condition Subsequent (Defeasible Fee) (Fee Simple Defeasible)

An estate on a condition subsequent conveys title, provided a specific condition is met. It does not provide a duration for which title is granted. An example would be a grant of property on the condition that it never be used for the sale of alcoholic beverages. If the condition is breached, the grantor must declare the breach and retake the property within a reasonable period of time.

Fee Simple Determinable

If a deed specifies that a grant shall be only "for as long as" or while a property is in a particular use, the length of the estate is really determined by the deed. Use for another purpose would automatically end the estate, and no action of the grantor would be necessary. An example is a deed to a city for the length of time the property is used as a road; if the road use were to cease, title would revert to the grantor.

Life Estates

In a life estate, the grantee customarily holds the estate only for his or her lifetime. Therefore, it cannot be inherited or encumbered by the life tenant beyond his or her lifetime. For example, if the life tenant leased the life estate for 20 years but died sooner, the lease would end with the life tenant's death.

It is possible to have a life estate based on the life of a person other than the life tenant, known as a *pur autre vie estate*. In such a case, the life tenant or his or her heirs will have the estate as long as this other person lives.

The life tenant must make repairs, pay taxes, and avoid committing waste, which is characterized by damage or failure to make repairs. Because the life tenant is under no obligation to insure the premises, future interest holders should secure their own insurance if they wish to be protected.

Lenders sometimes lend on a life estate but require that the life tenant take out a life insurance policy that will pay off the loan in the event of the life-tenant's death. As an alternative, a lender might require that any future interest holders join in signing the mortgage.

Reversionary and Remainder Estates   On the death of a life tenant, the property reverts to the grantor or to the grantor's heirs (if either retained a reversionary interest) or to a named third party who has a remainder interest.

If the conveyance shown in the diagram were from *A* to *B* for life and then to *C*, *C* or *C's* heirs would be certain of receiving the estate so they would have a vested remainder interest. If,

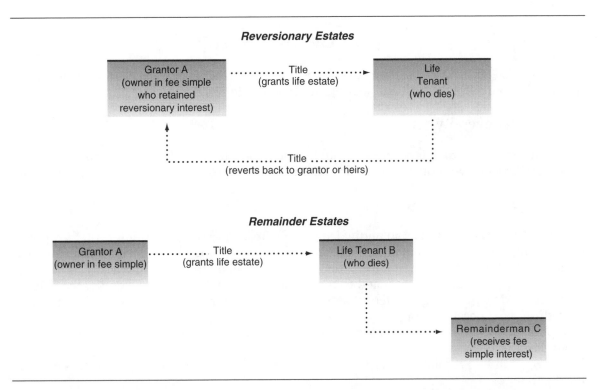

however, the conveyance were from *A* to *B* for life and then to *C* if *C* is still alive, *C* must outlive *B* in order to obtain the property. In this case, *C* would have a contingent remainder interest.

Creation   A life estate may be created by will, by grant where the grantor conveys a life estate, or by reservation where the grantor conveys the real property but reserves a life estate. In addition, a number of states recognize dower and curtesy as legal life estates created by law.

Dower   A wife's right to a life estate or an ownership interest in her husband's home upon his death is known as *dower*. Some states don't provide dower interests, and dower varies among the states where it is provided.

Curtesy   A husband's right to a life estate in the wife's property upon her death is known as *curtesy*. Usually, a one-third interest applies to curtesy. Not all states provide the right of curtesy.

In some states, homestead rights also create a legal life estate, giving a widow and minor children the right to occupy the homestead for life after the husband's death.

Termination   A life estate can be lost by merger. If the same party acquired both the life tenant's interest as well as the interests of the reversionary or remainder interest holder, the life estate would be lost through a merger. The single owner would now have a fee simple estate. Through the merger, the lesser interest is merged into the greater fee simple interest. A person cannot own a property in fee simple and also have a lesser interest as a life tenant.

Nonfreehold or Less-Than-Freehold Estates

Leasehold interests of tenants are nonfreehold estates. Unless specifically prohibited, leasehold interests can be transferred freely and may be inherited. While freehold estates are considered real property, leasehold interests of the tenant are considered to be personal property. The leased fee estate of the lessor, however, would be a freehold estate and is real property.

FORMS OF OWNERSHIP

While estates describe the *degree* of ownership interest, ownership can be in many forms, as discussed in the following sections. (See Figure 1.1 on page 11.)

Tenancy in Severalty

Tenancy in severalty is sole ownership by one individual or entity. A corporation or even a partnership can own property as a sole owner in either the corporate or the partnership name.

Joint Tenancy

Joint tenancy is defined as an undivided ownership by two or more people with the right of survivorship. An undivided interest is a share in the whole property rather than ownership in a particular portion of the property. **Survivorship** means that on the death of one joint tenant, his or her interest immediately ceases and passes to the surviving joint tenants. Because the interest ceases immediately on the joint tenant's death, it cannot be transferred by will. Thus, probate procedure is not necessary for joint tenancy interests.

Because it can live forever, a corporation cannot hold title in joint tenancy, so survivorship is not possible.

If *A*, *B*, and *C* are joint tenants, the estate passes under the survivorship right, as shown in the diagram.

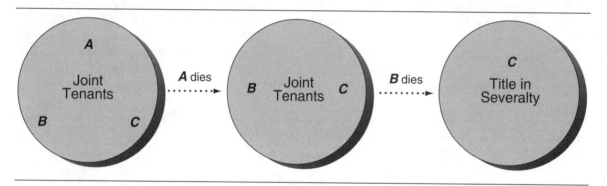

Creation   Four unities must occur for a joint tenancy to exist:

1. **Time** The joint tenants must have obtained their interests at the same time.
2. **Title** The joint tenants must have obtained their interests by the same document, usually a deed.
3. **Interest** The interests of the joint tenants must be equal.
4. **Possession** The joint tenants must have equal and individual rights to possession.

To create a joint tenancy, it is necessary to indicate this intent clearly. In some states, however, a conveyance to husband and wife is presumed to be as joint tenants unless the deed states otherwise. Other states require that a deed creating a joint tenancy be signed by the grantees, showing their agreement to this form of ownership.

Cessation   A joint tenancy ceases when the four unities are no longer present as to two or more parties. As an example, the sale by one joint tenant would result in a buyer who did not obtain his or her interest at the same time or by the same document as the other joint tenants, so the purchaser would be a tenant in common, not a joint tenant.

Encumbering the Joint Tenancy   A joint tenant can encumber his or her interest. While a creditor of a joint tenant could foreclose on a lien or obtain a judgment in order to break up the joint tenancy and attach the property, the death of a joint tenant before the creditor forces sale of the property would result in the property passing free of the debt or encumbrance to the surviving joint tenant(s).

Tenancy in Common

Undivided interest by two or more parties without the right of survivorship is called a *tenancy in common*. Conveyances to two or more parties that do not specify how title is to be taken give the parties title as tenants in common, however, in some states, conveyances to spouses result in tenancy by the entirety or community property. Tenants in common may have equal or unequal ownership interests. If a deed does not specify the percentage of ownership, tenants in common are generally presumed to have equal shares.

Possession is the only one of the four unities required for joint tenancy that is also required for tenants in common. Tenants in common have equal and individual rights of possession. Because there is no survivorship, on the death of a tenant in common, his or her interest passes to the heirs by will, trust, or probate rather than to surviving tenants in common. A tenant in common can sell or mortgage his or her interest without affecting the rights of the other tenants in common.

All owners must join in encumbering or selling the entire property. The evolution of a tenancy in common from joint tenancy is shown in the following diagram.

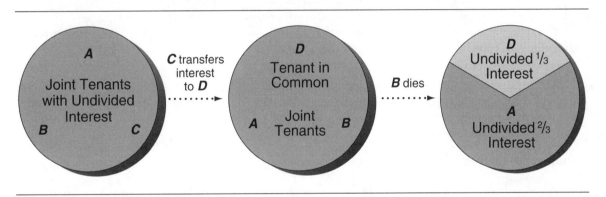

In this situation, *D* becomes a tenant in common because the unities of time and title do not apply to *D*. After *C* transfers interest, the four unities continue to apply to *A* and *B* until *B's* death.

Partition   A court action to break up a joint tenancy or tenancy in common is called *partition*. Courts favor partition in kind, that is, splitting the property, but where this is not possible or would result in loss of value, the court will order a sale and a division of the sale proceeds.

Community Property

> If your state is a community property state, community property questions are likely to appear on the state-specific portion of your examination rather than in the general portion of your examination.

Originally a Spanish concept, community property has been adopted by a number of states. Community property status requires that the owners be married. Property acquired during marriage is considered equally owned by both spouses. Property acquired prior to marriage is considered separate property, as is property received by either spouse as a gift or an inheritance during the marriage. Income from separate property is also regarded as separate property.

Either spouse can will his or her half of the community property to third parties. When a spouse dies intestate (without a will), his or her share of the community property will go to his or her heirs in accordance with state law.

Because neither spouse can partition the community property, spouses cannot separately convey their community property interest. An agreement of one spouse to sell or give community property, therefore, would not be binding on the other spouse.

Separate (noncommunity) property of a spouse might become community property if commingled (mixed).

Tenancy by the Entirety

> Like community property, questions on tenancy by the entirety are most likely to be on the state-specific portion of your examination if your state recognizes tenancy by the entirety.

In many states, when title is conveyed to a husband and wife without designating the form of ownership, each owns the entire parcel as a tenant by the entirety. Neither spouse can separately convey an interest during the other's lifetime. On the death of a spouse, the survivor owns the property. This is similar to the survivorship of joint tenancy. Divorce would change the ownership to a tenancy in common because the survivorship was based on marriage.

Generally speaking, a creditor cannot reach property held in tenancy by the entirety unless the creditor is a creditor of both husband and wife.

> **Note:** While valuable for general knowledge, the following material from *Partnerships Through Real Property Securities* is more likely to be on broker examinations than on salesperson examinations.

Tenancy in Partnership

A partnership is an agreement of two or more co-owners to conduct a business for profit. Agreements to share in the profit create a presumption of a partnership. Title to partnership property may be held in the name of the partnership and can be conveyed without the signatures of the partners' spouses, although real property cannot be conveyed or encumbered without the consent of all partners.

Partners have equal rights to use partnership property for partnership purposes. In the absence of an agreement to the contrary, they share equally in the control of the partnership and in its profits.

A partnership requires consent; therefore, one partner cannot assign his or her interest to another. Personal creditors of a partner cannot attach partnership property for that partner's personal debts.

General Partner   A general partner is an active partner and has unlimited personal liability for the debts of the partnership. One general partner can personally obligate the other general partners.

Limited Partner   A limited partner is an inactive partner who contributes money to the partnership. States that have adopted the Uniform Limited Partnership Act require the filing of a certificate listing the limited partners. Limited partners have limited liability and are liable only

Figure 1.1: Common Ownership Forms

	TENANCY IN COMMON	JOINT TENANCY	COMMUNITY PROPERTY	TENANCY BY THE ENTIRETY
Parties	Any number of persons (can be husband and wife)	Any number of persons (can be husband and wife)	Husband and wife only	Husband and wife only
Division	Undivided interest (equal or unequal)	Undivided interest (must be equal)	Undivided interest (interests are equal)	Undivided interest (interests are equal)
Title	Each co-owner has a separate legal title to an undivided interest	There is only one title to the whole property	Title is in the "community" (similar to title being in a partnership)	There is only one title to the whole property
Possession	Equal right of possession	Equal right of possession	Equal right of possession	Equal right of possession
Conveyance	Each co-owner's interest may be conveyed separately by its owner	Conveyance by only one co-owner breaks the joint tenancy	Both husband and wife must joint in conveyance; separate interests cannot be conveyed	Both husband and wife must join in conveyance; separate property interests cannot be conveyed
Purchaser Status	Purchaser becomes a tenant in common with the other co-owners	Purchaser becomes a tenant in common with the other co-owners	Purchaser can acquire whole title of community only	Purchaser can acquire whole title only
Death	Upon co-owner's death, his or her interest passes by will to the devisees or heirs; no survivorship right	Upon co-owner's death, his or her interest ends and cannot be willed; survivor owns the property by survivorship	Upon co-owner's death, half goes to survivor in severalty; up to half goes by will or succession to others (consult attorney with specific questions)	Surviving spouse owns property in severalty; may not pass to third party by will
Successor Status	Devisees or heirs become tenants in common	Last survivor owns property in severalty	If passing by will, tenancy in common between devisee and surviving spouse	Survivor owns property in severalty
Creditor Rights	Co-owner's interest may be sold on execution sale to satisfy creditor; creditor becomes a tenant in common	Co-owner's interest may be sold on execution sale to satisfy creditor; joint tenancy is broken, and creditor becomes a tenant in common	Co-owner's interests cannot be seized and sold separately; the whole property may be sold to satisfy debts of either the husband or wife, depending on the debt (consult attorney with specific questions)	Co-owner's interests cannot be seized and sold separately; the whole property may be sold to satisfy debts of both the husband and wife (consult an attorney with specific questions)
Presumption	Favored in doubtful cases unless husband and wife (see Community Property and Joint Tenancy)	Must be expressly stated and properly formed (in some states, deed to husband and wife presumed to be joint tenancy)	Strong presumption that property acquired by husband and wife is community property in community property states	In many states, presumed if a joint tenancy between a husband and wife

to the extent of their investments. Limited partnerships are regarded as securities because the investors have no control over the enterprise. A limited partnership must have a general or managing partner.

Taxation of Partnerships   Partnerships do not pay separate income tax, although they must file a return. The tax is assessed directly against the partners even when profits are retained in the partnership for partnership activities.

Death of a Partner   In a general partnership, the death of a partner dissolves the partnership. The heirs of a general partner have no rights to the partnership business but are entitled to the value of the deceased partner's share in partnership assets. Limited partnership interests may be inherited.

Joint Venture   A joint venture is an association formed for a single undertaking rather than a continuing business. A joint venture is treated by the law in most cases as a partnership; however, one joint venturer cannot contractually obligate the other joint venturers to a contract.

Franchise

A franchise is an independent business that is entitled to use a designated trade name and a common marketing plan. Many real estate offices are franchises.

Syndicate

A syndicate is made up of two or more people organized to make an investment. Although a syndicate could be a general partnership, ordinarily it is a limited partnership. The syndicator is the general managing partner, and the investors have limited liability. Syndicates are subject to state regulations.

Corporation

A corporation is an artificial but legal person created by state law. Because it is a separate entity, its shareholders have no personal liability for corporate debts. If individuals who control a corporation mix corporate funds with noncorporate funds, a court could "pierce the corporate veil" and hold them personally liable because they were not acting as a separate entity. Corporate profits are taxed, as are dividends received by the stockholders. This is known as **double taxation.**

In dealing with a corporation, a real estate agent should consider checking the bylaws to ascertain the power of the person(s) he or she is dealing with. If an act were outside the authority of the corporate representative, the corporation would not be liable for the act.

A deed to a corporation not yet in existence is void because a deed must have a definite grantee.

S Corporation   A small, closely held corporation of 75 or fewer shareholders can become an S corporation, provided all shareholders elect to be taxed as partners. Shareholders avoid the double taxation of a standard corporation but retain the protection of being exempt from personal liability for corporate debts. S corporations cannot receive more than 20 percent of their income from passive sources. Real estate investment income is considered passive income.

Limited Liability Company

This is a business entity in which the members have limited liability, as in a corporation, but are treated like a partnership for tax purposes.

A limited liability company (LLC) obtains the benefits offered by an S corporation without the qualifying or operational restrictions of limited partnership. Laws regarding forming or converting a business to an LLC vary by state.

Real Estate Investment Trust

Ownership in a real estate investment trust (REIT) is held in trust form for the beneficiaries by a trustee. Under federal law, a REIT must have 100 or more investors. It is taxed on retained earnings only and avoids double taxation of corporations if it distributes 95 percent or more of its ordinary income to the investors. At least 75 percent of the assets must be in real estate.

Investors in REITs are given shares (certificates of ownership) that may be traded freely. A number of REITs are listed on the American, NASDAQ, and New York stock exchanges. Interests in REITs are regarded as securities.

Trust   Besides real estate investment trusts, property can be held in trust by a trustee for the benefit of one or more parties. The trustee may have broad or restrictive powers, depending on the restrictions set forth in the trust document.

A living trust, whereby the trustor gives the property to himself or herself and others but retains the control and benefits of ownership, is used as an estate-planning tool to avoid probate and limit estate taxes.

Real Property Securities

These are investments in which investors are inactive participants, such as limited partnerships, investment contracts, and real estate investment trusts. Condominiums sold as investments with a mandatory rental pool agreement are also real property securities because the investor gives up management control to another.

Real property securities must be registered with the federal Securities and Exchange Commission (SEC) unless they are exempt from registration. Securities sold within a single state, or intrastate, are exempt, as are private offerings to a limited number of investors who have significant net worth. Individual states also have requirements for security registration as well as exemptions from registration. Even though a security may be exempt from SEC registration, it is still subject to federal disclosure and antifraud legislation as well as state regulations. Real estate licensees may need special licenses to sell real property securities, depending on state law.

Special Forms of Ownership

State and local statutes govern land divisions for the purpose of sale, lease, or financing.

Standard Subdivision   A standard subdivision is a land development with no areas owned in common.

Common Interest Subdivision   Any subdivision having interests owned in common by the owners is considered a common interest subdivision. Common interest subdivisions have homeowners' associations (HOA) that provide for maintenance of the common areas. Owners are assessed their share of the costs, and the assessments are considered liens against the property. Recorded bylaws set forth responsibilities of the association.

Undivided Interest Subdivision   An undivided interest subdivision is one where individual owners have an undivided interest in the entire subdivision and a nonexclusive right of occupancy. An example would be a 1/2,500 ownership share in a campground with the right to use whatever campsite happens to be available.

Condominium   A condominium is a development in which there is individual fee simple ownership of a unit and shared ownership of common areas with other owners as tenants in common. The developer files a master deed and condominium declaration that sets forth separate and common ownership areas, as well as the condominium bylaws and restrictions. The land is regarded as a common area. Owners pay their own mortgages and property taxes. (The definition of a condominium varies among states and in some states may include land ownership.)

Common elements in a condominium are commonly owned areas for the use and benefit of all the owners. **Limited common elements** are commonly owned areas reserved for use by designated owners, such as designated parking spaces and storage lockers.

Planned Unit Development (Planned Development Project)   A Planned Unit Development (PUD) subdivision offers individual lot ownership, with common areas owned by all owners as tenants in common. An example would be a subdivision with a community-owned swimming pool.

Cooperative   In a cooperative development, each owner owns stock in a corporation and has the right to occupy a unit under a proprietary lease. Unlike condominium ownerships, co-op taxes and mortgage payments are generally made by the corporation, not by individual owners. A disadvantage is that co-op owners don't have title, so they can't mortgage their interests; however, they can borrow on their stock. Because stock rather than real estate is owned, cooperative ownership is really personal property. Most cooperatives require approval of the board to transfer the stock and possession and also may impose a stock transfer fee.

Time-Share   Also known as **interval ownership,** a time-share is an undivided interest in a unit (usually as tenants in common), coupled with the exclusive right of occupancy for either a designated or floating period each year. Time-share owners have an undivided interest in the common area. Time-share interests can be leasehold estates, where the right of occupancy ends after a stated number of years, or fee simple ownership. Customarily, time-share properties are vacation units in which individual buyers enjoy occupancy for certain weeks each year. Some states provide a rescission period for purchasers of time-share and/or undivided interest subdivisions because of marketing practices sometimes used for these types of developments.

Your Pertinent State Information

1.   What is the mobile-home requirement for real property?

2.   Is the government survey system used in your state?

3.   Failure by a husband and wife to indicate how a title should be held creates what type of ownership?

4.   Does your state allow limited liability companies?

5.   May a real estate licensee sell real property securities?

6.   How is condominium defined by your state?

7.   Does your state recognize dower and curtesy rights?

8.   Does your state recognize community property or tenancy by the entirety?

CHAPTER 1 QUIZ

Real Property and Ownership

1. Real property interests include:

   (A) cultivated annual crops
   (B) leasehold interests
   (C) mortgages
   (D) fences

2. What is a form of ownership that is restricted to husbands and wives?

   (A) Joint tenancy
   (B) Tenancy in severalty
   (C) Tenancy in common
   (D) Tenancy by the entirety

3. What would result from a condition in a deed?

   (A) Fee simple
   (B) Defeasible fee
   (C) Chattel real
   (D) Nonfreehold estate

4. What does *datum* refer to?

   (A) Carpenter's tool
   (B) Aircraft used for survey purposes
   (C) Level surface from which elevations are measured
   (D) File of recorded documents

5. An investor's personal assets could be subject to a creditor's claim in a:

   (A) general partnership
   (B) syndicate
   (C) real estate investment trust
   (D) corporation

6. How does an S corporation differ from other corporations?

   (A) Its investors have no personal liability.
   (B) The double taxation aspect of other corporations is avoided.
   (C) It has a separate life from that of the investors.
   (D) Its tax rates are higher than for other corporations.

7. A tenant in a commercial building installed a large sign that was anchored to the building with steel rods. Which of the following terms properly describes the sign?

   (A) Fixture
   (B) Trade fixture
   (C) Real property
   (D) Emblement

8. What type of real property description would include reference to an iron stake?

   (A) Metes and bounds
   (B) Informal
   (C) Lot, block, and tract
   (D) Government survey

9. A tenancy in common differs from a joint tenancy in that:

   (A) there is a survivorship right if a tenant in common dies without a will
   (B) tenants in common may have unequal interests
   (C) tenants in common have divided interests
   (D) tenants in common must acquire their interests at the same time

10. Chattels real differ from appurtenances in that they:

    (A) transfer with the land
    (B) include growing trees
    (C) are personal property
    (D) are freehold interests

11. Rights, benefits, and improvements that go with the land are known as:

    (A) chattels
    (B) emblements
    (C) appurtenances
    (D) encumbrances

12. Which of the following would be classified as real property?

    (A) Trade fixtures
    (B) Water rights
    (C) Chattels real
    (D) Mortgages

13. Three of the tests of a fixture are:

    (A) adaptability, intent, and attachment
    (B) adaptability, cost, and attachment
    (C) size, weight, and adaptability
    (D) intent, cost, and attachment

14. All of the ownership rights that transfer with a fee simple estate are known as:

    (A) fixtures
    (B) emblements of title
    (C) remainder rights
    (D) the bundle of rights

15. Items that were formerly personal property but are now regarded as real property would be described as:

    (A) emblements
    (B) fructus industriales
    (C) fixtures
    (D) trade fixtures

16. An example of a real property security would be:

    (A) condominiums sold with a mandatory rental pool arrangement
    (B) general partnership shares in investment property
    (C) a pur autre vie estate
    (D) a vested remainder interest

17. Part of a legal description on a deed stated "38° 7'." What type of description was it?

    (A) Metes and bounds
    (B) Informal description
    (C) Lot, block, and tract
    (D) Government survey

18. A brother and sister hold land as joint tenants. The sister conveys one-half of her interest to her husband. Ownership would now be held by the:

    (A) brother, sister, and her husband as tenants in common
    (B) brother and sister as joint tenants and by her husband as a tenant in common
    (C) brother, sister, and her husband as joint tenants
    (D) brother and sister as joint tenants

19. An owner granted a life estate to another but retained a future interest, which was a:

    (A) remainder interest
    (B) chattel real
    (C) defeasible estate
    (D) reversionary interest

20. *K*, who had a life estate for the life of *L*, leased the property to *M* for 5 years. What would happen if *K* were to die?

    (A) *M's* lease would terminate.
    (B) *K's* heirs would be entitled to *K's* interest.
    (C) The remainder interest holder would obtain title.
    (D) *L* would obtain title.

21. A person other than the grantor has a future interest in a life estate. That interest would be a:

    (A) fee simple
    (B) fee simple determinable
    (C) remainder interest
    (D) reversionary interest

22. A life estate was lost by merger. Merger occurred when the:

    (A) original grantor died
    (B) life tenant died
    (C) remainder interest holder purchased the life tenant's interest
    (D) life tenant vacated the premises

23. The statutory right of a widow in the estate of her deceased husband is a:

    (A) dower right
    (B) curtesy right
    (C) tenancy at sufferance
    (D) remainder interest

24. *J* had to pay a stock transfer fee when he sold his unit. What type of development was it?

    (A) Condominium
    (B) Planned unit development
    (C) Cooperative
    (D) Time-share

25. A leased farm is sold. The growing crops belong to the:

    (A) seller
    (B) buyer
    (C) tenant
    (D) buyer and tenant equally

26. Owning property as tenants in common permits each owner to:

    (A) have title in severalty to half the property
    (B) have the right of survivorship
    (C) own unequal shares
    (D) avoid personal liability

27. Which of the following rights is considered personal property?

    (A) Air rights
    (B) Water rights
    (C) Mineral rights
    (D) Tenant rights

28. A swimming pool in a condominium development would be regarded as a(n):

    (A) common element
    (B) limited common element
    (C) leasehold element
    (D) emblement

29. *L*, *M*, and *N* are joint tenants. *N* sells his interest to *O*, then *M* dies. Which of the following statements is true?

    (A) *M's* heirs, *O* and *L*, are joint tenants.
    (B) *M's* heirs and *L* are joint tenants, but *O* is a tenant in common.
    (C) *L's*, *O's*, and *M's* heirs are tenants in common.
    (D) *L* and *O* are tenants in common.

30. What is a partition action?

    (A) A subdivision of lots by a developer
    (B) A court proceeding to break up a co-ownership
    (C) The conversion of rental apartments to condominiums or cooperatives
    (D) The conveyance of a partial interest to form a co-ownership

31. Which of the following would be considered a limited common element in a condominium?

    (A) Bearing walls between adjoining tenants
    (B) Community swimming pool
    (C) Parking space designated for a particular unit
    (D) Land under the units

32. A buyer of a residential unit received a share of stock and occupancy based on a lease. What type of development was the unit in?

    (A) Cooperative
    (B) Condominium
    (C) Planned unit
    (D) Time-share

33. Joint tenancy and tenancy in common are similar in that:

    (A) interest passes to heirs on death of an owner
    (B) interests of owners must be equal
    (C) a sale of an interest requires approval of other owners
    (D) all owners have equal rights of possession

34. Of the following forms of ownership, which is restricted to husbands and wives?

    (A) Joint tenancy
    (B) Tenancy in severalty
    (C) Tenancy in common
    (D) Community property —

35. *J* deeded property to *K*. The deed provided that if *K* ever used the property for the sale of alcoholic beverages, title would revert to *J*. The estate created by this conveyance is a(n):

    (A) estate on a condition subsequent
    (B) fee simple absolute
    (C) life estate
    (D) nonfreehold estate —

36. The lot and block reference in a legal description relates to:

    (A) a metes-and-bounds description
    (B) a recorded subdivision map —
    (C) the government survey system
    (D) correction lines and datum plane

37. *S* and *M* plan to buy a home together but want to be able to will their property individually to their own children from previous marriages. They should hold title as:

    (A) tenants by the entirety
    (B) joint tenants —
    (C) tenants in common
    (D) tenants in severalty

38. *J* and his sister *K* were co-owners of a lot. *K* became the sole owner automatically when *J* died because they owned the lot:

    (A) in severalty
    (B) in joint tenancy —
    (C) as community property
    (D) in tenancy by the entirety

39. *L*, *M*, and *N* owned property as joint tenants. *M* died, followed by the death of *N*. Title to the property would be held by:

    (A) *L* in severalty —
    (B) *L* and the heirs of *N* as tenants in common
    (C) *L* and the heirs of *N* in joint tenancy
    (D) *L* and the heirs of both *M* and *N* as tenants in common

40. Interval exclusive occupancy coupled with a tenancy-in-common interest describes a(n):

    (A) estate for years
    (B) tenancy at sufferance
    (C) cooperative
    (D) time-share ownership —

41. What is the highest form of ownership?

    (A) Fee simple determinable
    (B) Fee simple absolute —
    (C) Fee on a condition subsequent
    (D) A nonfreehold estate

42. The court will grant a request for a partition when title is held:

    (A) in severalty
    (B) as community property
    (C) as a tenancy by the entirety
    (D) as a joint tenancy

43. A property description in a deed mentioned a point of beginning. Which method was the description based on?

    (A) Lot and block
    (B) Informal method
    (C) Government survey
    (D) Metes and bounds —

44. An example of an estate in real property would be:

    (A) joint tenancy
    (B) fee simple
    (C) severalty ownership
    (D) community property —

45. A legal description outlines the boundaries of a property. What type of description is it?

    (A) Government survey —
    (B) Lot and block
    (C) Metes and bounds
    (D) Baseline and meridian

46. *J* had given *K* a life estate, and *L* was named to receive the interest on *K's* death. Given these facts:

    (A) *L* has a reversionary interest
    (B) *L* has a remainder interest -
    (C) *K* can defeat *L's* interest by deed or will
    (D) *K* cannot borrow on her interest

47. By purchasing the reversionary interest of the grantor, the former life tenant would now have a:

    (A) tenancy by the entirety
    (B) less than freehold estate
    (C) fee simple -
    (D) fee simple determinable

48. *J* purchased a property with *K* as joint tenants. When *J* died, it was discovered that an encumbrance had been placed against *J's* interest in the property and that *J's* will provided that the property interest should pass to *L*. How would title to the property be held?

    (A) *K* in severalty free of the encumbrance
    (B) *K* in severalty subject to the encumbrance
    (C) *K* and *L* as tenants in common free of the encumbrance
    (D) *K* and *L* as tenants in common subject — to the encumbrance

49. A condominium would be described as a(n):

    (A) undivided interest in the whole
    (B) undivided interest in common areas — and separate interest in individual units
    (C) separate interests in the whole
    (D) divided interest in common areas and undivided interest in each unit

50. Homeowner associations meet the needs of:

    (A) common interest development ⁓
    (B) emblement ownership
    (C) metes-and-bounds descriptions
    (D) nonfreehold estates

CHAPTER 1 QUIZ ANSWERS

Real Property and Ownership

1. (D) An appurtenance that goes with the land. (page 1)
2. (D) Community property also is restricted to husbands and wives. (pages 10, 11)
3. (B) The estate could be lost. (page 6)
4. (C) Elevations are based on the official datum, or datum plane, and a bench mark carries that information. (page 5)
5. (A) A general partner has unlimited personal liability. (page 10)
6. (B) Chapter S corporations are taxed like partners. (page 12)
7. (B) A tenant can remove a trade fixture but is liable for removal damage to real property. (page 2)
8. (A) An iron stake would be referenced as a monument or point in a metes-and-bounds description. (page 2)
9. (B) Or equal interests. (page 9)
10. (C) Chattels real are personal property related to real property. such as mortgages and tenant lease rights. (page 1)
11. (C) Appurtenances belong with the real estate. (page 1)
12. (B) As well as mineral rights and easements. (page 1)
13. (A) Intent is often said to be the most important of these three tests. (page 2)
14. (D) They are the rights of ownership. (page 1)
15. (C) They have been joined to the realty. (page 1)
16. (A) Owner of a security does not have any management control. (page 13)
17. (A) Degrees and minutes measure the angles between monuments. (page 3)
18. (A) There are no longer two owners possessing the four unities of joint tenancy. (The brother has an undivided one-half interest, and the sister and her husband each have undivided one-quarter interest.) In some states, the sister could convey her interest to her husband and to herself as joint tenants, but in this case, she conveyed only one-half of her interest. (page 8)
19. (D) The interest reverts back to the owner. (pages 6–7)
20. (B) The life estate is based on *L's* life. (page 6)
21. (C) A third-party future interest is a remainder interest. An interest that reverted to the grantor would be a reversionary interest. (page 6)
22. (C) The life interest and remainder interests are merged into a single interest. (page 7)
23. (A) In some states, a wife is entitled to a percentage of her husband's real property and/or a life estate in a husband's home on the husband's death. (page 7)
24. (C) *J* owned a share in a cooperative. (page 14)
25. (C) Growing crops are emblements. (page 2)
26. (C) Tenant-in-common interests need not be equal. (page 9)
27. (D) Tenant rights are chattels real, the others are real property. (page 1)
28. (A) Common areas for all owners. (page 14)
29. (D) When *N* sold to *O*, *N* broke the joint tenancy as to his or her interest, and *O* had a one-third interest. When *M* died, *L* took the share by survivorship. *L* has a two-thirds interest, and *O* has a one-third interest. (pages 8–9)
30. (B) This is an action to divide the land of a tenancy in common or joint tenancy when the owners cannot agree. The court could physically divide the property (if feasible) or order a sale. (page 9)
31. (C) Commonly owned but reserved for use of a particular unit. (page 14)
32. (A) Stock ownership plus proprietary lease. (page 14)
33. (D) The only one of the four unities present in tenancy in common is possession. (page 9)
34. (D) Tenancy by the entirety is also only for husband and wife (marriage is essential). (page 9)
35. (A) The estate is presently valid but can be lost. (page 6)
36. (B) The legal description references the recorded map. (page 2)
37. (C) There is no right of survivorship for tenants in common. Choices (A) and (B) would go to the survivor, and (D) is ownership by one person only. (page 9)
38. (B) Tenancy by the entirety is only for spouses. (page 8)
39. (A) On *M's* death, *L* and *N* held title as joint tenants. When *N* died, *L* owned the property in severalty. Interest of joint tenant passes by survivorship to remaining joint tenant(s). (page 8)
40. (D) A time-share can be a leasehold or fee simple interest for specified periods of time. (page 14)

41. (B) Fee simple ownership has no time limitation and can be freely transferred and can be inherited. (page 6)
42. (D) Or tenancy in common. (page 9)
43. (D) It measures from point to point. (page 3)
44. (B) Fee simple is the degree of ownership (estate), the others are forms of ownership. (page 5)
45. (C) It encircles the parcel. (page 3)
46. (B) *L* is third person. (page 6)
47. (C) Life estate was lost by merger into greater fee simple interest. (page 7)
48. (A) Title passes free of *J's* encumbrance to the survivor. It does not pass by will. (pages 8–9)
49. (B) Condominium owners own their own air space, but common areas are owned with other owners as tenants in common. (page 14)
50. (A) HOA are present and collect assessments whenever there is a common interest development. (page 13)

Land Use Controls and Restrictions

Land use is controlled by both public and private restrictions.

PUBLIC CONTROLS

Planning   A master plan is a comprehensive growth and use plan for a community indicating residential, commercial, and industrial areas. The master plan allows a community to consider its future goals and is implemented through zoning.

Master planning can consider both future development and redevelopment. It takes into account the coordination of all public services; protection of the environment; and the health, safety, morals, and general welfare of the people. Master planning can encourage growth or provide for growth limitations as well as include requirements that discourage premature development.

By allowing advantageous uses, zoning can encourage redevelopment by making it economically feasible to tear down existing structures. Redevelopment also can be pushed through special assessment districts and enterprise zones that are areas in which special tax or other benefits encourage redevelopment.

Besides providing for orderly growth and uses that are presumed to be consistent with the needs of the people, proper planning can protect property values.

Subdivision Control   Most states require approval prior to the sale of subdivision parcels. These requirements are intended to protect the purchasers and often require disclosures. The physical aspects of the subdivision are subject to local government approval.

Environmental Impact Statement   The National Environmental Policy Act (NEPA) of 1969 calls for an environmental impact statement (EIS) if a federal development is likely to affect the environment.

Many states also require that the developer prepare an environmental impact report (EIR) for any development likely to affect the environment. The EIR can be required by a planning commission to aid in decision making. In some states, private citizens can obtain a court order to demand an EIR. The report evaluates all aspects of the proposed development—schools, services, transportation, utilities, pollution, noise, future growth effects, jobs, wildlife, and ecology. A **negative declaration** states that a development will have no significant negative effect on the environment.

Rural Land Planning   Soil conditions should be considered in providing the best soils for agriculture. By exclusionary zoning (excluding other uses), land can be kept for agriculture. By buying an owner's development rights, it is possible for a governmental body or conservation group to ensure that property remains in a natural or an agricultural use. The same results can be obtained by purchasing an easement right that prohibits development (conservation easement).

Zoning

Whereas restrictive covenants are private restrictions on land use, zoning is a public restriction that is enforceable under the *police power* of the state (to preserve the health, safety, morals, and public welfare). Even though the exercise of police power could diminish value, an owner is not entitled to compensation. Zoning is delegated to local, city, and/or county government. There are no federal zoning laws.

Ordinarily, a local planning commission sets zoning. If an owner objects to the zoning assigned to his or her property, an appeal can be made to the planning commission or a zoning board.

Zoning Variance   A variance is a permanent exception to the zoning. For example, if an owner has a lot that is 9,800 square feet and the zoning ordinance requires 10,000 square feet, the local zoning authority might grant an exception (a variance). To obtain a variance, the owner is required to show that failure to grant the variance would deprive the owner of the reasonable benefits of use enjoyed by other owners.

Conditional Use Permit   A conditional use permit is a special permission for a use otherwise not allowed under the zoning. The zoning laws must have considered the use and provided criteria for granting such permits. A public hearing, with appropriate notice to area residents, is usually required for rezoning, zoning variances, and conditional use permits.

Rezoning   This is an actual change in zoning. If the owner's request for zoning is turned down, the owner can appeal to the city council, the county board of supervisors or a special zoning appeals board. After exhausting all administrative remedies, the owner can appeal to the courts. Courts will overrule the planning commission decisions if a determination is made that the zoning was arbitrary or irresponsible.

Legal Nonconforming Use   A legal use that was in existence prior to current zoning that prohibits the use is allowed to continue under what is known as a *grandfather clause*, but it may not be expanded. Zoning will not be retroactive to completely bar a legal use previously in effect. A use, however, can be abated or eliminated if it is a nuisance.

Zoning provisions can allow a reasonable period of time in which the use must cease, allowing the owner to recoup the investment. If a nonconforming use structure is destroyed, it may not be rebuilt. Once a nonconforming use is abandoned, it usually cannot be reinstated.

Zoning Types and Terms

- **Downzoning**   Zoning to a more restrictive, lesser use is an act of downzoning. An example is rezoning from commercial use to single-family residential use. An owner is not entitled to compensation for loss in value suffered by downzoning the use.
- **Upzoning**   Rezoning to a less restrictive use such as from single-family use to multifamily use is known as **upzoning.**
- **Cluster zoning**   Zoning that allows grouping of residences but maintains density with green or open areas.
- **Conservation zoning**   Open zoning that excludes development to keep an area in natural or agricultural state.

- **Spot zoning**   Zoning of a parcel that is inconsistent with surrounding use. Courts might refuse to permit spot zoning.
- **Bulk zoning**   Zoning for density using setbacks, height restriction, parking requirements, etc.
- **Inclusionary zoning**   Zoning that requires that something be included in a development, such as a percentage of homes for low-income buyers.
- **Exclusionary zoning**   Zoning that specifically prohibits a use such as adult bookstores.
- **Cumulative zoning**   Zoning that allows less restrictive use, such as apartment zoning that allows single-family dwellings.
- **Noncumulative zoning**   Zoning that allows only the stated use.
- **Buffer zone** A strip of land or land use that separates different land uses such as a greenbelt between single-family residential use and multifamily structures.

Health and Safety/Building Codes

Building codes have been enacted by state and municipal governments under their **police power** to protect the health, safety, and general welfare of the people. Building codes, which set minimum acceptable standards, cover a wide spectrum: construction standards and methods, plumbing, electrical, heating, fire alarm, fire suppression, sewage disposal, and ventilation, to name a few.

Local building inspectors are the primary enforcers of compliance with code standards, although the local fire department might have jurisdiction over fire-related codes and the local health department over health codes. A building permit would be issued even though a structure violated private restrictive covenants. Restrictive covenants would be enforced privately.

Local building inspectors issue building permits, and before a new structure can be occupied, a Certificate of Occupancy must be obtained, certifying the building is fit for occupancy and complies with the codes.

Specification Code   Specification codes call for particular methods of construction or materials and can be very restrictive.

Performance Code   This code specifies performance requirements that give greater latitude to builders so long as standards of performance are met.

PRIVATE CONTROLS

Restrictive Covenants

Restrictive covenants, also known as **CC&Rs (covenants, conditions, and restrictions)** or **deed restrictions,** are private, voluntary agreements (contracts) governing land use. Zoning, on the other hand, is a mandatory public control of land use. When the CC&R's and zoning differ, the more restrictive of the two will prevail.

Restrictive covenants are usually intended to be beneficial restrictions because they seek to enhance land value and enjoyment by setting minimum or maximum requirements. Restrictive covenants are considered to be **encumbrances.** While beneficial, they nevertheless restrict the rights that owners would otherwise have. Typically, restrictive covenants control things like property use, single-family and other types of residences, setback, minimum lot size, minimum house size, maximum height, outbuildings, fences, the keeping of animals, and even landscaping and architectural styles.

Creation   Although they may be placed by agreement of all of the landowners subject to the restrictions, restrictive covenants are normally placed on land by subdividers who record the declaration of restrictions and then sell the parcels subject to the restrictions.

Duration   Restrictive covenants run with the land. That means the rights and duties imposed are passed on to subsequent landowners. These rights and duties may go on forever unless state statute sets a maximum time limit or the restriction sets its own time limitation.

Enforceability   Because covenants are promises that can be enforced by anyone who is subject to them, they are normally enforced through an injunction. An injunction is a court order that either forbids a person from performing an act or compels him or her to do so. Courts ordinarily will not grant relief, if any, of the following circumstances are present:

- The parties have waived their rights to enforce the covenants because of failure to enforce previous breaches of the covenants.
- **Laches** would prevent a party from asserting a right. Laches is a delay in bringing action that works to the detriment of another party. As an example, if a neighbor knew your new garage would be in violation of the restrictive covenant and waited until the garage was built before seeking a court order to have it removed, the court would likely bar enforcement of the restrictions by your neighbor because of laches.
- Changes have been made in the area that would cause the enforcement to be unreasonable.
- The court determines that the restrictions are against public policy or are a violation of the law.

Racial restrictions are considered void and unenforceable (*Shelley v. Kraemer*, U.S. Sup. Ct., 1948).

Restrictions that unreasonably restrict future conveyances (alienation) will not be enforced. As an example, a restriction against a transfer to other than a direct descendant of a grantor placing the restriction would be an unreasonable restraint on future conveyances.

A restriction that creates a monopoly by allowing a use on a single property and prohibiting the use on similar properties would likely be declared void.

Termination   Restrictive covenants could be terminated by any of the following:

- Merger of interests—one party acquiring all of the parcels covered by the restrictions
- Quitclaim deeds—an owner acquiring quitclaim deeds in his or her property from all other owners covered by the restrictions
- Agreement of termination or modification by all the parties covered, unless the restrictions allow a percentage of owners to modify or remove them.
- Expiration of a set time period established in the restrictions (some states limit the time period for private restrictions)

Conditions   A condition differs from a covenant in that it provides for forfeiture of title in the event of breach. Because courts dislike forfeiture for being too harsh, they generally will try to treat a condition merely as a covenant to avoid forfeiture.

WATER RIGHTS

Water rights are very important in many areas of the country and are based on state law. Some of the terms that are important in understanding water rights include the following:

- **Riparian rights**   These rights ensure that a landowner receives reasonable use of water flowing through, adjacent to, or under his or her property.
- **Littoral rights** A landowner's rights to reasonable use of water from a lake, an ocean, or a pond bordering the property (nonflowing water) are known as *littoral rights*. In some areas, the term **riparian** is used to describe both littoral and riparian rights.
- **Groundwater**   *Groundwater* refers to underground, nonflowing water. The right of a landowner to the reasonable use of this underground water is known as the **right of correlative user.** (Several states follow the common-law rule that a property owner has absolute rights to water below the surface that is not in a defined channel and would not be limited by reasonable use.)
- **Prior appropriation**   This theory, used in several arid western states, says that the first water users have priority rights over later users of water from the same source.
- **Accretion**   This refers to the gradual buildup of land by action of water. The land added belongs to the riparian or littoral rights owner.
- **Reliction**   This is land that forms after water recedes (such land belongs to owners of waterfront property); it is also called **dereliction.**
- **Avulsion**   This is the sudden tearing away of land by action of water, such as a change in a river's course. The owner retains title to land washed away by sudden avulsion and may reclaim it—for example, by returning a river to its original course.
- **Erosion**   Erosion is the gradual loss of land by action of water. The former owner loses title to land that is lost by this process.
- **Surface water**   Surface water has no defined channel. Landowners can be liable for damage caused by diverting the natural flow of surface water.
- **Floodwater**   Water that overflows a defined channel is floodwater. In most cases, landowners can dike property against floodwater.
- **Wetlands**   Swampy areas and areas that seasonally are covered with water support diverse plant animal and bird life. Such areas are subject to federal, state, and local controls aimed at preservation.
- **Flood Plains**   Level areas bordering waterways that are subject to inundation will often be subject to government restrictions on development.

LIENS

A lien is a monetary claim against a property. The property is security for a debt or an obligation. The debt that gives rise to the lien may be a result of agreement between the debtor and creditor, as in a mortgage, or it may arise as a result of operation of law, as in a tax lien. While the lienholder has no right of ownership, the lienholder does have a limited right to force the sale of the secured property to pay the obligation should the owner default.

Liens intentionally placed or that are allowed to be placed against a property, such as a mortgage lien, would be considered voluntary liens, while liens arising by action of law, such as a judgment on a tax lien, would be considered involuntary liens.

Liens applying to one specific property, such as a mechanic's lien, mortgage lien, or property tax lien, would be specific liens, while liens applying to all the property of the debtor, such as a judgment lien, would be considered general liens.

Mechanic's Lien

A mechanic's lien is a statutory lien (established by state law) used to secure payment for labor, services, or materials used in construction, repair, or improvement of real property. It is based on the theory that the mechanic (the supplier of material or services) has enhanced the value of the property, and to deny his or her rights would be to unjustifiably enrich the property owner. A mechanic's lien is specific to the property on which the work was performed. The mechanic must acknowledge the lien before a notary, file (record) the lien within a prescribed time, and generally verify that the facts stated are correct.

Verification is swearing to the truthfulness of a statement. Property owners can protect themselves against mechanics' liens by requiring lien waivers from contractors, subcontractors, and suppliers of material. In many states, unlicensed contractors cannot file a mechanic's lien. If a mechanic's lien is not satisfied, the lienholder can force the sale of the property affected.

Some states require that the mechanic provide a preliminary notice to the owner that his or her work will subject the property to a lien. Some states allow filing of a **notice of completion,** which sets the time period for the filing of liens.

Some states allow mechanics' liens to be placed against a property even though the owner did not consent to the work. This usually applies to work ordered by a tenant or a buyer under a contract for deed (land contract). However, most of these states allow the owner to protect his or her interests by recording and posting a **notice of nonresponsibility** within a certain time after becoming aware of the work.

> Know the priority of mechanics' liens in your state for the state specific portion of your examination.

Priority of Mechanics' Liens   *Mechanics' liens* must be filed within a time period, specified by state law, after the work is completed. In some states, mechanics' liens take priority over prior recorded mortgages, but in most states, priority is based on recording.

Priority of mechanics' liens varies greatly among states. In some states, all mechanics' liens have equal priority; other states assign different priority based on criteria such as the following:

- Date on which the contractor started work
- Date on which the first work was performed (no matter who did it; this might include delivery of construction material to the site)
- Date of the construction contract
- Date on which the lien was filed

Judgment

In a lawsuit, a plaintiff brings a legal action against a defendant based on a claim. A *judgment* is a final order by a court that the defendant must pay the plaintiff an amount of money. When an **abstract of judgment** is recorded, the judgment becomes a general lien on all real and personal property owned by the debtor within the county where the abstract of judgment was recorded. A judgment can be recorded in more than one county. The duration of the judgment lien and renewals vary from state to state. By a **writ of execution,** the judgment creditor can have property sold by the sheriff to satisfy the judgment.

Attachment

An *attachment* is a lien placed on the property of a debtor before a judgment has been rendered. The purpose of the attachment is to assure the plaintiff that, by bringing the property under custody of the court, there will be property to levy against after a judgment is rendered. An attachment is generally available only for unsecured claims based on an existing contract. Some states grant an attachment only when it is believed the defendant will flee or otherwise dispose of the property. To obtain an attachment, a party might be required to post a bond.

Lis Pendens

A *lis pendens* is a recorded notice of a pending lawsuit concerning an interest in real property. It serves as constructive or public notice of an interest claimed in the subject property by a party other than the owner of record. Any purchaser of the property would take title subject to any rights the person who filed the lis pendens has against the property.

Additional Liens

Mortgages and trust deeds and property taxes are specific liens against real estate. However, income tax liens are general liens against all of the debtor's property.

Priority of Liens

Priority of liens works similarly to priority of recordation of title. The first recorded lien generally has priority over liens placed in the public record at a later time, except for certain special cases such as tax liens and mechanics' liens. Liens for property taxes and special assessments take priority over other liens, no matter when they were incurred; however, the priority of most liens is based on time and date of recording. Because a lien is secured by property, the lienholder has the right to force foreclosure if the owner fails to meet his or her obligations. In a foreclosure, liens are paid off from the sale proceeds in their order of priority. If the foreclosing lienholder buys the property at the foreclosure sale, title is taken subject to prior liens, but liens of lesser priority are lost. To be effective, the lien must be recorded in the county where the property is located.

EASEMENTS

An easement is an irrevocable right or interest one party has in another's land. A typical easement is a right of way to enter, called **ingress,** and exit, called **egress,** property over another person's property. Easements normally run (transfer), with the land. For an exception, see "Easement in Gross" below.

Dominant Tenement   The estate that uses another's land for an easement is held by the dominant tenement holder. By using a right of way, that person "dominates" the land use of another.

Servient Tenement   The land that is used by (or that "serves") the land of another is the servient tenement.

Types of Easements

Easement in Gross   This is an easement without a dominant tenement. While land of another is subject to the easement (servient tenement), no land is benefited. This is the case for easements for signs or utility lines. Because an easement in gross has no dominant tenement, the easement is personal to the easement holder and does not run, or transfer, with the land, although it can be personally transferred.

Appurtenant Easement   Any easement other than an easement in gross would transfer with the land. Such an easement would be appurtenant, that is, joined to and benefitting the dominant tenement.

Affirmative Easement   The right to use the land of another for some stated purpose is an affirmative easement. For example, a right of entry over such land is an affirmative easement.

Negative Easement   The right to prohibit an owner from a certain use, such as a height restriction to preserve light or view, is a negative easement.

Implied Easement   Although not expressly stated, an implied easement can be created by intent of the parties. A grantor conveys the implied right to use those apparent and visible easements that are necessary for reasonable use of the property conveyed. (See "Creation of Easements" that follows.)

Easement by Necessity   In some states, an easement by necessity is an implied easement whereby the easement right is essential to beneficial use of the property. Generally, it involves a property that has become landlocked by a prior conveyance. The property of the dominant and servient tenements must have been under common ownership in the past. The courts generally take the position that a prior grantor simply neglected to provide for the easement right.

Solar Easement   A solar easement is an easement to protect an owner's access to sunlight for solar collectors.

Conservation Easement   A negative easement that prohibits development. It provides that land be kept in natural state or for agricultural use only.

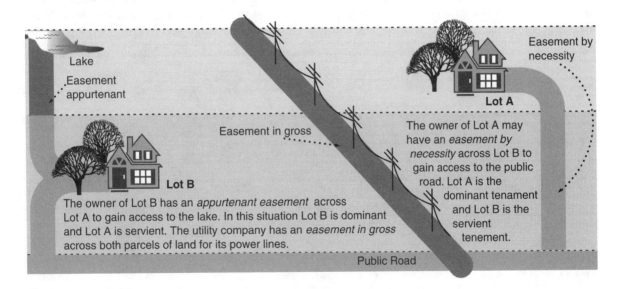

Creation of Easements

Easements may be created by any of the following means.

Grant or Reservation in Deed   This method either conveys the easement right or conveys the land and reserves the easement.

Agreement   If two neighboring landowners consent to a shared driveway or a party wall on their property line, an easement is created by agreement.

Implication Sometimes an easement is created by law whereby a single owner of two parcels of land creates a necessary use over one of the parcels and then conveys a property separately. For example, assume that the owner of parcels A and B, shown in the figure on this page, builds homes on both parcels. Assume further that parcel B's driveway goes across parcel A. If the owner sells parcel B, the court likely would determine that there was an implied easement over parcel A.

Necessity Creating useless, landlocked property is against public policy. In many states, it is possible to obtain an easement by necessity to gain access to such property by a court action. If any other access is possible, an easement by necessity will not be granted. Should another access to the property be later acquired, this access will terminate the easement by necessity.

Prescription This is an easement created by adverse use that is use against the interests of the servient tenement. Generally, the use must be adverse, hostile, open, notorious, continuous, and uninterrupted for a period of time prescribed by state statute. The user can be treated as a trespasser until the easement is perfected.

In many states, tacking on is permitted, which means one user can use property for a period of time and a successor uses it for an additional period of time to satisfy the statutory period for uninterrupted use. In many states, nonuse of the prescriptive easement for a statutory period will terminate the easement.

Eminent Domain A government body can take private property or an easement for a necessary public use; however, just compensation must be given. Eminent domain is not police power because police power does not require compensation. The power of eminent domain is often given to utilities, schools, hospitals, railroads, etc., because they serve a public good.

Term of an Easement

Easements may be created for a specific term of years, after which they end. In some states, easements cannot exceed a statutory period, whereas in others, they can go on forever.

Easements end upon the happening of specific events, such as one of the following:

- **Expiration** Easement ends once a stated or statutory period ends.
- **Agreement** A quitclaim deed from the holder of the dominant tenement to the holder of the servient tenement extinguishes the easement.
- **Abandonment** In some states, intentional nonuse for a statutory period ends the easement. In other states, nonuse will terminate only an easement created by prescription.

- **Destruction** If the servient tenement is destroyed, so is the easement.
- **Merger** If one owner acquires ownership of the dominant *and* servient tenements, the easement is lost because ownership includes the lesser right of the easement.
- **End of Purpose** An easement created for a particular purpose ends once that purpose no longer exists.

LICENSE

A license is a use granted by an owner's permission. Because it is permissive, the license grants no rights to the owner. Unlike an easement, the grantor may revoke it. Because the use is permissive and not considered an adverse use, it is not hostile; therefore, a license holder cannot obtain a prescriptive easement.

ENCROACHMENT

Encroachment is trespass by placing improvements, such as a building or fence, on or over another's land. The property owner can take court action, known as **ejectment,** to have the encroachment removed. Inaction could result in the trespasser gaining a right to continued use.

Courts can order an encroachment removed, but if the encroachment is minimal and/or the cost of removal significant, a court might order money damages or even allow an unintentional encroacher to purchase the land.

NUISANCE

A person cannot use property in such a manner that it unreasonably interferes with the reasonable use of others' property. Such unreasonable use is a trespass to the senses and is known in law as a *nuisance.*

Normally, a nuisance is a nonphysical invasion—a smell, light, dust, vibration, radio interference or dangerous activity. A **private nuisance** affects a relatively small area of the community, whereas a **public nuisance** affects a larger area. An **abatement action**, to require removal of the nuisance, or an injunction, to cease the activity, can be brought against a private nuisance by another property owner, but usually the city or county would have to bring the action against a public nuisance.

REAL PROPERTY TAX COMPUTATIONS

Real estate taxes are **ad valorem taxes;** that is, tax is assessed according to the value of the property. The tax assessor sets the value for each nonexempt property. Assessed value could be market value or a percentage of market value. Many states have state boards of equalization that ensure that valuations are set uniformly throughout the state. Property owners can appeal assessments, but not the tax rate, within a specified period of time through an appeal board. The total of the assessed valuations in a jurisdiction is known as the assessment roll, assessment tax base or tax roll.

Tax Rate

To determine the tax rate, the taxation authority divides the budgetary needs by the assessment roll:

$$\frac{\text{Budget Needs}}{\text{Assessment Roll}} = \text{Tax Rate}$$

For example, if a community needed $850,000 and had a tax base of $20,000,000, the tax rate per dollar of assessed valuation would be $.0425.

$$\frac{850,000}{20,000,000} = .0425$$

Tax rates are often expressed in mills. A **mill** is 1/10 of a cent, or $.001. The tax rate of $.0425 per dollar of evaluation could be expressed as 42½ mills. To determine the taxes, simply multiply the tax rate by the assessed valuation.

$$\text{Assessed Value} \times \text{Tax Rate} = \text{Annual Tax Amount}$$

Using the .0425 per dollar rate, the taxes on a home assessed at $80,000 would be $80,000 times .0425, which equals $3,400.

Assessed valuation is not necessarily the same as market value; it could be a much lower or even a higher figure.

Equalization Factor   In some areas where assessments are not considered equitable, an equalization factor is used. The assessed value is multiplied by the factor to determine the value for tax purposes.

Homeowners Tax Exemptions   Many states allow monetary tax exemptions for home-owners and/or veterans.

Tax Sale

If the taxes are not paid, they become a specific lien on the property. After a specified period, a sale at public auction is held. The tax collector issues a tax deed or quitclaim deed to the purchaser. States that allow the property owner a statutory period of redemption after the sale generally issue a certificate of the sale to the purchaser. A tax deed is not provided until the redemption period has expired.

Because real estate taxes typically are considered a priority lien, title at a tax sale passes to the purchaser free of any mortgages, mechanics' liens, or judgment liens against the former owner.

Special Assessments

Like property taxes, special assessments are property liens that take precedence over other liens. Special assessments cover improvements that directly benefit a property (road improvement, sidewalks, sewer, etc.). Assessments are based on benefits received and are often made on a front-foot (road frontage) basis. Because special assessments are specific liens, nonpayment can result in a public sale of the property.

Your Pertinent State Information

1.   What are your state's as well as your local subdivision's approval requirements and disclosures?

2.   What are the restrictive covenants' time restrictions?

3.   What kind of priority does the mechanic's lien have in your state?

4.   What are the notice requirements for mechanics' liens?

5.   What are the time restrictions on filing mechanics' liens?

6.   What are the requirements and applicability of your state's notice of nonresponsibility?

7.   What is the duration of a judgment lien?

8.   What are the attachment requirements and duration?

9.   What is the statutory limit on easements?

10. Is an easement by necessity allowed?

11. What are the special requirements for prescriptive easement?

12. Is tacking on allowed for prescriptive easement?

13. What are your state's homeowner tax exemptions?

14. What are the redemption rights (if any) after a tax sale?

CHAPTER 2 QUIZ

Land Use Controls and Restrictions

1. A utility company has the recorded right to erect poles on an owner's property and run electrical lines over it. The utility company has a(n):

   (A) negative easement
   (B) prescriptive easement
   (C) easement in gross
   (D) license

2. A property has an assessed value of $137,500. With an equalization factor of 117 percent and a tax rate of .037 per dollar of value, what are the taxes?

   (A) $1,608.75
   (B) $5,952.37
   (C) $16,087.50
   (D) $16,875.00

3. A lien on real property can be created by:

   (A) a contractor who makes improvements
   (B) restrictive covenants
   (C) an encroachment
   (D) unauthorized use

4. *T* had an easement over the land of *U*. *T* purchased *U's* land and resold it to *V* without mentioning the easement. What would be the result?

   (A) *T's* easement remains intact because the easement remains once it is a matter of record.
   (B) *T* has lost the easement rights.
   (C) *U* now has easement rights over the land of *V*.
   (D) *V* now has an easement right over the land of *U*.

5. A landowner who properly takes water from a river flowing through the property is exercising a(n):

   (A) littoral right
   (B) prescriptive right
   (C) riparian right
   (D) avulsion

6. A property has littoral rights. This means that the property:

   (A) is subject to restrictive zoning
   (B) borders a sea or an ocean
   (C) has ownership restrictions spelled out in the deed
   (D) has oil and mineral rights

7. A property was appraised for tax purposes at 80 percent of its $140,000 purchase price. The millage rate is 25.8. What will the annual taxes be on the property?

   (A) $2,064
   (B) $2,890
   (C) $2,900
   (D) $3,612

8. A lien differs from other encumbrances in that a lien:

   (A) is a monetary claim
   (B) can be enforced by an injunction
   (C) is a permissive right
   (D) restricts use

9. An exception to the zoning granted by a planning or zoning commission would be known as:

   (A) a variance
   (B) a nonconforming use
   (C) rezoning
   (D) downzoning

10. A zoning change from single-family use to multifamily use would be:

    (A) downzoning
    (B) bulk zoning
    (C) conservation zoning
    (D) upzoning

11. An easement that prohibits development of the servient tenement would be a(n):

    (A) easement by necessity
    (B) affirmative easement
    (C) conservation easement
    (D) implied easement

12. A writ of execution would be used to enforce a(n):

    (A) lis pendens
    (B) attachment
    (C) judgment
    (D) zoning

13. The term *lis pendens* refers to:

    (A) a valid property listing
    (B) an executory contract
    (C) construction work in progress
    (D) a recorded notice of a pending lawsuit

14. *J* built a service station in compliance with existing zoning. A subsequent change in the zoning excluded service station use on the site. What are *J's* rights?

    (A) *J* is entitled to have the zoning changed.
    (B) *J's* use is a nonconforming use.
    (C) *J* has an automatic variance.
    (D) The city is required to give *J* a conditional use permit.

15. *F* had an easement allowing *F* to place communication equipment on top of an adjacent 30-story building owned by *G*. The building was destroyed by fire. What are *F's* rights?

    (A) *F* can force *G* to rebuild.
    (B) *F's* rights terminated with the destruction of the building.
    (C) If another building is built on the site, *F's* rights would be renewed.
    (D) *F's* rights were lost by merger.

16. *K* sold land to *L* with a restrictive covenant that the property cannot be conveyed to non-Caucasians. *L* wishes to sell to a buyer who is not a Caucasian. Which of the following statements describes *L's* rights?

    (A) *L* can go to court to have the restriction declared void.
    (B) If *L* sells to a non-Caucasian person, then *L* would be liable to *K* for damages.
    (C) If *L* sells to a non-Caucasian person, title would revert to *K*.
    (D) *L* can ignore the restriction and sell to any qualified buyer.

17. To remove a nuisance, a property owner would bring an action for:

    (A) attachment
    (B) abatement
    (C) encroachment
    (D) injunction

18. *J's* nonconforming use predated the present zoning. *J's* right to the use:

    (A) can be abated if the use is a nuisance
    (B) must immediately cease
    (C) can be expanded
    (D) can be reinstated even if abandoned

19. A condition differs from a covenant on the point of:

    (A) writing
    (B) acknowledgment
    (C) forfeiture
    (D) time limitations

20. A recorded instrument that places private restrictions on land use would be a(n):

    (A) zoning restriction
    (B) restrictive covenant
    (C) attachment
    (D) nuisance

21. A lien that covers all real and personal property of the debtor within the county where recorded would be a(n):

    (A) mechanic's lien
    (B) judgment lien
    (C) attachment
    (D) lis pendens

22. What kind of zoning would require that a developer build 10 percent of the homes in a subdivision for low-income families?

    (A) Exclusionary
    (B) Cumulative
    (C) Inclusionary
    (D) Conservation

23. Restrictive covenants can be enforced by:

    (A) the local building inspector
    (B) anyone who knows of them
    (C) anyone who is subject to the restrictions
    (D) the local zoning commission

24. An example of a public nuisance would be a:

    (A) neighbor building a driveway over the property of another
    (B) factory that emits hazardous chemical smoke
    (C) neighbor who conducts a business from the home
    (D) neighbor who plays loud rock music constantly

25. An enforceable restrictive covenant could prohibit:

    (A) transfer outside bloodlines
    (B) a property from being used as a church
    (C) an owner from transferring or encumbering a property
    (D) ownership by a female

26. A permissive use that gives no future rights to the user would be a(n):

    (A) restrictive covenant
    (B) nonconforming use
    (C) license
    (D) encroachment

27. Which of the following is the decimal equivalent of 3 mills?

    (A) .3
    (B) .03
    (C) .003
    (D) .0003

28. An easement created by adverse use would be an easement by:

    (A) necessity
    (B) prescription
    (C) reservation
    (D) grant

29. When J sold land to K, the deed failed to give K the right of access to the land over a road on J's land. The court later determined that K had the right to use the road because there was a(n):

    (A) express easement
    (B) easement by reservation
    (C) prescriptive easement
    (D) easement by implication

30. J uses K's land under an easement right. K's land is considered a(n):

    (A) dominant tenement
    (B) servient tenement
    (C) prescriptive right
    (D) affirmative right

31. An offensive nonphysical invasion of the land of another would be a(n):

    (A) encroachment
    (B) license
    (C) nuisance
    (D) abatement

32. An easement without a dominant tenement would be an:

    (A) implied easement
    (B) easement by necessity
    (C) appurtenant easement
    (D) easement in gross

33. Priority of judgment liens would be based on the:

    (A) date of the debt
    (B) date of the lien recording
    (C) amount of the debt
    (D) reason for the debt

34. A judgment lienholder foreclosed and purchased property at the sale. Which of the following describes the foreclosing lienholder's rights?

    (A) Title is free of all but tax liens.
    (B) Title is clear of all liens.
    (C) Title is subject to property tax liens and prior liens.
    (D) Title is subject to all liens.

35. J bought K's property but was not aware that L had filed a lis pendens action concerning the property prior to the purchase. The result would be that:

    (A) L would take title to the property
    (B) J's title would be subject to L's claim
    (C) the lis pendens would be terminated by the transfer
    (D) the title would be held in trust for the benefit of L

36. The correct chronological order of events involving a judgment would be:

    (A) judgment, lis pendens, attachment
    (B) attachment, judgment, execution
    (C) attachment, judgment, lis pendens
    (D) lis pendens, judgment, attachment

37. Which of the following is a general lien?

    (A) Mechanic's lien
    (B) Property tax lien
    (C) Special tax assessment
    (D) Judgment lien

38. While a lot is zoned for apartments, single-family homes can be built because the zoning is:

    (A) inclusionary
    (B) cumulative
    (C) exclusionary
    (D) noncumulative

39. Which of the following liens is a voluntary lien?

    (A) Tax lien
    (B) Mortgage lien
    (C) Judgment lien
    (D) Attachment

40. *L* knew that *M* was going to build a new structure that would be an encroachment over *L's* land. *L* waited until the structure was completed before bringing an action to remove the encroachment. A court ruling against *L* would be based on:

    (A) prior appropriation
    (B) laches
    (C) a lis pendens
    (D) *M's* littoral rights

41. An example of downzoning would be:

    (A) placing height limitations on property
    (B) zoning from single-family to multiple-family use
    (C) zoning from multiple-family to single-family use
    (D) zoning requiring a percentage of low-income housing

42. The zoning in a subdivision allows duplexes, but the restrictive covenants restrict the use to single-family dwellings. An owner in the subdivision:

    (A) can build either a duplex or a single-family home
    (B) can convert a single-family home to a duplex
    (C) is restricted to single-family use
    (D) can bring an action to abate the restrictive covenants

43. The property tax amount would be determined by:

    (A) dividing the assessment roll by the budget needs.
    (B) multiplying the assessed value by the tax rate
    (C) dividing the assessed value by the tax rate
    (D) dividing the tax rate by the assessed value

44. *Tacking on* refers to:

    (A) an addition to a structure
    (B) an additional party to a document
    (C) obtaining an easement by prescription
    (D) a codicil to a will

45. What is required before a tenant can move into a newly completed building?

    (A) The builder must supply lien waivers.
    (B) The lender must approve.
    (C) An occupancy permit must be obtained.
    (D) The owner must post a completion bond.

46. An easement in gross differs from other easements in that it:

    (A) is attached to a person, not a property
    (B) is a revocable easement
    (C) has a definite termination date
    (D) is an appurtenant easement

47. A city can enact ordinances intended to provide for health, safety, morals, and general welfare under its:

    (A) injunction power
    (B) police power
    (C) power of eminent domain
    (D) riparian right

48. Land being added to other land by the gradual action of water is known as:

    (A) evulsion
    (B) accretion
    (C) littoral rights
    (D) prior appropriation

49. An owner who goes to court to obtain access for landlocked property would request a(n):

    (A) negative easement
    (B) dedication
    (C) easement by necessity
    (D) adverse possession

50. A homeowner converted the basement into a rental unit. This violated a restrictive covenant. Another homeowner wishing to enforce the covenant would commence an action for:

    (A) liquidated damages
    (B) specific performance
    (C) forfeiture
    (D) injunction

CHAPTER 2 QUIZ ANSWERS

Land Use Controls and Restrictions

1. (C) This easement has no dominant tenement so it is an easement in gross. It is also an affirmative easement. (page 28)
2. (B) To determine taxes, multiply the equalization factor by the assessed value and then apply the tax rate. (page 32)
3. (A) This would be a mechanic's lien. While restrictive covenants are encumbrances, they are not liens. Liens are monetary claims. (pages 26–27)
4. (B) The easement was lost by merger. Ownership includes the lesser interest of the easement holder. (page 31)
5. (C) Riparian rights apply to flowing water. (page 26)
6. (B) This is the reasonable right to use of a nonflowing body of water adjoining a property. (page 26)
7. (B) .80 × $140,000 = $112,000; $112,000 × .0258 = $2,889.60. (page 32)
8. (A) With the right of foreclosure. (page 26)
9. (A) Zoning is not changed, but an exception is made. (page 23)
10. (D) Upzoning is a change to a less restrictive use. (page 23)
11. (C) A conservation easement prohibits development. (page 29)
12. (C) The sheriff would seize and sell a debtor's nonexempt property. (page 27)
13. (D) It indicates that a claim is being made against a particular property. (page 28)
14. (B) A nonconforming use is normally allowed to remain under a grandfather clause. (page 23)
15. (B) Destruction of servient tenement ends the rights of the holder of the easement. (page 31)
16. (D) Racial restrictions are void and unenforceable. (page 25)
17. (B) Abatement is a court action to remove a nuisance. (page 31)
18. (A) Grandfather clause allows continued use unless use is a nuisance. (page 23)
19. (C) If the condition is breached, title could revert to the grantor. (page 25)
20. (B) Private restrictions are placed by restrictive covenant. (page 24)
21. (B) Judgment liens are general liens. (page 27)
22. (C) Inclusionary zoning requires that development include some element. (page 24)
23. (C) Enforcement action is usually an injunction. Anyone subject to restriction can enforce it against others. (page 25)
24. (B) This would be a nuisance to a large part of the community (a public nuisance is a matter of degree). (page 31)
25. (B) Specified uses, such as only single-family dwellings, can be enforced, but racial restrictions and unreasonable restraints on alienation (transfer) are not enforceable. (pages 24–25)
26. (C) A license is permissive and not a right. It can be ended at will. (page 31)
27. (C) A mill is 1/10 of a cent (.001). (page 32)
28. (B) Adverse, hostile use for a statutory period of time can create an easement right. (page 30)
29. (D) The use was intended or implied but not stated. (page 29)
30. (B) *K*'s land serves the land of *J*. (page 28)
31. (C) A nuisance could be smell, noise, vibration, sight, or use that endangers others. (page 31)
32. (D) It is personal, and the right does not transfer with land. (page 28)
33. (B) Later lienholder's rights are subject to the rights of prior lienholders. (page 28)
34. (C) The purchaser at a foreclosure sale takes title subject to liens having priority over the foreclosing lien. (page 28)
35. (B) *J* had constructive notice of *L*'s claim. (page 28)
36. (B) A lis pendens as well as an attachment occurs prior to a judgment. Execution follows the judgment. (page 27–28)
37. (D) It applies against all of a debtor's property. (page 27)
38. (B) Cumulative zoning allows less restrictive uses. (page 24)
39. (B) The other liens are involuntary. (page 26)
40. (B) *L*'s delay in bringing action worked to *M*'s detriment. (page 25)
41. (C) This is a change to a more restrictive use. (page 23)
42. (C) When zoning and restrictive covenants differ, the more restrictive use prevails. (page 24)
43. (B) Rate times assessed value. (page 32)

44. (C)   Adverse use by two or more successors in interest may be joined to fulfill the statutory period required. (page 30)
45. (C)   This is normally provided by the building inspector's office. (page 24)
46. (A)   It can be personally transferred. (page 28)
47. (B)   There is no compensation for loss in value due to exercise of police power. (page 23)
48. (B)   It belongs to the littoral or riparian rights owner. (page 26)
49. (C)   It may be granted when no other access is possible. (page 30)
50. (D)   The homeowner would seek a cessation of rental activity. (page 25)

Income Taxation and Transfer of Title

> While knowledge of income tax considerations is extremely important for real estate salespersons, there will be only a few questions on the salesperson's exam relating to this subject. There will be greater emphasis on income tax matters on the broker's examination.

INCOME TAX CONSIDERATIONS

Unless subject to an exemption, gains or profit from the sale of property are taxable. While losses from the sale of business or investment property can be used as deductions against other income, a tax loss cannot be taken for the sale of a personal residence.

Determining Gain

The amount of the taxable gain is computed by deducting the seller's adjusted cost basis or book value from the net sales price. **Adjusted cost basis** is the original cost plus improvements, less depreciation.

Although improvements may enhance the value and increase the cost base, repairs will not. Repairs are considered operating expenses and are deductible expenses for income and investment property in the year expended. For example, if a home originally cost $100,000 and the buyer spent $10,000 in improvements, the adjusted cost basis would be $110,000.

$$\underset{\text{Cost}}{\$100,000} + \underset{\text{Improvements}}{\$10,000} = \underset{\substack{\text{Book Value} \\ \text{(Adjusted Cost Basis)}}}{\$110,000}$$

If the owner then sold the property for $150,000, there would be a taxable gain of $40,000, the difference between sales price and book value (adjusted cost basis). The seller's sales costs would reduce the taxable gain. As an example, if the seller incurred commission and closing costs of $8,000, the gain in the example above would be reduced to $32,000.

Taxpayer Relief Act of 1997

Under the Taxpayer Relief Act of 1997, homeowners were given an advantageous exemption from taxation.

To be eligible for this new exemption, a homeowner must have occupied a residence for a total of 24 months during the preceding 5-year period.

Occupancy does not need to be continuous. For example, it could be for six months per year over a period of four years. Purchase of a replacement residence is not required for this exemption. The exemption from taxation is:

- married couples, $500,000;
- single persons, $250,000.

As an example, if a married couple paid $450,000 for a home and spent $70,000 in improvements, they would have a cost basis of $520,000. If they sold the property for $1,000,000, their capital gain of $480,000 would be exempt from taxation providing they had met the two-out-of-five year residency rule. Their gain was $480,000, and as a married couple, they have a $500,000 exemption from taxation:

Cost of home	$ 450,000
Improvements	70,000
Adjusted cost basis	520,000
Sale price	1,000,000
Adjusted cost basis	520,000
Capital gain	$ 480,000

Unmarried co-owners could each claim $250,000 as an exemption to obtain a total exemption of $500,000 on a sale.

This is not a one-time exemption. As an example, a married couple could purchase and occupy a house for two years, sell it at a profit, repeat the process over and over again, and still be entitled to exempt gains from taxations of up to $500,000 for each sale.

Income Tax Deductions (Homeowners)

Interest is a tax-deductible expense for homeowners, with some limitations:

- The interest limit on a home-purchase loan(s) is up to $1 million for the home and one second home loan(s), provided the loan balance does not exceed the cost of the residences plus improvements. Therefore, if a homeowner had a $2 million purchase loan, only the interest on $1 million would be deductible.
- For home equity loans, interest is deductible for loans not to exceed a total of $100,000 (principal residence plus one second home), provided that the combined home loans don't exceed the fair market value of the homes.

Discount points paid by a buyer are considered to be prepaid interest and are also deductible as interest in the year paid.

Property Taxes   Property taxes are a deductible homeowner expense. No other cash expenses or depreciation may be taken on a residence that is not used for business or income purposes.

INVESTMENT PROPERTY

Equity   This is an owner's interest in a property. It is the difference between the fair market value and the amount owed on the property (mortgage-trust deeds, liens).

Income   Gross scheduled income is the scheduled gross based on anticipated 100 percent occupancy. Adjusted gross income is the gross income adjusted for an estimated vacancy factor and collection loss and is known as the **effective gross income.** Net income is what an investor actually realizes from a property, considering all expenses. While interest payments are considered an expense for investment property, payments on principal are not.

Cash Flow   Cash flow is **net spendable income** after all cash expenses are deducted. This would include payments on the principal.

Liquidity   Real estate investments are considered illiquid because of the relatively long time it takes to turn the investment into cash by a sale. Investors can, however, borrow on their equity.

Appreciation   Real estate values have generally increased more rapidly than the rate of inflation.

Depreciation   Investment property can be depreciated for tax purposes, which can shelter income from taxation. Depreciation is a deduction for wear and tear of improvements. Homeowners cannot depreciate their personal residences.

Interest and Taxes   These are tax-deductible expenses for income and investment property as well as personal residences.

Leverage Because real estate purchases are generally financed, an investor is able to purchase property with a value far greater than the down payment. This allows the investor to take advantage of appreciation on the total value, not just the investor's equity.

> **Note**: Information on capital gains tax and tax-deferred exchanges is more likely to be needed on the broker's than on the salesperson's examination.

Capital Gains

A capital gain is the profit from the sale of a capital asset (such as real estate). The costs of improvements are added to the value of the property (i.e., the cost basis) for tax purposes. Repair costs are deductions from income that are taken in the year of the expenditure. Assume an investment property was originally purchased for $120,000, and the owner spent $38,000 in improvements and took $42,000 in depreciation. The cost basis would be

$$\underset{\$120,000}{\text{Cost}} + \underset{\$38,000}{\text{Improvements}} - \underset{\$42,000}{\text{Depreciation}} = \underset{\$116,000}{\text{Cost Basis}}$$

If the owner sold the property for $120,000, the same price for which it was originally purchased, there still would be a $4,000 taxable capital gain.

$$\underset{\$120,000}{\text{Sales Price}} - \underset{\$116,000}{\text{Cost Basis}} = \underset{\$4,000}{\text{Taxable Gain}}$$

The capital gains tax rate is 20 percent for assets held more than 12 months (10 percent if the taxpayer is in the 15 percent tax bracket).

Property held for one year or less is taxed as regular income.

Property acquired after December 31, 2000, that is held for more than five years will have a maximum tax rate of 18 percent (8 percent if the taxpayer is in the 15 percent tax bracket).

Capital Loss

While a homeowner who sells at a loss cannot take tax advantage of the loss, owners of investment property can use a capital loss to offset a capital gain from the sale of another property. As an example, if an owner, in one year, sold one investment property at a $100,000 loss and a second investment property at a $100,000 gain, the loss would offset the gain, so no tax would be due. If the taxpayer has no gain in the year of the sale to offset the loss, the gain can be carried forward to the succeeding year.

Imputed Interest

Interest received is taxable as regular income, but a capital gain is taxed at a lower rate. Some sellers who are carrying back financing will raise the sale price and lower the rate of interest to have a lower total tax liability. To discourage this attempt to avoid taxes, the IRS requires that the lender charge a minimum rate of interest, based on IRS regulations. If a lower rate is charged, then the lender will be taxed for an imputed rate of interest even though it was not received.

Tax Deferred Exchange

By exchanging property, one can defer capital gains. A *tax-deferred exchange* (1031 exchange) can involve only property held for income and investments, and it must be like-for-like property, real property for real property.

Each party to an exchange keeps the old cost basis, increased by the amount of boot given or decreased by the amount of boot received. **Boot** is any item of personal property (usually money) given to even up a trade. Debt relief (assuming a lower indebtedness on the property received than on the property given) is considered boot.

Boot is taxable as gain to the party receiving it.

Section 1031 of the Internal Revenue Code provides for a delayed exchange known as a **Starker exchange.** A seller of property can indicate that the proceeds be held by an escrow holder to purchase another property. The property must be designated within 45 days of the closing, and the completion must occur within 180 days of the closing. In a delayed exchange the seller must never have control of the money.

Depreciation

An owner of income or investment property can deduct depreciation as an expense for tax purposes. This deduction is based on the premise that value decreases with age and depreciation allows the owner to recoup his or her investment.

For tax purposes, accountants must use a 27½-year life for residential rental property and a 39-year life for nonresidential property. Only improvements such as buildings can be depreciated; land is never depreciated. Improvements are considered to be **wasting assets** because value declines with age. However, land is regarded as being a permanent asset. Because residential property improvements can be depreciated 100 percent over 27½ years, accountants can depreciate 3.636 percent of the value each and every year until fully depreciated:

$$\frac{100\%}{27.5} = 3.636\%$$

Therefore, if the value of the improvements were $100,000, we could take $3,636 in depreciation as an expense each year for tax purposes.

Depreciating equal amounts each year over the life of an improvement is known as the **straight-line method** of depreciation.

Accelerated Depreciation   Prior to the Tax Reform Act of 1986, methods of accelerated depreciation were allowed that provided for greater depreciation in the early years of an asset's life. Accelerated depreciation is no longer allowed for newly acquired assets, although owners who properly used accelerated depreciation prior to tax law changes are allowed to continue the use.

Sinking Fund   This is the setting aside and investing of a sum of money each year so that by the time an asset needs replacement, the amount set aside plus the compound interest it earns will be enough for that purpose.

Reserve for Replacement   This is an accounting expense for tax purposes that sets up a reserve fund to replace short-lived assets such as air conditioners, roofs, appliances, etc. The amount reserved must be sufficient to maintain the anticipated income. A reserve differs from depreciation in that depreciation is a loss in value while a reserve defers income by setting it aside in advance of needs.

Tax Shelter

For business and income property, all expenses are deductible, including depreciation. A *tax shelter* reduces the income by showing a bookkeeping loss, such as depreciation.

Prior to the 1986 Tax Reform Act, investors could use their real estate losses to shelter other income—without limit. Noncash losses from depreciation could be used to reduce taxpayer liability to the government. Now, real estate losses, which are considered passive losses, can be used only to offset passive income (income from other real estate activities), with two exceptions:

1. Lower income investors have retained a limited ability to shelter other nonproperty income. Investors with a gross adjusted income of less than $100,000 can use passive real estate losses to shelter up to $25,000 of other income, such as wages. For taxpayers having between $100,000 and $150,000 of adjusted gross income, this shelter has been phased out. With each $2 of adjusted gross income exceeding $100,000, the $25,000 limit is reduced by $1. Investors who do not actively manage their property (this includes real estate syndicate investors) cannot use their passive losses to shelter active income.
2. Investors who qualify as real estate professionals can use passive losses to offset other income without limitations.

Income Tax Liens

Income tax liens, when recorded, become general liens against all property of the debtor. The property can be sold at a sheriff's sale to satisfy the lien. Purchasers take title subject to all existing prior liens.

FEDERAL ESTATE TAX (INHERITANCE TAX)

The value of estate property is calculated based on the value of the decedent's interest in the property (decedent's equity) at the time of his or her death.

Estates valued at $600,000 or less are exempt from federal estate taxation. (Exemptions increase gradually to $1,000,000 by the year 2006.) In addition, that portion of an estate that passes to the decedent's spouse is exempt from federal estate taxation.

Many states also impose taxes on estates.

GIFT TAXES

The federal government has a gift tax that taxes the donor. Some states also have gift taxes that tax either the donor or donee.

The federal gift tax has a $10,000 annual exemption per donee, so a person having five children could give each of them $10,000 per year ($50,000) without taxation. Because the $10,000 limitation applies to individual donors, the donor's spouse also could give an annual $10,000 gift to each donee, making a total of $100,000 in federal tax-free gifts each year. Real property can be conveyed by gift by giving a fractionalized interest to a donee each year.

The purpose of giving gifts often is to reduce the estate so that estate taxes are reduced or eliminated.

DOCUMENTARY TRANSFER TAX

Most states have a transfer tax on real property sales. The tax is generally based on the seller's equity being conveyed. If there were to be new financing, the tax will be based on the entire purchase price, but where loans are to be assumed, the tax would be on the seller's equity. Deeds will not be accepted for recordation without evidence that the tax has been paid.

TRANSFER/ALIENATION

Alienation is the legal term for transferring ownership or interest in real property and is most commonly achieved as a result of a sale or lease.

Transfers may be voluntary acts of the grantor or involuntary, where the property is taken away without the owner's consent.

Dedication   Dedication is a voluntary transfer of real property or property rights to a governmental unit. Customarily, either a right-of-way, such as an easement, or an actual title is transferred. Dedication can be for roads, school sites, parks, hospitals, and so on. Dedication might be required as a condition for approval of a development by a city or county. The recording of an approved subdivision map showing areas dedicated to the public is regarded as **statutory dedication.**

Involuntary Alienation

Involuntary alienation refers to transfers without the owner's consent.

Adverse Possession   Title can be acquired from another without permission by adverse possession. Several conditions must be met:

- The use must be continuous and uninterrupted for a period of time prescribed by statute. Some states allow continuous use by means of *tacking on.* The period of use of prior users may be added to that of a successor to satisfy the statutory possession period.
- The use must be exclusive.
- The use must be hostile. The owner's permission would cancel the hostile nature of the use.
- The use must be open and notorious so that a diligent owner would know that another person was in possession of the property.

Some states require that adverse possession be under some claim of right to the property or color (appearance) of title, or provide a shorter statutory period for use when under a claim of right (e.g., a deed from a person who falsely claimed ownership).

A number of states add the requirement that the adverse user pay the taxes. Claiming rights and paying taxes generally enhance the claims of adverse users.

A new owner cannot obtain broader rights by adverse possession than the former owner had. Therefore, if former owner *A* had only half the mineral rights, by adverse possession, owner *B* would take title to the property with only half the mineral rights.

To obtain **marketable title,** an adverse possessor must bring an action to quiet title that asks a court to determine ownership or obtain a quitclaim deed from the prior owner.

Title cannot be taken from the government by adverse possession; nor, ordinarily, can it be taken from an incompetent or a minor because neither can defend property properly.

Sheriff's Sale (Judgment Foreclosure)   When an abstract of judgment is recorded, it becomes a lien against real and personal property in the county where it is recorded. The creditor can get execution on the judgment. The sheriff can seize nonexempt property of the debtor and dispose of it by public sale to satisfy the judgment. Real property generally is then transferred by a sheriff's deed, which transfers no greater right than the debtor had. The purchaser at the sheriff's sale takes title subject to existing liens. In most cases, there is a period of redemption after a sheriff's sale during which the debtor can regain the property upon payment of the sales price plus costs and interest.

Homestead Exemption   In many states, homeowners are protected against unsecured creditors forcing the sale of their homes by homestead exemptions. If the amount of a home-owner's equity is the same or less than the statutory exemption, the unsecured creditor cannot force the sale of the homestead. In some states, the homeowner must record a declaration of homestead to be protected. In some states, a homestead creates a legal life estate.

Usually, the homeowner must reside on the premises to file a homestead declaration (a homestead would not be possible, therefore, on a vacant parcel). In some states, a lessee can file a homestead on his or her long-term lease rights.

Declarations of homestead do not offer protection against secured creditors, including mortgages, mechanics' liens, and judgments recorded prior to the homestead declaration, and property tax liens.

Foreclosure   A mortgagor or trustor (borrower) who defaults on a mortgage or trust deed may be foreclosed by the mortgagee (lender) through a public sale. The purchaser at a foreclosure sale takes title subject to all encumbrances that are senior to the foreclosing lien (priority liens such as property taxes and prior recorded liens), but junior encumbrances, recorded after the foreclosing lien was filed, are wiped out.

Condemnation   Under the police power of the state, a property may be condemned and ordered vacated or destroyed if it is unfit or unsafe for use or occupancy. An owner whose property is so condemned is not entitled to compensation.

Another type of condemnation proceeding is the taking of private property for public use under the power of eminent domain.

Eminent Domain   A government unit may take ownership of private property for public purposes without the owner's consent. This power may be delegated to public utilities, schools, hospitals and other institutions.

The owner is entitled to the property's fair market value as of the time it is taken. The owner can object to the amount offered and has the right to a court determination of fair value in a condemnation proceeding.

Eminent domain is not authorized under the police power of the state. Under police power, restrictions placed on property are to protect the public health, safety, morals, and general welfare and no compensation is given.

Severance Damage   When only part of the owner's land is taken by eminent domain and the taking results in a reduced value for the remaining land, the owner is entitled to compensation for this additional loss.

Inverse Condemnation   An owner can take action to force the condemnation of his or her property if government action has caused loss in value or the inability to use the property. Such an action might occur, for example, when a government takes away a former public access and the result is a landlocked parcel.

DEEDS

Deeds are voluntary transfer documents for an interest in real estate. A deed is used only once. When you buy, you receive a deed from the seller. When you sell, you give a new deed to the buyer. A deed is used to transfer only real property. Personal property is transferred by a **bill of sale.**

Requirements for a Valid Deed

Delivery   A valid conveyance or transfer of title requires that the deed be delivered to the grantee by the grantor during the grantor's lifetime. Mailing generally constitutes delivery. For delivery to occur, there must be intent to pass title immediately. A recorded deed is presumed to have been delivered.

Acceptance   Because the law does not force a person to take title, a valid deed requires acceptance. Acceptance can be any words or conduct of the grantee that indicates intent to accept. For example, a grantee offering to sell or lease the deeded property indicates acceptance of the deed. Failure to repudiate a grant within a reasonable time after learning of the grant also could indicate acceptance. Acceptance can be presumed where the grant clearly benefits the grantee.

Conveyance   A deed must have a **granting clause**, words indicating that title is to pass.

Writing   All deeds must be in writing.

Unambiguous Description   The property must be described so that boundaries can be known. Although a few states require a legal description on a deed, such a description generally is not required to convey title. However, it is required to obtain title insurance.

Habendum Clause   Many states require that a deed define the interest or estate granted (such as fee simple or life estate). This is the function of the habendum clause, which usually includes the phrase "to have and to hold." In some states, the deed is presumed to convey a fee simple interest if the extent of the grant is not specified.

Competent Grantor   The grantor must be legally capable of conveying title. Grantees do not always have to be competent parties—for example, title can pass to a minor by gift.

Definite Grantee   The grantee must be readily identifiable. Although property can be conveyed to a grantee using a fictitious name, the grantee must be a definite, specific person.

Signed The deed must be signed by the grantor. The grantee does not have to sign. A forged deed is void and conveys nothing, nor does an altered deed. For example, a deed in which the property description was changed without the grantor's consent would be considered void.

Not Required for a Valid Deed

Witnesses In most states, a deed need not be witnessed (unless the grantor signs with an X).

Recording Recording a deed makes the deed a matter of public record. The recording process gives an implied notice, known as **constructive notice,** to others of the interest conveyed. A deed must be recorded to give constructive notice of the transfer to third parties. However, recording is not required between the grantor and the grantee, who already have knowledge of the transfer.

Address of Parties Some states require the address of the grantee to record the deed. The purpose is to determine where tax statements are to be sent, but the deed need not be recorded to be valid between the parties.

Seal Most states do not require a seal for a deed.

Acknowledgment Acknowledgment is the admission by the grantor, before a notary, that he or she is the grantor and that the signing (execution) is an act of free will. Acknowledgment is not required to have a valid transfer between the parties, but in most states, it is required to record the deed.

Consideration In some states, the consideration must be stated in the deed, whereas in others, it need not be. Love and affection is considered to be good consideration but it is not regarded as valuable consideration.

Date The deed need not be dated. It is considered dated as of the date of recording.

Types of Deeds

Warranty Deed Under a warranty deed, the grantor personally guarantees or warrants clear title. There are five basic covenants or promises in a warranty deed:
1. **Covenant of seisin** The grantor warrants that he or she has rightful ownership of the property and has the right to convey.
2. **Covenant of quiet enjoyment** The grantor warrants that the title will be good against third parties and will indemnify the grantee should any third party establish a superior claim.
3. **Covenant against encumbrances** The grantor warrants that the property is free of liens or other encumbrances except as stated in the deed.
4. **Covenant of warranty forever** The grantor promises to indemnify the grantee for any loss because of failure of title at any future time.
5. **Covenant of further assurance** If any further instrument or act is needed to perfect title, grantor promises to provide it at grantor's expense.

General Warranty Deed The grantor binds himself or herself and all heirs to defend the title of the grantee (and that of his or her heirs) against claims of others.

Special Warranty Deed The grantor warrants that he or she has made no undisclosed transfer of title or encumbrance (limitation on use or title). Warranty of title is limited to matters concerning title during the grantor's ownership. There is no warranty as to title defects prior to the grantor's ownership.

Grant Deed   Used in a few states, normally in conjunction with a policy of title insurance, the grant deed contains two warranties:

1. The grantor has not previously conveyed the property.
2. The grantor has placed no undisclosed encumbrances against the property.

The grant deed, as well as warranty deeds, generally convey **after-acquired title**—meaning that if, after a sale, the grantor obtains a better interest, such as a quitclaim deed from an encumbrance holder, the after-acquired interest automatically passes to the grantee.

Quitclaim Deed   This deed transfers whatever interests, if any, the grantor may have in property without making any claims of having any interest or ownership. Quitclaim deeds are frequently used to remove **clouds on title** (anything that appears to impair the title) or to give up an easement.

Bargain and Sale Deed   This deed is similar to a quitclaim deed in that the grantor does not guarantee title but is different because the grantor implies that he or she has an interest in the property. There is no such implication in a quitclaim deed.

Sheriff's Deed   Given at a sheriff's sale, the sheriff's deed carries no warranties or representations. It gives only the interest that was foreclosed. There could still be encumbrances.

Tax Deed   A tax deed is given at a property tax sale. Property taxes and special assessments generally are priority liens taking precedence over even prior recorded liens. In most states, a tax sale would wipe out liens such as mortgages.

Gift Deed   Title can pass by gift. Lack of valuable consideration will not in itself invalidate or void a transfer. (While a promise to make a gift requires consideration to be enforceable, a completed transfer without consideration is valid.) If it can be shown that an insolvent grantor made the gift in an effort to defraud creditors, the gift could be set aside and the creditors could seize the property. Most deeds conveying real property as a gift would describe the consideration as "love and affection."

Executor's Deed or Administrator's Deed   This deed is given by a personal representative of a deceased owner during probate.

Recording of Deeds

There is no time limit for recording, but no constructive notice of an interest is made until the deed has been recorded. Generally, the county recorder will time and date stamp the deed for recording and enter the deed alphabetically in grantor and grantee indexes, although other forms of record keeping exist.

Unrecorded Deed   Between the grantor and the grantee, an unrecorded deed would convey title to the grantee.

Grantor ——————▶ Deed ——————▶ Grantee

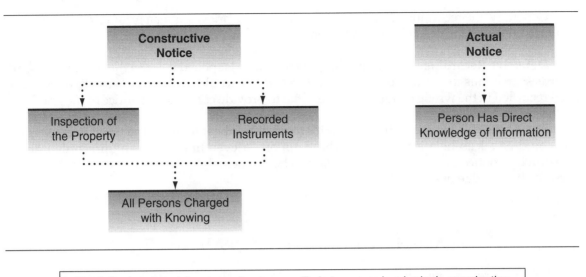

The following material on recording is more likely to appear in a broker's examination than in a salesperson's examination.

A deed *that is not recorded* is considered void as to a later recorded transfer to a purchaser who acts in good faith without having any actual or constructive notice of the prior conveyance. As an example:

> *J* sells to *K* (the deed is not recorded). *J* later sells to *L* (the deed is recorded). If *L* paid value and had no actual or constructive notice of the prior sale, *L* would have title and *K* would have only a claim against *J*.

> The reasoning for the above is that if anyone suffers, it should be buyer *K* who sat on his or her rights and failed to record, rather than diligent buyer *L*, who by checking the records (and property) would have no constructive or implied notice of any prior sale.

> Assume that when *L* purchased from *J*, *L* knew of the prior unrecorded deed from *J* to *K*. In this case, *K* would prevail over *J* because of *L's* actual notice of *K's* interest.

Priority of Recording   The time and date of recording generally determine the priority of an interest. However, possession is also considered to be constructive notice. Assume the following:

July 1:   *J* ————————▶ Deed ————————▶ *K*
July 5:   *J* ————————▶ Deed ————————▶ *L*

If *K* took possession on July 3, *L* would have had constructive notice of *K's* prior interest, and the deed to *L* would have conveyed nothing.
Assume the following:

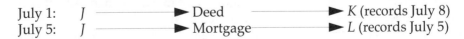

July 1:   *J* ———————▶ Deed ———————▶ *K* (records July 8)
July 5:   *J* ———————▶ Mortgage———————▶ *L* (records July 5)

Because *L* recorded the mortgage prior to *K's* recordation of the deed, *K* has title subject to *L's* prior recorded mortgage. This priority of recording is often referred to as "the race of the diligent."

Generally, the recording of a gift deed would not take priority over a prior unrecorded deed or mortgage given for valuable consideration.

Defective Recording   If a grantor or grantee's name is spelled incorrectly, so that a diligent records search fails to reveal a party's interest, recording would not give constructive notice. A deed recorded in the wrong county also would fail to provide constructive notice of the grantee's interest.

Possession also gives constructive notice to others of the interest of the party in possession that could be a leasehold interest, a purchase option, or even title under an unrecorded deed. Constructive notice is notice implied by law, whereas actual notice occurs when a party has personal knowledge of a fact.

ABSTRACT AND TITLE INSURANCE

Sellers in real estate transactions must show buyers that they are conveying **marketable title**. This is often accomplished through an abstract of title. An *abstract* is a chronological summary of every recorded document dealing with a property, prepared by an abstractor who searched the records showing the **chain of title,** which is the history of recorded ownership. An attorney then gives an opinion as to the marketability of the property. In preparing an abstract, the abstractor's only liability is failure to show a recorded document. The attorney's opinion is, therefore, based on only what is reported in the abstract.

Title insurance is more than an opinion—it is a limited **guarantee** of marketable title. The title insurance company checks the records and issues a **preliminary title report.** This is not a policy of insurance but a statement of the condition of the title (setting forth liens and encumbrances); it affirms that the insurance company will issue a title policy with the noted exceptions and/or conditions. In some states, such notation is known as a **title binder.** Title policies are issued at the closing of the transaction or date of title commitment.

Title policies with a one-time premium protect the purchaser and/or lender and insure against past defects in the title up to the amount of insurance purchased. Title insurance protects only the named insured or heirs. Therefore, a policy of title insurance taken out by a previous owner offers no protection to a new buyer.

Standard Policies

Standard policies of title insurance generally protect against forgery, lack of capacity, failure of delivery, recorded but unreported liens, tax liens, and undisclosed spousal interests.

Extended Coverage

Because the standard policy does not cover matters not of public record, lenders frequently require an extended-coverage American Land Title Association (ALTA) policy that includes rights of parties in possession, unrecorded liens, unrecorded easements, claims that a proper survey or inspection would have revealed (the property is surveyed for this coverage), mining claims, and water rights. Similar extended coverage is also available for the purchaser.

Lenders often insist on a **spot survey** as a condition of making a loan. A spot survey shows the location of improvements, easements and encroachments.

Title insurance does not protect the purchaser against zoning restrictions, against defects the purchaser knew of but failed to tell the insurer about, or against exceptions stated in the policy.

Table 1.1 will help you understand the coverage of standard and extended coverage policies.

Table 1.1: Owner's Title Insurance Policy

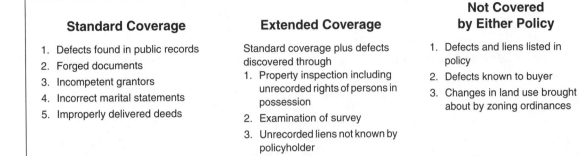

Standard Coverage	Extended Coverage	Not Covered by Either Policy
1. Defects found in public records 2. Forged documents 3. Incompetent grantors 4. Incorrect marital statements 5. Improperly delivered deeds	Standard coverage plus defects discovered through 1. Property inspection including unrecorded rights of persons in possession 2. Examination of survey 3. Unrecorded liens not known by policyholder	1. Defects and liens listed in policy 2. Defects known to buyer 3. Changes in land use brought about by zoning ordinances

Curing Title Defects

Title problems (cloud on title) can be rectified by any one of three methods:

1. A quitclaim deed from a person who claims to or appears to have an interest to the holder of the paramount (strongest) title (thus removing any possible interest that person had)
2. An action to quiet title in which the court determines the rights of the parties and issues a declaratory judgment
3. The recording of an affidavit that clarifies or removes an uncertainty

INHERITANCE

Probate is the legal procedure for disposing of the estate of a decedent and for paying his or her just debts as well as validating any will. If the decedent died **testate,** having written a valid will, the decedent would appoint an **executor** as his or her personal representative to administer and dispose of the estate. If the deceased died without a will, he or she is said to have died **intestate,** and the court would appoint a personal representative known as an **administrator** to administer and dispose of the estate.

An estate may be made up of two types of property:

1. **Devise**—real property given by will
2. **Bequest or legacy**—personal property given by will

The apportionment and division of an estate in probate, after paying costs and debts, is known as *distribution.*

Wills

A **will** is a testamentary disposition determined by the deceased prior to death. The testator must be of sound mind and understand the nature and the disposition of his or her property.

A **formal will** must be signed by the testator and witnessed by a prescribed number of witnesses.

A **holographic will** does not require witnesses but must be written entirely in the hand of the testator.

Nuncupative wills are oral deathbed wills and are valid in a few states as to personal property of limited value. Where valid, a nuncupative will must be reduced to writing by the witnesses.

A will can be canceled at any time prior to the testator's death. A new will cancels a prior will.

A **codicil** is an amendment to a will that requires the same formalities as a will.

In some states, a spouse can elect to take statutory dower or curtesy rights rather than what the will provides.

Intestate Succession

If a person dies without a will, he or she is said to have died *intestate* (without a testament). Property in his or her estate passes (is distributed) in accordance with the laws of intestate succession and distribution. Intestate succession varies among the states, with provisions for spouses and lineal descendants such as children. In the event no living descendants are found, provision is made for parents and collateral heirs, those related through a common ancestor. Intestate or hereditary succession is known as **descent**.

Generally, if a blood heir is dead but has left children, the children take by right of representation and share equally in the share their parent would have received.

Escheat   Because all property should have an owner, when a person dies intestate and has no known heirs, after a statutory period, the title to real and personal property reverts (escheats) to the state.

Abandoned personal property could also escheat to the state.

Your Pertinent State Information

1.   Does your state have special treatment for capital gains?

2.   Does your state have a two-year homeowner exemption on gains from the sale of a personal residence?

3.   Does your state have a gift and/or inheritance tax?

4.   Does your state have a documentary transfer tax? If so, what is the tax rate?

5.   What is the most common deed of conveyance?

6.   What are the special requirements for adverse possession?

7.   Is tacking on for adverse possession permitted in your state?

8.   What is the period of redemption after a sheriff's sale?

9.   What is the amount of your state's homestead exemption?

10.   What are the state's homestead requirements?

11.   What are the special state deed requirements?

12.   What are the requirements for a formal will?

13.   Is a holographic (handwritten) will valid?

14.   Is a nuncupative (oral) will valid?

15.   What are the provisions for intestate succession?

CHAPTER 3 QUIZ

Income Taxation and Transfer of Title

1. What percent of a capital gain would be the tax if an investor who is in the 28 percent tax bracket held the property for 12½ months?

   (A) 12½ percent
   (B) 20 percent
   (C) 25 percent
   (D) 28 percent

2. A spot survey differs from other surveys in that it shows:

   (A) longitude and latitude
   (B) only the approximate location
   (C) the location of improvements, easements and encroachments
   (D) that it is a true copy of a prior physical survey

3. A standard policy of title insurance covers:

   A) defects that would be revealed by a correct survey
   (B) rights of parties in possession
   (C) zoning restrictions
   (D) incompetent grantors

4. *J* died intestate and without heirs. The state took title to *J's* property by:

   (A) dedication
   (B) escheat
   (C) police power
   (D) eminent domain

5. *J* paid $190,000 for her home in 1989. She spent $41,000 on improvements to the home. She sold the home in 1994 for $184,000 and incurred closing costs of $11,900. *J* has:

   (A) a tax loss of $17,900
   (B) a tax loss of $35,100
   (C) a tax loss of $47,900
   (D) no loss for tax purposes

6. A warranty deed contains a covenant of further assurance, which means that:

   (A) the grantor promises to indemnify the grantee for any loss suffered because of failure of title
   (B) the grantor warrants the property is free of liens and encumbrances other than those stated in the deed
   (C) the grantor warrants he or she has rightful ownership
   (D) if any further instrument or act is needed to perfect title, the grantor promises to provide it

7. A high rate of inflation would be of greatest value to investors who have:

   (A) invested in long-term, fixed-income investments
   (B) purchased property without the use of leverage
   (C) purchased property using moderate leverage
   (D) purchased property using a high degree of leverage

8. An owner has a passive loss of $25,000 on an investment property. If the owner has an adjusted gross income of $125,000, how much of this loss can be used to shelter other than real estate income?

   (A) 0
   (B) $12,500
   (C) $25,000
   (D) $50,000

9. *J* traded her commercial lot to *K* for raw acreage. *K* gave *J* $10,000 to balance out the trade. Based on the above:

   (A) both parties will pay tax because the trade was not like for like
   (B) *J* will be taxed on $10,000
   (C) *K* will be taxed $10,000
   (D) the trade would defer all taxes

10. The act of signing a deed would be the:

    (A) execution
    (B) ratification
    (C) verification
    (D) habendum

11. *T* recorded an approved subdivision map that showed that certain areas of the subdivision were being dedicated to public use. This would be regarded as:

    (A) the exercise of police power
    (B) eminent domain
    (C) statutory dedication
    (D) inverse condemnation

12. *L* and *M*, a married couple, sold their home for $2,400,000. When they purchased the home 7 years previously, they paid $1,200,000. Assuming no improvements were made, their taxable gain would be:

    (A) nothing
    (B) $700,000
    (C) $1,200,000
    (D) $1,900,000

13. After meeting the statutory requirements of adverse possession, an adverse user could obtain marketable title by:

    (A) tacking on
    (B) continued open notorious and hostile use
    (C) a quiet title action
    (D) inverse condemnation

14. A property was declared unfit for occupancy and was boarded up. This action was a(n):

    (A) eminent domain
    (B) inverse condemnation
    (C) exercise of police power
    (D) statutory dedication

15. *G* gave a deed to *H* for valuable consideration. Because *H* did not take possession or record the deed:

    (A) *H* would have greater right than a later purchaser from *G* who records first
    (B) if *G* later gave a gift deed to *J*, *J*'s rights would be greater than *H*'s rights
    (C) the deed would be void
    (D) between *G* and *H*, *H* has good title

16. What is an abstract for a property?

    (A) Policy of title insurance
    (B) Condensation of every recorded document dealing with the property
    (C) Opinion of title
    (D) Commitment to issue a title policy

17. In which clause in a deed would the phrase to have and to hold appear?

    (A) Safety clause
    (B) Habendum clause
    (C) Execution clause
    (D) Description clause

18. On the same day, *J* deeded the same vacant lot to *K*, *L*, and *M* in that order. *M* was the first to record, followed by *K* and *L*. Who has superior rights to the property?

    (A) *K* because *K* was the first purchaser.
    (B) *M* because *M* was the first to record.
    (C) *K*, *L*, and *M* take equal shares as a matter of equity.
    (D) *J* retains title because *J*'s fraud cannot pass title.

19. *J*, who paid $47,000 for a property, has since refinanced the property. The present balance on the mortgage is $128,000. If *J* sold the property for $95,000, what would be the tax consequence of the sale?

    (A) *J* would have a loss of $33,000.
    (B) *J* would have a gain of $48,000.
    (C) *J* would have a gain of $81,000.
    (D) *J* would have a gain of $128,000.

20. An investor has total cash obligations of $187,000 on a property with an income of $225,000. The $38,000 difference is known as:

    (A) cash flow
    (B) equity
    (C) arbitrage
    (D) liquidity

21. Q intends to borrow $80,000 on her home at 9 percent interest to pay off credit card loans. As to this home equity loan, Q should realize that the:

    (A) loan will increase her tax liability in the event of sale
    (B) interest payments on the home equity loan may be tax-deductible expenses
    (C) cost basis of the home will be increased by $80,000
    (D) $80,000 in proceeds is subject to regular income taxation

22. The purchaser's down payment is considered what type of funds?

    (A) Borrowed
    (B) Leveraged
    (C) Equity
    (D) Capital

23. For tax purposes, residential property is depreciated based on a life of:

    (A) 15 years
    (B) 27½ years
    (C) 31 years
    (D) 39 years

24. An adverse user can take title by his or her adverse use from:

    (A) a minor
    (B) a foreign owner
    (C) the government
    (D) a person declared to be incompetent

25. A special warranty deed warrants that the grantor:

    (A) has not made any undisclosed transfer of title or encumbrance
    (B) will guarantee that there are no undisclosed liens
    (C) will make good any loss suffered by the grantee because of title defects
    (D) will provide any further instrument or act needed to perfect title

26. A requirement of a valid deed is that the deed be:

    (A) dated
    (B) acknowledged
    (C) recorded
    (D) signed by the grantor

27. N sold a property to O before N acquired the title from P. When N acquired the title it automatically went to O because the deed to O was:

    (A) notarized
    (B) a quiet claim deed
    (C) a bargain and sale deed
    (D) a warranty deed

28. A property has a variety of liens against it. Which of the following deeds would give the grantee the greatest protection against the existing liens?

    (A) Gift deed
    (B) Quitclaim deed
    (C) Tax deed
    (D) Bargain and sale deed

29. A standard title insurance policy offers protection to:

    (A) grantees who receive title from the insured
    (B) the party that conveyed title to the insured
    (C) lenders
    (D) heirs of the insured

30. *R* traded a lot to *S* for an apartment building. *R* assumed *S*'s $86,000 mortgage, and *S* assumed *R*'s $115,000 mortgage. No other consideration passed between the parties in this trade. How would this trade be taxed?

    (A) *R* has a $29,000 taxable gain.
    (B) *S* has a $29,000 taxable gain.
    (C) *S* will be taxed as if he received fair market value of the lot.
    (D) Neither *R* nor *S* has any taxable gain.

31. A handwritten, signed but unwitnessed testamentary document would be a:

    (A) formal will
    (B) nuncupative will
    (C) holographic will
    (D) codicil to a nuncupative will

32. Adverse possession requires:

    (A) permission
    (B) nonexclusive use
    (C) a use that is hidden from the owner
    (D) hostile use

33. A deed in which the grantor implies having an interest in the property conveyed but offers no warranties as to title is a:

    (A) quitclaim deed
    (B) bargain and sale deed
    (C) warranty deed
    (D) deed of trust

34. Acknowledgment is required to:

    (A) convey legal title
    (B) execute a deed
    (C) deliver a deed
    (D) validate a deed for recording

35. Taking property by eminent domain requires:

    (A) adverse use
    (B) compensation
    (C) the exercise of police power
    (D) a foreclosure proceeding

36. Real property that is transferred by will would be a:

    (A) bequest
    (B) legacy
    (C) devise
    (D) descent

37. A grantee of a deed alters the legal description to include additional property and then records the deed. What is the effect of this deed?

    (A) It grants only the property originally described.
    (B) It grants all the property described, but the grantor may void the added portion.
    (C) The grant is voidable.
    (D) No property is transferred by the deed.

38. A deed that has a covenant of quiet enjoyment is a:

    (A) quitclaim deed
    (B) bargain and sale deed
    (C) warranty deed
    (D) sheriff's deed

39. Quitclaim deeds and bargain and sale deeds are similar in that they both:

    (A) convey after-acquired title
    (B) convey a grantor's partial interest
    (C) include a warranty of merchantability
    (D) bind the grantor's heirs to defend the title conveyed

40. The testator appoints a personal representative known as the:

    (A) administrator
    (B) testatee
    (C) executor
    (D) referee

41. How does eminent domain differ from the exercise of police power?

    (A) Eminent domain is exercised for purposes of health, safety, morals, or general welfare.
    (B) Compensation is given under eminent domain.
    (C) Eminent domain is exercised by a government unit.
    (D) Eminent domain can limit an owner's rights in property.

42. A valid deed can be made to:

    (A) *L* using the fictitious name *Y*
    (B) a fictitious person
    (C) either *H* or *T*
    (D) *J* for property, the exact description and nature of which are to be determined by later agreement

43. Part of a property was taken by eminent domain. If the owner received compensation for the reduced value of the remaining property it would be considered:

    (A) severance damage
    (B) punitive damage
    (C) condemnation damage
    (D) inverse condemnation

44. One requirement for valid transfer of title by deed is:

    (A) witnesses
    (B) the address of the grantee
    (C) words of conveyance
    (D) recordation

45. When *P* died, a signed and acknowledged but unrecorded deed was found among his effects giving his house to a local charity. *P's* will provides that the entire estate was to go to a nephew. The house goes to the:

    (A) charity because acknowledgment is a presumption of delivery
    (B) charity because his intent was clear
    (C) nephew because *P* died owning the house
    (D) charity because delivery is not a requirement for charitable gifts

46. One of the differences in the requirements for obtaining an easement by prescription and a title by adverse possession is that title by adverse possession requires:

    (A) hostile use
    (B) open and notorious use
    (C) exclusive use
    (D) continuous use for the statutory period

47. Money that transfers by will would be regarded as a:

    (A) freehold
    (B) legacy
    (C) devise
    (D) descent

48. A standard policy of title insurance protects a purchaser against:

    (A) zoning prohibitions
    (B) an existing encroachment
    (C) rights of parties who are in possession
    (D) forgery in the chain of title

49. An owner wanted a municipality to take her property because planning changes took away her only access. She would ask for:

    (A) severance damage
    (B) inverse condemnation
    (C) dedication
    (D) adverse possession

50. *J* deeded property to *K*. *K* recorded the deed in the wrong county. Which of the following statements is true as to this deed?

    (A) The deed provides constructive notice of *K's* interest.
    (B) The deed is void and fails to transfer any interest.
    (C) *J* can void the transfer.
    (D) As between *J* and *K*, the deed transferred title.

CHAPTER 3 QUIZ ANSWERS

Income Taxation and Transfer of Title

1. (B) Holding period is more than 12 months. (page 43)
2. (C) It shows more than just location, size, and boundaries. (page 52)
3. (D) (A) and (B) would be covered by an extended coverage policy, but no policy covers zoning. (page 52)
4. (B) Escheats to state. (page 54)
5. (D) A homeowner cannot take a loss on the sale of a residence, but a gain is taxed. (page 41)
6. (D) One of five warranties. (page 49)
7. (D) The investors get appreciation benefits of inflation and pay back the loan with cheaper dollars. (page 43)
8. (B) Each $2 of adjusted gross income over $100,000 reduces the nonproperty income tax shelter by $1. (page 45)
9. (B) The party who receives boot is taxed on the boot received. (page 44)
10. (A) To execute is to sign. (page 49)
11. (C) But common-law dedication is based on an agreement. (page 46)
12. (B) Their gain was $1,200,000. They have a $500,000 exclusion, so $700,000 would be taxed. (page 42)
13. (C) To have a salable property, an adverse user also could obtain a quitclaim deed from the owner of record. (page 47)
14. (C) Condemnation as being uninhabitable is the exercise of police power, and no compensation is given. (page 47)
15. (D) Recording is not necessary as to rights between grantor and grantee. (page 49)
16. (B) It is a history of the recorded documents but does not warrant title. (page 52)
17. (B) Defines the extent of interest given. (page 48)
18. (B) *M* had no constructive notice of other buyers. (page 51)
19. (B) The gain is determined as the difference between cost basis and the sale price. (page 43)
20. (A) Spendable cash. (page 43)
21. (B) *Q* can deduct interest on equity loans up to $100,000, provided all combined loans don't exceed fair market value of the home. (page 42)
22. (C) An owner's equity is the difference between value and indebtedness. (page 42)
23. (B) Thirty-nine years is used for nonresidential property. (page 44)
24. (B) Others are protected. (page 47)
25. (A) Others are general warranty deed covenants. (pages 49–50)
26. (D) To be valid, recording and date are not required. (page 49)
27. (D) Warranty deed conveys after-acquired title. (page 50)
28. (C) Because tax sale wipes out junior liens. (page 50)
29. (D) Protect only insured and insured's heirs. (page 52)
30. (A) *R's* debt relief is boot and is taxable as a capital gain. **Note:** the property would be regarded as like for like. (page 44)
31. (C) By definition. (page 53)
32. (D) Hostile, exclusive, and open use for statutory period. (page 46)
33. (B) There is no implication of having an interest in a quitclaim deed. (page 50)
34. (D) An unrecorded deed is a valid transfer between the parties, but it does not give constructive notice. (page 49)
35. (B) Fair market value must be paid under eminent domain. (page 47)
36. (C) Devise is real property. Bequest and legacy refer to personal property. (page 53)
37. (D) A forged or altered deed does not transfer anything. (page 49)
38. (C) The grantor guarantees title against other claims. (page 49)
39. (B) Both convey whatever interest the grantor has. (page 50)
40. (C) The administrator would be appointed by the court when a person dies without a will (intestate). (page 53)
41. (B) (C) and (D) are points in common. (pages 47–48)
42. (A) A valid deed requires a clear, unambiguous property description and a definite grantee, not "either". A deed can be given to a real person using a fictitious name. (page 48)
43. (A) To cover the value loss of the property remaining. (page 48)

44. (C) Between the parties recording is not necessary, but without recording, there is no constructive notice. (page 48)
45. (C) The deed was never delivered to the charity, so *P* died owning the property. (page 48)
46. (C) There can be multiple users for an easement by prescription. (page 46)
47. (B) A bequest can also be money. A devise is real property. (page 53)
48. (D) Choices (B) and (C) are covered by extended coverage policies, but no policy covers zoning. (page 52)
49. (B) Take the property because the government made it unusable. (page 48)
50. (D) There was a valid transfer, but faulty recording would not provide constructive notice to a later purchaser. (page 49)

Valuation and Appraisal

VALUE

Appraisal is the supported estimation of value of a real estate at the time of the appraisal. *Value* is regarded as worth, or the present worth of future benefits. **Price** is what actually is paid for a property and might differ from value because of special buyer or seller needs, unusual financing, or imperfections of the real estate market.

Types of Value

Market Value   The price a willing, informed buyer would pay to a willing, informed seller in an open market, allowing a reasonable marketing time, is known as *market value*. Appraisal is concerned primarily with market value.

Market *price* is not the same as market *value*. Market price is the price actually paid, and it could be more or less than market value because of motivation, knowledge, or bargaining strength of the parties.

Objective and Subjective Value   Objective value is the actual market value. *Subjective value* or **utility value** is the personal use value of the benefits of ownership. The appraiser estimates the objective value that the typical buyer will be willing to pay for the benefits offered.

Book Value   Book value is the original property cost plus the cost of any improvements, minus any depreciation taken. Book value, the value carried on the owner's books, bears no relationship to market value and is not used in appraising.

Assessed Value   This is the value placed by a tax assessor. Assessed value, often influenced by the price paid, may differ from market value.

Loan Value   Loan value is less than market value, as it is customarily a percentage of market value, leaving a margin for lender security.

Principles of Value

The following briefly describe principles applied in appraising property.

Economics of Scale   A larger development or multiple units generally can be built at a lower price per square foot or per unit.

Principle of Anticipation   Value is based more on anticipated or expected future benefits than present benefits derived.

Principle of Balance   Value is best created and maintained when land, labor, capital, and management are in balance. When any of these is in excess, or when there is a shortage, value will be distorted.

Principle of Change   Real estate value does not remain constant. An appraiser must consider how changing economic and social conditions affect the value of property.

Principle of Competition   When extraordinary profits are derived from an investment, competition will be created that will increase the supply, thus lowering profits.

Principle of Conformity   A property will achieve and maintain its maximum value when it is in a homogeneous or uniform area of similar-use property, such as in a subdivision.

Principle of Contribution   Maximum value is achieved when improvements return the highest net in relationship to the investment. A decision to add amenities to a property should be based on the cost of the amenities and the anticipated increase in value that would result.

Principle of Integration and Disintegration   Property goes through phases of development (integration), stability (equilibrium) and decline (disintegration). This principle also is referred to as the principle of the three-stage life cycle: development, maturity, and old age.

Principle of Progression   The value of a home will be increased by more expensive homes in the area. Economically, it is often desirable to have the least expensive home in an area.

Principle of Regression   The value of a home will be held down by the presence of homes having lesser value in the area. The principle of regression is the opposite of the principle of progression.

Principle of Substitution   A person will not pay more for one property than for another comparable property of equal utility and desirability.

Principle of Supply and Demand   An increase in supply without a change in demand will decrease prices. A decrease in supply without a change in demand will increase prices. An increase in demand without a change in supply will increase prices. A decrease in demand without a change in supply will decrease prices.

Highest and Best Use   The use that results in the greatest net value being attributed to the land is the highest and best use.

Assemblage and Plottage   Assemblage is the process of joining several contiguous, or touching, parcels of property together under common ownership to form one larger parcel. The larger parcel is likely to have a resulting value greater than the sum of the values of the smaller parcels because of the difficulty in assembling larger parcels in developed areas. The increase in value by assemblage is known as *plottage* or **plottage increment.**

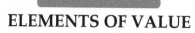

ELEMENTS OF VALUE

The least important factor in determining property value is cost, or price paid. Cost represents what was spent in the past, not the present worth. There are four essential elements of value:

1. **Demand**   Without demand, there is no value. To be meaningful, demand must be coupled with purchasing power.
2. **Utility**   To have value, a property must have a useful purpose; even an ornament serves a purpose.
3. **Scarcity**   If many similar properties are on the market, the value of each will be less than if only a few such properties were available.
4. **Transferability**   To have value, the title or possession must be capable of being transferred. An interest that cannot be transferred has no value.

> Acronym, DUST: Demand, Utility, Scarcity, and Transferability.

Four Special Forces That Influence Value

1. Physical

Topography   Steep grades mean higher development costs. Subdividers like gentle rolling land that breaks the monotony but does not result in excessive costs.

Shape   Rectangular lots are more valuable than irregularly shaped parcels. An exception would be lots on cul-de-sacs that are valued because of diminished traffic.

Size   The width and depth of a lot determine possible uses.

Exposure   How a property is situated as to light, air, view, and so on affects value. For example, the south and west sides of streets generally are more valuable for foot traffic business because they offer shoppers more shade on hot afternoons.

Soil   The ability of soil to support a structure affects construction costs. Compaction tests by a civil engineer would measure this ability. Fertility of soil generally has only a slight effect on value other than for agricultural land.

Corner Influence   A corner location has greater value for commercial purposes because of greater exposure for signs and displays as well as easier access.

Location   Location is the site of a property in relationship to other uses and physical features. Appraisers often state that the three most important factors in determining value are location and location.

2. Economic   The economy affects value in that it directly affects demand. For a particular property, the local economy tends to be more important than the national economy. The economy of a particular community might run counter to the national economy. A primary measurement of the national economy is the gross domestic product (GDP), which is the sum of all goods and services produced by our nation during a certain period. Changes in the GDP are indicators of changes that have occurred in the national economy.

Changes in unemployment levels indicate trends in the local economy. Real estate values tend to rise during periods of inflation, when the purchasing power of the dollar decreases. A principal measurement of inflation is the consumer price index (CPI).

Interest rates affect value because lower rates encourage more buyers to enter the marketplace, resulting in greater demand that results in rising prices. The opposite can also be true as to high interest rates.

3. Political Government regulations—zoning, taxes, growth limitations, building codes, health codes, public housing, rent control, and the like—also affect value.

4. Social Social factors that influence value include population movements, size of households, attitude toward recreation, etc.

> Acronym, PEPS: Physical, Economic, Political, and Social.

Neighborhood

A neighborhood is an area characterized by social conformity. It might have defined boundaries, such as a particular street, a river, or a particular subdivision. Other neighborhoods might merge together with imprecise boundaries. Similarity of interests provides neighborhood cohesiveness; similarities might include income, education, children, or recreational interests. If residents of an area have pride in their neighborhood, the neighborhood is likely to remain stable; a neighborhood that loses common interests tends to decline. A decline in the percentage of home ownership and an increase in rental units often indicate a declining neighborhood.

APPRAISAL METHODS

Three appraisal methods are used to arrive at property value:

1. Sales comparison approach (market data or direct sales comparison)
2. Cost approach (replacement cost)
3. Income approach (capitalization of income)

> Acronym, MCI: Market, Cost, and Income.

Sales Comparison Approach (Market Data or Direct Sales Comparison)

In the sales comparison approach, which is the oldest and easiest-to-learn appraisal method, a property's value is arrived at by comparing the sales prices of similar properties recently sold. In selecting the comparables, the appraiser considers terms of sale, special features, quality, age, size, and location, making adjustments when properties or features are not equally desirable. **Amenities** are property features that provide greater satisfaction in living or pride of ownership: a beautiful garden, mature trees, a magnificent view, a fountain, or an extra bath, for example. In the market comparison method, the amenities are considered in arriving at the value.

The appraiser adjusts prices paid for property comparable with the property being appraised by adding and subtracting from the comparable property sale price based on the presence or absence of features and amenities compared with the property being appraised.

The sale price of a comparable property would be adjusted upward if the comparable lacked a feature or was less desirable than the subject property and would be adjusted downward if the comparable had a positive feature or was more desirable than the subject property. This adjusted price is known as the **adjusted selling price.**

Subject Property	Comparable Property	Adjustment to Comparable
2-car garage	3-car garage	–
2 1/2 baths	2 baths	+
	More desirable location	–
12,000-sq.-ft. Lot	9,000-sq.-ft. lot	+

The appraiser considers depreciation as it applies to both the property being appraised and the comparables in making adjustments. There could be physical depreciation, such as is caused by age and wear and tear; functional obsolescence that is built in, such as an undesirable floor plan; and economic obsolescence, which would be forces outside the property, such as neighborhood problems. All of these could pull value down.

Forced sales such as foreclosures should not be used for comparables because they seldom reflect market value.

The comparison method is the best appraisal method for single-family dwellings. It also can be used for land as well as improved properties where sales exhibit a high degree of similarity.

Disadvantages are difficulty of locating similar recent sales and adjusting amenities and sales terms.

Many real estate agents use the sales comparison method to prepare a **competitive market analysis (CMA),** in which comparable sales data are used to estimate the likely sales price of a particular property. The principle of **substitution** is basic to the analysis because buyers will not pay more for a property than they would have to pay for an equally desirable property.

Cost Approach

If there are no comparables and there is no income, the cost approach would likely be used. The cost approach is the best method for appraising new or special-use structures (e.g., library, county stadium.) The cost approach tends to set upper limits on value. An exception would be a market where prices are rising rapidly. Although the cost approach can be effectively used for new homes, the market comparison approach is more effective for older homes. If the cost approach were applied to an older home, an appraiser would have to determine the accrued depreciation, which tends to be subjective and reduces the reliability of the appraisal.

The cost approach is a three-step appraisal process:

Cost To Replace – Accrued Depreciation + Land = Value

1. Determine the present cost to replace improvements, that is, to build a structure of the same utility and desirability using today's material, methods, and design. *Replacement cost* differs from *reproduction cost,* the cost to duplicate the structure with exactly the same design and materials.
2. Deduct *accrued depreciation*—that is, depreciation that already has occurred; *remainder depreciation* is depreciation that will occur in the future.
3. Add the value of the land, which is arrived at by using the market comparison approach.

Replacement Cost   The replacement cost can be arrived at by several different methods.

Quantity Survey Method   This is the most detailed and time-consuming method to determine replacement costs, where all costs fees, labor, material, subcontracts, interest, etc., are priced separately.

Builders would use the quantity-survey method when actual construction of a structure is contemplated. This is developed by considering all direct and indirect contracting costs.

Unit in Place (Segregated Cost) Method   This method uses costs per unit, such as per square foot, per cubic foot, per bath, per room, per electrical outlet, and so on. Some appraisers consider price per square foot to be a separate method (the comparative unit method).

Index Method   The present cost to build is arrived at by applying increases or decreases in the construction cost index since the structure was built to its original cost to build.

Accrued Depreciation   For appraisal purposes, only improvements are depreciated, **never land**. To arrive at the depreciation of a structure, the economic life of the structure must be determined. **Economic life** is the period during which the improvements contribute to the net income. **Age-life tables** provide the economic life—often 40 to 50 years—for various types of structures and construction. To determine the amount of accrued depreciation, the effective age of the structure must be estimated. **Effective age** is the structure's age for appraisal purposes. Effective age can differ from chronological age, depending on the care given to maintenance and repair. As an example, an appraiser might indicate the effective age of a 10-year-old structure as 7 years because it has been well maintained. A similar 10-year-old structure might be given an effective age of 15 years because of excessive wear and tear.

The appraiser analyzes the condition of the property, considering physical deterioration, functional obsolescence, and external factors, to determine the accrued depreciation. This is known as the **observed condition method.** For example, if the economic life is determined to be 40 years, each year's depreciation amounts to 2½ percent of the replacement cost.

$$\frac{100\%}{40} = 2\tfrac{1}{2}\%$$

If the property had an effective age of ten years, it would have depreciated 25 percent.

$$2\tfrac{1}{2}\% \times 10 = 25\%$$

Sample Problem   A 15,000-square-foot warehouse would cost $40 per square foot to build today. Its economic life is 50 years, and its effective age is 8 years. The land is valued at $170,000 (arrived at by the market comparison method). The property is valued as follows:

15,000 × $40	= $600,000 cost to replace
50-year life	= 2% depreciation per year
8 years × 2%	= 16% depreciation
.16 × $600,000	= $96,000 accrued depreciation
$600,000	Cost to build today
− 96,000	Accrued depreciation
$504,000	Present value of structure
+170,000	Land value
$674,000	Total present value of land and improvements

Income Approach

The income approach is generally the best appraisal method for income-producing property. An exception is a single-family rental home, for which the market comparison method is usually preferred because of the availability of comparables.

The income approach is based on the net operating income (NOI) of the property being appraised. To estimate value, an appraiser determines the appropriate rate of return, the capitalization rate, and divides it into the NOI:

$$\frac{NOI}{Capitalization\ Rate} = Value$$

Annual Net Operating Income To determine annual NOI, an appraiser deducts total annual expenses from the gross annual income, including an allowance for vacancies and collection losses as well as management expenses. The only costs not deducted are payments on the loan principal and interest expenses, known as **debt service** and depreciation. In determining the gross income, an appraiser is more interested in anticipated future income than in past income.

Capitalization Rate The capitalization rate is the rate of return an investor wants on a particular property. For a high-risk investment, an investor might want a 20 percent return, whereas an 8 percent return for a secure investment might be acceptable. When interest rates are high, investors use a higher capitalization rate to reflect a higher desired return on investment.

Besides indicating a return on an investment, the capitalization rate can be increased to provide for depreciation that is the return of the investment. For example, if an investor wanted an 8 percent return on an investment and the property was expected to have a 50-year useful life (economic life), the investor could add 2 percent to the rate, raising the rate to 10 percent. This added 2 percent provides for the recapture of the investment over 50 years.

Capitalization rates for comparable sales can be determined by dividing the sales price into the NOI of the comparable properties.

$$\frac{NOI}{Sales\ Price} = Capitalization\ Rate\ Used$$

Sample Problem An appraiser anticipates that an eight-unit apartment building will have monthly rentals of $400 per unit, a 10 percent vacancy and collection loss factor, plus total expenses of $600 per month. Find its value using a capitalization rate of 12 percent.

8	× $400	= $ 3,200	monthly scheduled gross income
$3,200	× 12	= $38,400	annual scheduled gross income

$38,400	Annual scheduled gross income
− 3,840	10% vacancy and collection loss
$34,560	Effective gross income (gross less vacancy and collection factors)
− 7,200	Expenses ($600 × 12)
$27,360	NOI

To determine the value after the NOI and the capitalization rate have been determined, divide the NOI by the capitalization rate.

$$Value = \frac{NOI}{Cap\ Rate} = \frac{\$27,360}{.12} = \$228,000$$

The value, using the income approach, is $228,000.
If the capitalization rate were 10 percent:

$$\frac{\$27,360}{.10} = \$273,600$$

If the rate used were 14 percent:

$$\frac{\$27,360}{.14} = \$195,428.57$$

Value moves inversely to capitalization rate; that is, value goes up if the rate goes down, and value goes down if the rate goes up. Similarly, if expenses go up, value goes down because net decreases; if expenses go down, value goes up because net increases.

Gross Rent Multiplier

A variation of the income approach multiplies the gross income by a figure known as the *gross rent multiplier (GRM)* to arrive at value. If a property has a gross annual income of $10,000 and can be purchased for $70,000, the seller believes that an annual GRM of 7 is appropriate.

$$\frac{\text{Sales Price}}{\text{Gross Rent}} = \text{Gross Rent Multiplier}$$

By knowing the average GRMs of similar properties that have sold, a prospective purchaser will have a general idea as to the value of a property being offered. Because a property might have unusually high or low expenses, a gross rent multiplier gives only a rough idea of value; it does not consider the actual net income. Because the gross rent multiplier requires comparables, it requires an active market. The GRM also can be expressed as a monthly factor.

Reconciliation

An appraiser might arrive at separate values using two or all three basic appraisal methods. If this happens, the appraiser will assign different weights to each method, a process known as *reconciliation* or **correlation.** As an example, an appraiser might use 80 percent of the value determined by market comparison, 20 percent of the value by the cost approach, and 0 percent of the value by the income approach (80% + 20% + 0% = 100% of value).

Deferred Maintenance

Owners often put off making repairs. In using the capitalization method or the gross rent multiplier, the appraiser deducts the estimated needed repair costs from the value derived to correct for the deferred maintenance.

Site Analysis and Valuation

It is often necessary to determine site value (the value of the land alone) for developed as well as vacant property. As an example, the cost approach requires a separate land valuation. A number of methods can be used for site valuation.

Sales Comparison   When there have been sales of similar sites, the sales comparison method can be used. The sales prices of comparable sites would need to be adjusted for factors such as size, shape, view, and topography, as well as other locational differences.

Development Method   This method of appraising a site requires that the appraiser determine the **highest and best use,** the use that results in the greatest net that is attributable to the site. The appraiser determines the cost of an improvement and then deducts the cost from the total value the property would have with that improvement. The balance is the site value for that use.

Sample Problem   Assume that constructing a $300,000 apartment building on a site will result in a total value of $450,000 for the building and site. In this case, the site value would be $150,000 ($450,000 [total value] minus the cost of construction, $300,000).

This would not be the highest and best use if $50,000 in improvements for a parking lot would give the site a value of $250,000. The value of the land would be $200,000 ($250,000 − $50,000), which would make the parking lot a higher and better use.

Land Residual Method   The income approach can be combined with the cost approach to determine the value of the land alone when it is improved with a structure. By multiplying the applicable capitalization rate by the value of the improvements, determined by the cost approach, the appraiser finds the income attributable to the improvements. The balance of the income, therefore, is attributable to the land. By capitalizing the income attributable to the land, the appraiser determines the value of the land.

Abstractive Method   By determining the value attributable to the improvements using the cost approach and then deducting this amount from the market value, an appraiser can determine the value attributable to the land alone.

Surplus Productivity (Principle of Surplus)   After deductions for labor, management, and capital investment, the balance of the value should be attributable to the land itself. It is based on the following formula:

$$Land + Labor + Capital + Management = Value$$

This method is really a variation of the abstractive method.

Depth Table   Appraisers use complex mathematical tables to determine value for lots of increased or decreased depth. The 4-3-2-1 approach to land value is a simplified method, where 40 percent of the value is in the first 25 percent of depth, 30 percent is in the next 25 percent, 20 percent is in the next 25 percent, and 10 percent is in the last 25 percent of depth.

Expressing Land Values   Land values are expressed differently for different types of property.

Agricultural Land   Land is priced per acre.

Commercial Land   Land is priced per square foot or per front foot.

Industrial Land   Land is priced per square foot or per acre.

Residential Lots   Land is priced per lot (exception: waterfront lots generally are priced per front foot).

100 Percent Location   This is an idiom meaning the very best commercial location within a community for a particular type of business.

Excess Land   This expression refers to having more land than is economically needed for a property (land that does not contribute to value).

Depreciation

Depreciation is a loss in value from any cause. There are various types of depreciation.

Physical Deterioration   Wear and tear from use, negligence, age, or other physical damage results in physical deterioration. Examples include dry rot, blistering paint, a leaking roof, and a sagging floor.

Functional Obsolescence   This is loss in value that was "built into" the structure by poor design, lack of needed facilities, outdated equipment, or changes in demand. Examples include bedrooms without closets, small rooms, and an awkward floor plan. An excessively expensive improvement (overbuilding) also is functional obsolescence.

External Locational Obsolescence (Economic or Social Obsolescence)   This type of loss in value is caused by forces outside the property itself. Examples include neighborhood change, traffic problems and parking problems.

The statement "more buildings are torn down than wear out" reflects economic obsolescence—the buildings are not worn out, but because of outside factors, they are no longer economical for their designed uses.

Curable Depreciation   Curable depreciation is loss in value that can be corrected economically. As an example, if the value of a property after repair work would exceed the land value plus the cost of the repairs, the depreciation would be regarded as curable because it would make economic sense. The existing improvements still have value.

Incurable Depreciation   Incurable depreciation is loss in value that cannot be reversed economically. If the value of a property after repairs were made would be less than the value of the land plus the cost of the repairs, it would not be economically feasible to make the repairs. Because forces outside the property itself cause economic obsolescence, an owner would ordinarily be unable to cure the external problem. Therefore, *economic obsolescence is generally regarded as being incurable depreciation.*

Computing Depreciation

The *straight-line method* of depreciation is used for appraisal purposes. With this method, an equal sum is depreciated each year over the life of the asset. Depreciation periods used for appraisal are taken from age-life tables and generally are longer than those used for income tax purposes.

APPRAISAL PROCESS

The appraisal process involves a number of steps:

- Define the problem. This involves determining the property and the property interest to be appraised, such as fee simple or leasehold. It also involves determining the value to be determined (market value, replacement cost, reproduction cost, etc.) and the purpose of the appraisal.
- Determine the data needed, and collect and verify the data.
- Determine the highest and best use for the property.
- Estimate the value by use of the three basic approaches to value.
- Reconcile the estimated values, and make a final value determination.
- Report the value.

> **Note**: The information about Certified and Licensed Appraisers is more likely to be needed in broker examinations than in salesperson examinations.

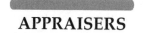

APPRAISERS

Certified and Licensed Appraisers

Title XI of the Real Estate Appraisal Reform Amendment of the Federal Financial Institutions Reform Recovery and Enforcement Act (FIRREA) of 1989 requires that state-licensed or state-certified appraisers be used for real estate transactions involving federal financial and public policy interests. Any loan regulated or insured by a federal agency as well as transactions involving Fannie Mae or Freddie Mac must meet the licensing or certification requirements. (This covers loans made by practically all financial institutions.)

There is no license or certification requirement for federally related appraisals less than $250,000, although Fannie Mae and Freddie Mac can require them. In addition, state law might require licensing or certification.

State-certified appraisers must be used for federally related transactions of $1 million or more and may be required by the particular federal agency for lower-dollar transactions.

Every state must enact legislation to provide for certification that is consistent with criteria established by The Appraisal Foundation, a private nonprofit corporation. Certification shall be in residential and general categories (general level includes income as well as residential property). An examination is required, without exception, for certification. For those federally related transactions that do not require a certified appraisal, the appraiser must be licensed. Criteria for licensing must be consistent with Title XI. Every state must set minimum appraiser standards, even for appraisals that are not federally related. The Appraisal Standards Board (ASB) of the Appraisal Foundation is responsible for the **Uniform Standards of Professional Appraisal Practice (USPAP).** Appraisers are required to conform to these standards.

Appraisal Reports

The following sections describe various kinds of appraisal reports and report content.

Narrative Report   A narrative report is self-contained, comprehensive, and complete, containing the background data leading to the appraiser's conclusions. These reports often include photos, maps, plot plans, floor plans, community economic information, and the appraiser's credentials.

Short-Form Report   This report is completed by filling in a standard form or check sheet.

Uniform Residential Appraisal Report (URAR)   URAR is generally required by FNMA, VA (Department of Veterans Affairs), HUD (Department of Housing and Urban Development), and FHLMC (Federal Home Loan Mortgage Corporation).

Content for Appraisal Reports

Federally related appraisals must conform to the USPAP. USPAP requires that every written report include the following:

- Clear description of the property being appraised
- Property interest appraised (fee simple, leasehold, etc.)
- Purpose of the appraisal (insurance, loan, etc.)
- Value being appraised (market value, reproduction value, replacement value, etc.)
- Effective date of the appraisal

- Source of data gathered and confirmation of the data and assumptions that affect the appraisal conclusions
- Appraisal conclusions
- Information that was considered and the reasoning
- Procedures followed
- Highest and best use for the property
- Other appropriate information (If the appraiser has a financial interest in the property, it must be fully disclosed.)
- Any deviations from the USPAP Appraisal Practice
- Valuation approach used and the reasons for exclusion of any valuation approach
- Signed certification of appraiser

Neither the purpose of the report nor the sales price should influence the appraised market valuation. An appraiser should not discuss the appraisal with anyone other than the principal for whom the appraisal was performed without the permission of the principal. It is also considered unethical for an appraiser to take an appraisal that is beyond the appraiser's ability, to pay a referral fee for business, to charge a fee based on a percentage of the appraisal value, or to have any undisclosed interest in the property being appraised.

Your Pertinent State Information

1. What are your state's appraiser licensing requirements?

2. What are your state's appraiser certification requirements?

3. What are your state requirements for appraisal reports (if any)?

CHAPTER 4 QUIZ

Valuation and Appraisal

1. A competitive market analysis is prepared by a real estate agent to estimate the likely sales price of a property. This analysis is based on the:

   (A) sales comparison method
   (B) gross rent multiplier method
   (C) cost approach
   (D) income approach

2. In appraising a home for a lender who wishes to make a purchase loan, the appraiser would be concerned with:

   (A) the amount of the loan requested
   (B) unpaid special assessments
   (C) the price the seller has agreed to pay
   (D) economic changes in the area

3. An example of external obsolescence would be:

   (A) numerous pillars supporting the ceiling in a store
   (B) roof leaks, making the premises unrentable
   (C) an older building with very small rooms
   (D) vacant and abandoned structures in the area

4. An appraisal of property is the:

   (A) supported estimate of value
   (B) utility value
   (C) selling price
   (D) cost plus improvements less depreciation

5. An appraiser would need to determine accrued depreciation when using the:

   (A) gross rent multiplier method
   (B) cost approach
   (C) income approach
   (D) sales comparison approach

6. In appraising property an appraiser would depreciate:

   (A) fences
   (B) agricultural land
   (C) land under a structure
   (D) a vacant lot

7. Which of the following actions by an appraiser would be unethical?

   (A) Refusal to make an appraisal that the appraiser feels is beyond his or her expertise
   (B) Appraising a property in which the appraiser has a disclosed interest
   (C) Accepting an appraisal where the fee will be a percentage of the value derived
   (D) Requesting payment in advance

8. An appraiser, in using the expression a "willing, informed buyer and a willing, informed seller," is referencing:

   (A) progression
   (B) supply and demand
   (C) the principle of highest and best use
   (D) market value

9. Which appraisal method would tend to set the upper limit of value on a new structure?

   (A) Gross multiplier
   (B) Income approach
   (C) Cost approach
   (D) Sales comparison approach

10. The advisability of including a tennis court with a planned apartment building may be determined by the principle of:

    (A) contribution
    (B) progression
    (C) substitution
    (D) change

11. A new, expensive home in a mixed area of commercial property and older, less expensive homes could have a market value less than the cost of the new home because of:

    (A) external obsolescence
    (B) the gross multiplier effect
    (C) progression
    (D) physical deterioration

12. A property has a net income of $30,000. One appraiser decides to use a 12 percent capitalization rate, while a second appraiser uses a 10 percent rate. Use of the higher rate results in:

    (A) a 2 percent increase in appraised value
    (B) a $50,000 increase in appraised value
    (C) a $50,000 decrease in appraised value
    (D) no change in appraised value

13. Which of the following reports would be the most comprehensive appraisal report?

    (A) Short form report
    (B) Narrative report
    (C) Uniform Residential Appraisal Report
    (D) Certified appraisal report

14. A value regarded as being a subjective value would be:

    (A) market value
    (B) assessed value
    (C) use value
    (D) book value

15. According to the principle of integration and disintegration:

    (A) the value of a property will eventually decline
    (B) property value is best maintained in homogeneous areas
    (C) extraordinary profits will disappear with competition
    (D) the maximum value would be based on cost of a comparable property

16. The reason the gross rent multiplier is an inaccurate measurement of value is that it fails to consider:

    (A) depreciation
    (B) unusual expenses
    (C) location
    (D) amenity values

17. According to the principle of conformity, the highest value is maintained by having a residence:

    (A) adjoining a shopping area
    (B) next to a church
    (C) across from a school
    (D) in the center of a residential development

18. Several $150,000 homes were built in an area where the existing homes had been valued at $400,000 to $500,000. The effect was that the value of the existing homes declined. Which real estate principle applies to this situation?

    (A) Regression
    (B) Competition
    (C) Substitution
    (D) Integration and disintegration

19. With an annual net income of $40,000 and a capitalization rate of 8 percent, the value of the property using the income approach would be:

    (A) $400,000
    (B) $440,000
    (C) $500,000
    (D) $520,000

20. The time period during which a structure shows income that is attributable to the structure itself is known as its:

    (A) economic life
    (B) effective age
    (C) period for depreciation
    (D) period of profitability

21. The last lot in a subdivision sold for almost twice the price paid for the first lot sold. This is an example of the principle of:

    (A) regression
    (B) diminishing returns
    (C) supply and demand
    (D) conformity

22. A property being appraised has a two-car garage, while a comparable has a three-car garage. In making adjustments, the appraiser would:

    (A) raise the value of the comparable
    (B) lower the value of the home being appraised
    (C) lower the value of the comparable
    (D) raise the value of the home being appraised

23. A good definition of *market value* would be the:

    (A) price paid by the owner
    (B) present worth of future benefits
    (C) assessed valuation
    (D) price offered by a prospective buyer

24. After determining the value of the improvements of an existing structure, the appraiser deducted this amount from the market value to determine the value attributed to the land. This appraisal method is known as:

    (A) surplus productivity
    (B) the abstractive method
    (C) the development method
    (D) the land residual method

25. The highest and best use is the use that provides the greatest:

    (A) benefit to the community
    (B) gross
    (C) value
    (D) capitalization rate

26. Demand is not effective in determining the value of real property unless it is combined with:

    (A) scarcity
    (B) a use
    (C) purchasing power
    (D) access

27. An investor making extraordinary profits from the first miniwarehouse in the area would be concerned with the principle of:

    (A) substitution
    (B) competition
    (C) surplus productivity
    (D) conformity

28. The principle of supply and demand predicts:

    (A) increasing price when supply increases
    (B) decreasing demand when supply increases
    (C) increasing demand when price decreases
    (D) decreasing price when demand increases

29. An appraiser wanted to know the capitalization rate applicable for a recent sale. The net income was reported at $21,000 and the property sold for $300,000. What capitalization rate applied to the sale?

    (A) 6%
    (B) 7%
    (C) 8%
    (D) 9%

30. The appraiser used 80 percent of the value arrived at by the market comparison approach, 20 percent of the value arrived at with the cost approach, and did not consider the value arrived at using the income approach. The process the appraiser was engaged in is known as:

    (A) the sum of the values
    (B) reconciliation
    (C) the abstractive method
    (D) the index method

31. The appraiser could calculate the annual gross rent multiplier that applied to a recent sale by:

    (A) capitalizing the annual gross income
    (D) dividing the annual gross income by the price paid
    (C) dividing the price paid by the annual gross income
    (D) multiplying the monthly gross income by 12

32. A seller agreed to sell a home with no down payment and below-market-rate seller financing. The favorable financing could be expected to affect the:

    (A) price but not the value of the property
    (B) value of the property but not the price
    (C) utility of the property
    (D) depreciation method

33. A property owner would have the greatest difficulty in correcting depreciation caused by:

    (A) chronological age
    (B) the built-in nature of the structure
    (C) forces outside the property boundaries
    (D) wear and tear due to use

34. An appraiser sets a replacement cost of a structure at $120,000 and appraises the land value separately at $80,000. The appraiser places an economic life on the structure at 50 years and states that it has an effective age of 10 years. Using the cost approach, the appraiser would appraise this property at:

    (A) $140,000
    (B) $160,000
    (C) $176,000
    (D) $200,000

35. In using the sales comparison approach to value to appraise a single-family residence, an appraiser might have to make adjustments for:

    (A) assessed valuation differences
    (B) a difference in possible rental income
    (C) date of sale
    (D) difference in the capitalization rate

36. Each unit in a fourplex rents for $225 per month. With a sales price of $81,000, the annual gross rent multiplier is:

    (A) 7.5
    (B) 30
    (C) 90
    (D) 360

37. Federal law requires that an appraiser be licensed or certified for:

    (A) any appraisal
    (B) any residential appraisals
    (C) any federally related appraisal
    (D) federally related appraisals of $250,000 or more

38. A buyer who looked at seven very similar homes in a three-year-old subdivision made an offer on the home with the lowest list price. The buyer was utilizing the principal of:

    (A) supply and demand
    (B) substitution
    (C) conformity
    (D) change

39. A separate value for the land is needed for the:

    (A) income approach
    (B) gross rent multiplier method
    (C) cost approach
    (D) market comparison approach

40. With fixed rents and a capitalization rate of 8 percent, an increase in taxes of $4,000 would result in the value of a property:

    (A) decreasing by $5,000
    (B) decreasing by $50,000
    (C) remaining unchanged
    (D) increasing

41. An appraiser counting the number of electrical outlets in a structure is using the:

    (A) market comparison method
    (B) income approach
    (C) cost approach
    (D) gross rent multiplier method

42. A property being appraised had 2,400 square feet, but a comparable used by the appraiser had only 2,250 square feet. The appraiser should:

    (A) disregard the comparable because of dissimilar size
    (B) use the comparable but ignore the slight size difference
    (C) adjust the sale price of the comparable upward because of size difference
    (D) adjust the sale price of the comparable downward because of the size difference

43. Which appraisal principle indicates the economic effect an improvement has on property?

    (A) Progression
    (B) Substitution
    (C) Surplus
    (D) Contribution

44. The use of more than one appraisal method with different weights assigned to each method describes:

    (A) reconciliation
    (B) a certified appraisal
    (C) the development method
    (D) the quantity survey method

45. In the market comparison method, amenities are balanced out:

    (A) to allow for appreciation
    (B) because of the principle of competition
    (C) because the market is not static
    (D) because no two properties are identical

46. The first step in appraising an apartment building using the income approach would be to determine the:

    (A) scheduled gross income
    (B) effective gross income
    (C) net income
    (D) vacancy factor

47. "The whole is worth more than the sum of its parts" refers to:

    (A) progression
    (B) assemblage
    (C) land residual
    (D) depreciation

48. Two adjacent residences in the center of a large development had similar values when they were built 60 years ago. They both have been maintained in similar condition and the site values are identical, but one is now worth far more than the other. The reason for the difference in value relates to:

    (A) physical deterioration
    (B) economic obsolescence
    (C) functional obsolescence
    (D) the principle of integration and disintegration

49. Which appraisal method would be used to determine the present value of future income?

    (A) Income approach
    (B) Cost approach
    (C) Quantity survey method
    (D) Sales comparison approach

50. Which description refers to reproduction cost?

    (A) Present cost to build a structure of similar utility and desirability
    (B) Depreciated present value of a structure
    (C) Present cost to produce a duplicate of a structure
    (D) Depreciated value of a structure plus the present land value

CHAPTER 4 QUIZ ANSWERS

Valuation and Appraisal

1. (A) It uses the price and terms of comparable sales. (page 66)
2. (D) This could indicate economic obsolescence as well as progression or regression. The others don't affect the property's value. (pages 66)
3. (D) External obsolescence deals with forces outside the property itself. (A) and (C) are functional obsolescence, whereas (B) is physical deterioration. (page 71)
4. (A) An appraisal is an estimate based on appraiser information. (page 62)
5. (B) It is the cost to build today less accrued depreciation, plus the value of the land. (page 66)
6. (A) While improvements are depreciated, land is never depreciated. (page 67)
7. (C) This could create the appearance of a conflict of interest. It is all right to have an interest in the property being appraised so long as there is open and full disclosure. (page 73)
8. (D) See definition of market value. (page 62)
9. (C) Cost approach tends to set upper limits on value. (page 66)
10. (A) What will the tennis court contribute to the anticipated net income? (Capitalize the anticipated increase in net income to determine the value of the tennis court.) (page 63)
11. (A) It is regression, which is economic obsolescence. (page 71)
12. (C) Increasing the rate decreases the value. Value moves inversely to the capitalization rate. (pages 68–69)

$$\frac{\text{Net}}{\text{Rate}} = \text{Value}$$

$$\frac{\$30,000}{.10} = \$300,000$$

$$\frac{\$30,000}{.12} = \$250,000$$

13. (B) It includes background and data use for conclusions. (page 72)
14. (C) It is also known as *utility value*. Market value is considered to be the objective value. (page 62)
15. (A) Property goes through three phases—integration, equilibrium, and disintegration. (page 63)
16. (B) Because of unusual expenses, the gross may bear little relationship to the net. (page 69)
17. (D) The principle of conformity states that value is maintained when a property is located in an area of similar properties. (page 63)
18. (A) The new lower-value homes negatively affected the value of the more expensive homes. (page 63)
19. (C) Divide the net by the capitalization rate to determine value. (page 68)

$$\frac{\$40,000}{.08} = \$500,000$$

20. (A) When the property no longer returns an income attributable to the structure itself, it has exceeded its economic life. (page 67)
21. (C) The demand exceeds the supply, which causes prices to increase. (page 63)
22. (C) The sale price of the comparable is adjusted to the property being appraised. (page 66)
23. (B) Whereas an appraiser estimates the value, (B) is its definition. What one buyer paid does not determine a property's value. (page 62)
24. (B) To determine land value, the value of the improvements is deducted from the market value of the property. (page 70)
25. (C) It is that use that will provide the greatest net attributable to the property. (page 63)
26. (C) Demand without purchasing power is only a wish. (page 64)
27. (B) Whenever extraordinary profits are being made. competition produces additional units that reduce profits. (page 63)
28. (C) When supply exceeds demand, prices drop. When demand exceeds supply, prices rise. As prices drop, there are more buyers (demand); as prices rise, there are fewer buyers. (page 63)
29. (B) Divide the net income by the price paid to determine the capitalization rate used. (page 68)

30. (B) Reconciliation involves use of applicable methods with the appraiser applying a weight to each method. (page 69)

31. (C) You also can get the monthly gross rent multiplier by dividing the price paid by the monthly gross income. (page 69)

32. (A) Advantageous sales terms could result in a higher price; however, the value of the property is intrinsic to the property and remains the same. (page 62)

33. (C) Because external obsolescence is caused by forces outside the property, it is extremely difficult for a property owner to correct it alone. (A) and (D) refer to physical deterioration and (B) to functional obsolescence. (page 71)

34. (C) Replacement cost less depreciation plus land equals value. A 50-year life means 2 percent depreciation per year; 2 percent times 10 equals 20 percent;.20 times $120,000 equals $24,000 (pages 66–67)

$$\$120,000 - \$24,000 + \$80,000 = \$176,000$$

35. (C) When the market has changed since a comparable sale, an adjustment is necessary. (pages 65–66)

36. (A) (page 69)

$$\begin{array}{lll} \$225 & \times & 4 = \$ \ \ 900 \text{ per month} \\ \$900 & \times & 12 = \$10,800 \text{ per year} \end{array} \quad \frac{\$81,000}{\$10,800} = 7.5 \text{ GRM}$$

37. (D) And certified appraisers must be used for federally related appraisals of $1 million or more. (page 72)

38. (B) A buyer will not pay more than what an equally desirable property can be purchased for. (page 63)

39. (C) It is the cost to replace less depreciation plus the value of the land. (page 66)

40. (B) The increase in expenses of $4,000 with fixed rents will mean a $4,000 reduction in net. The value of $4,000 income by capitalizing $4,000 (divided by .08) equals $50,000. (page 68)

41. (C) This would be the unit cost-in-place method to determine the replacement cost. (page 67)

42. (C) When the comparable has a lesser feature (or lacks a feature) raise the sale price of the comparable. If the comparable is better, lower the sale price of comparable. (page 66)

43. (D) This is used to determine the economic viability of an improvement. (page 63)

44. (A) It is also known as *correlation.* (page 69)

45. (D) Appraisers add or subtract from comparable sales prices for the presence or absence of amenities compared with the property being appraised. (pages 65–66)

46. (A) The scheduled gross then must be adjusted for a vacancy factor. (page 68)

47. (B) The added value due to assemblage is plottage value. (page 63)

48. (C) It would be built-in obsolescence by design (outmoded or less desirable floor plan or design). Other choices are ruled out by the facts. (pages 70–71)

49. (A) When we capitalize the net, we determine the present value of future income. (page 68)

50. (C) Reproduction cost is the cost to duplicate a structure exactly, while replacement cost deals with one having similar utility and desirability. (page 66)

Contracts/Agency and Fair Housing

CONTRACTS

Real estate transactions are ruled by specific documents such as leases, listings, and offers to purchase. Such documents spell out the contractual rights and obligations agreed to by parties to certain transactions. Therefore, much of this chapter addresses the general area of law known as **contract law.** An understanding of contracts is essential in dealing with real estate. In simple terms, a contract is an agreement enforceable by law.

Types of Contracts

Bilateral Contract A contract that contains a promise made in exchange for a promise is a bilateral contract. Sales agreements are bilateral—promises to buy given for promises to sell. Similarly, an exclusive right-to-sell listing is a bilateral contract in which the owner agrees to pay a commission if the agent is successful and the agent in return agrees to use his or her best efforts to locate a buyer.

Unilateral Contract A contract that contains a promise contingent on the performance of an act is a unilateral contract. Acceptance of the promise is not in the form of another promise but in the form of an act. For example, assume a property manager promised to pay a man $100 to remove trash from a property. If the man removed the trash, he would be entitled to the $100 even though he was not obligated to perform. His or her performance of an act made the acceptance.

Executed Contract An executed contract is one that has been fully performed. As an example, a purchase contract would be executed upon closing.

Executory Contract An executory contract has yet to be fully performed but is not in default. As an example, prior to the closing a purchase contract would be executory.

Express Contract An express contract is one specifically agreed to, either verbally or in writing. Because they are required by the statute of frauds to be in writing, real estate contracts are express contracts. The statute of frauds is covered later in this chapter.

Implied Contract An implied contract is one that is understood because of actions of the parties, although a specific agreement is not stated. For example, in requesting a carpenter to make repairs, you might fail to specify a fee. It is implied, however, that you will pay a fair price for the services received.

Valid Contracts

Contracts that meet all legal requirements are valid and enforceable, which means that either party can hold the other party responsible for his or her agreement. Four requirements must be met before a contract is valid.

1. **Competent Parties**   Contracting parties must have mental and legal capacity to enter into a valid contract. Persons found to be mentally incompetent cannot contract. Legal capacity is determined by legal age, which is set by law. In most states, the legal age for contracting is 18. In some states, deeds by minors are considered void, while in other states, deeds by minors are considered voidable, which means that the minor may elect to be bound by the agreement or to void the agreement at the minor's option. A minor can buy real estate from an adult; however, the minor has the option of voiding the transaction. Therefore, great care must be exercised when dealing with a minor. A minor could, of course, receive real estate as a gift. In some states, emancipated minors, such as married minors, are allowed to contract as adults.

Individual state laws govern the right of convicted prisoners to contract. These rights generally are restricted.

2. **Mutual Agreement**   To have a valid contract, there must be a meeting of the minds, that is, mutual assent, normally evidenced by an offer and acceptance. A unilateral mistake on the part of one party only will not allow that person to get out of the contract. As an example, if a buyer mistakenly believed that the zoning would allow a particular use, and the seller had done nothing to indicate that the buyer's secret plans were possible, the buyer could not void the agreement because of his or her error. However, a mutual mistake of fact or impossibility of performance makes the contract unenforceable. As an example, assume the buyer and seller both believed an irregularly shaped parcel contained the necessary square footage to construct a duplex. If they later discovered that the actual square footage was less than believed, so that a duplex could not be built, the buyer could likely void the agreement based on the mutual mistake.

3. **Consideration**   For an agreement between two parties to be binding, the parties must give or promise something of value, called *consideration*. A promise unsupported by consideration really is a promise to make a gift and, therefore, is unenforceable. Consideration does not have to be fair, although grossly inadequate consideration could be evidence of fraud or undue influence.

Love and affection are deemed to be "good consideration." However, they are not deemed to be the "valuable consideration" required to support a contract. Valuable consideration is a right, an interest, a profit, or an agreement to refrain from a lawful act, any one of which the promisor considers valuable. Consideration, then, need not be money, but it must have worth.

4. **Legal Purpose**   To be enforceable, a contract must be for a legal purpose. A contract made for an unlawful purpose is illegal and would be void and unenforceable by either party.

As an example, a contract in violation of state or federal antitrust laws would be void and unenforceable.

Finally, some contracts have a fifth requirement: they must be in writing to be enforceable in a court of law.

Statute of Frauds

In old England, real estate was considered the basis of all wealth. Real estate transactions were so important that the statute of frauds required every real estate contract to be in writing to be enforceable. Every state has a statute of frauds that requires particular agreements to be written and to be signed by the party to be held to the agreement.

Verbal contracts can be valid and enforceable, unless they are required by the statute of frauds to be in writing. State statutes of frauds usually require that the following be in writing:

- All agreements for the sale of real estate. In most states, listing agreements must be in writing because real estate is involved; however, a few states allow oral listing agreements that are one year or less in term.
- Any lease for more than one year. (However, some states allow verbal leases for more than one year.)
- Contracts that by their terms cannot be fully performed within one year of the parties entering into the agreements.
- Promises to pay the debt of another.
- Promises made in contemplation of marriage.
- Contracts for the sale of personal property for more than $500.

Although executory verbal real estate contracts are unenforceable, fully executed agreements are valid transfers. For example, a verbal promise to sell a house for $100,000 cannot be enforced, but once the consideration has been paid and the title transferred, the transaction is complete and cannot be set aside because it was based on a verbal agreement.

The courts may allow enforcement of a verbal real estate purchase contract, even though the statute of frauds requires a written agreement, in cases where there has been partial performance based on the verbal agreement. This is the doctrine of **estoppel** whereby a person is prohibited (estopped) from disavowing his or her verbal promise after the other party has acted to his or her detriment based on that promise.

As an example, assume there was a verbal agreement for the sale of a lot for $30,000. Assume also that the prospective buyer, with the knowledge of the seller, spent $40,000 bringing utilities to the lot and preparing the site for construction. A court would likely determine that the seller was **estopped** from raising the defense of the statute of fraud because of the buyer's reliance on the verbal agreement. Of course the buyer would have to prove the existence of the verbal agreement.

Void Contracts

Any contract that fails to meet one or more contractual requirements is void and unenforceable by either party to the agreement.

Voidable Contracts

Voidable contracts are valid unless voided. Only one party—the innocent party to the transaction—can void the agreement or elect to be bound by it. (The innocent party is the one not guilty of a wrongful act.) The following factors are among those that may make contracts voidable.

Duress or Menace Contracts entered into under force (duress) or threat of force (menace) may be voided by the injured party.

Fraud Fraud is an intentional statement or omission that persuades or influences another to act to his or her harm. It can also be a false statement made by a person who did not know whether it was true or false. Concealing a material defect or fact could also be fraud (negative fraud).

Fraud can be a criminal as well as a civil wrong. The injured party may void a contract entered into because of fraud.

Fraud as to the nature of the contract could make the contract void rather than voidable. An example would be an owner representing a purchase contract as an option to buy.

Misrepresentation   Misrepresentation is a misstatement or concealment of an important fact so that another party is led to act to his or her detriment. Whereas fraud requires the element of intent to deceive, misrepresentation could be a false statement made by someone who believed it to be true. Misrepresentation also allows a contract to be voided and, like fraud, could subject the wrongdoer to civil damages.

If a person knew that a statement was false or that a material fact was being concealed, the contract would not be voidable by that person because he or she was not deceived into acting to his or her detriment.

Puffing   Puffing is merely a statement of opinion ("This is a good value"). It is not generally considered sufficient basis to void a contract, even though the statement influences another party to act to that party's detriment.

Undue Influence   Undue influence is where a person does not act voluntarily because of an overpowering relationship. If *L* enters into an unfair contract with *M* against *L*'s own free will because of their confidential relationship (client/attorney, broker/owner, doctor/patient, parent/child), *L* can void the agreement.

Minor Status   A minor may disaffirm a contract within a reasonable period of time after reaching contractual age; however, a minor cannot disaffirm a contract for necessity, such as food or clothing.

Unconscionable Contracts   If a contract is so harsh that a court considers it unconscionable (shockingly unfair), the court will refuse to enforce it.

Offer and Acceptance

An offer is made by an offeror and expresses that person's willingness to enter into a particular agreement. The offeree is the person to whom the offer is made. When the offeree accepts the offer, a contract is formed. Unless the offer specifies a particular period of time for acceptance, it is considered to be held open for acceptance for a reasonable time. A newspaper advertisement usually is not regarded as an offer but merely an invitation to negotiate.

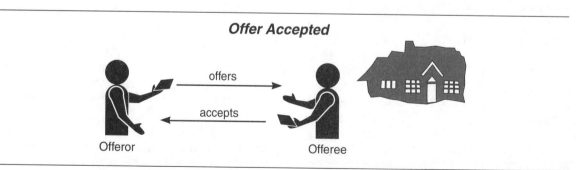

Offer Accepted

offers →

← accepts

Offeror   Offeree

If an offer states a time for acceptance but fails to indicate that "time is of the essence," the courts could allow acceptance after the period for acceptance expires. If "time is of the essence" is stated in the offer, acceptance must occur within the period specified or the offer is canceled automatically.

If the offer fails to specify the form for acceptance (letter, telephone call, telegram, or even performance), the offer may be accepted in any reasonable manner. Acceptance does not take place until the offeror is notified, which usually is by delivery of a signed, accepted copy of the offer to the offeror. The statute of frauds requires that offers and acceptances for the sale of real estate be in writing.

Revocation of Offer Because the offeror did not receive any consideration for making the offer, the offeror can withdraw or revoke the offer any time prior to its acceptance. This applies even when the offeror promised to keep the offer open for a specified period of time. The act of placing an acceptance in the mail is acceptance; however, a mailed revocation of an offer does not take effect until it is received.

Death of Offeror The death of the offeror or offeree *prior to* acceptance voids the offer automatically. The death of the offeror or offeree *after* acceptance does not affect the agreement, which becomes binding on the estate of the deceased party. However, if a contract called for the personal services of one of the parties to the contract, such as the services of a well-known architect, that party's death would terminate the agreement. The death of a corporate officer of the offeror or offeree corporation does not terminate the offer because a corporation is regarded in law as a separate being.

Counteroffer A conditional acceptance that varies from the original offer due to a new or changed requirement customarily is regarded as a counteroffer and not an acceptance. Because a counteroffer is really a rejection of the original offer, the original offeree now becomes an offeror with a new offer. The original offeror (now the offeree) can either accept the new offer and form a binding contract or reject that offer. Once an offer is rejected, it is considered dead, and any later acceptance constitutes a new offer.

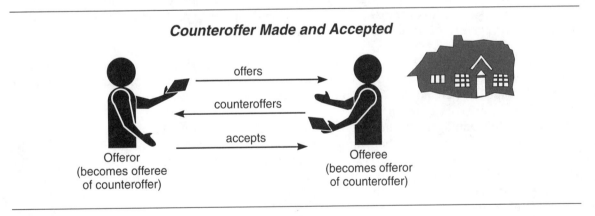

Options

An option keeps an offer open. It is a right to buy or lease property at a specified price during a designated period of time. The option right is given to the optionee (potential buyer) by the optionor (owner).

To create a valid option, the optionee must have given the optionor something of value as nonrefundable consideration to keep the offer open. Once given, an option cannot be revoked by the optionor, which makes the option an irrevocable offer.

An option is a unilateral contract until it is exercised because while the optionor is bound by an irrevocable offer, the optionee need not exercise the option. Once the option is exercised, it becomes a bilateral contract with both optionor and optionee bound to their promises.

Right of First Refusal

A right of first refusal gives the holder the right to buy or lease a property only if the owner decides to sell or lease it to another person. It is the right to match an offer, within a designated period of time, that an owner is otherwise prepared to accept. The owner, however, is under no obligation to sell or lease the property. This differs from an option, where the owner must sell or lease if the optionee wishes to exercise the option.

Rights of first refusal are often found in leases giving the tenant first chance at any purchase or later lease agreement the owner wishes to accept.

Remedies for Breach of Contract

A breach of contract is the failure of a party to comply with a material (key) contractual provision. Following are some legal remedies for broken contractual promises.

Compensatory Damages Money awarded by the court to the injured party to make up for the loss suffered is called *compensatory damages*.

Assume a seller agreed to sell a lot for $100,000 and later refused to honor the agreement. If the buyer had to pay $110,000 for a similarly desirable lot, the buyer could seek compensatory damages in the amount of $10,000.

The injured party has a duty to try to keep the damages as low as reasonably possible when a contract is breached. This effort is referred to as **mitigation of damages.** For example, if a tenant breaks a lease, the landlord has a duty to use reasonable effort to obtain a new tenant.

Punitive or Exemplary Damages   Courts may award damages beyond compensatory damages to punish (punitive) or make an example of (exemplary) a party who committed a willful and/or an outrageous act or breach of an agreement.

Nominal Damages   If a breach does not result in an actual dollar loss, token amount— called *nominal damages*—are awarded. For example, a court might award nominal damages for a wrongful trespass where no money damages occurred.

Liquidated Damages Liquidated damages are breach-of-contract compensation agreed on by the parties at the time of their agreement. Construction contracts often include a daily liquidated damages amount if a job is not completed on time, and purchase contracts customarily provide for the buyer to give up the earnest money deposit in the event of the buyer's breach. If liquidated damages are set too high, the courts might determine that they are actually penalties, which are unenforceable.

Specific Performance If an owner enters into a contract to sell his or her real property and later refuses to convey the property, the buyer can request performance (specific performance) rather than money damage. Because every parcel of real estate is unique, money damages are not always an adequate remedy. Courts will, therefore, grant the remedy of specific performance for real estate contracts. Courts generally will not grant specific performance if the consideration is not considered adequate.

Injunction An injunction is a court order to stop doing a certain activity (cease and desist). Injunctions may be permanent or temporary.

Declaratory Relief   This remedy consists of a court determination of rights and duties of the parties before actual damages occur.

Reformation   An action to correct a mistake in an agreement or a deed is called *reformation.* The action amends an agreement to conform to the original intention.

Rescission   Rescission cancels the contract and restores the parties to the positions they held prior to entering into the contract. One party can use a breach by the other party as the basis for rescinding the contract. **Restitution** is the return of consideration when a contract is rescinded.

Waiver   A party to a contract can waive a contractual breach by the other party and choose to remain bound by the contract. For example, a buyer might waive the seller's failure to correct a defect and, in doing so, insist on closing.

A party also can waive any provisions for his or her sole benefit. For example, if an agreement was contingent on the buyer obtaining an 80 percent loan at no more than 7 percent interest, the buyer could waive the contingency if such a loan could not be obtained and choose to go ahead with the transaction. Waiver leaves the parties as they are; rescission puts them back the way they were.

Accord and Satisfaction   Accord and satisfaction are the agreement to accept a lesser consideration than that specified in a contract. Such agreement is common in construction contracts when there is disagreement as to proper performance of the work.

Novation   Substitution of a new contract for an old one is called *novation.* Parties to a novation agree to cancel the old contract in favor of the new agreement, as when a buyer and a builder make a contract for a model home that is different from the one originally chosen and named in a contract. Novation also is considered to occur when all parties agree to the substitution of a new party for one of the original contract parties and to the full release of the original party from all obligations under the agreement. (Novations may be used in loan assumptions in which the seller is released from all loan obligations by the substitution of the buyer.)

Statute of Limitations   A state statute of limitations defines the period of time during which various types of legal action must be brought. The statute of limitations starts on the date an obligation is due. If no payment is made or no legal action taken during the prescribed period, the right to enforce the agreement is lost. As an example, assume that your state has a four-year statute of limitations on written contracts. If a person was obligated under a written contract to pay the sum of $10,000 to another person by a specified date, the person entitled to the $10,000 would be barred from forcing a collection if more than four years had elapsed from the date the money was due.

Interpretation of Contracts

Generally speaking, the courts will try to interpret contracts in accordance with the intent of the parties. Words will be given their common meaning within the trade or profession involved.

If more than one meaning is possible in interpreting a contract, the contract is ambiguous. The courts attempt to resolve ambiguities based on the intent of the parties. If the ambiguities are such that intent cannot be identified, a contract is considered unenforceable because it lacks mutual agreement.

Typed material takes priority over the printed form, and handwritten portions take priority over typed content because these additions to a printed or typed contract clearly indicate the intent of the parties.

Written words take priority over numerals. For example, if a contract states, "forty-six thousand dollars ($40,000)," $46,000, *not* $40,000, would stand as the contractual amount.

In the event of an ambiguity between two or more documents, a later agreement generally takes precedence over a prior agreement because it assumed that the later, or latest, one indicates the final intent of the parties.

Obvious typographical errors can be disregarded.

Ambiguities in a contract usually are decided against the party drafting the instrument.

Assignment of Contracts

Assignment of a contract is the transfer of all the interests of one of the contractual parties to a third person. Contracts that do not specifically prohibit assignment can be transferred without the approval of the other contracting party. However, contracts that are personal in nature (for particular personal services) cannot be assigned. For example, if a party contracted with a particular distinguished real estate broker to negotiate a lease, that broker could not assign the contract to another broker because the contract would be considered personal in nature.

In an assignment, the assignee takes the place of the assignor and is primarily liable for the contractual duties of the assignor. The assignor, however, retains secondary liability, which means that the assignor could be held to the contract should the assignee fail to perform. This situation differs from a novation, in which a new party is completely substituted for the old party, who is released from all contract liability.

AGENCY

An *agency* is a personal relationship freely entered into whereby the **agent** acts for another, the **principal.** To appoint an agent, the principal must have contractual capacity (mental and legal capacity).

The principal is liable for the acts of his or her agent within the scope of the agency (**doctrine of respondent superior**).

It does not matter whether an agent receives compensation. An agent who acts without compensation has the same duties to the parties as an agent who is paid by the principal.

A real estate broker acts as agent of an owner or buyer, or the broker may, in some states, even act as a dual agent. The salesperson would be a subagent of the broker's principal. The listing broker would be the agent of the principal. Salespersons and other brokers may be subagents.

Facilitator/Intermediary/Transaction Broker

This is a relatively new concept that has been adopted in a few states. The facilitator, intermediary, or transaction broker works with both the buyer and seller as a middleman rather than as an agent. The broker has no advocacy or fiduciary duties but must nevertheless be fair and honest with both buyer and seller. Some states require that the broker take an agency position, which precludes being a facilitator, intermediary, or transaction broker.

Cooperating Broker

Multiple-listing services (MLSs) may offer cooperating brokers subagency. If the cooperating broker declines subagency, the cooperating broker would be an agent of the buyer; otherwise, the cooperating broker would be a subagent of the seller or listing broker, depending on the agreement. In some states it is possible for the cooperating broker to elect to be a dual agent.

If the cooperating broker represents a prospect buyer under a buyer's listing, then the cooperating broker would decline subagency.

Unless state law provides otherwise, agreements between brokers to split commissions need not be in writing to be enforceable because they deal in money, not an interest in real estate.

Power of Attorney

A *power of attorney* is a particular written agency agreement whereby the principal authorizes another person, the agent, to act in the place of the principal as an **attorney-in-fact.** A specific power of attorney applies to one particular act, such as signing a deed in place of the principal. A general power of attorney allows the attorney-in-fact to obligate a principal in almost any way that the principal could have obligated himself or herself. In real estate, a power of attorney is occasionally used when the principal is unavailable. A power of attorney that authorizes the attorney in fact to convey real property must be recorded for the attorney-in-fact to convey a marketable title. In some states, an agent cannot sign a deed.

Seller and Buyer Agency

Historically, real estate agents had been seller agents with fiduciary duties to the seller and a duty to the buyer of fair play and to disclose negative information regarding the property that they were aware of.

There has been a significant growth of buyer agency where the broker is the agent of the buyer, regardless of who is paying the commission, and has a duty to fulfill the needs of the buyer in as advantageous a manner to the buyer as possible. Where an agent represents either a buyer or seller it is known as a **single agency.**

Dual Agency

In some states, it is possible for a broker to elect to be a dual agent. A dual agency is also known as a **limited agency.** As a dual agent, the broker would have agency duties to both buyer and seller or lessor and lessee. While dual agency agreements prohibit the broker from passing on confidential information received from one principal to the other principal, dual agencies can create a serious conflict of interest. Where dual agency is possible, the broker must obtain consent from both principals to the dual agency representation. If a principal were unaware of a broker's dual agency, the principal would likely have the right to the return of any compensation paid as well as the right to void any contract entered into.

A broker could inadvertently create a dual agency if the broker's words and/or actions led a party to believe that the broker was representing him or her. If this should happen, the broker could be held to have agency duties to both parties to the transaction.

To avoid accidentally creating a dual agency or allowing a party to have a misconception of the broker's role, most states require that the broker disclose in writing his or her agency status to both buyer and seller prior to the signing of a purchase agreement. This disclosure applies to both listing and selling agents. The agency relationship specified could be buyer's agency, seller's agency, dual agency, designated agency, or even a nonagency facilitator role where applicable.

Designated Agency (Split Agency)

This agency relationship is not authorized in all states. It allows a listing salesperson for a firm to be the designated agent (sole agent) of the seller. If another salesperson from the same firm procures a buyer, that salesperson could be the designated agent of the buyer.

Broker/Salesperson Relationship

The employment contract between real estate broker and salesperson specifies either an employee or independent contractor relationship. Employees customarily operate under the control and direction of employers, whereas independent contractors are hired for specific jobs and generally are not under direction as to how the jobs are to be accomplished. Some states consider real estate salespeople to be employees despite agreements that specify otherwise. The reasoning is that because a broker has a duty of supervision, the salesperson must be an employee. Because real estate salespeople are paid by commission, they are not entitled to unemployment compensation benefits.

The Internal Revenue Service will treat real estate salespeople as **independent contractors,** exempt from deducting withholding tax or making employer Social Security contributions, if three criteria are met:

1. They are licensed as salespeople or broker associates.
2. Pay is related to sales success, not to hours worked.
3. A written contract states that for tax purposes, the salesperson will be treated as an independent contractor.

A salesperson may receive payment for acts requiring a real estate license only from his or her own broker. It is regarded as a violation of state law for a salesperson to be paid by another broker or directly by an owner for an act requiring a real estate license.

Types of Agents

Specific Agent (Special Agent)   An agent who has authority only for designated acts is a specific agent. An example is a listing agent, who customarily has authorization to locate a buyer or a property but not to consummate a sale on the owner or buyer's behalf.

General Agent   A general agent has all the authority necessary to conduct a business or trade. A general manager of a real estate office or a property manager might be a general agent. The term **universal agent** describes a broad general agency where the agent is appointed to do all acts a principal can lawfully delegate to another.

Agency Creation

An agency can be created in a number of ways.

Express Agency   An express (a stated) agency is created by written or verbal agreement. A listing, for example, creates an express agency where the broker is the agent of the principal.

Agency by Implication   An agency that is understood by the words or conduct of the parties, although not specifically agreed to, is an agency by implication. By actions or words of an agent, a prospective buyer could reasonably be led to believe the seller's agent was representing him or her. In such a case, an implied agency could be formed that would obligate the agent to both buyer and seller (dual agency). Similarly if a broker who wished to act as a facilitator, by words and or actions, reasonably leads a person to believe that the broker was representing him or her, then there could be an implied agency to that party.

An **ostensible agency** is an implied agency created by actions of the parties even though the principal might not have intended an agency relationship. For example, if an owner knows a broker is showing his or her property to prospective buyers without authorization and does nothing to prevent the showing, a prospective buyer reasonably could believe that an agency relationship exists. The owner could be held liable for the agent's acts.

Agency by Estoppel   A person might be estopped (prohibited) from denying an agency exists if that person's words or actions reasonably led a third person to act to his or her detriment based on the third person's belief as to the existence of the agency. As an example, assume owner *J* told prospective tenant *K* that *L* was *J's* exclusive commercial leasing agent when, in fact, no agency had ever been established. Based on *J's* representation, *K* gave *L* a $10,000 deposit on a lease. Neither *L* nor the deposit can now be located. *J* would likely be barred from denying the existence of the agency, by estoppel, because *J's* words led *K* to act.

Agency by Ratification   An agency is created when a principal's acceptance of the benefits of an unauthorized agent's act or an act beyond the agent's authority ratifies an agency relationship. For example, assume that agent *P* entered into a lease claiming to be the owner's agent but had no actual authorization from the owner. If, after learning of the transaction, the owner accepts rent under the lease, the owner will have ratified the agency.

Duties of the Agent

Fiduciary Duty   An agent has a fiduciary duty to his or her principal. A fiduciary duty is one of trust. There are five elements to the fiduciary duty.
1. **Care**   The agent must exercise "due care" which is reasonable and diligent care in carrying out the duties of the agency.
2. **Obedience**   The agent has a duty to obey the lawful instructions of the principal. An agent who fails to obey instructions or who exceeds the authority given by the principal could be liable for resulting damages. If instructions given to the agent require that the agent perform or be an accomplice to an illegal act, the agent must withdraw from the agency.
3. **Accounting**   The agent must account for all funds received or disbursed on behalf of the principal.
4. **Loyalty**   The agent must be loyal to the principal. The agent cannot disclose to third parties any facts about the principal or the agency that are not in the principal's best interest. An agent may not act for more than one party in a transaction without the knowledge and approval of all the parties. The agent must place the interest of the principal above his or her personal interest should interest conflict. Making a **secret profit,** regardless of amount, violates the agent's fiduciary duty.
5. **Disclosure**   The agent has a duty of full disclosure and must inform the principal of any facts likely to influence the principal's decision-making process. As an example, if a seller's agent realizes that a buyer is willing to pay more than is being offered, a seller's agent would have a duty to inform the seller of this fact. Every offer received must be transmitted promptly to the principal. In many states, this disclosure extends to verbal as well as written offers and subsequent offers received after another offer has been accepted.

> As a learning tool, consider the acronym "COALD".

Agent's Duties to Buyer   Even though a broker's primary duties under a sale listing are to his or her principal, the seller's agent has a duty to deal with buyers in good faith. Therefore, the agent must disclose to the buyer any known facts of a material nature. In several states, an agent has the affirmative duty to make a reasonably diligent inspection of the property and to disclose to the prospective buyer any detrimental information discovered by the inspection. If an agent knows that an intended use by a prospective buyer is not feasible or possible, the agent has the affirmative duty to disclose that fact. An agent may not disclose that a former owner or tenant had AIDS. State laws differ as to disclosure requirements regarding the violent death of a former occupant, as well as psychologically impacted, stigmatized property such as a haunted house.

An agent cannot volunteer information as to the presence of minorities in an area, as this would be regarded as "steering," which violates the Civil Rights Act of 1968.

Even when an agent only relays representations made by an owner, the agent can be held **liable for misrepresentations** if the agent knew, or should have known, the information to be false.

Learn your state's consumer protection laws as they relate to real estate transactions. For example, does your state require specific disclosures by agents and/or sellers?

Secret Agent   An agent who does not reveal that he or she is acting in an agency capacity can be held personally liable for his or her actions. Third parties have the option of holding the undisclosed agent liable or taking action against the principal; they cannot do both. **Blind ads** that fail to indicate agency are prohibited.

Termination of the Agency

Agencies can be terminated in a number of ways.

Expiration   If the agency is for a specified period of time, as in an exclusive listing, expiration of that period ends the agency.

Repudiation   Because an agency requires consent of both principal and agent, either party can end the agreement at any time. Courts will not force an agency to continue; however, the party who wrongfully breached the agency agreement could be held liable for damages.

An exception to the principal's right to terminate an agency is an **agency coupled with an interest.** For example, if an agent advances an owner funds in an effort to stop a foreclosure in order to obtain the listing, the agent is coupling a financial interest to the agency. Thus, the principal cannot terminate the agency.

Death   An agency is a personal service relationship; therefore, the death of either the principal or the agent terminates the agency. Because a corporation is a separate legal entity, the death of a corporate officer does not affect the agency.

Performance   The agency terminates when the agent has performed his or her duties, usually to procure a buyer at the price and terms stated in the listing or at any other price and terms the principal agrees to accept.

Impossibility   Impossibility of performance, such as destruction of the property, terminates the agency.

Incapacity   If the agent becomes incapacitated and no longer can serve, the agency terminates. If the principal becomes mentally incapacitated, the agency terminates.

Bankruptcy of either the agent or principal may or may not terminate the agency, depending on the decision of the bankruptcy court.

Termination of the agency does not terminate all agency duties. For example, loyalty would prevent the former agent from disclosing to others information received in confidence and from using such information to his or her advantage, even after the agency has ended.

LISTINGS

A sales *listing* is a contract by which a principal (an owner) employs an agent (a broker) to procure a buyer for his or her property. When a salesperson takes a listing, the listing is the property of the broker, not the salesperson. The broker, not the salesperson, is the agent. Because of the state statutes of fraud or specific rules, in most states real estate listings must be in writing. Most verbal listings, therefore, are unenforceable although in several states, short-term verbal listings are enforceable. It is possible to have a verbal property management contract if the agent leases for one year or less.

Listings do not give brokers rights in the listed property; therefore, listings cannot be recorded.

If, after accepting an offer, the seller refuses to sell, the broker cannot force the sale. Although the broker may be entitled to sue for a commission, specific performance is a legal remedy of the buyer after the seller has accepted an offer. Because a listing requires consent, either broker or owner can cancel a listing at any time, however, that person could be liable for damages if the contract was canceled without proper cause.

Types of Listings

In an **exclusive listing,** the owner agrees that only one agent will be appointed. There are two types of exclusive listings: exclusive-right-to-sell listings and exclusive agency listings.

All exclusive listings must have a definite termination date, and the broker must give the owner a copy at the time the listing is signed. Exclusive listings are considered to be bilateral contracts if a broker promises his or her best efforts to obtain a buyer or property in return for an owner's promise to pay a fee should the broker succeed.

Exclusive-Right-To-Sell Listing   Under an *exclusive-right-to-sell listing,* the agent is entitled to a commission if, during the term of the listing or any extension thereof, the agent or anyone else procures a buyer who is ready, willing, and able to purchase the listed property under the terms of the listing or any other terms to which the principal agrees.

Because the broker is assured a commission regardless of who sells the property, this type of listing is most often sought.

Exclusive-Agency Listing   The *exclusive-agency listing* appoints the broker as the owner's sole agent to sell the property. It differs from the exclusive-right-to-sell listing in that the owner retains the right to sell the property himself or herself without being obligated to pay a commission.

Open Listing   Unless a listing agreement specifically states that it is exclusive, the listing is assumed to be open. Open, or nonexclusive, right-to-sell listings may be given concurrently to more than one broker. However, only the broker who procures a buyer is entitled to a commission. If the owner sold the property independently of the agent, no commission would be paid.

To earn a commission under an open listing, the broker must be the **procuring cause** of the sale; that is, the broker's efforts must have started an uninterrupted chain of events that resulted in the sale. An open listing can simply be a letter from an owner. It is not necessary for the owner to receive a copy or for the listing to contain a definite termination date. Either principal or agent can cancel an open listing at any time. An open listing is regarded as a unilateral contract if the broker is not obligated to use any effort to locate a buyer. The broker's act of obtaining a buyer forms the acceptance of the offer.

Net Listing   A net listing can be an exclusive or an open listing. The term *net* refers to the broker's fee. Under a net listing, the broker gets all the money exceeding a net amount that the owner is to receive. Because the agent is likely to be more interested in his or her own profit than the owner's best interests, net listings are considered by many to be unethical. In a number of states, they are illegal. Even where legal, they should be avoided, as any extraordinary broker profit will likely result in a lawsuit by the seller.

Buyer Listing   While a great many real estate agents still only represent sellers, there is a growing interest in buyer agency, whereby the agent agrees to use his or her efforts to locate a property that meets the needs of the buyer at the best price. Buyer listings may be exclusive-right-to-locate-property listings, exclusive-agency listings, or open listings.

Multiple Listing Services

Listings that authorize brokers to employ subagents or to cooperate with other brokers may be submitted to MLSs that publish and distribute listings. MLSs are usually associated with the local board of REALTORS®. In the absence of any authorization to cooperate with others, the broker has no right to share the listing with other agents.

It is considered a restraint of trade for listing organizations to set minimum commissions, to exclude brokers from access to their services, or to even conspire to participate in these activities. In some states, an MLS cannot exclude an open listing.

Listing Provisions

Provisions that may be included in a listing include the following:

- **Description**   While a legal description of the property is not required, the description of the listed property must be clear and unambiguous.
- **Price**   The owner determines the price at which the property is to be offered.
- **Commission**   Must be negotiable between owner and agent.
- **Safety or protection clause**   This provision provides that the agent is entitled to a commission when the owner sells to a buyer after the expiration of the listing in cases where the agent negotiated with that buyer and provided the buyer's name to the owner within a stated time period. Safety clauses may provide that the owner is relieved of liability if the property is relisted with another broker.
- **Buyer damages**   This clause may provide for a division of damages received between owner and broker when a buyer defaults on a purchase.
- **Hold-harmless clause**   This clause provides for owner reimbursement to the agent for the agent's liability when the agent repeats false or incomplete information furnished by the owner.
- **Title**   The listing specifies how evidence of a marketable title will be shown.
- **Attorney's fees**   Listings frequently provide that in the event of a legal action between the parties, the prevailing party will be entitled to attorney's fees.
- **Arbitration**   Arbitration clauses provide for either voluntary or mandatory arbitration of broker/owner disputes.

DISCLOSURES

As a general rule, you should disclose to a buyer anything you would conceivably want to know if you were a buyer. The following are mandated disclosures:

Lead Paint

For housing built prior to 1978, sellers and lessors must disclose any known lead paint hazards to buyers or lessees. A lead paint disclosure booklet entitled *Protect Your Family from Lead Paint* must be given to buyers and lessees.

Note: Federal law does not require testing for or removal of lead paint.

Flood Hazard Area

The seller must disclose to the buyer that improved real estate (or mobile homes) is located in a flood hazard zone as indicated on maps published by the Federal Emergency Management Agency (FEMA).

Flood Disaster Insurance

Where a seller has previously received federal flood disaster assistance, the seller must notify a buyer about the requirement to obtain and maintain flood insurance.

Home Inspection Notice

For the sale of one to four residential units, including mobile homes, that involve FHA financing or are HUD owed, the borrower must sign a notice entitled *The Importance of a Home Inspection*.

Megan's Law

Megan's Law is a federal law that allows the release of information to the public about convicted sex offenders. Various states have adopted and implemented statutes that allow the public to call and obtain information about child molesters and other sex offenders living in their area. Several states require that buyers and lessees of real property be informed as to where such information can be obtained.

Miscellaneous Disclosures

In addition to the fiduciary duty disclosures required to be made to the seller and the disclosures of known defects that must be made to the buyer, many states have mandated disclosures concerning financing, environmental hazards, state subdivision, and so on. In addition to state disclosures, federal disclosures are required under the **Real Estate Settlement Procedures Act.** In many states, sellers must disclose to buyers any known material property defects, including work performed without a required building permit.

PURCHASE CONTRACTS

Real estate purchase agreements are offers by the purchaser (offeror) to buy at definite prices and terms. Like any offer, a purchase offer can be revoked prior to acceptance, but if accepted by the seller (offeree) during the period designated for acceptance, a binding contract is formed.

Purchase Deposits

While a deposit is not necessary to have a valid purchase contract, deposits known as **earnest money** normally accompany offers to purchase. (Sales requiring court approval, such as estate sales, normally have deposit requirements.) A deposit indicates good faith on the part of the purchaser and may provide readily available damages for the seller should the buyer default on the purchase agreement.

The owner must be informed of the form of the deposit if other than cash. A deposit check may be held uncashed prior to acceptance at the direction of the purchaser, if stated in the offer, and after acceptance at the direction of the seller. If not otherwise instructed by the purchaser, an agent can do one of three things with a deposit:

1. The agent can deposit it directly into the broker's real estate trust account. By requiring separate trust accounts, trust monies held by brokers are protected from creditors of the brokers. Money from numerous transactions is usually deposited in the same real estate trust account, but at least one state requires a separate account for each transaction.

    A broker might not be required to maintain a trust account if deposits received are made out or paid directly to an escrow or other closing agent.

    State law generally requires that trust accounts be demand deposits (checking accounts) in federally insured institutions. A buyer might specify that his or her deposit be placed in an interest-bearing account as a condition of the offer. Any interest that accrues to trust account funds prior to closing would be credited to the party depositing the funds (buyer) unless otherwise agreed to.

2. The agent can deposit it directly into a neutral depository (escrow).

3. In some states, the agent can turn over the money to the principal.

The broker must, of course, protect the buyer's deposit and return it promptly if an offer is not accepted.

Commingling   Commingling is the mixing of trust funds with personal or general business funds and is grounds for disciplinary action by the state-licensing agency. Holding checks uncashed without authorization or failing to deposit cash received into a trust account within a reasonable or statutory period of time could also constitute commingling.

Conversion   Conversion is the actual misappropriation, or theft, of trust funds. Besides being the basis for disciplinary action against the broker, it would also be the basis for criminal action.

Disposition of Trust Funds   Should a sale fail to close after a contract has been entered into, the broker should obtain agreement of both buyer and seller as to the disposition of the deposits being held by the broker. If the parties are unable to agree, in most states the broker may institute an **interpleader action,** which asks the court to decide the rights of the parties.

OFFER-TO-PURCHASE PROVISIONS

Some of the provisions that may be found in offers to purchase include the following:

Liquidated Damages   The agreement may provide for the forfeiture of the buyer's deposit as the seller's sole remedy should the buyer default on the agreement. By agreeing to liquidated damages, the seller gives up the right to sue for actual damages sustained due to the buyer's breach, should it occur.

Contingencies   Frequently, purchase agreements are contingent upon financing or other conditions.

Time Is of the Essence   This clause provides that failure to accept or perform under the agreement by a specified date(s) will be a breach of the contract. Without this clause, the courts might excuse reasonable delays.

Closing/Possession   Unless a date for closing is set, closing must occur within a reasonable period of time. If a date for possession is not given, possession is upon closing.

Antitrust Laws

Antitrust laws were developed because of abuses that were prevalent when a business became a monopoly, thus controlling a marketplace, or where groups of businesses conspired to control prices and/or competition. The principal antitrust law is the **Sherman Antitrust Act,** which is a federal law. (There are also state antitrust acts.) Violation of the Sherman Act can result in a fine up to $100,000 (up to $1,000,000 for corporations) and up to three years in prison. An individual injured by an antitrust violation is entitled to triple the amount of actual damages plus costs and attorney fees.

Antitrust violations include the following actions:

- **Price-fixing**   The illegal practice of setting prices. As an example it would be illegal for a group of brokers to agree on minimum commissions or to withhold cooperation from brokers who did not abide by these rules.
- **Market allocation**   Agreements of firms to divide the marketplace on a geographic or type-of-service basis are illegal because they reduce or eliminate competition.
- **Group boycotting**   Agreeing not to do businesses with another business to reduce competition is illegal. As an example, if a group of brokers agree that they will not allow a particular broker to show their listings, it is a *group boycott.*
- **Tie-in agreements**   These illegal agreements require that a business buy goods or services in order to obtain other goods or services. If a builder wished to buy a lot to build a home and the broker required the builder to list the home with the broker as a condition of lot purchase, it would likely be an illegal tie-in sale.

FEDERAL FAIR HOUSING

Civil Rights Act of 1866

The *Civil Rights Act of 1866* gave all citizens the same rights as those enjoyed by white citizens—to inherit, purchase, lease, sell, or hold real and personal property.

For many years, this act was ineffective because of narrow court interpretation. *Jones v. Mayer* (U.S. Supreme Court, 1968) held that based on the 13th Amendment, the act was valid. A victim of discrimination in the sale of housing can take the case to federal court for damages, obtain an order that prohibits sale to another, or force the owner to sell to the plaintiff. There is no limit to punitive damages under this act.

Civil Rights Act of 1964

This act prohibited discrimination in housing wherever there was government assistance. It applied to FHA (Federal Housing Administration and VA (Department of Veteran's Affairs) programs as well as other government assistance programs, such as urban renewal.

Civil Rights Act of 1968

Title VIII of the *Civil Rights Act of 1968* is known as the federal Fair Housing Act.

Application   The act covers housing only.

Coverage   The act prohibits discrimination based on national origin, color, religion, and race when selling or leasing residential property. A 1974 amendment extended protection based on sex, and in 1988, the act was expanded to include familial status and the handicapped.

Exemptions

- Religious groups having nonprofit housing may limit sale or lease to members of their religious group, providing the religion is open to others without discrimination.
- Private clubs can discriminate in favor of their members in the sale or lease of housing for noncommercial purpose and limit sale or leasing.
- Owner-occupants of one to four residential units can discriminate in renting rooms or units if no agent is involved and no discriminatory advertising is used.
- Owners of single-family homes who own three or fewer rental units can discriminate if they are not in the business of renting and neither an agent nor discriminatory advertising is used. Owners who occupy a home at the time of the transaction are limited to the exemption of one sale within any 24-month period.

The *Jones v. Mayer* decision held that without exception, the Civil Rights Act of 1866 prohibits all racial discrimination. Therefore, a person discriminated against may seek remedy under the 1866 act, or state law, even though the discriminatory acts were among those covered by the exemptions in the 1968 law.

Prohibitions   The federal Fair Housing Act prohibits these activities:

- Broker discrimination as to clients and customers
- Refusal to show, rent, or sell by falsely representing that a property is not available
- Discrimination in access to multiple-listing services
- **Steering**—that is, directing people of certain races, religions, and such away from (or toward) particular areas
- Discriminatory advertising (prohibited even for those exempt from the act); discrimination includes ads that indicate a property is close to a religious institution or ethnic or racial area, as well as ads that indicate a preference, which would discriminate   against any protected group
- Retaliatory acts against those making fair housing complaints, or intimidation to discourage complaints
- Discriminatory sale, lease, or loan terms
- **Blockbusting,** which induces panic selling by claiming that prices will drop or crime will increase as a result of certain groups entering the area
- **Redlining**—that is, refusing to loan or insure within a certain area
- Coercion, intimidation, or other interference with a person's rights in buying, selling, or leasing

Enforcement   HUD (Department of Housing and Urban Development) may initiate complaints on its own, or aggrieved parties can take the following actions:

- Bring a complaint to HUD within one year of the discriminatory action. (The 1968 Act is administered by the secretary of the Department of Housing and Urban Development.)

A hearing on the complaint is held before an administrative law judge, who can assess civil penalties from $10,000 to $50,000, as well as actual damages and compensation for humiliation suffered because of discriminatory practices.

- Bring a civil action in a state or federal district court within two years after the alleged occurrence. The court could award actual damages plus punitive damages as well as court costs and attorney's fees and/or a permanent or temporary injunction or restraining order to decease or refrain from an activity.
- HUD may use minority as well as nonminority testers to determine if the treatment of buyers and renters is equal.

Many states also have fair housing laws that provide remedies in state courts. Any one discriminatory act could violate one or more state laws as well as federal laws.

1988 Fair Housing Amendment Act

The *Fair Housing Amendment Act of 1988* added fair housing protection for persons physically or mentally handicapped as well as protection based on familial status.

Handicapped   The term *handicapped* refers to mental as well as physical handicaps affecting one or more major life functions. While drug addiction is not regarded as a handicap, alcoholism, cancer, and speech, vision, hearing, and mobility impairments as well as AIDS and HIV infection are regarded as handicaps.

Modification of a Unit   Handicapped tenants may modify their units at their own expense to allow themselves reasonable use of the premises. They may also make alterations to common areas for access. While the landlord may require restoration, at the tenant's expense, of internal alterations, the tenant need not restore the common areas to their previous condition upon vacating the property.

Seeing Eye Dogs/Support Animals   Rules against pets cannot be applied to Seeing Eye dogs or support animals. Handicapped persons cannot be charged an increased security deposit because of a Seeing Eye dog or support animal or because they altered their units to obtain reasonable benefits of use. However, a tenant would be liable for any damage done to the property by a Seeing Eye dog or support animal.

Prohibited Acts   It is illegal to ask whether an applicant has a handicap or to question the severity of a handicap.

It is unlawful for a landlord to refuse reasonable accommodation in terms of rules, policies, practices, or services necessary to ensure equal enjoyment opportunity for a unit. For example, a landlord may have to provide special parking access for a disabled tenant for his or her reasonable enjoyment of a unit.

Landlords may not advertise that a particular unit is unavailable to handicapped persons or those with familial status. Landlords may, however, advertise that a unit is handicap accessible, as well as its family benefits.

New Units   The 1988 amendment requires that new multifamily units (four or more) be readily accessible in public and common areas for use by handicapped individuals.

Familial Status   The term *familial status* refers to persons younger than age 18 living with a parent or guardian, to persons in the process of obtaining legal custody, or to pregnant persons.

Apartments that have sections designated "adults only" or "family section" would be in violation of the law because they would still be discriminating as to familial status regarding particular units. Steering prospective tenants toward a family or an adult area in an apartment complex and away from another area also violates the act.

Apartments can have rules for children's use of facilities if there is a nondiscriminatory reason for the difference in rules. The act does not prohibit owners from setting maximum occupancy of units so long as the rule is reasonable and enforced without discrimination.

Exemptions   There are several exemptions to the prohibition of refusing to rent or sell based on familial status:

- Housing provided under any state or federal program that the secretary of HUD determines is specifically designed and operated to assist elderly persons
- Housing having at least 80 percent of the units occupied by at least one person aged 55 or older
- Housing intended for and occupied solely by persons aged 62 and older

Americans with Disabilities Act

The act, which applies to both physical and mental disabilities, prohibits any discrimination that would deny the equal enjoyment of goods, services, facilities, and accommodations in any existing place of public accommodation (which is defined as nonresidential facilities that affect commerce). Owners and operators (including management companies) of commercial facilities must make the facilities accessible to the extent readily achievable. **Readily achievable** is defined as easily accomplished, without a great deal of expense. This would be based on costs of compliance when related to property value and the financial abilities of the person(s) involved.

New construction must be readily accessible and usable unless it is "structurally impractical" (practicality would relate to the cost of making access possible); alterations must also comply with the guidelines.

Elevators are not required for either new or existing structures having fewer than three stories or fewer than 3,000 square feet per story.

The act also applies to employment discrimination if there are 15 or more employees. The employer must alter the workplace to provide reasonable accommodations for a handicapped employee unless it creates an undue hardship on the business.

The act can be enforced by either an action by the U.S. attorney or by a civil action by a private citizen and could result in

- $50,000 in civil penalties for the first discriminatory act;
- $100,000 for each subsequent violation;
- compensatory damages; and
- attorney's fees.

Equal Housing Opportunity Poster

A current equal housing opportunity poster (supplied by HUD) must be exhibited prominently in every broker's place of business. Failure to display the poster can shift the burden of proof to the broker should a discrimination complaint be made. A sample poster is shown.

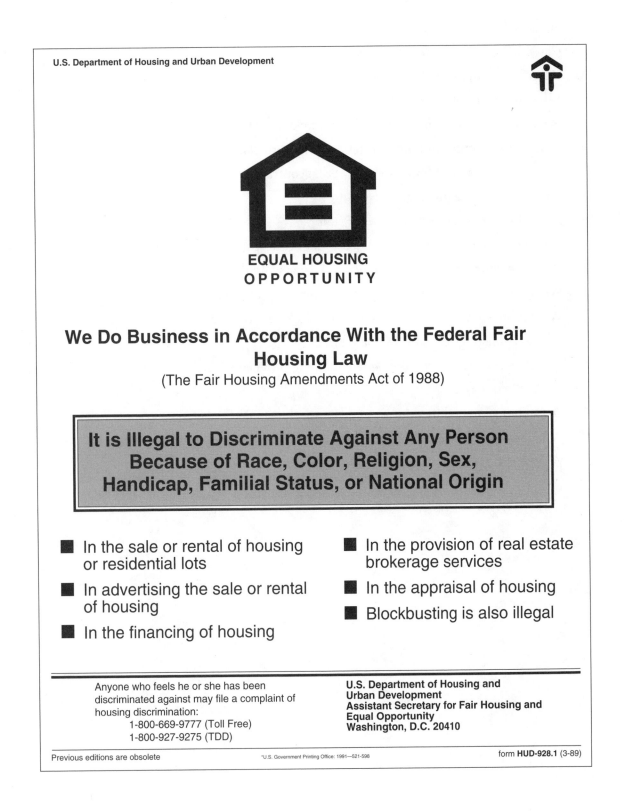

Your Pertinent State Information

1.   What is the contractual age in your state?

2.   Can minors purchase real estate (void or voidable)?

3.   Describe an emancipated minor in your state.

4.   What are the rights of prisoners to contract?

5.   What special provisions relate to the statute of frauds?

6.   What is the statute of limitations on written contracts?

7.   What is the statute of limitations on verbal contracts?

8.   May a broker be a dual agent?

9.   May a broker be a facilitator in your state?

10.   Does your state allow the designated-broker concept?

11.   What are your state's special agency provisions and disclosures?

12.   What is the agent's duty regarding discovery of property defects?

13.   What is an agent's responsibility when disclosing violent death?

14.   Are verbal listings possible in your state?

15.   What are your state's requirements for listing provisions?

16.   Are net listings legal?

17.   Does your state require additional buyer disclosures?

18.   What are your special state requirements for real estate purchase contracts?

19.   What are the provisions of your state's fair housing law(s)?

CHAPTER 5 QUIZ

Contracts/Agency and Fair Housing

1. Mutual assent to a real estate contract is indicated by:

   (A) attestation
   (B) offer and acceptance
   (C) acknowledgment
   (D) seals

2. An example of an executory oral contract that is enforceable is a:

   (A) lease for 6 months starting in 6 months
   (B) sale of a lot for less than $500
   (C) lease for 2 weeks starting in 12 months
   (D) sale of drapes for $600

3. A salesperson may be compensated for real estate service by:

   (A) the owner
   (B) another broker
   (C) another salesperson
   (D) the salesperson's employing broker

4. After an offer is accepted, the seller finds out that the broker was the undisclosed agent for the buyer as well as the agent for the seller. What are the seller's rights?

   (A) The seller can withdraw without obligation to broker or buyer.
   (B) The seller can withdraw but is subject to liquidated damages.
   (C) The seller can withdraw only with concurrence of the buyer.
   (D) The seller is subject to specific performance if he or she refuses to sell.

5. A voidable contract could be described as:

   (A) valid unless voided
   (B) void unless validated
   (C) illegal
   (D) unenforceable by either party

6. A remedy that puts the parties back in the positions they were prior to entering into a contract is:

   (A) specific performance
   (B) waiver
   (C) rescission
   (D) accord and satisfaction

7. By agreement, one party to a contract was discharged and another party took her place, an act known as a(n):

   (A) rescission
   (B) reformation
   (C) novation
   (D) accord and satisfaction

8. The Americans with Disabilities Act prohibits employment discrimination by:

   (A) all employers
   (B) employers having 5 or more employees
   (C) employers having 10 or more employees
   (D) employers having 15 or more employees

9. Failure of a broker to post an equal housing opportunity poster could result in:

   (A) automatic revocation of the broker's license
   (B) shifting the burden of proof as to discrimination from the plaintiff to the broker.
   (C) suspension of the broker's license
   (D) criminal penalties

10. In renting residential units, a property manager may properly:

    (A) charge families higher security deposits than single renters
    (B) require handicapped tenants who remove interior doors for accessibility to restore the premises at the end of a lease
    (C) refuse to rent to pregnant persons
    (D) designate adult and family sections in an apartment complex

11. Owners wish to list an expensive home but have requested that the home be sold to Caucasians only. The agent should:

    (A) refuse the listing
    (B) explain that it is unlikely that non-Caucasians can afford the house
    (C) advise the owners to sell it themselves
    (D) accept the listing and ignore the owner's request

12. An owner may properly refuse to rent to a prospective tenant because the prospective tenant:

    (A) has AIDS
    (B) is mentally handicapped
    (C) is a recovering alcoholic
    (D) is a drug addict

13. To force a broker to increase commissions charged, several brokers agreed that they would refuse to cooperate with the offending broker. Their action would be regarded as:

    (A) price-fixing
    (B) market allocation
    (C) group boycotting
    (D) a tie-in arrangement

14. A seller's agent owes a duty to the buyer of:

    (A) loyalty and obedience
    (B) confidentiality and accounting
    (C) fairness and honesty
    (D) disclosure and due care

15. Persons or groups specifically exempted from discriminatory practices by the Civil Rights Act of 1968 include:

    (A) all nonprofit groups
    (B) religious groups limiting leases on nonprofit housing to members of its religion
    (C) owners of furnished units
    (D) hotel and motel operators.

16. A white couple responded to a broker's ad for a property in a predominantly minority neighborhood. The broker should:

    (A) try to direct them to another property in a white neighborhood
    (B) explain that the neighborhood is predominantly minority
    (C) tell the prospects they would be uncomfortable in the neighborhood
    (D) show the property

17. A biracial family inquires about a home in a predominantly white area. The agent should:

    (A) explain the problems their presence in the neighborhood could cause
    (B) inform the owners of the buyers' racial status prior to showing
    (C) treat the prospective buyers the same as anyone else
    (D) attempt to interest the prospects in homes in integrated areas

18. In determining rental rates and security deposit requirements a landlord may properly:

    (A) require an increased security deposit for tenants with pets
    (B) require an increased security deposit for tenants with children
    (C) provide that a single-person occupancy will be entitled to a $100 reduction in rent.
    (D) have a monthly surcharge above basic rent of $25 per resident

19. Under federal law, a landlord may properly refuse to:

    (A) rent to pregnant women
    (B) allow visually handicapped tenants to keep guide dogs because pets are not allowed
    (C) rent to anyone younger than age 55 because the units are intended for the elderly and 80 percent of the units have a tenant older than 55 years of age
    (D) rent to persons having AIDS

20. Under the 1988 amendment to the Civil Rights Act of 1968, an apartment owner would be acting within the law by:

    (A) refusing to pay for modifications to an apartment that would allow a handicapped person the full enjoyment of the unit
    (B) asking whether a renter has a handicap and attempting to determine its severity
    (C) refusing to make reasonable accommodations in rules, policies, practices, or services to allow a handicapped person equal opportunity to use a dwelling
    (C) refusing to rent to a person whose handicap is mental rather than physical

21. Broker *N* has installed ramps over stairs to her office, moved furniture for easier access within the office, and installed a paper cup dispenser by the water fountain. She performed these actions to comply with:

    (A) Title VIII of the Civil Rights Act of 1968
    (B) the Americans with Disabilities Act
    (C) the Civil Rights Act of 1964
    (D) the 1988 Fair Housing Amendment Act

22. In soliciting listings of homes in an area where minorities had recently purchased homes, Broker *S* told his salespeople to solicit only Caucasian owners for listings as they will likely want to leave the area. This action would be regarded as:

    (A) steering
    (B) blockbusting
    (C) redlining
    (D) intimidation

23. A buyer's earnest money deposit was placed in the broker's escrow account when a purchase offer was received. The owner gave a counteroffer, but the buyer refused it and has requested return of her deposit. The seller has requested that the deposit should not be returned to the buyer. The broker should:

    (A) give the deposit to the broker's principal
    (B) return the deposit to the buyer
    (C) keep the deposit in the escrow account
    (D) file an interpleader action

24. A purchase contract provision stating that the buyer shall forfeit the deposit if the buyer fails to complete the purchase is known as:

    (A) liquidated damages
    (B) the safety clause
    (C) punitive damages
    (D) the subordination clause

25. Failure to include a time period for acceptance in an offer to purchase would:

    (A) void the offer
    (B) keep the offer open for acceptance during a reasonable period of time
    (C) allow the offer to be accepted any time prior to revocation
    (D) require immediate acceptance or the offer would expire

26. A court ordered *L* to pay *M* $100,000 in excess of *M*'s out-of-pocket damages that resulted from *L*'s breach of a contract with M. What is this $100,000 called?

    (A) Liquidated damages
    (B) Compensatory damages
    (C) Punitive damages
    (D) Nominal damages

27. *L* purchased a commercial lot from *M* based on *M*'s fraudulent representation as to lot size, zoning, and sewer connections. *L* cannot use the parcel purchased. What remedy should *L* seek?

    (A) Reformation
    (B) Waiver
    (C) Rescission
    (D) Specific performance

28. *S*'s offer to purchase states that it will be kept open three days for acceptance. One day after making the offer, and before acceptance, *S* wants to withdraw it. The real estate agent should inform *S* that:

    (A) the offer may be withdrawn without penalty
    (B) revocation means the forfeiture of earnest money
    (C) only in the event of death can the offer be revoked prior to acceptance
    (D) the offer is irrevocable

29. An owner died one month after signing a six-month exclusive right-to-sell listing. The day after the owner's death, the listing agent procured a buyer for the full list price. The administrator of the owner's estate does not wish to sell. What are the rights of the parties?

    (A) The buyer can obtain specific performance.
    (B) The listing broker has earned a commission.
    (C) The listing broker can obtain specific performance.
    (D) The administrator need not sell and is not liable for a commission.

30. A purchase contract for the sale of land was valid when it was entered into, but the seller refused to convey the land as agreed. Although there have been no changes in the law, the executory contract is now unenforceable. The reason why the buyer is not entitled to a legal or equitable remedy could be:

    (A) the seller's death
    (B) the statute of frauds
    (C) the statute of limitations
    (D) an assignment of interests

31. An owner listed the same property with three separate agents. The owner gave an exclusive-right-to-sell listing to broker *L*, an exclusive-agency listing to broker M and an open listing to broker *N*. Broker *N* sold the house and collected a commission while the other listings were still in effect. What are the rights of *L* and *M* as to a commission?

    (A) *L* and *M* both are entitled to a split of the commission from *N*.
    (B) *L* and *M* are entitled to a second commission to be split between them.
    (C) *L* and *M* are each entitled to a full commission.
    (D) *L* and *M* are not entitled to any commission.

32. On June 1, *J* mailed *K* an offer to buy *K*'s property. *J* gave *K* 15 days for acceptance. On June 3, *J* mailed a letter to *K* revoking the offer. On June 4, before receiving the revocation, *K* mailed a written acceptance of *J*'s offer. Based on these facts:

    (A) a valid contract was formed because the offer was irrevocable for 15 days
    (B) *J* is bound to the purchase agreement because the offer was accepted prior to revocation
    (C) the offer cannot be accepted because the acceptance was mailed after the revocation was mailed
    (D) if the revocation is received prior to receipt of the acceptance, no contract will be formed

33. One salesperson in a brokerage office is serving as an owner's agent, while another salesperson in the same office is serving as the buyer's agent for the same transaction. This would be an example of a:

    (A) limited liability transaction
    (B) facilitator transaction.
    (C) designated agency
    (D) controlled business arrangement

34. An agency that cannot be terminated by an owner is a(n):

    (A) exclusive listing
    (B) agency coupled with an interest
    (C) power of attorney
    (D) express agency

35. *J* agreed to sell a lot to *K*. *J*, who mistakenly believed the lot was zoned for multi-family apartments told *K* that the lot was zoned for a 16-unit apartment building. However, *K* knew the correct zoning and nevertheless entered into the purchase agreement. Before closing, what are the rights of the parties?

    (A) Either *J* or *K* can void the contract.
    (B) Only *K* can void the contract.
    (C) The contract is void because of the misrepresentation.
    (D) The agreement as made would be enforceable by either *J* or *K*.

36. A contract is void if it involves:

    (A) misrepresentation of the purchaser's intentions
    (B) an illegal purpose
    (C) duress
    (D) undue influence

37. In interpreting a contract, a court would consider that:

    (A) a contract should be interpreted in favor of the party drafting the instrument
    (B) a later document takes precedence over an earlier document
    (C) numerals take precedence over written words
    (C) a printed clause would take precedence over a handwritten portion of an agreement

38. *J* agreed to sell *K* a lot for $6,000. *J* later refused to sell, and *K* purchased a similar lot for $8,000. A court awarded *K* $2,000 in damages. Which term describes the damages?

    (A) Nominal
    (B) Punitive
    (C) Compensatory
    (D) Liquidated

39. The amount of commission is determined by:

    (A) local custom
    (B) the multiple-listing service
    (C) the Department of Real Estate
    (D) negotiation

40. A broker obtained an offer on an apartment building from a syndicate of which the broker was a member without informing the seller of this interest. Before the closing of the accepted offer, the owner discovered the broker's interest and refused to sell. If the broker sued the owner for the commission, the court would:

    (A) order revocation of the broker's license
    (B) order payment of the commission to the broker
    (C) release the owner from the obligation to pay the commission
    (D) order that the buyer obtain specific performance

41. *L* and *M* agree that *L* will buy *M's* farm for $400,000 cash, with the sale to take place in three months. This is an example of what type of contract?

    (A) Bilateral, express, executed
    (B) Bilateral, express, executory
    (C) Unilateral, express, executory
    (D) Unilateral, implied, executed

42. A clause requiring punctual performance of a contract is known as the:

    (A) time-is-of-the-essence clause
    (B) contingency-date clause
    (C) reasonable-time-for-performance clause
    (D) excusable-delay clause

43. *J*, who operated his brokerage office as a sole proprietorship, died. His daughter *K*, also a broker, wishes to take over all her father's listings. She should:

    (A) inform all the owners that she is the successor in interest to her father
    (B) obtain the approval of the probate court
    (C) inform the state that she has taken over responsibility for the listings
    (D) renegotiate all the listings

44. A right to buy a property at a yet-undetermined price, where the seller is free not to sell, is a:

    (A) lease option
    (B) right of first refusal
    (C) purchase contract
    (D) sale-leaseback

45. A builder failed to follow the agreed landscaping plans. The purchaser decided to accept the variance and pay the full contract price. This is known as:

    (A) accord and satisfaction
    (B) waiver
    (C) novation
    (D) reformation

46. A contractual disagreement led to a builder's reducing the contract price by $1,000. This agreement would be:

    (A) unenforceable because of a lack of consideration
    (B) an accord and satisfaction
    (C) a novation
    (D) a waiver

47. An owner refuses an offer, even though it is exactly in accordance with a valid exclusive-right-to-sell listing. What are the owner's rights?

    (A) The owner does not have to sell.
    (B) The owner is liable to the buyer for money damages.
    (C) The owner likely would be sued by the broker for specific performance.
    (D) The owner is liable to the buyer for specific performance.

48. Broker *M* told buyer *N* that a home was in a "great neighborhood." After purchasing the home, *N* found out that there had been several recent crimes in the area. The statement of broker *M* would be regarded as:

    (A) misrepresentation
    (B) a mutual mistake
    (C) fraud
    (D) puffing

49. An oral contract for the sale of real estate is:

    (A) illegal
    (B) unenforceable
    (C) valid for property of low value
    (D) enforceable if witnessed

50. Broker *L* works with both buyers and sellers to complete sales transactions but does not have any agency obligations. Broker *L*:

    (A) is a dual agent
    (B) is acting as a facilitator
    (C) still has a fiduciary duty to both parties
    (D) has no disclosure duties to either party

CHAPTER 5 QUIZ ANSWERS

Contracts/Agency and Fair Housing
1. (B) This indicates a meeting of the minds. (page 82)
2. (A) A lease for one year or less that can be fully performed within one year can be oral. (page 83)
3. (D) The only person who can pay a salesperson for an act requiring a real estate license is his or her broker. (page 90)
4. (A) Because of the undisclosed agency, the seller can withdraw without obligation and the broker could be subject to disciplinary action. (page 89)
5. (A) Only one party can void it at that party's option. (page 83)
6. (C) Waiver, however, leaves them as they are. (page 87)
7. (C) This is a substitution of parties to a contract or of contracts. (page 87)
8. (D) Smaller employers are excluded from the act's requirements. (page 100)
9. (B) The broker could have to prove he or she did not discriminate. (page 100)
10. (B) If a nonhandicapped person would not want the alteration, the tenant can be required to restore the premises. (page 99)
11. (A) If the owner or another agent sold based on racial exclusion, they would violate the fair housing laws. (page 98)
12. (D) Drug addiction is specifically excluded from handicapped protection. (page 99)
13. (C) A Sherman Antitrust Law violation. (page 97)
14. (C) The others are fiduciary duties owed to the principal. (page 91)
15. (B) However, religious groups are not exempt under the 1866 act and many state fair housing laws. (page 98)
16. (D) The other actions listed would be steering, which are prohibited by the Civil Rights Act of 1968. (page 98)
17. (C) The other actions are steering. (page 98)
18. (A) The others discriminate based on familial status. (pages 99–100)
19. (C) This is a specific exemption to the 1988 amendment. (page 100)
20. (A) It is the handicapped person's responsibility to modify the unit. (page 99)
21. (B) The ADA requires access to places of public accommodation. (page 100)
22. (B) While subtle, the broker is nevertheless inducing owners to sell based on entry of minority groups to the area. (page 98)
23. (B) Because the offer was rejected by the counteroffer, the deposit must be returned. (page 96)
24. (A) The parties agreed in advance what the seller's damages would be in the event of a buyer breach. (page 105)
25. (B) The offer can still be revoked prior to the acceptance. (page 84)
26. (C) This punishes *L* for outrageous conduct. (page 86)
27. (C) The other remedies would not benefit *L*. (page 87)
28. (A) An offer can be withdrawn any time prior to acceptance unless consideration was given to keep it open. (page 85)
29. (D) The death of the principal terminated the agency. (page 92)
30. (C) While the contract is valid, the statute of limitations makes it unenforceable. (page 87)
31. (C) By signing the two exclusive listings the owner became obligated to both for a full commission if a sale was consummated in accordance with the listings. (page 93)
32. (B) Acceptance takes place upon mailing, but revocation takes place upon receipt. (page 85)
33. (C) This concept allows for separate agency representation of buyer and seller within the same office. (page 89)
34. (B) The agent has an interest in the property. (page 92)
35. (D) Because *K* knew of the false statement, it was not relied on. (page 84)
36. (B) Answers (C) and (D) would make the contract voidable. (page 82)
37. (B) It shows the final meeting of the minds. (page 88)
38. (C) This makes up the actual cash loss to *K*. (page 86)
39. (D) Owner and broker are free to agree on commission. It is considered an illegal restraint on trade for brokers to agree as to minimum commissions. (page 94)
40. (C) The broker could also be disciplined by the state licensing authority but not as a decision in a civil suit. (pages 89, 91)

41. (B) It is a promise for a promise, stated so it is express and executory because it has yet to be performed. (page 81)
42. (A) A delay in performance would place the delaying party in default. (page 97)
43. (D) The listing ended with the death of the agent. (page 92)
44. (B) The right to buy is triggered only if the owner wishes to sell to another. (page 86)
45. (B) The purchasers waived the breach by the builder. (page 87)
46. (B) The builder agreed to accept a lesser consideration. (page 87)
47. (A) The owner could be liable to the broker for a commission, but there is no contract with the buyer. (page 93)
48. (D) This was a statement of opinion, not a warranty. (page 84)
49. (B) It is not a violation of the law (illegal), but it cannot be enforced. (page 83)
50. (B) But L has duties of fair dealing, which would require disclosure of material facts to both parties. (page 88)

Financing/Settlements

FINANCING INSTRUMENTS

For financing purposes, real estate typically is **hypothecated**—that is, the borrower retains possession while the lender holds security interest.

The three basic instruments used to finance real estate are the **mortgage,** the **trust deed** or **deed of trust**, and the **land contract,** also known as the **contract for deed.** (There are regional differences in terminology.)

A **note** is the primary evidence of the debt. It is a promise to pay a sum of money. The security for the note is the financing instrument (mortgage/trust deed).

MORTGAGES

The mortgage is a two-party instrument whereby the **mortgagor (the borrower)** gives an interest and a note to a **mortgagee (the lender)** in exchange for a loan. The promissory note is the evidence of the debt, and the real estate interest (the mortgage) is given as security for that debt.

Mortgage Theories

Lien Theory   In the majority of states, the borrower retains title and gives the lender a lien on the property. The lien is perfected when the mortgage is recorded in the county where the real estate is located. When the borrower has paid off the loan, the lender gives the borrower a **satisfaction of mortgage,** which, when recorded, removes the lien.

Title Theory   In title theory states, the borrower transfers title to the lender on a condition subsequent, usually by a trust deed. This means that when the condition is met (payment of the mortgage note), title reverts back to the borrower.

Intermediate Theory   Under the intermediate theory, title remains with the borrower, as in the lien theory, but it automatically transfers to the lender in the event the borrower defaults.

No matter what mortgage theory is used, the borrower has the right to convey the property. However, this might require that the mortgage note be paid off.

TRUST DEEDS

A *trust deed*, also called a *deed of trust* or **trust indenture,** is a three-party instrument whereby the **trustor (borrower)** gives a note to the **beneficiary (lender)** and, as security for the note, conveys title and/or a power of sale to a **trustee (third person).**

When the trustor has paid the note in full, the beneficiary directs the trustee to return the interest held to the trustor, generally accomplished with the trustee's **deed of reconveyance.** Should the trustor default on the note (mortgage) the beneficiary would order the trustee to conduct a sale. The purchaser at such a sale would receive a **trustee's deed.** The trustee is said to hold only a "bare" or "naked" legal title because the trustee's rights are so limited.

Many lenders prefer trust deeds to mortgages because they generally provide for a quick and inexpensive sale and, in most states, avoid lengthy mortgage redemption periods. However, a disadvantage is that deficiency judgments may not be allowed when foreclosure is by trustee sale.

Trust Deed

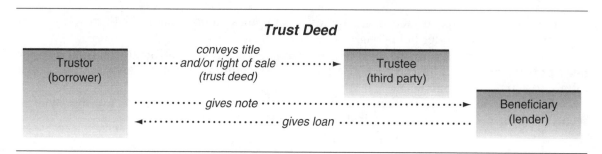

Trust deeds are used in more than half the states, although mortgages are also allowed in many of these same states.

LAND CONTRACTS (SALES CONTRACTS)

Also known as *land sales contracts* or **contracts for deed,** land contracts are financing agreements whereby the seller retains the legal title as security for the borrower's promise to pay. Under a land contract, the borrower has an interest known as **equitable title.** The contract is signed by both **vendor (seller)** and **vendee (buyer).** Unlike mortgages and trust deeds, a land contract generally does not require a separate note.

Land Contract

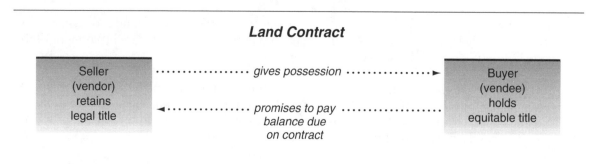

Because land contracts provide for relatively quick forfeiture of the buyer's interests in event of default, they often are used in sales with low down payments.

A deed is not given until the property is paid for or the loan balance is reduced to an agreed amount. This can create a danger to the buyer in that the seller might be unable to provide good title. Land contracts could provide that the deed be given to an escrow, which would offer the purchaser some protection.

Courts in many states have placed restrictions on the quick and easy forfeiture provisions of land contracts, and in some cases, judicial foreclosure is required. Land contracts should be recorded to protect the buyer's interests, but often they are not. They must be acknowledged by the vendor to be recorded.

FORECLOSURE SALE

If the borrower defaults on the note, mortgage foreclosure normally involves a public auction after statutory notice is given. The lender could bid the amount owing on the foreclosing loan; other bidders would have to bid cash. Should the sale bring more than the amount owed on the foreclosing loan, the balance would go to pay off junior encumbrances in the order of their priority. Any further excess would be paid to the borrower. In some states, money received from a foreclosure sale must be applied first to delinquent property taxes because taxes are priority liens.

The priority of liens is determined by the time and date of recording—the first recorded lien is the priority lien, and all other liens become junior to it. When a lien is foreclosed, the encumbrances (liens) junior to the foreclosing lien are wiped out. A purchaser at a foreclosure sale takes title subject to the encumbrances that are senior to the loan being foreclosed, but all junior encumbrances are eliminated.

For example, suppose there were five mortgages on a property:

1. Mortgage 1 recorded 1 Sep 1986
2. Mortgage 2 recorded 3 Aug 1990
3. Mortgage 3 recorded 15 May 1992
4. Mortgage 4 recorded 9 Jul 1994
5. Mortgage 5 recorded 24 Dec 1999

If mortgage 3 foreclosed, the purchaser would take title subject to mortgages 1 and 2, and mortgages 4 and 5 would be wiped out.

The lender on a junior lien that contains a default clause could protect his or her interest prior to foreclosure by making the payments on the senior lien in default and then foreclosing on the junior lien. This would leave the former junior lienholder as the owner, subject to any senior encumbrances. Because unpaid property taxes and special assessments are priority liens, they are not affected by a foreclosure.

Redemption In some states, after a judicial foreclosure (foreclosure by court action), borrowers have a statutory period during which to redeem the property by paying the foreclosure sales price plus interest and penalties. In some states, the borrower is allowed possession during the redemption period, which can be as long as one year. In other states, redemption must be prior to the foreclosure sale. Redemption after the foreclosure sale requires paying off the lien in full. Some states allow the borrower to reinstate the loan prior to the foreclosure sale by making the loan current and paying costs and interest.

Deficiency Judgments If the amount realized at a foreclosure sale is not sufficient to satisfy the debt owed to the foreclosing mortgagee, it is possible for a deficiency judgment to be granted for the difference between the sales price and the amount owing. The foreclosed mortgagor not only loses the property that secured the mortgage but is still liable for the deficiency. Several states prohibit deficiency judgments, and many others place strong limitations on their use.

Deficiency judgments generally are not allowed where the foreclosing mortgagee purchases the property for less than its fair market value or where the foreclosing mortgagee is the seller (purchase-money loan) who is simply taking the property back by bidding at the foreclosure sale.

In cases of trust deeds, deficiency judgments generally are not allowed when foreclosure is by exercising the power of sale in the trust deeds (nonjudicial foreclosure).

A loan for which a deficiency judgment is not possible is considered **nonrecourse financing,** which means the borrower has no personal liability under the loan. The lender's sole remedy is to foreclose on the property.

Strict Foreclosure   In several states, strict foreclosure is allowed, whereby the court orders the borrower's interest to be terminated without a sale. Some New England states allow foreclosure by entry. If the lender can peaceably take possession, after a required period of time, the borrower's interests are terminated. Deficiency judgments are not allowed in cases of strict foreclosure or foreclosure by entry.

Deed in Lieu of Foreclosure   To avoid the credit stigma of a foreclosure sale, an owner sometimes deeds his or her interest to the lender. Although a foreclosure sale wipes out junior liens, accepting a deed in lieu of foreclosure could give title to the lender with the subsequent liens intact.

Nonjudicial Foreclosure   In some states, mortgages can provide for a nonjudicial foreclosure procedure similar to the trust deed foreclosure sale described earlier.

FEDERAL RESERVE

The actions of the Federal Reserve can affect lender requirements as well as the interest charged for loans.

The Federal Reserve has the power to raise or lower the discount rate, which is the rate charged by member banks to borrow funds, and to raise or lower the reserve requirements of member banks. These actions affect the amount of money available to lend. The Fed can also buy and sell government securities that also affect the money supply. Further, to fight inflation, it could reduce the money supply and raise interest rates. Conversely, it can expand the economy by reducing interest rates. Lower interest rates lower monthly payments and make more people eligible for financing, which tends to increase sales. Raising interest rates has an inverse effect and would increase the demand for rental housing.

LOAN TYPES, TERMS AND PROVISIONS

Loans are categorized in a number of ways so that a single loan might be referred to as more than one loan type.

Loan Types

Purchase-Money Loan   With a purchase-money loan, the seller finances the buyer. No money changes hands, and the interest rate is often less than for hard-money loans. The term *purchase-money loan* is used in some areas to denote any loan made for the purpose of purchase.

Amortized Loan   A loan in which the regular equal payments fully pay the loan during the period of the loan is said to be *amortized.* Each payment on an amortized loan applies a greater amount to principal and a lesser amount to interest than the prior payment.

Partially Amortized Loan A loan whose payments do not fully liquidate the loan and that thus requires a final balloon payment is partially amortized.

Straight or Term Loan This is a loan where interest only is paid. The principal is due in full on the due date.

Graduated Payment Mortgage (GPM) These mortgage loans have lower payments during the early years. The payments, which are not sufficient to pay the interest, result in a negative amortization during the early years. This means that the amount owed actually increases. These loans are well suited to young buyers with rising incomes because low initial payments allow the buyers to qualify for a larger loan than would otherwise be possible.

Growing Equity Mortgage (GEM) These loans have initial payments based on a long-term amortization schedule, such as 30 years. They provide for periodic payment increases that apply directly to the loan principal, allowing the GEM to be paid off in a relatively short period.

Biweekly Mortgage This type of mortgage loan provides for half of the monthly payment to be made every two weeks. The result is that 26 payments are made every year (13 months), which either shortens the amortization period or decreases the payments.

Renegotiable Rate Mortgage (RRM) Also known as a **rollover** or **two-step loan,** this instrument is short term (usually 5 to 7 years), with payments based on a 25-year or 30-year period. When the term expires, the lender rewrites the loan at the then-current interest rate or the loan may be paid off.

Adjustable-Rate Mortgage (ARM) With ARMs the interest rate can be adjusted up or down during the loan term. Special terms that apply to ARMs are as follows:

- **Index** The index is the interest rate that the loan interest is based on, such as federal cost of funds.
- **Margin** The margin is an amount added to the index to determine the rate of interest for the loan, such as 2½ percent.
- **Adjustment period** Loans often set the frequency of interest adjustments to every six months or annually.
- **Cap (rate cap)** The cap is the maximum amount of an interest increase or decrease. There is usually a payment cap on a periodic adjustment (such as 1 percent) as well as a lifetime cap over the period of the loan (maximum cap is generally 5 percent).
- **Introductory rate** This rate that is also called a "teaser" rate, is generally set below the index rate plus the margin. It allows a lower qualifying income for borrowers and lower initial payments. One problem with the low introductory rate is that borrowers frequently experience payment shock at the first adjustment to their payments.
- **Negative amortization** Some ARMs allow negative amortization when the payment is kept less than the interest because of caps on payments, while other ARMs do not allow negative amortization. If there is negative amortization, the loan principal increases rather than decreases.

Convertible Mortgage This is an adjustable-rate loan where the borrower may convert the loan to a fixed-rate mortgage at a later date.

Participation Mortgage On large commercial projects, lenders may insist on sharing ownership, as limited partners, as well as receiving interest on the loans. The participation loan may carry a lower interest rate than otherwise required.

Shared Appreciation Mortgage (SAM)   This is an amortized loan in which the investor or lender makes the down payment for a buyer or gives the borrower a lower rate of interest in exchange for an agreement whereby the investor will share in the appreciation of the property value. The agreement usually sets a date for the property to be sold.

Reverse-Annuity Mortgage (RAM) or Reverse Mortgage   With RAMs, owners borrow against the equity in their homes by receiving monthly payments. This mortgage provides a means for elderly people to keep their homes. The mortgage is paid off when the mortgagors die or when the property is sold.

Blanket Mortgage   A blanket mortgage is secured by more than one property. Normally it would include a **release clause,** providing for the release of parcels from the mortgage upon the payment of stated amounts.

Wrap-Around Mortgage or All-Inclusive Mortgage   This is a second loan written to cover the amounts of a first and second loan. The buyer makes the total payment to the seller, who then makes the payment on the first loan. This arrangement allows the seller to make money on the interest differential between the rate on the first loan and the rate on the second loan as well as to get the interest on his or her equity.

Open-End Mortgage   An open-end loan can be increased to an agreed-on ceiling.

Open Mortgage   An open loan can be prepaid without penalty.

Package Mortgage   A package mortgage is secured by both personal property and real property.

Construction Mortgage   The payments that are made as work progresses are known as **obligatory advances**. The final payment usually is not made until the lien period expires. Construction loans are made at a higher interest rate than permanent financing. Construction loans are usually first loans.

Take-Out Loan   This is the permanent financing obtained by the owner who "takes out" the construction loan.

Bridge Loan (Swing Loan or Gap Loan)   A bridge loan is a short-term loan between other loans, for example, a loan between the construction loan and suitable permanent financing (take-out loan). Bridge loans have higher interest than permanent financing.

Piggyback Loan   A loan with two lenders, one taking the bottom portion (greater security) and the other taking the remainder.

Seasoned Loan   A seasoned loan is an existing loan with a payment history. On the secondary mortgage market, it might sell at a premium when compared to a similar new loan.

Nonrecourse Loan   Under a nonrecourse loan, the borrower is not personally liable on the loan so a deficiency judgment is not possible.

Personal Property Loan   The Uniform Commercial Code (UCC) provides that recording a **financing statement** creates a lien against personal property, including property that becomes a fixture.

Loan Terms

Loan terms define common loan expressions.

Interest   Interest is the charge paid to borrow money. The interest rate is a percentage of the amount borrowed.

Compound Interest   This is interest computed on the principal plus accrued interest. An amortized mortgage carries **simple interest**—the only time the interest is compounded is when payments are not made.

Usury   State law regulates maximum interest rates that can be charged by various categories of lenders. Interest charged in excess of the maximum rate is usurious and cannot be collected because the practice is illegal. Usury is treated as a misdemeanor or felony. In most states, however, a loan with usurious rates is not invalid; the loan must still be repaid, although state law might prohibit interest, limit interest to the amount legally collectible, and/or provide penalties for usurious interest already collected.

Negative Amortization   If payments are insufficient to cover the interest, the unpaid interest is added to the loan balance. Instead of the principal decreasing, it increases.

Discounting a Mortgage   Selling an existing mortgage for less than its face value results in discounting the mortgage.

Compensating Balance   Banks might require that a borrower maintain a balance of a percentage of the loan in a savings or checking account at the bank. The net effect of maintaining such an account at a relatively low or no interest rate would be to raise the effective rate of interest on the loan.

Private Mortgage Insurance (PMI)   Several firms offer lenders mortgage protection coverage (similar to FHA insurance) against the default of the mortgagor. Lenders will often accept a lower down payment when there is mortgage insurance. Under federal regulations, a borrower may request cancellation of PMI when the principal balance reaches 80 percent of the original value. The lender must automatically terminate PMI when the balance reaches 78 percent of value.

Mortgage Warehousing   This is interim financing by a mortgage company. Mortgage bankers borrow on their inventory of loans rather than sell the loans when they believe interest rates will fall (thus increasing the resale value of their inventory).

Points   Points are units of measure (one point equals 1 percent of the loan). Points are charged by lenders to cover lender expenses, increase lender yield, and/or allow a lower mortgage rate (known as **buying down** the mortgage).
As a rule of thumb, each point increases the lender's yield by approximately 1/8 of 1 percent in interest. Although this one-time charge is considered interest when paid by a buyer, points paid by a seller may be considered a sales cost that would be reflected in any capital gain.

Origination Fees   These fees are lender charges for making a loan. They cover the lender's initial costs, such as a credit check and application processing. Appraisal costs may be included or treated as separate costs.
Unlike points, origination fees are not treated as interest for the purchaser. They cannot be used as a deductible expense for income tax purposes, but they do affect the purchaser's cost basis and could lower any eventual capital gain.

Loan Assumptions   A buyer who assumes a loan agrees to be primarily liable for payment of the loan; the seller remains secondarily liable. Because the buyer has agreed to pay, a deficiency judgment is possible against the buyer in event of default.

A loan without a due-on-sale clause does not prohibit assumption, so it may either be assumed or the buyer could take "subject to" the loan.

"Subject to" Loan   When a buyer purchases "subject to" an existing loan, the buyer acknowledges the existence of the loan but does not agree to pay it. In the event of foreclosure, the buyer loses the property but is not liable for a deficiency judgment. In a "subject to" sale, the seller remains primarily liable on the loan and could be held liable for a deficiency judgment. If a loan contains a due-on-sale clause, a buyer cannot take title with the loan remaining.

Loan Provisions

Loan provisions are conditions included in the loan documentation and / or note. Basic loan provisions include amount of loan, interest rate, monthly payments, term of the loan, etc. The following are some of the additional provisions that may be included in a loan.

Late Charges   Grace periods (the number of days allowed for a late payment) as well as charges for late payments generally are set forth in the loan agreement and may be regulated by state statutes. Courts will not allow excessive late charges.

Defeasance Clause   The defeasance clause provides for the release of the lien when the obligation under the note is discharged by payment.

Prepayment Penalty   Without special authorization or state statute to the contrary, the borrower has no right to repay a loan in any manner other than as set forth in the note. Prepayment clauses allow early repayment but may specify a penalty—for example, "six months' interest based on the amount prepaid." Prepayment penalties cannot be charged if an early payment is required under a due-on-sale clause. Many states regulate prepayment penalties.

"Or More" Clause   The use of words such as "payments of $550 or more per month" allows the mortgagor to prepay a loan without penalty.

Lock-in Clause   A lock-in clause allows prepayment but requires that all interest be paid as if the original loan schedule were followed (actually a severe prepayment penalty). Many states strictly regulate or prohibit the use of such clauses. Where lock-in clauses are permitted, they generally are used in commercial loans by long-term lenders (such as insurance companies and pension funds that want the long-term interest).

Due-on-Sale (Alienation) Clause   A loan with a due-on-sale clause must be paid in full if the property is sold; therefore, such a loan cannot be assumed.

A lender often will allow an assumption rather than accelerate the payments if the interest rate is favorable to the lender or if the loan is assumed at a higher rate of interest.

Acceleration Clause   This clause accelerates all loan payments (entire amount due) if a borrower defaults, for example, fails to make payments by a given date. The entire loan can be declared due and payable immediately, which will often lead to foreclosure. (There may be state restrictions on accelerating payments.) A due-on-sale clause is a type of acceleration clause.

Nondisturbance Clause   This clause is an agreement by the mortgagee to honor subsequent leases should the mortgagee foreclose.

Assignment of Rents   This clause provides that the lender shall have the right to collect rents and apply them to the debt should the borrower default. Otherwise, the borrower could collect and keep the rent receipts until the foreclosure sale.

Balloon Payment   A balloon payment is a large payment, often at the end of an unamortized or partially amortized loan. Although a loan payment might be based on a long amortization period, the loan might state "balance all due and payable seven years from date hereof," which would require that the buyer either come up with cash or be able to refinance the loan. A balloon payment could also be used for a deferred down payment. Many states have restrictions on balloon payments.

Power-of-Sale Clause   This clause allows for a relatively quick nonjudicial foreclosure should the borrower default (not allowed in all states).

Release   If a mortgage or trust deed covers more than one property (blanket mortgage), release clauses allow individual properties to be freed from the lien on payment of specified sums. Without a release clause, the entire loan balance must be paid off to sell one parcel.

Subordination   This clause changes the priority of a loan, making it secondary to a later recorded loan. It is often used with land sales where the seller agrees to take a lien that will be subordinate to a later recorded construction loan. Subordination clauses subject the seller to great risks.

Impound Account   Also known as a **borrower's escrow account** or **reserve account,** an impound account is a trust account kept by the lender for taxes and insurance when taxes and insurance are part of the borrower's payment to the lender. In some states, these accounts are required to bear interest.

Default Clause   This clause allows a junior lienholder to cure a default of the borrower on a prior lien. If the prior lien had foreclosed, the junior lien would be wiped out.

PRIMARY AND SECONDARY FINANCING

Most funds for real estate financing come indirectly from private and business savings deposited with institutional lenders.

Primary financing refers to the first loan on a property, such as a first mortgage. *Secondary financing* refers to second mortgages.

Characteristics of secondary financing often include the following:

- Shorter term compared with primary financing
- A greater likelihood of having a balloon payment with a large final balance
- Higher interest rate compared with primary financing, because of greater lender risk

As a rule, primary financing uses amortized loans—that is, loans that are paid off over the loan period with equal monthly installments applying to principal and interest.

Do not confuse primary and secondary financing with the primary and secondary mortgage markets. Key distinctions are as follows:

- Primary financing—first loans
- Secondary financing—second or junior loans
- **Primary mortgage market**—loans made directly to borrowers
- **Secondary mortgage market**—the purchase and sale of existing loans

CONVENTIONAL LOANS

Loans made without government guarantees or insurance are conventional loans. They generally have a lower **loan-to-value (LTV) ratio** than government-insured or government-guaranteed loans, which means that larger down payments are required.

Commercial Banks

Although commercial banks make numerous purchase-money mortgage loans, they prefer higher-interest loans such as construction loans, home equity loans, and business loans. Deposits are insured by the Federal Deposit Insurance Corporation (FDIC).

Mutual Savings Banks

These banks are owned by investor/depositors and pay dividends rather than interest. Located primarily in the Northeast, they prefer low-risk real estate loans such as government-insured and government-guaranteed mortgages.

Savings and Loans (Thrifts)

Although originally restricted to housing loans, Savings and Loans (S&Ls) or Thrifts have been deregulated and can now make loans on other types of property. S&Ls are able to make home loans with lower down payments than most other lenders. FDIC also insures S&L deposits.

Insurance Companies

Insurance companies prefer large commercial and industrial loans as well as some new-home loans. They seldom make individual loans on older homes and generally do not make construction loans. Insurers often purchase loans from mortgage bankers and/or make loans through mortgage brokers.

Mortgage Bankers and Brokers

Mortgage bankers (mortgage companies) use their own funds to make loans, which they usually sell to investors. For a fee, mortgage bankers service the loans they sell. Mortgage brokers are different in that they are middlemen (often real estate licensees) who, for a fee, bring together borrowers and lenders. Mortgage brokers *seldom* service the loans they arrange.

GOVERNMENT LOANS

The government does not make *government loans*. Most of what are referred to as government loans are government-insured or government-guaranteed loans. FHA (Federal Housing Administration) and VA (Department of Veterans Affairs) loans are made by lenders subject to government supervision. FHA loans are government-insured, whereas VA loans are government-guaranteed.

Federal Housing Administration (FHA) Loans

Title I loans are home improvement loans with a maximum term of 15 years.

Title II loans are home purchase loans limited to **one to four residential units.** Generally, they are 15-year or 30-year loans but can be up to 40 years.

Characteristics of FHA Loans

1. FHA loans are government-insured. A one-time **mortgage insurance premium (MIP)** is collected at settlement or added to the mortgage. An additional ½ percent is added to the mortgage payments based on the amount of the down payment. FHA insurance insures the lender against losses suffered if the borrower defaults.
2. The loans cover housing only, including mobile homes and apartments (one to four residential units).
3. An FHA appraisal is required.
4. The property must meet minimum property requirements (MPRs).
5. They are high loan-to-value ratio loans. The maximum FHA loan percentages are based on purchase price and are subject to change. (The purchaser must, however, have a minimum cash investment of 3 percent, but it can come from a gift.)
6. 100 percent of reasonable closing costs may be financed.
7. FHA local field offices set a maximum loan amount on single-family dwellings based on the region.
8. Secondary financing is not allowed at time of loan origination.
9. Loan discount points may be paid by the buyer, seller, or both, subject to mutual agreement.
10. They are fully amortized loans. Balloon payments are not allowed.
11. They are long-term loans and, therefore, require lower monthly payments than many shorter-term conventional loans.
12. No prepayment penalty is allowed.
13. Taxes and insurance are included in the payments.
14. The assumability of FHA loans depends on the origination date of the loans:
    - Loans made prior to December 15, 1989, are fully assumable without qualifying by the purchaser.
    - Loans made after December 15, 1989, are assumable only by owner-occupants who qualify for the loans (investors cannot assume loans). Unless there is a novation (substitution of liability), a seller could be held liable on a loan.
    - The FHA cost for loan assumption without buyer qualification is $125. Loans assumed with buyer qualification requirements incur FHA costs of actual costs or $500, whichever is less.
15. The loans are made by institutional lenders. The FHA will issue a six-month *conditional commitment* to insure a loan for a property, provided the buyer, when found, qualifies for the loan. A **firm commitment** to insure may be obtained for a property when there is a definite buyer.
16. Lenders may be allowed to determine if a loan qualifies for FHA insurance. This process, known as **direct endorsement,** speeds up loan processing.

Characteristics of VA Loans

1. The veteran, if not on active duty, must submit a copy of his or her discharge and obtain a **certificate of eligibility**.
2. An appraisal and a **certificate of reasonable value (CRV)** are required. The veteran is not obligated to complete the purchase if the sales price exceeds the CRV. The veteran can, however, pay the difference in cash.
3. Institutional lenders usually make the loans.

4. The VA guarantee

Loan Amount	Guarantee
Up to $45,000	50% of loan
$45,000–$144,000	Minimum guarantee of $22,500, maximum guarantee is 40% of loan up to $36,000
More than $144,000	25% of loan up to a maximum of $50,750

5. There is no limit on the amount of a VA loan, so long as it does not exceed the CRV. The limit is on the guarantee.
6. VA loans can be for farm, home, or business. VA housing loans are limited to one to four residential units, and residences must be owner occupied.
7. No down payment is required for VA loans up to $203,000, but lenders may require a down payment. (A 5 percent down payment is required for manufactured housing.)
8. Secondary financing is not allowed at the time of purchase.
9. The loans are long term (30 years for home).
10. The loans are amortized (no balloon payments).
11. The veteran may pay a 1 percent loan origination fee. Payments of points are negotiable between the buyer and seller. While the veteran can pay points, unlike FHA loans, points may not be financed as part of the loan.
12. The veteran pays a percentage of the loan as a **funding fee** to the Department of Veterans Affairs at the time of the loan (the fee can be included in the loan). The funding fee varies from 1.25 percent to 1.875 percent based primarily on the amount of down payment.
13. VA loans made prior to March 1, 1988, are fully assumable by anyone, without qualification.

    Loans made after March 1, 1988, are assumable only if the buyer qualifies for the loan. The veteran is no longer liable for any deficiency judgment should the qualifying buyer default, except in the case of fraud.
14. A veteran can restore loan eligibility by paying off the loan upon sale or can ask for a substitution of entitlement if another veteran assumes the loan. A processing fee can be charged for loan assumptions.
15. VA loans charge no prepayment penalty.
16. Prepayment can't be less than $100 or one installment.
17. Payments include taxes and insurance.
18. No buyer loan broker fee (commission) can be charged to the veteran buyer.

Farm Service Agency (FSA)

The FSA was formerly known as the Federal Agricultural Mortgage Corporation—Farmer Mac. It is a subsidiary agency of the Department of Agriculture and both guarantees loans made by private lenders and makes loans directly when they are not available from private sources. FSA is involved in loans in rural areas to low-income and moderate-income families.

Table 6.1 FHA and DVA Loan Programs

	FHA	VA
Government involvement	FHA insured-mutual mortgage insurance premium (MIP) paid by borrower. Up-front premium paid on closing as well as a fee with payments	VA guarantee ($50,750 maximum guarantee)
Who is eligible?	Anyone who qualifies	U.S. veterans who will be owner-occupants
Who makes the loans?	Approved lending institutions	Approved lending institutions
Loan costs	1 percent loan origination fee plus mortgage insurance premium	1 percent loan origination fee plus funding fee to VA
Loan purpose	Housing only (includes mobile homes and 1-unit to 4-unit apartments)	Farm, home (1 to 4 units), or business (if for a home, it must be owner occupied)
Maximum loan allowed (subject to change)	1 unit $160,950 (varies by area)	No limit to loan, but loan can't exceed CRV (appraisal)
Interest rates	Negotiable	Negotiable
Term of loan	Usually 30 years	Maximum 30 years
Down payment	3 percent first $25,000; 5 percent from $25,000 to $125,000; 10 percent remainder	No down payment required for loans up to $203,000 (lender can require down payment)
Prepayment penalty	None	None
Secondary financing	Not allowed at time of sale	Not allowed at time of sale
Assumable (loans made prior to specified dates are assumable by anyone)	Loans made after Dec. 15, 1989, assumable only by owner-occupants who qualify for the loans	Loans made after March 1, 1988, assumable only if buyers qualifiy for the loans

SECONDARY MORTGAGE MARKET LOANS

There are a number of organizations, as well as individuals, engaged in the secondary mortgage market, which involves the buying and selling of existing mortgages.

Fannie Mae   FNMA (Federal National Mortgage Association) is a private corporation that sells corporate shares as well as participation certificates to raise money. **Participation certificates** are securities backed by a pool of mortgages. It creates a marketplace for existing mortgages by buying and selling FHA, VA, and conventional mortgages in the secondary mortgage market. The loan limit for purchase of single-family homes was $252,700 at the time of printing, but the limit is subject to annual adjustment.

Freddie Mac   FHLMC (Federal Home Loan Mortgage Corporation), a private government chartered corporation, provides a secondary mortgage market for federal savings associations. It now buys FHA, VA, and conventional mortgages and uses them as security to sell bonds and participation certificates.

Conforming and Nonconforming Loans   Conforming loans are conventional loans that meet the purchase standards of Fannie Mae or Freddie Mac. Because of strict underwriting requirements and the fact that there is a ready market to resell these loans, the interest rate for conforming loans may be less than the rate for nonconforming loans.

Nonconforming loans don't meet Fannie Mae or Freddie Mac purchase requirements so sometimes they are held by the lender (portfolio loans) rather than resold in the secondary mortgage market. Single-family home loans over $252,700 are known as **jumbo loans.**

Ginnie Mae   GNMA (Government National Mortgage Association) is a division of the Department of Housing and Urban Development (HUD). It guarantees government-assistance loans where other financing is unavailable and utilizes **mortgage-backed securities (MBS).**

Ginnie Mae increases liquidity in the mortgage market by its MBS program. It will guarantee securities issued by private intermediaries such as banks or mortgage companies that are backed by pools of mortgages.

LENDER REQUIREMENTS

In evaluating borrowers, lenders are interested in the three Cs—collateral, capacity, and character.

Collateral   The value of the *collateral (security for the loan)* is crucial. The lender wants a margin for safety in its loan-to-value (LTV) ratio. A lower LTV might mean better loan terms. A higher loan-to-value ratio would be possible with government-insured or government-guaranteed loans as well as with loans having private mortgage insurance (PMI).

Capacity   Capacity deals with a borrower's income and indebtedness; the incomes of both spouses and joint borrowers are considered. Generally, lenders will not consider overtime earnings, and only a portion (usually 50 percent) of dividend income from stocks will be considered. In qualifying borrowers for home loans, lenders generally use two ratios—the **front-end ratio,** which is the ratio of the borrowers' gross monthly income to the **principal, interest, taxes,** and **insurance** loan (PITI) payment, and the *back-end ratio,* which is the ratio of gross monthly income to the PITI loan payment plus all monthly long-term credit obligations (beyond 10 months). The front-end ratio is generally 28 percent, which means the borrower cannot pay more than 28 percent of gross monthly income for the loan payment. The back-end ratio is generally 36 percent, which means that no more than 36 percent of the gross monthly income can be used for loan and monthly credit payments. Special situations and local customs could result in different ratios being used.

Character   Character deals with borrowers' credit history—which looks at how they have paid obligations in the past.

LAWS RELATING TO REAL ESTATE FINANCING

Truth-in-Lending Act (Regulation Z)

Regulation Z, a part of the federal **Consumer Credit Protection Act of 1968,** requires that the lender provide the borrower with a disclosure statement showing credit costs in percentage as well as total finance charges. It is enforced by the Federal Trade Commission.

Finance charges include interest, loan fees, finders fees, any price differential for buying on credit, points, service fees, and premium for credit life insurance (if a condition of the loan). Disclosure also must include late payment charges and prepayment penalties. Not included in finance fees are title insurance costs, credit report costs, and legal and recording fees.

Truth-in-lending applies to loans where credit is extended with a finance charge or credit payable in **more than four installments.** If the amount or percentage of down payment, the number of payments or period of repayment, or the amount of payment or finance charges is included in any advertisement, the ad must include three elements:

1. Amount or percentage of down payment
2. Terms of repayment (number, amount and due dates of payments)
3. **Annual percentage rate (APR)** (the true interest rate considering points and other loan costs; the nominal rate is the rate stated on the note)

Advertising the APR alone will not trigger the above disclosure requirements. Escrow impounds for taxes and insurance are not considered loan costs so need not be listed.

The requirement to supply the borrower with a truth-in-lending disclosure statement showing all loan facts applies to creditors that regularly extend credit. This means creditors extending credit more than 25 times, or more than 5 times if the loan is secured by a dwelling, within the preceding year. However, the total amount of finance charges for the term of the loan need not be shown for first mortgages or loans used to purchase real property.

Truth in lending makes **bait-and-switch** advertising a federal offense. This is advertising property that agents don't intend to sell or that is not available in order to attract buyers for other property.

Three-Day Rescission Right   If the loan is for consumer credit secured by the borrower's residence, the borrower has the right to reconsider and cancel. This right is valid until midnight on the third business day following loan completion. The rescission right does not apply to first mortgages but does apply to second mortgages.

Exemptions   Loans exempt from all truth-in-lending disclosure requirements are business loans, agricultural loans, construction loans, personal property loans exceeding $25,000, loans secured by more than four dwelling units, interest-free loans, and loans with four or fewer installments. Nonowner-occupied housing is considered a business and thus exempt from disclosure. Carryback financing for most sellers (not more than five sales per year) also is exempt.

Equal Credit Opportunity Act

The *Equal Credit Opportunity Act (ECOA)* prohibits discrimination against any loan applicant on the basis of race, color, religion, age, national origin, sex, marital status, or dependency on public assistance (source of income).

Lenders cannot ask questions concerning marital status, pregnancy, or divorce. Lenders cannot arbitrarily reject secondary income. A lender must notify the applicant within three days of action taken on a loan request. If the loan is denied, the reason for denial must be listed. The borrower has the right to rebut (appeal) the reasoning for loan denial.

SETTLEMENTS

A real estate settlement is the closing of a transaction where a deed conveying the title is exchanged for cash and/or a security instrument and all costs are paid and/or prorated.

Prior to closing, the buyer will ascertain that the title is marketable through either title insurance or an attorney's title opinion based on the abstract of title. The buyer will also want to ascertain before closing that the property is in the condition agreed on and that any special contractual conditions have been met. A final walk-through inspection is often arranged by the agreement of the parties.

Sometimes, a real estate settlement is the responsibility of the listing broker; however, in most areas, settlements are handled by escrow or title companies (closing agents) or attorneys. Presettlement includes these activities:

- Ordering the preliminary title report for title insurance or an update of the abstract and a title opinion
- Obtaining statements from lenders as to loan balances being assumed or paid off, as well as assumption costs and/or prepayment penalties
- Prorating taxes, insurance, rents and the like as applicable. In most states, the seller is responsible for costs and is entitled to income for the date of closing, but in a few states, the closing day is the buyer's responsibility. (For examination purposes, the seller should be treated as responsible for the day of closing unless the question states otherwise.)
- Arranging for the transfer of insurance policies being assumed (The seller bears the risk of loss prior to closing. However, if the buyer is given possession prior to closing, the risk of loss could be borne by the buyer.)
- Obtaining leases and arranging for their assignment
- Preparing bills of sale for personal property
- Obtaining a certificate of occupancy (may be required for new structures)
- Drafting all deeds, notes, mortgages, and so forth. In a real estate settlement, the person giving an instrument normally pays to draft it and pays notarization fees. The party receiving the instrument customarily pays for its recording.
- Drafting settlement statements
- Obtaining certificates required by state law, such as smoke detector certificates and municipal lien certificates
- Complying with disclosure and reporting requirement (state and federal)

At the settlement, all signatures are obtained and funds disbursed. The closing agent generally arranges for the recording of all documents.

In a face-to-face closing, both the buyers and sellers have an opportunity to examine the closing statement prior to the exchange of title and consideration. Lenders customarily attend face-to-face closings to make certain that existing loans are properly paid off and that new loans are properly signed. Lenders generally require that evidence of property casualty insurance be provided prior to closing. Lenders also may require that they be protected by a lenders' policy of extended coverage title insurance.

The closing agent generally provides separate closing statements for the buyer and the seller, showing all debits and credits and the amount to be paid or received. Credits are pluses (amounts a party is entitled to). Debits are minuses (amounts to be paid or subtracted from amounts due).

Credit and debits are different for buyer and seller. For example, whereas the seller is entitled to the sales price (credit), the buyer is responsible for this amount (debit).

When a buyer assumes a loan or gives the seller a new second mortgage, it reduces the amount needed for a purchase. Therefore, the transaction is a credit against the sales price for the buyer and a debit to the seller against funds to which the seller is entitled.

While loans against the property may be paid off by the seller prior to closing, generally the closing agent writes checks to pay off existing loans that are not being assumed. The payoff of existent loans is a debit to the seller, as it reduces the amount the seller is entitled to.

The accompanying closing statement indicates common debits and credits of closing. Chapter 8 includes settlement math problems.

Transfer Tax   Most states and local communities have a real property transfer tax. The seller generally pays this tax, although local custom varies. The tax is usually based on the seller's equity being transferred, although in some areas, it is based on sales price. If the tax were based on equity, when loans are assumed, the tax would be charged on the difference between sales price and the loans being assumed; but if the property were to be refinanced, it would be based on the full purchase price.

IRS Reporting   Settlement agents (brokers, attorneys, and escrows) must report the closing price (gross sale price) to the IRS on **Form 1099S**. (Applies to one to four residential units.)

Personal Property   Personal property included in a real estate transaction would be transferred by a written **bill of sale** that describes the property being transferred, indicates it is being conveyed, names the vendee (buyer), and is dated. The vendor (seller) signs the bill of sale.

Real Estate Settlement Procedures Act

The Real Estate Settlement Procedure Act (RESPA) requires lender disclosure of loan costs (separate from financing costs) to buyers and sellers for federally related real estate purchase loans of **one to four residential units** involving a new first loan. **"Federally related loans"** refers to loans made by a federally insured or federally regulated lender and to federally guaranteed or insured loans, as well as to loans that are to be resold to Fannie Mae, Freddie Mac, or Ginnie Mae. (Like Regulation Z, escrow impounds for taxes and insurance are not considered loan costs so need not be listed.)

RESPA requires that a HUD information booklet, *Settlement Costs and You,* must be given to the borrower. (Generally, it is given at the time of loan application.) The borrower also must be given a **good-faith estimate** of settlement costs within three business days of loan application. If the lender or broker requires the use of a *particular* service provider (required provider), such as an insurance company, attorney, title company, etc., the lender or broker must disclose its relationship with that service provider and estimate the costs involved. Where a broker has more than a 1 percent interest in a service provider, that interest must be disclosed, and the borrower must be allowed to obtain the services from other providers.

HUD's **Uniform Settlement Statement,** which covers all loan costs and fees, must be given to the borrower on or before settlement. RESPA specifies the following:

- The purchaser has a right to review the statement on the business day prior to closing.
- Every charge must be justified by a service rendered.
- The buyer cannot be required to purchase title insurance or other services from a particular company.
- The lender cannot give or accept kickbacks for referring a service. An exception would be referral fees to a genuine employee.
- The lender cannot charge for preparing the disclosure statement.
- Limits are placed on the amount of advance taxes and insurance payments the lender can collect. The lender cannot collect more than two months' advance taxes and insurance in addition to prorated amounts based on date of closing.

The law does not apply to business property, vacant land, dealers buying for resale, refinancing, junior loans, or loan assumptions where the lender charges less than $50.

Servicing Disclosure   The lender must disclose to the borrower if the loan is to be assigned or sold and the fact that the right to service the loan may be assigned.

Controlled Business Arrangement (CBA)   A real estate company can offer a package of services to a customer, such as title insurance, property insurance, mortgage banking, and home inspection service (one-stop shopping). RESPA allows such a package, provided the borrower understands the relationship between the service providers and that other service providers are available. Fees, however, may not be exchanged for referrals. While the broker may have an ownership interest in a service provider, the broker may receive compensation only on a profit-sharing basis. The controlled business arrangement must function as a separate business.

Computerized Loan Origination (CLO)   When a fee is charged to a borrower for access to computerized loan origination services, a disclosure must be provided to the borrower in a format set forth by RESPA. The disclosure must inform the borrower that the fee can be avoided by approaching lenders directly.

Adjustable Rate Loan Disclosure   For adjustable rate loans, the lender must provide a copy of the Federal Reserve Board booklet entitled *Consumer Handbook on Adjustable Rate Mortgages* to the borrower. The booklet explains the various loan terms and how the caps work. The consumer is warned about negative amortization and payment shock at the first adjustment period after the initial rate.

SELLER'S CLOSING STATEMENT

Debit Seller	*Credit Seller*
Title insurance or abstract costs*	Purchase price
Survey fee (if required)	Balance in loan impound accounts
Payoff on existing loan	Prepaid insurance (if policy is assumed)
Prepayment penalty	
Loan being assumed	
Seller financing	
Earnest money received from buyer	
Commission to be paid broker	
Taxes (could be credit or debit)	Taxes (could be credit or debit)
Documentary transfer stamps (transfer tax)	
Cost to notarize deed	
Cost to draft deed	
Recording costs of new mortgage (if seller financing). Note: The party who gives an instrument generally pays to prepare and acknowledge it. The party receiving it pays to record it.	
Termite inspection fee	
Termite correction work required	
Recording satisfaction of mortgage being paid off	
Prepaid rents	
Rental security deposits	
Attorney's fees	
Unpaid utility bills	
New loan points (as agreed by the parties or required by law)	
Cash to be received at closing	

*In some areas, the buyer pays the title insurance.

BUYER'S CLOSING STATEMENT

Debit Buyer	*Credit Buyer*
Sales price	Loans being assumed
Recording deeds received	Money paid to seller or deposited with agent
Drafting new mortgages	
Notarizing new mortgages	New mortgage to be given
Balance in impound accounts of loans being assumed	Interest on loans being assumed (if paid in arrears)
Insurance policies being assumed	
Attorney's fees	Prepaid rent
Interest paid in advance	Rental security deposits
Advance taxes and insurance for impound account	Unpaid utility bills
Appraisal fee for new loan	
New loan costs	Taxes (could be credit or debit)
Taxes (could be credit or debit)	
New survey (could be paid by seller)	Balance paid at closing
Fuel oil in tank	
Title insurance (extended coverage policies)	

Your Pertinent State Information

1. What are the regulations and disclosures applicable to mortgage loan brokers?

2. Identify your state's special loan programs.

3. What are your state's usury rates?

4. What happens when a usurious rate of interest is paid?

5. What are the allowable late charges?

6. What are the allowable prepayment penalties?

7. Is a lock-in provision enforceable? If so, when?

8. What are your state's restrictions on balloon payments?

9. Do impound accounts bear interest?

10. What theory is followed as to mortgages?

11. What are your state's trust deed procedures?

12. What are your state's trust deed foreclosure notices and reinstatement rights?

13. What is your state's common reference for "land contract"?

14. What are the land contract foreclosure procedures?

15. What is the notice requirement for mortgage foreclosure?

16. What are the mortgage foreclosure sale procedure and effect?

17. What are the mortgage reinstatement and redemption rights?

18. What are your rights to deficiency judgment?

19. Is a strict foreclosure possible?

20. May mortgages be foreclosed through nonjudicial foreclosure?

21. What are your nonjudicial foreclosure procedures?

22. Describe any state loan disclosures requirements.

23. Who handles closings in your state?

24. Who is responsible for the day of closing?

25. What are the disclosures or certificate requirements for closing?

CHAPTER 6 QUIZ

Financing/Settlements

1. The *effective rate of interest* describes:

   (A) APR
   (B) the nominal rate of interest
   (C) compound interest
   (D) the usury rate

2. An advantage of FHA financing to a buyer is:

   (A) a federal limitation on the interest
   (B) that there are no loan origination fees
   (C) that the property must meet minimum property requirements
   (D) that the buyer does not pay points

3. What is the benefit of having FHA insurance?

   (A) It pays off the loan if the buyer dies or becomes disabled.
   (B) It pays for any needed corrective measures not revealed by FHA appraisal.
   (C) It protects the lender against foreclosure losses should the buyer default.
   (D) It is a comprehensive homeowners' policy.

4. A veteran wishes to buy a home with a VA loan. The owner will not lower the price below $75,000, but the CRV is for $73,000. The veteran:

   (A) cannot buy the home
   (B) could have the seller carry a $2,000 second mortgage
   (C) could borrow $2,000 from another lender
   (D) could pay $2,000 as a down payment

5. A buyer defaulted on a loan and the lender foreclosed. Why would this foreclosure adversely affect the seller's credit rating?

   (A) The buyer took subject to the seller's loan.
   (B) The buyer used the seller as a personal reference with the lender.
   (C) There was a novation on the loan.
   (D) The buyer's loan was an adjustable loan.

6. A borrower was offered an adjustable-rate mortgage that provided for a margin of 2¼ points. It was to be based on an index that was at 4¾ percent. The lender was offering an introductory rate 1¾ percent less than would otherwise be payable. What is the introductory rate being offered?

   (A) 3%
   (B) 5¼%
   (C) 7%
   (D) 8¾%

7. An owner can be relieved of primary responsibility for a mortgage by finding a buyer who is willing to:

   (A) take "subject to" the loan
   (B) assume the loan
   (C) subordinate the loan
   (D) give a wraparound mortgage

8. A mortgage insurance premium (MIP) is associated with what type of loan?

   (A) VA
   (B) FHA
   (C) Conventional
   (D) Freddie Mac

9. A builder purchased a lot with seller financing. The seller's loan would allow for a later construction loan to be the priority loan. The loan obtained contained a:

   (A) release clause
   (B) defeasance clause
   (C) subordination clause
   (D) due-on-sale clause

10. IRS Form 1099S is used to:

    (A) report real property exchanges
    (B) compute tax on capital gains
    (C) report sales prices
    (D) claim investment credits

11. How many installment payments must there be before truth-in-lending disclosure is required?

   (A) Two
   (B) Three
   (C) Four
   (D) Five

12. The borrower has three business days to rescind a consumer loan that placed a lien on her residence. Which law provides for this right or rescission?

   (A) RESPA
   (B) The Truth-in-Lending Act
   (C) The Equal Credit Opportunity Act
   (D) The Uniform Commercial Code

13. A note given with a mortgage would be the:

   (A) security for the loan
   (B) primary evidence of the debt
   (C) hypothecation agreement
   (D) guarantee of payment

14. A broker offers buyers one-stop shopping by handling title insurance, home inspection, mortgage origination and other services to buyers. This is an example of:

   (A) a limited liability company
   (B) a controlled business arrangement
   (C) designated agency
   (D) dual agency

15. A seasoned loan is a:

   (A) priority loan
   (B) long-term loan
   (C) loan that includes incentives for early payment
   (D) loan with a payment history

16. An owner was in default on a mortgage payment. The lender could call the entire loan balance due if the loan contained a(n):

   (A) due-on-sale clause
   (B) "or more" clause
   (C) defeasance clause
   (D) acceleration clause

17. On a real estate closing transaction involving an exclusive-right-to-sell listing, the commission would be a debit to the:

   (A) buyer and a credit to the seller
   (B) seller and a credit to the buyer
   (C) seller
   (D) buyer

18. On a buyer's closing statement, the buyer would be debited for:

   (A) loans being assumed
   (B) a down payment given to the agent
   (C) a new loan being given to the seller
   (D) the sales price

19. Which of the following lenders uses its own funds to fund loans that will be sold in the secondary mortgage market?

   (A) Mortgage broker
   (B) Department of Veterans Affairs
   (C) Fannie Mae
   (D) Mortgage banker

20. A buyer would have to seek new financing if the seller's existing loan:

   (A) contained an alienation clause
   (B) was seller carryback financing
   (C) had a prepayment penalty
   (D) was a nonconforming loan

21. The Equal Credit Opportunity Act makes it illegal for lenders to refuse credit or discriminate because an applicant is:

   (A) a single parent who refuses to supply income verification
   (B) a family that has had persistent and recent credit problems
   (C) a single woman
   (D) unemployed and without any known income

22. The seller holds legal title to real property after the sale under a:

   (A) trust deed
   (B) mortgage (lien theory)
   (C) land contract
   (D) bill of sale

23. What kind of loan provides that a borrower is restored his or her loan eligibility benefits when the loan is paid off?

    (A) Construction loan
    (B) Conventional loan
    (C) VA loan
    (D) Growing equity mortgage

24. An example of negative amortization is a loan:

    (A) where the amount applied to interest declines each month
    (B) that is only partially amortized
    (C) where the payments are insufficient to cover the loan interest
    (D) where monthly payments are "plus interest" rather than "including interest"

25. Which type of loan features a profit split between the borrower and lender when the property is sold?

    (A) Shared appreciation mortgage
    (B) Graduated payment mortgage
    (C) Growing equity mortgage
    (D) Adjustable rate mortgage

26. Seller financing where the seller takes back a loan written for the amount of existing loans plus part or all of the seller's equity is known as:

    (A) compensating balance
    (B) a wraparound mortgage
    (C) an open mortgage
    (D) a blanket mortgage

27. The interest on an amortized loan is:

    (A) simple
    (B) compound
    (C) discounted
    (D) prepaid

28. An insurance company agreed to provide the developer financing for a shopping center at 13 percent interest plus an equity position. This arrangement is what type of loan?

    (A) Participation
    (B) Package
    (C) Variable
    (D) Open-end

29. An ad used a term that triggered full disclosure of loan terms. The ad stated:

    (A) low down payment
    (B) payments like rent
    (C) $10,000 down
    (D) 8 percent APR

30. A lender charged an illegal rate of interest. This would be known as:

    (A) a buydown
    (B) usury
    (C) subordination
    (D) impound interest

31. An elderly couple has difficulty paying their expenses although they own their home free and clear. A solution to their problem, without requiring them to move, would be a(n):

    (A) participation mortgage
    (B) growing equity mortgage
    (C) reverse-annuity mortgage
    (D) adjustable-rate mortgage

32. The rescission provisions of truth-in-lending apply to what type of loan?

    (A) Purchase money
    (B) Construction
    (C) Business
    (D) Home equity

33. The activities of Fannie Mae include:

    (A) insuring mortgages
    (B) guaranteeing mortgages
    (C) raising and lowering the federal discount rate
    (D) purchasing mortgages originated by others

34. The effect of equal monthly payments on an amortized loan is that they:

    (A) reduce the loan principal in equal monthly amounts
    (B) compound the interest
    (C) apply decreasing amounts to the interest
    (D) apply decreasing amounts to the principal

35. A mortgage foreclosure would terminate a lease on the foreclosed property when the lease was:

    (A) entered into prior to the mortgage
    (B) for more than one year
    (C) entered into after the mortgage
    (D) recorded

36. A deed of trust moves title and a limited power of sale from the:

    (A) mortgagor to the mortgagee
    (B) trustor to the trustee
    (C) trustor to the beneficiary
    (D) beneficiary to the trustor

37. An impound account is the property of the:

    (A) mortgagor
    (B) mortgagee
    (C) beneficiary
    (D) trustee

38. A type of loan that provides for increases in loan payments when interest rates rise would be a(n):

    (A) graduated payment mortgage
    (B) growing equity mortgage
    (C) adjustable-rate mortgage
    (D) shared appreciation mortgage

39. On a closing statement a buyer would be credited with the:

    (A) sales price
    (B) fee for recording the deed
    (C) cost of fuel oil in the tank
    (D) earnest money paid

40. A deed of reconveyance is signed by the:

    (A) trustor
    (B) trustee
    (C) beneficiary
    (D) vendor

41. A foreclosed owner's rights after a foreclosure sale relate to:

    (A) redemption
    (B) a deficiency judgment
    (C) hypothecation
    (D) defeasance

42. What advantage might a land contract have to a buyer, compared with a conventional mortgage?

    (A) Lower down payment
    (B) Amortization
    (C) Longer term
    (D) More protection from foreclosure

43. A home sold for $142,000. The lender demanded that the buyer pay 1¾ points for an 80 percent loan. What amount did the buyer pay in loan points?

    (A) $1,750
    (B) $1,902
    (C) $1,988
    (D) $2,485

44. A lender had a claim against the borrower after the property securing the loan was sold at a foreclosure sale. The lender had a:

    (A) subordination agreement
    (B) deficiency judgment
    (C) wraparound loan
    (D) right of redemption

45. A lender is able to decide if a loan to be made is eligible for FHA insurance. This ability of the lender is known as:

    (A) direct endorsement
    (B) prequalification
    (C) MIP
    (D) funding

46. A defeasance clause in a mortgage provides for:

    (A) the lien to be increased by later advances
    (B) the lien to be released by payment of the note
    (C) the assumption of the mortgage with the permission of the mortgagee
    (D) a private foreclosure sale

47. A loan applicant has sufficient income for a loan, but the income is in the form of public assistance. What law prohibits the lender from discriminating against the applicant because of the source of the income?

    (A) Uniform Commercial Code
    (B) Equal Credit Opportunity Act
    (C) RESPA
    (D) Regulation Z

48. What law requires that a "good-faith estimate" be given to a borrower for a federally related loan?

    (A) Truth-In-Lending Act
    (B) Real Estate Settlement Procedures Act
    (C) Equal Credit Opportunity Act
    (D) Fair Credit Reporting Act

49. Increasing the points asked for a loan in the absence of any economic change should have what effect on the loan?

    (A) Increase the risk
    (B) Reduce the interest
    (C) Increase the payments
    (D) Shorten the loan term

50. Which of the following formulas would be used to determine the front-end qualifying ratio for a loan?

    (A) $\dfrac{\text{PITI (Monthly Payment)}}{\text{Gross Monthly Income}}$
    (B) $\dfrac{\text{PITI + Monthly Debt}}{\text{Gross Monthly Income}}$
    (C) $\dfrac{\text{Net Monthly Income}}{\text{Monthly PITI Payment}}$
    (D) Gross Monthly Income – Loan Guarantee

CHAPTER 6 QUIZ ANSWERS

Financing/Settlements

1. (A) The annual percentage rate (APR) is the true rate of interest, adjusting the nominal rate for loan costs. (page 125)
2. (C) Homes receiving FHA loans must meet minimum property requirements. (page 121)
3. (C) FHA insurance protects the lender up to insurance limits. (page 121)
4. (D) While secondary financing is not allowed at the time of a VA loan, and VA loans greater than the CRV are not permitted, the veteran may still purchase the home by paying the difference in cash. (page 121)
5. (A) The seller remained liable on the loan. (page 118)
6. (B) The margin 2¼ percent plus the index of 4¾ percent equals 7 percent. The introductory rate is 1¾ percent less. (page 115)
7. (B) The buyer would become primarily liable, whereas the seller would remain secondarily liable. (page 118)
8. (B) The MIP is unique to FHA insurance. (page 121)
9. (C) This makes the purchase-money loan secondary to a construction loan. (page 119)
10. (C) The settlement agent must report the sale to the IRS. (page 127)
11. (D) Disclosure is required only for loans having more than four payments. (page 125)
12. (B) Rescission does not apply to home purchase loans. (page 125)
13. (B) The note is the promise to pay; the mortgage is the security for the note. (page 111)
14. (B) The buyer must be told that other service providers are available. (pages 127–128)
15. (D) Because of the reduced likelihood of default, a seasoned loan could sell at a premium over a new loan on the secondary mortgage market. (page 116)
16. (D) Payments all become due upon a default. (page 118)
17. (C) The commission is a seller's obligation (debit) and is never a credit. (page 128)
18. (D) The other answer options are credits that reduce the amount the buyer needs to close. (page 129)
19. (D) Mortgage brokers seldom use their own funds. The VA only guarantees loans. (page 120)
20. (A) An alienation clause is a due-on-sale clause that prohibits loan assumption. (page 118)
21. (C) Discrimination based on sex or marital status is specifically prohibited. A loan may be refused based on credit history (character) or capacity to pay. (page 125)
22. (C) Under a land contract, the vendor retains title and the vendee is given possession. (page 112)
23. (C) Veteran is then eligible for a new VA loan. (page 122)
24. (C) The loan balance increases each month. (page 117)
25. (A) A shared appreciation mortgage allows the lender to share in the increase in value. (page 116))
26. (B) The seller benefits by an interest higher than that provided by the existing low-interest loans. (page 116)
27. (A) The interst is paid each month so as not to compound. (page 114)
28. (A) The lender gets interest plus becomes a limited partner, sharing in the profits. (page 115)
29. (C) Amount of payments or down payment triggers full disclosure. Interest as an APR does not. (page 125)
30. (B) A rate that exceeds a statutory limit. (page 117)
31. (C) They could receive payments as with an annuity. (page 116)
32. (D) It applies to consumer credit secured by the borrower's residence. (page 125)
33. (D) It is active in the secondary mortgage market. (page 123)
34. (C) They also result in increasing amounts applied to the principal. (page 114)
35. (C) Foreclosure wipes out junior interests. (pages 113, 118)
36. (B) The trustee holds naked legal title in trust until the trustor pays the beneficiary or default causes a sale. (page 112)
37. (A) The borrower actually owns the prepaid insurance and taxes that are paid to the lender, which holds them in trust. (page 119)
38. (C) Up to the increase allowed by the cap because the index would rise. (page 115)
39. (D) This reduces the balance due the seller. (page 129)
40. (B) It returns legal title from the trustee to the trustor when the trust deed has been paid off. (page 112)
41. (A) Statutory right to redeem property (some states). (page 113)

42. (A) Sellers often sell with lower down payments on land contracts because of easy foreclosure in many states. (page 112)
43. (C) Eighty percent of $142,000 equals $113,600; $113,600 times .0175 equals $1,988. (page 117)
44. (B) A judgment for the difference between amounts realized at the foreclosure sale and the amount due on the note. (pages 113–114)
45. (A) Direct endorsement shortens the loan processing time because FHA approval is not required. (page 121)
46. (B) The mortgage is canceled when the note is paid. (page 118)
47. (B) The lender cannot discriminate based on the public assistance source of the income. (page 125)
48. (B) Estimate of settlement costs must be given within three business days of loan application. (page 127)
49. (B) Points are really prepaid interest. (page 117)
50. (A) Answer (B) describes the back-end ratio. (page 124)

Property Management
and Leases

PROPERTY MANAGEMENT

A broker has the same legal duties to an owner in *property management* as to a client in listing a property for sale. The property manager generally handles these responsibilities:

- Renting units and collecting rents
- Arranging for maintenance and repairs
- Hiring and firing on-site personnel
- Providing a complete accounting to the owner

A property management agreement ordinarily would give the agent the right to advertise, lease to prescribed time and dollar limitations, collect rents, handle maintenance and repairs, contract for services (might have a dollar and/or time limit), hire and discharge personnel, pay bills and expenses, give tenant notices, etc.

A property manager is the agent of the owner and therefore has agency responsibilities. The property management contract should require that the agent account for all income and expenses paid, provide statements to the owner, keep tenant deposits and other owner funds in a trust account, use diligence in carrying out the provision of the agreement, and obey all laws and regulations.

The owner should agree to provide the manager with applicable records, carry adequate liability insurance and workers compensation to protect owner and broker, indemnify the broker for any costs or expenses relating to the management, and pay all fees as agreed by contract.

Managers customarily receive a percentage of the gross income based on the type of property and management duties. A minimum management fee and a leasing commission also might be included as compensation. A minimum management fee is important when property is vacant. A separate leasing commission is customarily a percentage of the rent for the entire lease. On long-term leases, the percentage tends to be lower for later years than for the first year.

The manager also might be entitled to compensation for evictions, supervising improvements, and fire damage rehabilitation, as well as representing the owner before public agencies. Kickbacks from suppliers would constitute a secret profit and would breach the agent's fiduciary duty.

LEASES

Leasehold Estates

There are four types of estates possible for lessees.

1. **Estate for Years** A lease interest for a definite period of time is called an *estate for years.* Such a lease does not automatically renew itself. Because an estate for years ends at the end of its specific term, no notice is required for termination. State laws provide for the maximum term of a leasehold interest, which is often 99 years.
2. **Periodic Tenancies** These leases are from period to period, such as month-to-month or year-to-year, and automatically renew themselves unless either party gives notice. Generally, notices to end the tenancy must be delivered or posted on the property within a specified number of days, often 30, prior to termination.
3. **Tenancy at Will** Tenancy at will describes a lease for an unspecified period where permissive possession was given without an agreement as to tenancy. An example of a tenancy at will is a seller who gives a buyer occupancy prior to a closing and without any rental agreement or a lessor who gives a prospective tenant possession prior to finalizing a lease. Statutory notice, typically 15 or 30 days, is required to terminate such a tenancy.

    Tenant-at-will interests may not be assigned and cease on sale of the property or the death of tenant or landlord. Other leases generally bind the estates of the parties.
4. **Tenancy at Sufferance** If a tenant properly comes into possession of real property, but wrongfully holds over or continues occupancy after expiration of the lease, a tenancy at sufferance arises. An example is a tenant who fails to leave at the end of a fixed term lease or one who gives notice but fails to leave. Occupancy by a former owner after a completed foreclosure or after condemnation under eminent domain also results in a tenancy at sufferance.

    A tenant at sufferance may be removed by an **ejectment action** without formal notice or by a formal eviction procedure. If an owner accepts rent from a tenant at sufferance, however, the tenant becomes a periodic tenant. If a periodic tenancy is established, a proper notice must be given prior to an action for eviction.

Types of Leases

Under a *lease,* the **lessor (owner)** subordinates his or her right of possession to a **lessee (tenant).** The legal term **demise** refers to the conveyance of a leasehold interest. There are several basic types of leases.

Gross Lease A *gross (flat) lease* is a fixed-rate rental in which the owner pays the taxes and insurance as well as agreed-on maintenance and repairs. Although a long-term gross lease ensures having a tenant, there is a danger of being tied to a low rental during an inflationary period. Most residential leases are gross leases.

Index Lease A long-term gross lease would be disadvantageous to an owner during an inflationary period where the tenant would be paying a below-market rent. This risk can be offset by use of an index lease with rent increase tied to an index such as the consumer price index (CPI).

Step-Up Lease A lease that has a fixed rent but has agreed upon rent increases at specified times is a *step-up lease* or graduated lease.

Net Lease   The *net lease,* a long-term commercial lease, provides that the owner shall receive a fixed or net amount as rent. The tenant pays the maintenance and operating expenses. To protect the purchasing power of the rent received, the net rent could be adjusted with the CPI. A **triple net lease** describes a net lease where the lessee also pays taxes and insurance as well as all maintenance and operational expenses.

Percentage Lease   The *percentage lease,* commonly used in shopping centers, gives the owner a percentage of the tenant's gross receipts. Generally, businesses with higher markups pay higher percentages. A percentage lease might include a minimum rent, a covenant to remain in business, advertising requirements, and hours of operation. As an incentive for greater volume, percentage leases often provide for reductions in the percentage paid as rent as the volume increases. To obtain a desirable anchor tenant, a major store that generates high traffic, a shopping center might offer extremely desirable terms. Having the anchor tenant would allow increased base rent for other tenants and increase their volume.

Sale-Leaseback   Under this arrangement, a commercial property is sold to an investor and the former owner becomes a tenant. Generally, a long-term net lease is used, with provisions for inflation-adjusted increases. The seller benefits because the sale frees capital for operational use, the rent is fully deductible as a business expense, and the balance sheet of the business will no longer show a long-term mortgage debt.

Oil and Gas Lease   Such a lease, sometimes referred to as a **vertical lease,** gives the lessee the right to drill and extract gas and oil, paying an initial lease fee plus a royalty fee based on what is taken. Oil and gas leases differ from mineral, oil, and gas rights, which are ownership rights separate from the property for which no fees or royalties are paid. While mineral, oil, and gas rights are regarded as real property, oil, and gas leases, like all other leases, are considered to be chattels real, which are personal property interests.

Ground Lease   A *ground lease* is the lease of the land alone. The tenant owns or separately leases the structures that have been legally separated from the land. One purpose in leasing rather than purchasing the land is that leasing reduces the initial investment. At the end of the ground lease, the improvements become the property of the lessor. **Ground rent** is not the same as ground lease. Ground rent is usually regarded as that portion of a lease amount that is attributable to the land.

Lease Provisions

Description of Premises   The lease must contain an unambiguous *description* of the premises leased.

Term   Unless a longer *term* is clearly stated, the lease generally is considered to be a periodic tenancy for the length of the rent-paying period. State laws govern the maximum length of a lease, which can be up to 99 years. Leases for agricultural purposes and oil and gas leases might have different maximum terms.

Quiet Enjoyment   The tenant is entitled to *quiet enjoyment* of the premises without interference from the lessor, and the lessor will defend the lessee's right of possession against claims of third parties. Quiet enjoyment is usually considered an implied covenant of the lease.

Habitability   Residential leases carry an implied, if not a written, *covenant of habitability.* State law specifies requirements, which usually include a weather tight structure; operational heat, plumbing, and electrical systems; as well as pest-free premises at the time of rental.

Use of Premises   Leases often contain clauses specifying the particular *use* that the tenants may have for the premises. If there is no limitation, the tenant can use the premises for any legal purpose.

Amount of Rent   The *rent,* or a formula to determine rent, must be set forth in the lease. A property manager must make certain that rents don't violate restrictions imposed by local rent control ordinances. Violations of rent ordinances could subject both the owner and property manager to penalties.

Repairs   Leases generally provide for who shall be responsible for what repairs. In residential property, the lessor is responsible for the roof, walls, and windows; the heating and cooling system; as well as any appliances included.

Renewal Options   Leases for fixed periods often provide for *renewal options* at specific rents or formulas to determine the rents for additional periods of time. A lease with an option to purchase sometimes includes a right of the lessee to have a portion of the rent applied as a down payment if the option is exercised. Rather than giving a tenant a purchase option, the lessor might give the tenant a **right of first refusal** that would not obligate the owner to sell.

Automatic Renewal   Some leases provide that they *automatically renew* for a like period unless notice to terminate is given. States generally require such a provision to be in bold face type.

Forfeiture   A lease may provide that a material breach of a provision of the lease can end the tenant's rights; nonpayment of rent is not generally considered to be such a breach. If a landlord collects rent after the tenant has breached a provision allowing *forfeiture,* the landlord may have waived the right to declare forfeiture.

Holdover Clause   A *holdover clause* provides for a significant rent increase should a tenant fail to give up possession at the end of the lease. It serves to discourage a tenancy at sufferance by forcing the tenant to vacate or negotiate a new lease.

Escalator Clause   An *escalator clause* provides for rent to fluctuate. It may be based on the consumer price index, or increases in owner costs relating to taxes, insurance, maintenance, and / or operational costs.

Exculpatory Clause   This is a hold-harmless clause by which the tenant agrees that the landlord shall not be liable for any loss or injury because of the condition of the premises. The tenant agrees to refrain from holding the landlord accountable for any losses suffered. In many states, an *exculpatory clause* is unenforceable in a residential lease.

Recapture Clause   A *recapture clause* in a percentage lease gives the lessor the right to terminate the lease if the lessee does not achieve a specified volume of sales.

Security Deposit   This deposit is paid by the lessee and held by the lessor to ensure that the property is returned to the lessor in good repair at the end of the lease, with the exception of normal wear and tear. The lessor can use the money to repair damage or for rent owed but must return the balance, if any. A *security deposit* is taxed to the lessor as income only if the lessee forfeits it. The last month's rent paid in advance is taxed when it is received.

Most states regulate the amount of the security deposit that can be collected for residential rentals, and several states require that the lessor pay interest on these funds. Nonrefundable cleaning or security deposits are not allowed in many states.

Fixtures   The lease may provide for the removal of improvements, or it may provide that improvements shall be considered *fixtures* and stay with the realty.

Insurance   A commercial lease might require that the lessee carry *insurance* that protects the lessor against injuries to others.

Signature   In many states, one party can be held bound to a written lease he or she did not sign if rent was paid or accepted after receipt of a copy of the lease signed by the other party.

Acknowledgment   In most states, recording a lease requires that it be *acknowledged* before a notary. In some states, leases beyond a statutory period must be recorded to give the lessees rights against subsequent purchasers.

Lease Termination

Merger   A lease is terminated if the lessor and the lessee become the same person. If a tenant under a long-term lease purchases the property and later sells it, the tenant would be without a lease. It would have been lost by *merger* because the former tenant couldn't own the property in fee simple and also be his or her own tenant with a lesser leasehold interest.

Breach   A lease may be terminated by either lessor or lessee for a material *breach* of lease provisions. The tenant may be evicted after statutory notice by an unlawful detainer action.

Eviction procedure varies from state to state, but generally there is notice, often three days, to quit, quit or cure, or quit or pay rent. If the tenant fails to comply, an **unlawful detainer action** is commenced, which is the court eviction procedure. The court then issues an order for the tenant to vacate. This order is called a **writ of possession** or **restitution**.

A breach by the landlord of a material lease provision or the implied right of quiet enjoyment, disturbing the tenant's reasonable use, could be treated by the tenant as an act of **constructive eviction**, and the tenant could vacate without further lease liability.

Notice   State law provides for a notice period (as well as the form of notice) to terminate or modify a periodic tenancy (such as month to month).

Destruction of Premises   In the absence of an agreement to the contrary, *destruction of the premises* would terminate the tenancy.

Eminent Domain   The taking of the premises under the power of *eminent domain* would terminate the lease; however, the tenant might be entitled to compensation for the value of the leasehold.

Condemnation   *Condemnation* for health or safety reasons also would serve to terminate the lessee's responsibility.

Commercial Frustration   Unforeseen events not contemplated at the time of the lease could be grounds to terminate a commercial lease. For example, if a lease specified the sale of a particular product only and that product became unavailable, the lessee might terminate for commercial frustration.

Bankruptcy   *Bankruptcy* of the tenant could terminate lease obligations.

Surrender   The landlord's acceptance of the return of possession prior to expiration of the lease would terminate all obligations under the lease.

Expiration of Term   The *expiration* of the lease term would end a tenancy for years.

Foreclosure   The *foreclosure* of a mortgage recorded prior to the lease agreement would terminate the lease unless the lender has agreed that the lease shall have priority.

Uniform Residential Landlord and Tenant Act

A number of states have adopted all or part of the *Uniform Residential Landlord and Tenant Act*, which is designed to provide uniformity as to the rights and duties of residential landlords and tenants. The act contains the following provisions:

- If no period for the rental is set it is a periodic tenancy on a month-to-month basis, unless rent is collected weekly (in which case it would be a week-to-week rental).
- If no rental amount is specified, the amount would be fair rent (which could be determined by a court).
- If either party signs a lease and the other party, after receiving the lease, pays or collects the rent, the other party shall be bound to the lease.
- The tenant need not agree to limit the landlord's liability (except as to common areas), and the lease may not require the tenant to give up rights under the act, agree to confess judgment on any claim arising under the lease, or pay the lessor's attorney's fees.
- Within five days of possession, the parties must make a joint inventory as to the condition of the premises and furnishings.
- The maximum security deposit shall be one month's rent for unfurnished units (one and one-half month's rent for furnished units) plus half a month's rent for tenants having pets. The lessor must promptly return the deposit at the end of the lease less damages (an itemized list must be provided). If lessor fails to do so, the lessee will be entitled to the return of the amount wrongfully withheld plus damages of one and a half times that amount. (Many states have modified the security deposit limitations and set time periods for return of security deposits.)
- The landlord may establish reasonable rules applicable to all tenants, but the landlord must give notice of the rules at the time of rental.

Tenant's Responsibility   The act provides the following tenant responsibilities:

- The tenant may not unreasonably withhold permission for the landlord to enter the premises.
- The tenant cannot apply the security deposit to the last month's rent.
- The tenant must comply with reasonable rules related at the time of rental.
- Use will be solely as a dwelling unless otherwise specified.
- The tenant will abide by housing and health codes, keeping the premises clean and properly disposing of garbage. The tenant must take reasonable care in using the premises.

Landlord's Responsibility   The act provides these landlord responsibilities:

- The landlord will give reasonable notice prior to entry and will not enter without permission except in cases of extreme emergency.
- The landlord will inform the tenant as to the name and address of that person responsible for managing the property and that person who shall receive legal notices.
- The landlord will make repairs necessary to keep the premises fit for habitation, as well as maintain common areas.
- The landlord is responsible for garbage receptacles. Running water, hot water, and heat are to be provided unless the lease makes these tenant responsibilities or the tenant has exclusive control over the water and/or heat installations.
- If the landlord fails to arrange for required services within a reasonable period of time, the tenant can arrange for the services and sue for damages.

- The landlord may not increase the rent of or evict a tenant who complains to a government agency or joins a tenant organization **(retaliatory eviction).**

Termination of Tenancy   The act provides for termination if any of the following occurs:

- The tenant breaches a material provision of the lease. The landlord may deliver notice that the tenancy will terminate in 30 days if a good-faith effort is not begun to correct the breach during the 30-day period, or the landlord could waive the breach and continue to hold the tenant to the other lease provisions.
- If the tenant's breach concerns failure to repair or replace damaged items, the landlord, after reasonable notice, can enter the premises and make necessary repairs and replacements and charge the reasonable cost of the work to the tenant.
- The tenant fails to pay rent. The landlord can terminate with a three-day notice.
- The property is destroyed or damaged where reasonable enjoyment of the premises is affected. The tenant may terminate the lease or vacate that portion of the premises with a reduction in rent.
- The tenant abandons the premises. The landlord must make reasonable efforts to rerent the premises at a fair rental (duty to mitigate damages). If the landlord fails to do so, the landlord accepts the abandonment as surrender of the premises, which terminates the lease and all future lease obligations.

Assignment and Sublease

Generally, the lease can prohibit *assignments* and *subleases.* If the tenant wrongfully assigns or sublets, the lessor can consider the action a breach and evict or waive the breach and accept the assignment or sublease. If the lease provides for assignments or subleases with the approval of the lessor, most courts have held that approval cannot be unreasonably withheld.

Unless a lease specifically prohibits assignments or subleases, the lessee can assign or sublease.

Assignment   In an assignment, the lessee transfers all of his or her interests to another. The assignee becomes the tenant of the lessor and pays the rent to the lessor in accordance with the original lease. Although the original lessee remains secondarily liable under the lease, the assignee is primarily liable.

Sublease   Also known as a **sandwich lease,** the sublease makes the lessee, under the **master lease,** a lessor who takes on his or her own tenant. The lessor, under a sublease, can lease all or a portion of the premises.

The sublessee pays the rent under the sublease to the sublessor, and the sublessor, the original lessee, pays to the lessor. The original lessee remains primarily liable for fulfillment of the lease terms. An advantage to a lessee of a sublease rather than an assignment is that the sublease could require more rent than the original lease.

Liability of Owners

Owners can be held liable for injuries caused by the condition of their property in accordance with state law. Under the **attractive nuisance doctrine,** owners have a special duty to children if the property is likely to attract young children, even if they are trespassers.

Figure 7.1: Assignment Versus Subletting

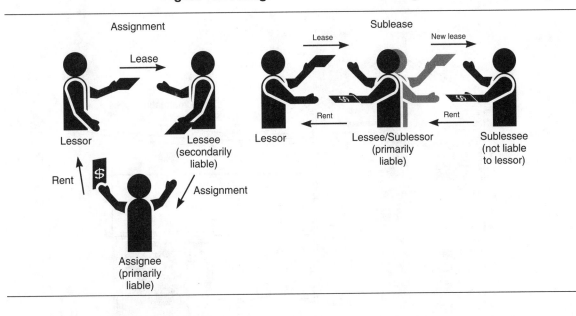

Hazardous Substances

The federal *Comprehensive Environmental Response Compensation and Liability Act (CERCLA)* of *1980 (Superfund)* provides for strict liability of owner, operator, and lessee for cleanup of hazardous substances generated, transported, or disposed of. A defense of innocence is possible for an owner as to a preexisting problem only if appropriate inquiry was made prior to acquiring the site.

Hazardous substances can include:

- **asbestos**—This fire-resistant material was at one time extensively used in insulation, floor and ceiling tile, and roofing. Asbestos dust has been found to cause respiratory problems including lung cancer.

  Removal of asbestos requires great care because removal can result in asbestos dust. An alternative is encapsulation where the asbestos material is sealed.
- **lead**—This substance was commonly used in oil-based paint and in plumbing solder. The greatest household danger is from lead dust due to deteriorating paint. Lead poisoning can result in brain, kidney, and nervous system damage.
- **radon gas**—A naturally occurring colorless, odorless gas that can enter homes through cracks in foundations or basements. Radon is considered carcinogenic.
- **electromagnetic fields (EMFs)**—EMFs are generated by the movement of electrical currents. The major concern involves high-tension power lines. There is a great deal of controversy about alleged cancer dangers from EMF.
- **underground storage tanks**—Leakage of fuel or chemicals from these often-forgotten tanks can result in soil and water contamination.
- **waste disposal sites**—Unless property used as a dumpsite is properly capped, dumped substances could endanger persons living in the vicinity as well as leach into the underground water supply.
- **fertilizers and pesticides**—Agricultural chemicals could present a health risk to current users of the land as well as present a problem to others because of runoff and pollution of groundwater.

Figure 7.2: Environmental Hazards

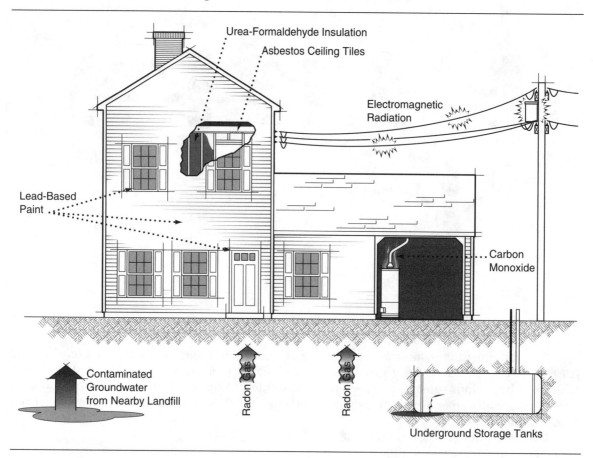

- **PCBs (polychlorinated biphenyls)**—PCBs were formerly used in electrical transformers and other electrical equipment. PCB leakage can create a serious health hazard. PCBs are considered to be carcinogenic.
- **urea formaldehyde foam**—Formerly used as insulation (or as a binder material in some particle board), this substance emits an irritating gas as it deteriorates.
- **chemical discharge**—Spills and careless disposal of various chemicals from commercial and industrial sources have created many significant environmental problems.

A number of states have statutes that expand owner liability and require disclosure of hazardous substances by sellers, lessors, and lessees. (See Figure 7.2.)

Insurance

Insurance is a personal contract whereby an insurer agrees to indemnify and protect an insured in the event of a specified loss. In exchange for payment of a premium, the risk of loss is shifted from the insured to the insurer. An agent should have an understanding of the following insurance types and terms:

Basic Fire Policy   This covers loss by fire, lightning, and smoke from a hostile fire.

Extended Coverage Policy   This includes coverage for wind, hail, water damage, and other specified perils.

Homeowners Policy   This provides a package of protection from losses beyond the extended coverage policy, including vandalism and theft coverage, personal property protection, and liability coverage.

Tenants Policy   This package of protection for tenants' personal property also may include liability protection.

Condominium Owner Policy   Similar to a tenant policy, this includes most of the general homeowners coverage except for loss of the structure, which is covered by a separate policy of the condominium owners' association.

Public Liability   This protects an owner as to members of the public who may enter the premises and be injured because of the condition of the premises. Lessors frequently require commercial tenants to carry such coverage with the lessor as a named insured.

Flood Insurance   The National Flood Insurance program makes flood insurance available through private insurance carriers under a government-subsidized program.

Earthquake Insurance   Although earthquake coverage can be included as part of another policy, it usually requires a separate policy.

Errors and Omissions   A real estate brokerage or property management office would carry this type of policy. It is similar to medical malpractice coverage in that it protects the insured from liability based on negligence. It does not protect the insured from his or her own fraudulent acts.

Home Warranty Plans   This buyer insurance plan covers structural, mechanical, and electrical problems over a stated period of time. It is issued to a buyer at the time a home is purchased.

Rent Insurance   Rent insurance protects the owner against lost income while a property is being repaired or rebuilt as a result of a casualty (an accidental) loss.

Mortgage Life Insurance   Mortgage life insurance is a term life insurance policy, or life and disability insurance, that pays off the mortgage if the insured dies or becomes disabled. It is really declining term insurance because coverage decreases as the mortgage is paid off.

Deductibles   Premiums can be reduced by having a deductible amount withdrawn from the coverage. The higher the deductible, the lower the premium.

Assumption   In some states, property insurance policies can be assumed, with approval from the insurer. An insured that cancels a policy gets a *short rate refund,* which is less than a prorated refund. If the insurance company cancels the policy, the insured is entitled to a full-prorated refund. To get full credit for the insurance, it is in the best interest of the seller that the buyer assumes the insurance policy.

Coinsurance   Coinsurance requires an insured to carry a particular percentage of the replacement value, usually 80 percent, to be fully reimbursed for a loss. If an insured carries less than the required percentage coverage, the insured can collect only that percentage of any loss suffered up to the amount of coverage.

Riders   These are amendments to policies that usually exclude or increase coverage.

Fidelity Bonds   By bonding an employee, an employer is protected against any employee's dishonesty.

Your Pertinent State Information

1.   What is the maximum period for leases?

2.   Describe the procedure for the recording of leases.

3.   What are the security deposit limitations in your state?

4.   How long does a landlord have after the end of tenancy to return the security deposit?

5.   What are the notice requirements for periodic tenancy?

6.   What hazardous substance disclosures are required in your state?

CHAPTER 7 QUIZ

Property Management and Leases

1. An estate for years would be created by:

   (A) express agreement
   (B) adverse possession
   (C) operation of the law
   (D) holding over

2. The tenant who remains in possession after the lease expires:

   (A) is on a periodic tenancy
   (B) has a freehold interest
   (C) is a tenant at sufferance
   (D) has a servient tenement

3. The effect of a lease assignment is that the:

   (A) entire lease interest is transferred
   (B) assignee makes rent payments to the assignor
   (C) assignee is a tenant of the assignor
   (D) assignor remains primarily liable on the lease

4. In accordance with the Uniform Residential Landlord and Tenant Act, a lessor may properly require that the tenant:

   (A) pay a security deposit equal to two months' rent
   (B) agree to a limitation on the owner's liability
   (C) pay any lessor attorney fees arising from a dispute
   (D) restrict use of the premises to residential purposes.

5. A lease prohibited assignment or subletting without the owner's prior approval. The lessee assigned without asking the lessor. The assignment is:

   (A) void
   (B) voidable
   (C) unenforceable
   (D) illegal

6. The Uniform Residential Landlord and Tenant Act provides that the tenant:

   (A) can agree to hold the landlord harmless for actions of the landlord
   (B) may apply the security deposit to the last month's rent
   (C) may not unreasonably withhold permission for the landlord to enter the premises
   (D) will make the repairs necessary to keep the premises fit for habitation

7. A sublessee is a(n):

   (A) assignee
   (B) owner
   (C) tenant
   (D) lessor on a sublease

8. An advantage offered to an investor buying a structure subject to a ground lease rather than buying the structure and the land is:

   (A) not having to pay for an unneeded structure
   (B) lower investment requirements
   (C) being able to deduct interest payments
   (D) the advantage of a continued rental income

9. A clause in a three-year lease provides that should the tenant retain possession after expiration of the lease, it will be on a month-to-month basis with a significant increase in rent. This clause is intended to discourage a:

   (A) lease renewal
   (B) lease extension
   (C) tenancy at sufferance
   (D) surrender of the premises

10. A lessee is relieved of all obligations under the lease when the:

   (A) lessee is evicted for rent arrearage
   (B) property is sold
   (C) lessee is constructively evicted
   (D) lessee can no longer afford to pay the rent

11. A lease in which the lessee's total monthly rent costs remain unchanged for the term of the lease is what type of lease?

   (A) Gross
   (B) Net
   (C) Percentage
   (D) Graduated

12. Broker L, who manages property for M, approaches tenant N for back rent a day after M dies. N refuses to pay. The broker should:

   (A) give N statutory notice to quit or pay rent
   (B) start an unlawful detainer action
   (C) turn the matter over to a collection attorney
   (D) take no further action

13. J leased to K, who subleased to L, who then subleased to M. The lease between K and L could be regarded as a(n):

   (A) sandwich lease
   (B) assignment
   (C) master lease
   (D) flat lease

14. Partial lease interests were transferred by a lessee. This is a(n):

   (A) step-lease
   (B) gross lease
   (C) assignment
   (D) sublease

15. The lessee pays for fire insurance under what type of lease?

   (A) Gross
   (B) Percentage
   (C) Triple net
   (D) Graduated payment

16. What type of long-term lease is best for a commercial tenant during an inflationary period?

   (A) Gross
   (B) Percentage
   (C) Index
   (D) Net

17. A property manager is in trouble because of compensation received. This compensation was a:

   (A) percentage of the gross
   (B) fee for leasing
   (C) fee for supervising repairs
   (D) kickback from a supplier

18. A mineral formerly used in home construction that can cause lung cancer is:

   (A) asbestos
   (B) lead
   (C) radon
   (D) urea formaldehyde foam

19. A former owner could be liable for the physical condition of the premises, even after ten years:

   (A) if a warranty deed was used to convey title
   (B) if the owner failed to specify "as is."
   (C) under the federal Comprehensive Environmental Response Compensation and Liability Act of 1980
   (D) under the Uniform Residential Landlord and Tenant Act

20. G leased a commercial building to S for ten years. After six months, S moved out without notice. G advertised for a tenant. G's actions relate to:

   (A) liquidated damages
   (B) mitigation of damages
   (C) punitive damages
   (D) severance damages

21. A child was injured when he fell through the floor in an abandoned house. If the owner was held liable for the injury, the house was probably considered a(n):

    (A) encroachment
    (B) attractive nuisance
    (C) hazardous substance
    (D) implied easement

22. One reason a company would sell and then lease back its real property would be:

    (A) the deductibility of interest
    (B) to reduce monthly expenses
    (C) liquidity
    (D) the tax benefits of depreciation

23. When a lease is assigned, who is responsible for rent obligations?

    (A) The assignee becomes primarily liable under the lease, and the assignor is released.
    (B) The assignor remains primarily liable under the lease.
    (C) The assignee becomes primarily liable under the lease, and the assignor retains secondary liability.
    (D) The assignee is liable only to the assignor, and the assignor is liable to the lessor.

24. A commercial lease for a definite period of time is terminated by:

    (A) death of the lessor
    (B) death of the lessee
    (C) a sale by the lessor
    (D) surrender

25. A lessor believes the desirability and sales volume of a large retail store will increase dramatically in the next few years. In negotiating a long-term lease for the premises, the lessor would ask for what type of lease?

    (A) Flat
    (B) Triple net
    (C) Percentage
    (D) Gross

26. *R* rented a summer cottage for the first two weeks in July. What type of tenancy does *R* have?

    (A) Estate for years
    (B) Estate at will
    (C) Periodic tenancy
    (D) Tenancy at sufferance

27. An example of constructive eviction would be a:

    (A) tenant who refuses to pay rent
    (B) tenant being given a notice to quit or pay rent
    (C) landlord cutting off the tenant's heat and water
    (D) tenant who remains in possession after termination of the lease

28. After receiving a three-year lease, a residential tenant moved in and paid the first month's rent, but failed to sign and return a copy to the lessor. As to the tenant's obligations the:

    (A) tenant can cease the tenancy after a 30-day notice
    (B) lease is invalid because it is an oral lease for more than one year
    (C) tenant can leave but must forfeit any security deposit
    (D) tenant remains bound to the provisions of the lease

29. A valid lease must include:

    (A) an exculpatory provision
    (B) the specified use of the premises
    (C) a definite termination date
    (D) a description of the premises

30. A lessee would have the greatest protection with a(n):

    (A) estate for years
    (B) estate at will
    (C) tenancy at sufferance
    (D) periodic tenancy

31. A purchaser concerned with EMFs would be interested in knowing about:

    (A) underground fuel storage tanks
    (B) use of urea formaldehyde foam insulation
    (C) electrical transmission lines
    (D) the presence of radon gas

32. A tenancy based on permissive occupancy without any tenancy agreement would be a:

    (A) month-to-month lease
    (B) freehold interest
    (C) tenancy at sufferance
    (D) tenancy at will

33. An owner died, which immediately ended a tenant's rights. What kind of tenancy was it?

    (A) Tenancy at will
    (B) Tenancy at sufferance
    (C) Periodic tenancy
    (D) Estate for years

34. A lease that ends on a specified date without the requirement of notice is a(n):

    (A) tenancy at will
    (B) estate for years
    (C) tenancy at sufferance
    (D) periodic tenancy

35. A residential lease has an implied covenant of:

    (A) acknowledgment
    (B) exculpation
    (C) merger
    (D) habitability

36. A residential tenant on a month-to-month tenancy generally has a:

    (A) gross lease
    (B) net lease
    (C) percentage lease
    (D) graduated lease

37. A tenant on a long-term lease purchased the building from his landlord and resold it to investors at a profit, making no mention of lease rights. The lease was terminated by:

    (A) commercial frustration
    (B) merger
    (C) surrender
    (D) recordation

38. In the absence of a notice to terminate, a lease that automatically renews itself would be a:

    (A) periodic tenancy
    (B) tenancy for years
    (C) gross lease
    (D) ground lease

39. A landlord included a clause in the lease that said the tenant would not hold the landlord liable for personal injury or property damage for any reason. This is considered a(n):

    (A) recapture clause
    (B) quiet enjoyment clause
    (C) exculpatory clause
    (D) holdover clause

40. A tenant has the right to meet the terms offered by any prospective new tenant when the current lease expires. What is this right called?

    (A) Holdover provision
    (B) Option
    (C) Right of first refusal
    (D) Extension agreement

41. The Uniform Residential Landlord and Tenant Act provides that:

    (A) it is a one-year lease when no rental period is agreed to
    (B) if no rental amount is specified, then no rent can be collected
    (C) the tenant must sign an exculpatory clause if requested to do so
    (D) the maximum security deposit for unfurnished units is one month's rent

42. A lease provids that every June 1, the monthly rent will increase by $50. What type of lease is this?

    (A) Flat lease
    (B) Net lease
    (C) Graduated lease
    (D) Index lease

43. A property management contract should include:

    (A) a list of properties currently managed by the manager
    (B) the obligations and responsibilities of the manager
    (C) the manager's professional qualifications
    (D) an ethnic breakdown of current tenants

44. What colorless, odorless gas causes cancer and enters a home through the foundation?

    (A) PCBs
    (B) EMFs
    (C) Radon
    (D) Urea formaldehyde

45. A landlord failed to deal with a serious rodent problem, claiming she could not afford an exterminator. A tenant could break a lease based on:

    (A) commercial frustration
    (B) constructive eviction
    (C) merger
    (D) destruction of the premises

46. The initial action in an eviction for non-payment of rent would be a(n):

    (A) unlawful detainer action
    (B) writ of possession
    (C) seizure notice
    (D) notice to quit or pay rent

47. A lessor wants a tenant to protect the lessor from claims of others based on problems concerning the premises. What type of insurance would the lessor want the lessee to carry?

    (A) Public liability
    (B) Errors and omissions
    (C) Homeowner policy
    (D) Fire and extended coverage

48. A tenant moved out with 18 months remaining on the lease. To mitigate damages, the landlord:

    (A) boarded up the premises to prevent vandalism
    (B) advertised the vacancy
    (C) sued the tenant for the amount owing
    (D) sued the tenant for amount owing plus balance on the lease

49. A tenant suffered from lead poisoning relating to the occupancy of an older apartment. The cause was likely:

    (A) insulation
    (B) radon leakage
    (C) flaking paint
    (D) related to EMF

50. An owner wanted to structure the lease to provide income benefits like an annuity but also wanted inflation protection. To a long-term net lease she added a provision relating to:

    (A) the Consumer Price Index
    (B) EMF
    (C) a right of first refusal
    (D) quiet enjoyment

CHAPTER 7 QUIZ ANSWERS

Property Management and Leases

1. (A) Because it is a lease for a specified period of time, there must be specific agreement. (page 139)
2. (C) In many areas, the holdover tenant can be treated like a trespasser. (page 139)
3. (A) The assignee makes rent payments to the original lessor. (pages 144, 145)
4. (D) Unless the lease authorizes other use. (page 143)
5. (B) The owner can consider it a material breach and terminate the lease or accept the assignment. (page 144)
6. (C) Entry must be for a reasonable purpose with reasonable notice. (page 143)
7. (C) The sublessee is the tenant of the sublessor (original lessee) on a sublease. (pages 144, 145)
8. (B) The purchase price would be less, but the buyer of the building would pay rent for the land use. (page 140)
9. (C) A holdover clause discourages the tenant from remaining in possession because of higher rent. It encourages agreement to a new lease. (page 141)
10. (C) Lessor breached lease so lessee, who vacates, is relieved of all further lease obligations. (page 142)
11. (A) It is also known as a *flat lease.* (page 139)
12. (D) The agency agreement terminated with the death of the principal. (page 138)
13. (A) It is a sublease lease that does not involve both the owner and the tenant in possession. Subleases are often referred to as *sandwich leases.* (page 144)
14. (D) While an assignment transfers all interests, a sublease can transfer a partial interest. (page 144)
15. (C) The lessee is liable for all maintenance and operational expenses plus taxes and insurance and gives the landlord a net amount. (page 140)
16. (A) The rent would not increase; therefore, it would not be good for the landlord. (page 139)
17. (D) The property manager cannot make a secret profit. (page 138)
18. (A) It was used as insulation and in floor and ceiling tile as well as acoustical spraying. (page 145)
19. (C) The former owner could be liable for hazardous waste deposited on the property. (page 145)
20. (B) The lessor has a duty to keep tenant damages as low as reasonably possible. (page 144)
21. (B) There is a special duty of owners when property is likely to attract children. (page 144)
22. (C) To obtain cash from an illiquid asset. (page 140)
23. (C) In a sublease, the original lessee (sublessor) would have remained primarily liable. (page 144)
24. (D) An acceptance of the premises by the lessor ending all lease obligations. (page 142)
25. (C) This would mean greater rent as retail volume increases. (page 140)
26. (A) A lease for a definite period of time. (page 139)
27. (C) Constructive eviction is wrongful conduct by a landlord that forces the tenant to move; it ends all lease obligations. (page 142)
28. (D) The tenant accepted the lease by performance of paying rent. (page 143)
29. (D) Description must be clear and unambiguous. (page 140)
30. (A) If lessee is not in default, lessee is assured possession for a set period. (page 139)
31. (C) Electromagnetic fields are believed by many to have serious effects on health (disputed). (page 145)
32. (D) It is personal and cannot be assigned. (page 139)
33. (A) Ceases on death of tenant or landlord. (page 139)
34. (B) Lease for a definite period of time. (page 139)
35. (D) Also implied covenant of quiet enjoyment. (page 140)
36. (A) Most residential tenants pay a flat rental. (page 139)
37. (B) When the tenant purchased the building, there was no longer a tenancy because the lesser interest (leasehold) was merged into the ownership. (page 142)
38. (A) Such as a month-to-month lease. (page 139)
39. (C) Not valid for residential leases. (page 141)
40. (C) Right of first refusal can be for leasing as well as purchase. (page 141)
41. (D) And 1½ months for furnished units (many states have modified these amounts). (page 143)
42. (C) Step-up lease is a graduated lease. (page 139)
43. (B) As well as the responsibilities of the owner. (page 138)
44. (C) It is a naturally occurring gas linked to lung cancer. (page 145)

45. (B) Tenant can treat breach as proper cause to end lease obligations. (page 142)
46. (D) Followed by the unlawful detainer action. (page 142)
47. (A) With the landlord as a named insured. (page 147)
48. (B) A duty to rerent to keep damages low as possible. Can only sue for rent due not future rent. (page 144)
49. (C) Most oil-based house paints in use prior to 1978 had high concentrations of lead. (page 145)
50. (A) The consumer price index is commonly used in leases, so rent reflects the actual purchasing power. (page 139)

CHAPTER

Mathematics of Real Estate

The mathematics required for your state license examination consists of an understanding of simple addition, subtraction, multiplication, division, some basic formulas, percentages and decimals. If you understand the text material and are able to work the problems at the end of this chapter, you should have no difficulty with mathematics on your examination.

DECIMALS AND PERCENTAGES

A fraction such as ½ can be converted to a decimal by dividing the numerator (top number) by the denominator (bottom number):

$$1 \text{ (Numerator)} \div 2 \text{ (Denominator)} = .5$$

Further examples:

$$¾ = 3 \div 4 = .75$$
$$⅝ = 5 \div 8 = .6250$$

To convert a decimal to a percentage, move the decimal point two places to the right and add a percentage sign: 0.6 becomes 60%.

To convert a percent to a decimal, move the decimal point two places to the left and drop the percentage sign: 60% equals 0.6 or you can use the % button on your calculator.

Percentage Problems

There are 3 components to a percentage problem:

1. The percentage rate
2. The whole number
3. The part of the whole number

If you know any two of the above numbers or one of the numbers and the rate, you can find the third component using these three formulas:

1. $\text{Rate} = \dfrac{\text{Part}}{\text{Whole}}$

2. $\text{Whole} = \dfrac{\text{Part}}{\text{Rate}}$

3. $\text{Part} = \text{Rate} \times \text{Whole}$

A simple way to determine these three formulas is to use a *T bar:*

$$\div \quad \underline{\qquad \text{Part} \qquad} \quad \div$$
$$\text{Whole} \quad \times \quad \text{Rate}$$

If the line between the two known items is horizontal, then you can find the missing item by dividing the top number (dividend) by the bottom number (divisor). If the rate were unknown (missing) you would then divide the part by the whole to determine the rate:

$$\text{Rate} = \frac{\text{Part}}{\text{Whole}}$$

If the whole were missing you could determine the whole by dividing the part by the rate:

$$\text{Whole} = \frac{\text{Part}}{\text{Rate}}$$

If the line between the known items is vertical, which is the case when the part is unknown, you would multiply the known items to find the unknown item (part):

$$\text{Part} = \text{Rate} \times \text{Whole}$$

Finding the Rate

Use the formula:

$$\text{Rate} = \frac{\text{Part}}{\text{Whole}}$$

If the part is 20 and the whole is 50 then $20 \div 50 = .40$ or 40%

Problem $12,000 was paid as commission on a $200,000 sale. What percent commission was paid?

$$\text{Rate} = \frac{\text{Part}}{\text{Whole}}$$

$$\text{Rate} = \frac{\$12,000 \ \text{(Part)}}{\$200,000 \ \text{(Whole)}}$$

Rate of commission = 0.06 or 6%

Problem   An investor earned $1,200 interest on a $20,000 investment for one year. What was the interest rate earned?

$$\text{Rate (interest)} = \frac{\$1,200 \ \text{(Part)}}{\$20,000 \ \text{(Whole)}}$$

Interest Rate = 0.06 or 6%

In real estate we base our percentage returns on net income, which is part of the whole.

$$\text{Rate} = \frac{\text{Net}}{\text{Whole}}$$

Divide Into the Net

Percentage returns (rates) could be based on total price paid, down payments or an owner's equity.

$$\text{Rate} = \frac{\text{Net}}{\text{Total Price}}$$

$$\text{Rate} = \frac{\text{Net}}{\text{Down Payment}}$$

$$\text{Rate} = \frac{\text{Net}}{\text{Owner's Equity}}$$

Problem   An investor earned $24,150 on a $350,000 investment for one year. What was his percentage return?

$$\text{Rate} = \frac{\$24,150 \;\; (\text{Part})}{\$350,000 \;\; (\text{Whole})}$$

Percentage Rate = 0.069, or 6.9%

Problem   An owner has an $80,000 mortgage against a property worth $120,000. If the property nets $4,000 per year, what is the owner's percentage return on equity?

Value $120,000 – $80,000 Mortgage = $40,000 equity

$$\text{Percentage Return} = \frac{\$4,000 \;\; (\text{Part})}{\$40,000 \;\; (\text{Whole})}$$

Percentage return is percent on the owner's equity.

Finding the Whole Number

The formula is

$$\text{Whole} = \frac{\text{Part}}{\text{Rate}}$$

If the part is 20 and the rate is 40%, then

$$\frac{20}{0.40} = 50 \text{ is the whole}$$

Problem   6 percent commission was paid on a sale. The commission totaled $12,000. What was the selling price?

$$\text{Whole (selling price)} = \frac{\$12,000 \;(\text{Part})}{0.06 \;\;(\text{Rate})} = \$200,000 \text{ (selling price)}$$

Problem   An investor received $1,200 in interest for one year on a 6 percent investment. How much was invested?

$$\text{Principal (Whole)} = \frac{\$1,200 \;\; (\text{Part})}{0.06 \;\;\; (\text{Rate})}$$

$20,000 was invested.

Problem   Assume a seller wanted to net $23,500 from the sale of a lot after she had paid a 6 percent commission:

$23,500 = 94% of sale price (since it is sale price after 6% commission is paid); 94% as a decimal is 0.94.

$$\text{Whole} = \frac{\$23,500 \text{ (Part)}}{0.94 \quad \text{(Rate)}}$$

The whole is $25,000; and after the 6 percent commission ($1,500) is paid, the seller will have $23,500 left.

Problem   Property sold for $80,000, which is 40 percent more than it cost the seller. What did the seller originally pay?

80,000 is 40% more than cost, or 140% of cost (1.4 as a decimal)

$$\text{Whole} = \frac{\$80,000 \text{ (Part)}}{1.4 \quad \text{(Rate)}}$$

Whole (original cost) = $57,142.86

Finding the Part

To find the part of the whole number, multiply the percentage rate as a decimal by the whole number. If the rate is 40 percent (0.40 as a decimal) and the whole number is 50, then $0.40 \times 50 = 20$.

Commission is a percentage of the selling price (part of the whole) and is determined by multiplying percentage rate × selling price (the whole number).

Commission = Rate × Selling Price

If the rate was 6 percent (0.06) and the selling price was $200,000, then the commission would be $12,000:

$$0.06 \times \$200,000 = \$12,000$$

Problem   Assume a home sold for $165,000, which was 12 percent less than its list price. If it had sold at its list price, how much would the broker be entitled to if there were a 6 percent commission agreement?

Step 1: Find the list price.

The home sold for 88 percent of list price (12 percent less than list price)

$$\text{Whole} = \frac{\$165,000 \text{ (Part)}}{0.88 \quad \text{(Percentage)}}$$

Whole (List Price) = $187,500

Step 2: Find the part of the Whole (Commission).

Multiply percentage (0.06) × $187,500 (list price) = $11,250 which is what the commission would have been if the property had sold at list price.

INTEREST

Interest is the percentage return received or paid for the use of money. It is normally given as an annual rate.

Finding the Interest

To determine the amount of interest earned, take the amount of the loan (principal) times the rate of interest times the time (period) of the loan.

$$I = PRT$$
Interest = Principal × Rate × Time

The interest earned on $20,000 at 6 percent for one year is

Interest = $20,000 × 0.06 (6% stated as a decimal) × 1 = $1,200

Interest earned over six months is

Interest = $20,000 × 0.06 × 0.5 (½ year) = $600

Finding the Principal

This is found using the formula

$$\text{Whole} = \frac{\text{Part}}{\text{Rate}}$$

If $6 were earned in interest over a one-year period and the interest rate was 6 percent, then

$$\text{Whole} = \frac{\$6}{0.06}$$

The whole (principal) would be $100.

Finding the Interest Rate

This is the application of the formula

$$\text{Rate} = \frac{\text{Part}}{\text{Whole}}$$

If $6 were earned in interest over a one year period on an investment of $100, then

$$\text{Percentage (Interest Rate)} = \frac{\$6}{\$100}$$

The percentage of interest would be 6 percent.

Finding the Time

If rate of interest, amount of interest earned, and principal amount are known, the period of investment can be found by dividing interest earned by the amount of the principal by the rate of interest.

$$\text{Time} = \frac{\text{Interest Earned}}{\text{Principal} \times \text{Rate}}$$

The T bar will help you remember the above formula for finding the time because it is the entire T bar graph:

$$\div \quad \overline{\quad\quad \text{Part} \quad\quad} \quad \div$$
$$\text{Whole} \quad \times \quad \text{Rate}$$

$$\text{Time} = \frac{\text{Interest Earned (Part)}}{\text{Principal (Whole)} \times \text{Rate}}$$

Earnings of $1,200 on a $20,000 investment at 6 percent means the investment must have been for one year:

$$T = \frac{\$1,200}{\$20,000 \times 0.06} = \frac{\$1,200}{\$1,200} = 1 \text{ year}$$

NOTE: If you are still uncertain of the correct formula, test the formula by inserting known figures. For example, you know that $100 (principal) at 6 percent (rate of interest) for one year (time) will earn $6 (interest earned). If a given formula works properly when these test numbers are inserted, the formula likely is correct.

Plus Interest

A payment of $100 per month plus interest at 12 percent on a $10,000 loan would mean a first-month payment of $200.

$100 principal

$100 interest $(0.12 \times \$10,000 = \frac{\$1,200}{12} = \$100$ per month

The second month's payment on the same loan ($9,900 balance) would be $199.

$100 principal

$99 interest $(0.12 \times \$9,900 = \$1,188$ per year: $\frac{\$1,188}{12} = \$99$ for the second month

The third month's payment on the loan ($9,800 balance) would be $198.01.

$100 principal

$98.01 interest $(0.12 \times \$9,800 = \$1,176.12$ per year: $\frac{\$1,176.12}{12} = \$98.01$ for the third month

With plus interest loans, the principal decreases by the same amount each month while the amount of interest paid decreases each month, as do the total payments.

Including Interest

For a $10,000, 12 percent loan, equal monthly payments of $110.11 would amortize (liquidate) the loan over 20 years. The payments would be constant and include principal and interest. The first month's payment would be applied as follows:

$100 interest ($10,000 $\times$ .12 = $1,200 per year: $\frac{\$1,200}{12} = \$100$ for one month

$10.11 principal (balance of $110.11 payment)

The second month's payment would be applied as follows:

$99.90 interest ($9,989.89 balance of principal $\times$ 0.12 = $1,198.79 per year:

$$\frac{\$1,198.79}{12} = \$99.90 \text{ for one month}$$

$10.21 principal (balance of $110.11 payment)

Thus, an amortized equal-payment loan will result in the amount applied to principal increasing each month and the amount applied to interest decreasing by a like amount.

TAXES

As stated in Chapter 3, taxes on real property are ad valorem, taxed according to value. A tax rate normally is expressed per dollar of evaluation, or it could be per $100 or $1,000 of evaluation. Tax evaluation is set by a tax assessor and need not be the same as market value.

Assume a property was assessed at 50 percent of its market value of $80,000. If the tax rate were 0.03794 per dollar of evaluation, you would multiply the rate by the evaluation to determine the taxes.

If the rate above were expressed per $100 of evaluation, it would be 3.794 per $100, or $3.79 and 4 mills per $100. Simply move the decimal point two places to the left to find the rate per dollar of evaluation, and multiply the rate by the evaluation to determine the property tax. A mill is 1/10 of a cent or 1/1,000 of a dollar. It is expressed as a decimal: $.001.

In some areas of the country an equalization factor is used to make the assessed value more realistic. The assessed value would be multiplied by the equalization factor to determine the value for tax purposes.

If property were assessed at $125,000 and the equalization factor was 1.34, then the value to which the tax rate would apply would be $167,500 ($125,000 × 1.34).

PRORATIONS

To prorate means to divide proportionally. In real estate we divide income and expenses between buyer and seller at closing.

Prorating problems are more likely to be on broker examinations than on salesperson examinations.

Items to be prorated at closing could include prepaid rent, taxes, insurance (when the policy is assumed), prepaid service policies, interest, etc.

For proration purposes use 365 days for the calendar year and the actual days in the month unless an exam question states otherwise. Your examination question will also indicate who is responsible for the date of closing.

Example: Assume a contract for a home alarm system was paid in advance for one year at a cost of $485.45.

$$\$485.45 \div 365 = \$1.33 \text{ daily cost}$$

Assume that the seller paid the contract in advance starting July 1, 1999, and the contract was assumed by the buyer with the buyer responsible for the September 10, 1999, closing date. The seller would be responsible for July, August, and 9 days in September.

$$
\begin{array}{lr}
\text{July} & 31 \text{ days} \\
\text{August} & 31 \text{ days} \\
\text{September} & \underline{9 \text{ days}} \\
\text{Seller responsible:} & 71 \text{ days}
\end{array}
$$

$$71 \times \$1.33 = \$94.43$$

The buyer would be responsible for the balance of the contract.

$$\begin{array}{r} \$485.45 \\ -94.43 \\ \hline \$391.02 \end{array}$$

The buyer would be debited with $391.02 (prorated unused portion of the contract) and the seller would be credited this amount at settlement.

Interest Proration

Interest on loans is, in most states, paid in arrears, which means that a loan payment due August 1 would cover the July interest. In the case of a loan assumption during the month of July the buyer would be paying the entire July payment with the August payment. Therefore, the seller would owe the buyer for that portion of the month that the seller was responsible for.

Assume closing was July 15. If the seller was responsible for the day of closing, then the seller would be responsible for 15 days' interest. If the buyer were responsible for the day of closing, the seller would only be responsible for 14 days' interest. To determine seller responsibility, you would divide the interest for the month of July by 31 to find the daily rate and then multiply by the number of days of seller responsibility. The seller would be debited this amount and the buyer credited this amount in the closing statement.

Note: In some areas prorations do not use calendar days but instead use the **banker's method**, which is based on every month having 30 days and there being 360 days in the year.

AREA AND VOLUME

Square Footage

To find the square footage of a square or rectangle, multiply the length (in feet) by the width (in feet).

For example, a 40′ × 140′ lot contains 5,600 square feet.

A right triangle is half of a rectangle. Therefore, the square footage of a right triangle is one-half the length times the width. The square footage of the 50′ × 60′ rectangle shown here is 3,000. Half of that number—1,500 square feet—is the area of the triangle.

When determining square feet of a building, we ordinarily use exterior measurements excluding garages and porches. *Floor space*, however, uses interior dimensions.

Square Yards

There are nine square feet in one square yard:

Be sure to convert square feet to square yards, or vice versa, to match the problem or answers.

Perimeter

The perimeter is the outer boundary of an area. To find the perimeter of an area, first determine all of the dimensions. For example, find the perimeter of the following parcel:

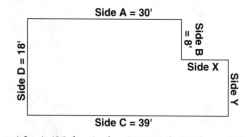

Side X is 9 feet because side A (30 feet) plus X equals 39 feet. Side Y would be 10 feet because side B (8 feet) plus Y equals 18 feet. Therefore, 30 feet (A) plus 8 feet (B) plus 9 feet (X) plus 10 feet (Y) plus 39 feet (C) plus 18 feet (D) equals 114 feet.

Assume a three-foot walk was to be built around the perimeter of the area and you needed to know the number of square feet for the walk. You would start by drawing the parcel and walk.

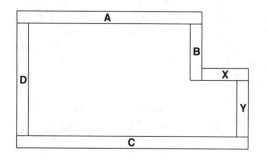

The walk on side A would be 36′ × 3′, or 108 sq. ft.
The walk on side B would be   8′ × 3′, or   24 sq. ft.
The walk on side X would be   9′ × 3′, or   27 sq. ft.
The walk on side Y would be 10′ × 3′, or   30 sq. ft.
The walk on side C would be 45′ × 3′, or 135 sq. ft.
The walk on side D would be 18′ × 3′, or   54 sq. ft.
              Total sq. ft. of walk =   378 sq. ft.

To find the number of square yards, divide by 9: $\dfrac{378}{9}$ = 42 square yards.

Volume

In some areas of the country, appraisers use a cubic foot method. To find the volume (cubic measure), multiply length by width by height. For example, a cubic yard contains 27 cubic feet (3′ × 3′ × 3′). Therefore, a room 10′ × 9′ × 8′ contains 720 cubic feet.

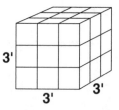

FINDING ONE DIMENSION OF A RECTANGLE

To find one dimension of a rectangular-shaped parcel when one dimension and the total square area are known, divide the known dimension into the area.

$$\text{Unknown Dimension} = \frac{\text{Area}}{\text{Known Dimension}}$$

The diagram on the right shows a rectangular parcel having a width of 100 feet and a total area of one acre (1 acre = 43,560 square feet). Therefore the depth of the rectangle would be:

1 acre

100'

$$\frac{43,560}{100} = 435.6 \text{ feet}$$

AMORTIZATION

Monthly Amortization Table for a $1,000 Loan

No. of Years	9%	10%	11%	12%
5	20.76	21.15	21.75	22.45
10	12.67	13.22	13.78	14.35
15	10.15	10.75	11.37	12.02
20	9.00	9.66	10.33	11.01
25	8.40	9.09	9.81	10.54
30	8.05	8.78	9.53	10.29

Using the amortization table, assume *C* borrowed $130,000 at 11 percent interest for 30 years and *D* borrowed $130,000 at 10 percent interest for 15 years. *D*'s total interest payments would be what percentage of *C*'s total interest payments?

Because payments are monthly, *C* would make 360 payments (12 × 30). Payments would be $9.53 per $1,000, or $1,238.90 per month (130 × 9.53).

$1,238.90 × 360 = $446,004   Total payments
                      −130,000   Principal
                      $316,004   Interest

D would make 180 monthly payments on a 15-year loan (12 × 15). Monthly payments would be $1,397.50 ($10.75 × 130).

$1,397.50 × 180 = $251,550   Total payments
                      −130,000   Principal
                      $121,550   Interest

C paid $316,004 interest.
D paid $121,550 interest.

D paid 38.5% of the interest *C* paid.

$$\frac{\$121,550}{\$316,004} = .3846, \text{ or } 38.5\%$$

CHAPTER 8 QUIZ

Mathematics of Real Estate

1. An office manager was paid $1,000 per month plus ¼ of one percent of all office sales. In November, she received $2,780. This amount was based on monthly sales of:

   (A) $ 556,000
   (B) $ 712,000
   (C) $ 912,000
   (D) $1,112,000

2. What investment is necessary for a yield of $500 per month at 6 percent interest?

   (A) $8,333.33
   (B) $60,000.00
   (C) $100,000.00
   (D) $120,000.00

3. A 30-acre rectangular parcel has 660 feet on the street side. What is the depth of the parcel in feet?

   (A) 738.42
   (B) 963.7
   (C) 1,240
   (D) 1,980

4. A list price was set to leave the owner with $90,000 after a 6 percent commission was deducted from the sales price. What was the list price?

   (A) $95,400.00
   (B) $95,745.00
   (C) $95,905.66
   (D) $96,000.00

5. Which is the correct formula to determine the interest rate?

   (A) Interest Rate = Interest Earned ÷ Principal
   (B) Interest Rate = Interest Earned × Principal × Time
   (C) Interest Rate = Interest Earned ÷ Time
   (D) Interest Rate = Interest Earned × Time

6. The next monthly interest payment on a loan balance of $17,835 is $132.28. The interest rate on the loan is what percent?

   (A 6.78
   (B) 7.4
   (C) 8.9
   (D) 13.48

7. On a 70-foot-by-70-foot rectangular lot, the side yard building setbacks are 10 feet. The front yard setback is 25 feet, and the rear setback is 20 feet. What is the maximum square footage possible for a one-story structure?

   (A) 1,000
   (B) 1,200
   (C) 1,250
   (D) 4,900

8. *J* purchased 4 lots at $12,000 each and divided them into 6 lots that were sold for $9,600 each. What was *J's* percentage of profit based on his cost?

   (A) 6%
   (B) 12%
   (C) 20%
   (D) 24%

9. *K* purchased a property for $175,000. *K* wishes to sell the property. If the total selling costs will equal 11 percent of the sale price, how much will the property have to appreciate in value for *K* to break even?

   (A) $19,612
   (B) $20,311
   (C) $21,629
   (D) $23,730

10. A mill would be expressed as:

   (A) $ .001
   (B) $ .01
   (C) $ .1
   (D) $1.0

11. A house purchased four years ago for $50,000 has increased in value by 10 percent each year since purchase. The house is now worth:

    (A) $66,550
    (B) $70,000
    (C) $73,205
    (D) $90,000

12. Builder *J* received a bridge loan for $72,500 at 12 percent interest. If his total interest costs were $5,075, how many months did it take *J* to pay off the loan?

    (A) 4½ months
    (B) 6 months
    (C) 7 months
    (D) 8 months

13. A property with a gross annual income of $20,000 has a value of $120,000. The only expense is the 11 percent interest payment on a $100,000 straight mortgage. What is the owner's percentage return on equity?

    (A) 16.6%
    (B) 20%
    (C) 22.2%
    (D) 45%

14. A one-acre site has a 40′ × 100′ building. The building occupies what percentage of the site?

    (A) .025%
    (B) 2.5%
    (C) 9.2%
    (D) 11.1%

15. *D* sold a note to *E* at a 32 percent discount. *D* received $5,304. What was the amount due on the note?

    (A) $1,697
    (B) $6,800
    (C) $7,420
    (D) $7,800

16. A 50-acre rectangular industrial site fronting on a highway is 1,000 feet deep. Assuming a sales price of $3,000 per acre, what is the price per front foot?

    (A) $ 68.87
    (B) $ 74.93
    (C) $ 150.00
    (D) $3,443.52

17. A fully rented ten-unit apartment building has rents of $500 per month. A 10 percent rent increase brings a 10 percent vacancy factor. The gross income:

    (A) remains the same.
    (B) increases 1%
    (C) increases 9%
    (D) decreases 1%

18. A driveway was one-half mile long and was two acres in total area. How wide was the road?

    (A) 11 feet
    (B) 21 feet
    (C) 33 feet
    (D) 37 feet

19. A six-foot-wide sidewalk is to be constructed inside the perimeter (on the lot line) of two adjacent sides of a 60′ × 100′ rectangular corner lot. The sidewalk will contain how many square feet?

    (A) 900
    (B) 924
    (C) 960
    (D) 1,600

20. A six-foot-wide sidewalk is to be constructed outside the perimeter on two adjacent sides of the lot described in question 19. The sidewalk will contain how many square feet?

    (A) 960
    (B) 996
    (C) 1,032
    (D) 1,660

21. How many cubic yards of concrete are needed in a 30-foot driveway 18 feet wide and 4 inches thick?

   (A) 7
   (B) 20
   (C) 180
   (D) 540

22. The last monthly interest payment on a mortgage was $825.77. If the interest rate was 7.2 percent, what was the balance due on the principal?

   (A) $118,764
   (B) $131,741
   (C) $137,628
   (D) $158,730

23. *J*, a seller, and *K*, a buyer, have agreed to split all closing costs, with the seller paying 60 percent and the buyer paying 40 percent. The costs are as follows: title insurance, $420; fees for drafting and recording documents, $222; miscellaneous costs, $248. How much more will *J* pay than *K*?

   (A) $178
   (B) $184
   (C) $196
   (D) $204

24. *L* purchased a lot for $9,000, and he listed the lot for sale at 40 percent more than he paid. Unable to find a buyer, he reduced his price by 30 percent. He found a buyer at the reduced price. After paying a 7 percent commission, what was the profit or loss?

   (A) Profit of $207.00
   (B) Profit of $270.00
   (C) Loss of $180.00
   (D) Loss of $797.40

25. *J* has agreed to buy *K's* house for $140,000 with a $20,000 down payment. The balance is to be paid under a contract for deed having interest payments only. Interest is to be at 9½ percent, with the total principal amount due in five years. How much interest will *J* pay under the life of the contract?

   (A) $46,812
   (B) $47,500
   (C) $57,000
   (D) $64,000

26. How many acres is 348,480 square yards?

   (A) 2.66
   (B) 8
   (C) 24
   (D) 72

27. Builders' blueprints frequently use the scale of ¼ inch equals 1 foot. If a plan indicated a family room 10½ inches by 3½ inches, what would floor tile cost at $7.60 per square yard?

   (A) $ 496.50
   (B) $ 622.32
   (C) $1,489.60
   (D) $4,468.80

28. A salesperson was to receive 30 percent of the office share of the commission for obtaining a listing. The salesperson listed a house for $185,000, and it was sold for $170,000 by another office with the selling office receiving one-half of the 6 percent commission. The salesperson's listing commission was:

   (A) $ 1,530
   (B) $ 3,060
   (C) $ 3,330
   (D) $10,200

29. A 90' × 60' building needs floor covering. Sixty percent of the building will be carpeted at a cost of $16 per square yard, and the remainder will be tiled at a cost of $8 per square yard. The cost of the floor covering will be:

    (A) $ 2,560
    (B) $ 5,760
    (C) $ 7,680
    (D) $23,040

30. A rectangular lot with 80 feet of frontage has adjoining rectangular lots of equal 160-foot depth on each side. One of these side lots contains 12,800 square feet, and the other has 9,600 square feet. The combined front footage of the three lots equals how many feet?

    (A) 140
    (B) 200
    (C) 220
    (D) 250

31. A man willed his estate as follows: 54 percent to his wife, 18 percent to his daughter, 16 percent to his son, and the remainder to his church. The church received $79,000. The daughter received:

    (A) $105,333
    (B) $118,500
    (C) $355,500
    (D) $658,333

32. A railroad divided three sections of land into parcels of 20 acres each and then sold 16 of the parcels for $4,000 each. The remainder sold for $5,000 each. What was the total sales price?

    (A) $ 64,000
    (B) $ 84,000
    (C) $264,000
    (D) $464,000

33. A 100-acre parcel is to be subdivided. Seventeen percent of the land will be utilized for streets. How many 80´ × 120' lots are possible?

    (A) 349
    (B) 376
    (C) 411
    (D) 437

34. An income property sold for $400,000 to an investor who planned on a 9 percent return on investment. An investor who wanted a 12 percent return would have paid how much for the property?

    (A) $300,000
    (B) $330,000
    (C) $360,000
    (D) $400,000

35. A broker listed a lot for $23,000 with a 7 percent commission agreement. The broker brought in an offer of $20,000. The owner agreed to accept the offer if the broker paid the delinquent property taxes of $240. The broker agreed. What percentage commission did the broker actually earn on this sale?

    (A) 5.8%
    (B) 6.2%
    (C) 6.4%
    (D) 6.7%

36. An investor owes $90,000 on a building worth $120,000. The net income is $6,000, which would give the investor a percentage return on equity of:

    (A) 10%
    (B) 20%
    (C) 30%
    (D) 40%

37. Five condominiums were sold at $165,000, $195,200, $225,000, $265,600, and $296,000. Together the units have annual property maintenance expenses of $15,400, which the owners share on a pro rata basis, based on the cost of their units. The lowest-priced unit had a monthly assessment of:

    (A) $ 57.56
    (B) $156.56
    (C) $184.65
    (D) $221.52

38. Of the following transactions, which will result in the greatest net proceeds to the seller?

	Sales Price	Commission	Closing Costs
A.	$110,000	7%	$1,280
B.	$108,000	6%	$1,308
C.	$106,000	4%	$ 820
D.	$105,000	3%	$ 980

39. The monthly amortized payments on a 7 percent, 30-year, $100,000 amortized loan are $665.31. How much would be paid for interest over the amortization period?

    (A) $ 96,851
    (B) $139,511
    (C) $159,674
    (D) $239,511

40. The last month's interest on a 12 percent amortized loan was $923.18. The balance due was:

    (A) $ 1,178.16
    (B) $ 7,693.00
    (C) $ 92,318.00
    (D) $110,781.00

41. A rectangular property sold for $6,400, or $0.40 per square foot. The parcel had a depth of 200 feet. What price did the buyer pay per front foot?

    (A) $16
    (B) $32
    (C) $40
    (D) $80

42. A fire insurance policy has a one-year premium of $430.70. The daily proration of the policy would be:

    (A) $1.14
    (B) $1.18
    (C) $1.20
    (D) $1.26

43. A property that offers a 7.5 percent return on the listing price has a monthly net of $810. The property is listed at:

    (A) $ 9,720
    (B) $ 10,800
    (C) $129,600
    (D) $138,400

44. *F* sold a lot for 30 percent more than she paid for it. She invested the entire sales price at 14 percent interest. The interest on this investment gave her $820 per year. What did *F* originally pay for the lot?

    (A) $4,505
    (B) $5,123
    (C) $5,857
    (D) $9,837

45. An apartment has an annual gross income of $64,000. The net income is 30 percent of the gross. An investor who wants an 11 percent return on the purchase price would pay no more than:

    (A) $174,545
    (B) $192,000
    (C) $581,818
    (D) $831,168

46. A 120′ × 80′ warehouse with a 15-foot-high ceiling is listed for sale at $55 per cubic yard. What is the list price per square foot?

    (A) $20.37
    (B) $27.00
    (C) $30.55
    (D) $53.33

47. *L* made a $30,000, 15-year home equity loan at 9 percent interest with monthly payments of $304.28. How much of *L's* second payment would apply to interest?

    (A) $224
    (B) $228
    (C) $247
    (D) $293

48. *J* purchased six acres of land for $1,800 per acre and divided them into 14 lots, which *J* sold for $1,150 each. *J's* return on the purchase price is what percent?

    (A) 18%
    (B) 21%
    (C) 25%
    (D) 49%

49. Two houses sold together for $245,000. One house sold for $15,000 more than the other house. What was the price of the least expensive house?

    (A) $109,000
    (B) $115,000
    (C) $118,000
    (D) $120,000

50. A business had sales of $1,500,000. The business had a markup of 90 percent of cost. What was the cost of merchandise sold?

    (A) $ 789,474
    (B) $ 812,622
    (C) $ 971,600
    (D) $1,120,333

CHAPTER 8 QUIZ ANSWERS

Mathematics of Real Estate

1. (B) $2,780 – $1,000 (salary) =
    $1,780 attributable to sales

    $$\text{Whole} = \frac{\$1,780 \text{ (part)}}{0.0025 \text{ (percentage as a decimal) ¼ of 1\%}}$$

    Whole = $712,000 Total office sales (page 158)

2. (C) $500 per month = $6,000 per year

    $$\text{Whole} = \frac{\$6,000 \text{ (part)}}{0.06 \text{ (percentage as a decimal)}}$$

    Whole = $100,000 investment yielding $6,000 per year at 6% (page 158)

3. (D)   Known dimension: 660'. Total area 30 acres, or $30 \times 43,560 = 1,306,000$ square feet. To find one dimension of a rectangle when total area and other dimensions are known, divide the known dimension into the total area. :

    $$\frac{1,306,000}{660} = 1,980' \qquad \text{(page 165)}$$

4. (B) $90,000 is left after 6% of the sales is taken out, so 94% of list price is $90,000.

    $$\text{Whole} = \frac{90,000 \text{ (part)}}{0.94 \text{ (percentage as a decimal)}}$$

    List price $95,744.68 rounded off to $95,745 (pages 158–159)

5. (A)   The rate is (Page 157)

    $$\text{Rate} = \frac{\text{Part (interest earned)}}{\text{Whole (principal)}}$$

6. (C)   Monthly interest of $132.28 $\times$ 12 = yearly interest of $1,587.36

    $$\text{Rate} = \frac{\$1,587.36 \text{ (Part)}}{\$17,835 \text{ (Whole)}} = 0.089 \text{ or } 8.9\% \qquad \text{(page 157)}$$

7. (C)   Building maximum width is 50 feet because there are 10-foot setbacks on each side. Maximum depth is 25 feet since front yard and rear yard setbacks total 45 feet (70' – 45'). Multiply width (50') by depth (25') to find square footage. (page 163)

8. (C)   4 lots at $12,000 each = $48,000 cost
    6 lots at $9,600 each = $57,600 selling price
    $57,600 – $48,000 = $9,600 profit
    To find percentage we divide the net by the cost:

    $$\text{Percentage} = \frac{\$9,600 \text{ (Net)}}{\$48,000 \text{ (Cost)}}$$

    or 0.02, which is 20%. (page 158)

9. (C)   To break even, the sale price must be $175,000 plus 11% of the sale price, so $175,000 = 89% of the sale price.

    $$\text{Whole} = \frac{\$175,000 \text{ (Part)}}{-.89 \text{ (Rate)}}$$

    Sale price would be $196,629. But the question asks for appreciation, so 196,629 – $175,000 = $21,629. (page 158)

10. (A) A mill is ⅒th of a cent and a cent is 0.01. (page 162)

11. (C) The house has appreciated in value by 10 percent each year. (page 159)

$50,000 + 10% = $55,000 value at end of 1st year
$55,000 + 10% = $60,500 value at end of 2nd year
$60,500 + 10% = $66,550 value at end of 3rd year
$66,550 + 10% = $73,205 value at end of 4th year

12. (C) To find the time, you can use the formula (pages 160–161)

$$\text{Time} = \frac{\text{Interest Earned}}{\text{Principal} \times \text{Rate}}$$

$$\text{Time} = \frac{\$5,075}{\$72,550 \times 0.12}$$

$$\text{Time} = \frac{\$5,075}{\$8,700} = 0.5833 \text{ of a year}$$

(1 month) ¹⁄₁₂ = 0.0833
Divide 0.5833 by 0.0833 to find time in months or:
$72,500 × 0.12 = $8,700 interest
$8,700 ÷ 12 = $725 interest cost per month
$5,075 ÷ $725 = 7 months

13. (D) Gross = $20,000
Expenses = 11% of $100,000 or $11,000. Net would be $20,000 – $11,000 = $9,000.
Equity is difference between value ($120,000) and the mortgage ($100,000), or $20,000. (page 158)

$$\text{Percentage Return} \quad \frac{\$9,000 \;\; \text{Net}}{\$20,000 \;\; \text{Equity}} = 0.45 \text{ or } 45\%$$

14. (C) 40′ × 100′ = 4,000 sq. ft., 1 acre = 43,560 sq. ft., Percentage = 4,000 (Part) = 0.092 or 9.2%; 43,560 (Whole) (pages 157, 163)

15. (D) Note sold at 32% discount, so it sold at 68% of amount due. (page 159)

$$\text{Whole} = \frac{\$5,304 \;\; \text{(Part)}}{0.68 \;\; \text{(Percentage as decimal)}} = \$7,800$$

16. (A) 50 acres = 43,560 × 50 = 2,178,000 sq. ft. (page 165)
To find one dimension of a rectangle divide the total area by known dimension.

$$\frac{2,178,000}{1,000} = 2,178 \text{ feet frontage}$$

Sale price was 50 × $3,000 or $150,000. To find price per front foot divide cost ($150,000) by front footage (2,178); $150,000 ÷ 2,178 = $68.87 per front foot.

17. (D) 10 × $500 = $5,000 per month
9 (10% vacancy) × $550 = $4,950 or $50 less in rent, which is 1% of $5,000. (page 156)

18. (C) Divide total area (87,120 sq. ft. because it is 2 acres) by known dimension (2,640′ because it is one-half mile. (page 165)

19. (B) 100′ × 6′ +54′ = 924 sq. ft. (We don't want to count the corner area twice.) (page 164)

20. (B) $100' \times 6' + 60' \times 6' + 6' \times 6' = 996$ square feet. (We don't want to miss the corner.) (page 164)

21. (A) $18' \times 30' = 540$ square feet. Four inches thick is ⅓ of a foot, so the cubic footage of the driveway would take ⅓ of 540 square feet. (page 164) :

$$\frac{540}{3} = 180 \text{ cubic feet.}$$

Because there are 27 cubic feet in a cubic yard, $180 \div 27$ equals 6.6 yards (but you would need 7 yards).

22. (C)   (page 158)

$$\text{Whole} = \frac{\text{Part}}{\text{Rate}}$$

$825.77 is interest for 1 month, so for a year it would be $825.77 × $9,909.24.

$$\text{Whole} = \frac{\$9,909.24 \text{ (Part – Interest)}}{0.072 \quad \text{Interest rate as decimal}}$$

23. (A) $420 + $222 + $248 = $890 total costs (page 159)

60% of $890 = $534
40% of $890 = $356
$534 – $356 = $178

24. (D) $9,000 paid × 1.40 (listed at 40% more than paid) = $12,600 (list price); $12,600 × 0.30 = $3,780 (reduction). (page 159)

$12,600 – $3,780 = $8,820 (sales price) $8,820 × 0.07 (commission) = $617.40 (commission)
$8,820 – $617.40 = $8,202.60
$9,000 – $8,202.60 = Loss of $797.40

25. (C) $140,000 – $20,000 = $120,000 balance

$120,000 × 0.095 × 5 = $57,000 (page 160)

26. (D)   348,480 sq. yd. × 9 (number of square feet in a square yard) = 3,136,320 sq. ft. Divide by the number of square feet in an acre. (page 163)

$$\frac{3,136,320}{43,560} = 72 \text{ acres}$$

27. (A)   Each inch would equal 4 feet, so 10½" = 42' and 3½", which equals 14'. (page 163)

42 × 14 = 588 sq. ft.
There are 9 square feet in a square yard, so:
588 ÷ 9 = 65.33 yards
65.33 × $7.60 = $496.50, cost of floor tile

28. (A) $170,000 × 0.06 = $10,200. The office share was one-half, or $5,100.
0.30 × $5,100 = $1,530 commission. (page 159)

29. (C) (page 163)

$$
\begin{array}{rcl}
90' \times 60 &=& 5,400 \text{ sq. ft.} \\
5,400' \div 9 &=& 600 \text{ sq. yards} \\
60\% \text{ of } 600 &=& 360 \\
360 \times \$16 &=& \$5,760 \\
40\% \text{ of } 600 &=& 240 \\
240 \times \$8 &=& \$1,920 \\
\text{Total:} && \$7,680, \text{ cost of floor covering}
\end{array}
$$

30. (C) The two side lots have 12,800 and 9,600 square feet, or a total of 22,400 square feet. (pages 163, 165)

The depth is 160'. Frontage is 22,400 divided by 160, or 140'. With the 80' of the central lot, the combined total is 220'.

31. (B) The church received 12 percent of his estate: (pages 158, 159)

12% of estate was $79,000

$$\text{Whole} = \frac{\$79,000}{.12} \begin{array}{l} \text{(Part)} \\ \text{(Percentage as decimal)} \end{array}$$

Total estate was $658,333. The daughter received 18 percent or $658,333.33 × 0.18.

32. (D) There are 640 acres in a section, so three sections equal 1,920 acres. (page 159)

$$
\begin{array}{l}
1,920 \div 20 = 96 \ \ 20\text{-acre parcels} \\
16 \text{ sold at } \$4,000 \text{ each } = \ \$\ \ 64,000 \\
80 \text{ sold at } \$5,000 \text{ each } = \underline{\$400,000} \\
\phantom{80 \text{ sold at } \$5,000 \text{ each }} \text{Total } = \ \$464,000 \text{ sales price}
\end{array}
$$

33. (B)
$$
\begin{array}{l}
100 \times 43,560 = 4,356,000 \text{ square feet} \\
17\% \text{ or } 740,520 \text{ sq. ft. for streets} \\
4,356,000 - 740,520 = 3,615,480 \text{ net} \\
80 \times 120 = 9,600 \text{ square feet} \\
3,615,480 \div 9,600 = 376.6 \text{ (page 159, 163)}
\end{array}
$$

34. (A)
$$
\begin{array}{l}
\text{Part} = \text{Rate} \times \text{Whole} \\
\text{Part} = 0.09 \times \$400,000 \\
\text{Part} = \$36,000, \text{ which is return} \\
\text{For 12\% return:}
\end{array}
$$

$$\text{Whole} = \frac{\$36,000}{0.12} \begin{array}{l} \text{(Return)} \\ \text{(Percentage as decimal)} \end{array} = \$300,000 \text{ (pages 158, 159)}$$

35. (A) 7% of $20,000 = $1,400

$$
\begin{array}{r}
\underline{-\ \ \ 240} \\
\$1,160 \text{ net}
\end{array}
$$

To find percentage return, divide into net by sale price.

$$\frac{\$1,160 \ \ \text{(Net)}}{20,000 \ \ \text{(Sale price)}} = 0.058 \text{ or } 5.8\% \qquad \text{(page 159)}$$

36. (B) (page 158)

$$\frac{\text{Net}}{\text{Equity}} = \text{Percentage Return}; \ \frac{\$6,000}{\$30,000} = .020$$

37. (C) The total cost of all units (whole) = $1,146,800 (page 157)

$$\text{Rate} = \frac{\$165,000 \ \ \text{(Part)}}{\$1,146,800 \ \ \text{(Whole)}}$$

Rate for unit is 0.14388 or 14.388% of total costs

$$
\begin{array}{ll}
\$\ \ 15,400 \times 0.14388 &= \$2,215.75 \text{ per year} \\
\$2,215.75 \div 12 &= \$184.65 \text{ per month}
\end{array}
$$

38. (A) $110,000 – 7% – $1,280 = $101,020. (page 159)

39. (B) $665.31 × 12 (months) × 30 (years) = $239,511 in total payments. Deduct the principal ($100,000) to determine the interest paid. (page 165)

40. (C) 12 percent per annum is 1 percent per month. So $923.18 is 1 percent of $92,318. Or

$$\text{Principal} = \frac{\text{Interest Earned}}{\text{Rate of Interest}}$$

$$\text{Principal} = \frac{\$923.18 \times 12 \text{ (1 year)}}{0.12}$$

$$\text{Principal} = \frac{\$11,078.16}{0.12} = \$92,318 \qquad \text{(page 158)}$$

41. (D) (page 165)

$ 6,400 ÷ $.40 = 16,000 sq. ft.
16,000 ÷ 200 = 80' wide
$ 6,400 ÷ 80 = $80 per front ft.

42. (B) Use 365 days unless question indicates otherwise. $430.70 ÷ 365 = 1.18 (page 162)

43. (C) Monthly net is $810, so $810 × 12 = $9,720 per year (page 158)

$$\text{Whole (list price)} = \frac{\$9,720 \text{ (Part)}}{0.075 \text{ (Percentage as a decimal)}}$$

44. (A) (pages 158-159)

$$\text{Whole} = \frac{\$820 \text{ (Part)}}{0.014 \text{ (Percentage as a decimal)}}$$

Whole (Sale price) = $5,857. This was 30% more than *F* paid or 130% of what *F* paid.

$$\text{Whole} = \text{(Price paid)} \frac{\$5,857 \text{ (Part)}}{1.3 \text{ (Percentage as a decimal)}}$$

F paid $4,505

45. (A) Net is 30 percent of $64,000, or $19,200 (pages 158, 159)

$$\frac{\$19,200}{0.11} = \$174,545$$

46. (C) 120' × 80' × 15' = 144,000 cubic feet. (page 163)

$$\frac{144,000}{27} = 5,333.33 \text{ cubic yards}$$

5,333.33 × $55 = $293,333.33 list price
120 × 80 = 9,600 sq. ft.

$$\frac{\$293,333.33}{9,600} = \$30.55 \text{ per sq. ft.}$$

47. (A) (page 161)

0.09 × $30,000	= $2,700	
$ 2,700 ÷ 12	= $225, first month's interest payment	
$ 304.28 – $225	= $79.28, applied to principal	
$ 30,000 – $79.28	= $29,920.72, balance after first payment	
.09 × $29,920.72	= $2,692.86	
$2,692.86 ÷ 12	= $224 interest	

48. (D) (page 158)

$ 1,150 × 14 = $16,100 sales price
$ 1,800 × 6 = $10,800 purchase price
$16,100 − $10,800 = $5,300 profit

To find the percentage return on the purchase price, divide the purchase price into the net.

$$\frac{\$5,300}{\$10,800} = 0.49, \text{ or } 49\%$$

49. (B)

2 Houses = $245,000
House + House + $15,000 = $245,000
2 Houses + $15,000 = $245,000
2 Houses = $230,000

Least expensive house sold for $115,000.

50. (A) Cost was marked up 90 percent, so merchandise sold at 190% of cost. (page 158)

$$\text{Whole} = \frac{1,500,000 \text{ (Part)}}{0.9 \quad \text{(Percentage as a decimal)}}$$

Review Tests

The five review tests have been weighted to reflect the emphasis given to the various areas on the ASI Salespersons examination.

We have attempted to arrange these five examinations in an ascending order of difficulty. As an example, if you take the Level I exam first, your score should be higher than your score would be if you took the Level V examination first.

Some of the questions we have included are more likely to be covered on a broker's examination than on a salesperson's examination, particularly questions in Levels IV and V.

DIFFICULTY LEVEL I

1. Which of the following broker actions is an example of blockbusting?

   (A) Refusing to sell or rent to prospects because of race
   (B) Refusing to rent to families with children
   (C) Soliciting listings based on a fear of racial change in an area
   (D) Directing people to an area based on race

2. The phrase "definite duration" refers to a(n):

   (A) life estate
   (B) estate for years
   (C) estate at will
   (D) periodic tenancy

3. A lease that automatically renews itself, in the absence of notice, would be a(n):

   (A) estate for years
   (B) net lease
   (C) month-to-month tenancy
   (D) percentage lease

4. C just sold a condominium for $80,000. This gave C a 20 percent profit on what C paid. What did C pay?

   (A) $ 64.000
   (B) $ 66,666
   (C) $120,000
   (D) $662,800

5. A house that gains in value because of higher-cost homes being built in the area is an example of the principle of:

   (A) change
   (B) contribution
   (C) progression
   (D) conformity

6. A business wishes to increase its liquidity while reducing its long-term debt. This would be possible with a:

   (A) piggyback loan
   (B) sale-leaseback
   (C) wraparound loan
   (D) nonconforming loan

7. In real estate, the term *steering* refers to:

   (A) directing buyers to properties that best meet their needs
   (B) engaging in the qualification process for buyers
   (C) directing people to or away from areas based on their race, religion, or national origin
   (D) dividing apartment buildings into adult-only and family areas

8. In a buyer's closing statement, the selling price is:

   (A) a debit to the buyer
   (B) a credit to the buyer
   (C) assumed by the seller
   (D) less the amount to be paid for commission

9. What deduction from income does a homeowner have for tax purposes?

   (A) Interest expense
   (B) Insurance cost
   (C) Depreciation
   (D) Maintenance expense

10. The requirement that a booklet entitled *Protect Your Family from Lead Paint* be given to buyers and lessees applies to:

    (A) single-family homes only
    (B) one to four residential units only
    (C) all property built prior to 1968
    (D) residential property built prior to 1978

11. An apartment owner takes an equal amount of depreciation as an expense each year. This is:

    (A) straight-line depreciation
    (B) a method to increase book value
    (C) known as *accelerated depreciation*
    (D) a violation of the IRS code

12. Which of the following is both a lien and an encumbrance?

    (A) A restrictive covenant
    (B) An easement
    (C) A lease
    (D) A mortgage

13. To locate buyers for other properties, a broker advertised a property that was not available but which would generate great interest. The broker's action violated:

    (A) RESPA
    (B) Truth-in-Lending
    (C) ADA
    (D) the Sherman Act

14. A property manager's duties include:

    (A) preparing the owner's tax returns
    (B) giving the owner legal advice
    (C) collecting rent
    (D) devising a tax strategy to minimize the owner's taxes

15. The first step in the appraisal process is to:

    (A) determine the highest and best use
    (B) do a reconciliation
    (C) define the problem
    (D) determine land value

16. A property manager may properly refuse to rent a second floor apartment to a(n):

    (A) unmarried pregnant woman
    (B) blind person with a guide dog
    (C) person who is ill with AIDS
    (D) person addicted to drugs

17. *Market value* is defined as:

    (A) assessed value less depreciation
    (B) the probable price a willing, informed buyer would pay to a willing, informed seller
    (C) subjective value
    (D) utility value of the property to the owner

18. An agent's sales commission is set by:

    (A) state law
    (B) professional rules and regulations
    (C) the MLS
    (D) negotiation

19. A lessee has the right to have a portion of the rent apply to a purchase. The lessee could have a(n):

    (A) option to purchase
    (B) residential lease
    (C) recapture clause
    (D) condemnation right

20. The basic fire policy of insurance covers:

    (A) lightning
    (B) water damage
    (C) earthquake damage
    (D) flood damage

21. If no period is set for a residential tenancy but rent is to be paid monthly, the lease is a:

    (A) month-to-month tenancy
    (B) lease for one month only
    (C) lease for one year
    (D) week-to-week rental

22. Functional obsolescence can be created by:

    (A) deterioration of the driveway
    (B) an overimprovement
    (C) deterioration of another property
    (D) forces outside the property itself

23. An apartment complex of 420 units has 21 vacancies. What is the vacancy rate?

    (A) 4 percent
    (B) 5 percent
    (C) 6 percent
    (D) 7 percent

24. A minor cannot list property the minor owns with a broker because:

    (A) a minor cannot appoint an agent
    (B) of the statute of frauds
    (C) of the statute of limitations
    (D) of laches

25. Which of the following is true of a blind ad?

    (A) It fails to include the owner's name.
    (B) It omits the property address.
    (C) It does not include a price.
    (D) It fails to indicate the advertiser is an agent.

26. A builder wanted the listing to reflect $85 per square foot for a 2,500-square-foot home plus $75,000 for the lot after the 6 percent commission was paid. What should the home be listed at to meet the builder's wishes?

    (A) $212,500
    (B) $287,500
    (C) $304,750
    (D) $305,851

27. In using the sales comparison approach an appraiser would use comparables from a:

    (A) foreclosure sale
    (B) sheriff's sale
    (C) similar neighborhood
    (D) tax sale

28. Salesperson *J's* contract with his broker *K* calls for a 50/50 split of all listing and sales commissions. *J* sells a home listed by broker *L* for $180,000. *L's* listing provides for a 6 percent commission. If *L* splits the sales commission 40/60, with 60 percent going to the selling office, what will *J* earn on the sale?

    (A) $ 3,240
    (B) $ 5,400
    (C) $ 6,480
    (D) $10,800

29. In an exclusive listing, the broker's promise to use diligence makes the listing:

    (A) a unilateral contract
    (B) a bilateral contract
    (C) voidable
    (D) an illusory contract

30. To have a valid deed there must be:

    (A) a seal
    (B) witnesses
    (C) recording
    (D) a description of the property

31. The quality of income is measured by the:

    (A) capitalization rate used
    (B) cash flow
    (C) income history
    (D) gross

32. A borrower has a right to see the Uniform Settlement Statement:

    (A) within three days of loan application
    (B) within seven days of loan application
    (C) seven days prior to closing
    (D) on the business day prior to closing

33. Which of the following is an example of involuntary alienation?

    (A) Dedication
    (B) Will
    (C) Deed
    (D) Sheriff's sale

34. When a person purchases property on a land contract of sale, the party making the payments customarily is known as the:

    (A) vendor
    (B) vendee
    (C) trustor
    (D) grantor

35. A father and son could hold title together:

    (A) in severalty
    (B) in tenancy by the entirety
    (C) as joint tenants
    (D) as community property

36. In using the income approach, an appraiser would be interested in:

    (A) accrued depreciation
    (B) the capitalization rate
    (C) reproduction cost
    (D) comparable sales

37. *J* breached a contract to sell a property to *K*. This resulted in a loss to *K* of $40,000, which a court awarded to *K*. What type of damages was awarded?

    (A) Liquidated
    (B) Compensatory
    (C) Punitive
    (D) Nominal

38. What is the function of a real estate appraisal?

    (A) Set market value
    (B) Determine market value
    (C) Estimate market value
    (D) Establish the cost

39. A home was sold for $90,000 with an 80 percent loan. The buyer paid $1,800 in points. How many points did the buyer pay?

    (A) .2
    (B) 2.2
    (C) 2.5
    (D) 2.8

40. Court-determined breach-of-contract damages that exceed the actual loss suffered would be:

    (A) liquidated damages
    (B) punitive damages
    (C) compensatory damages
    (D) specific performance

41. In depreciating a residential income property for tax purposes, you would base the depreciation life on:

    (A) age-life tables
    (B) the observed condition of the property
    (C) 27½ years
    (D) 39 years

42. A commercial property was purchased for $85,000 and has depreciated to $28,000 book value. If it is sold for $75,000, there is a(n):

    (A) $10,000 taxable loss
    (B) $18,800 taxable gain
    (C) $28,200 taxable gain
    (D) $47,000 taxable gain

43. In determining the external obsolescence for a commercial property, an appraiser would be interested in knowing:

    (A) if the structure has deferred maintenance
    (B) the net income
    (C) if the property is being properly managed
    (D) if commercial tenants in the area are doing well economically

44. To *alienate* property means to:

    (A) borrow against it
    (B) transfer it
    (C) improve it
    (D) appraise it

45. When would a vendee buying under a land contract receive a deed?

    (A) On closing
    (B) After the statutory period
    (C) On default
    (D) When the contract is paid in full

46. A lender under a deed of trust is known as the:

    (A) trustor
    (B) mortgagor
    (C) trustee
    (D) beneficiary

47. Who would be an attorney-in-fact?

    (A) Person acting under a court order
    (B) Attorney at law acting in a legal capacity
    (C) Agent appointed by a power of attorney
    (D) Attorney acting in a state where he or she is not legally licensed to practice

48. Because depreciation is a very important advantage of real estate investments, a real estate professional should know that:

    (A) residential property uses a 39-year life for depreciation
    (B) if an asset has appreciated, it cannot be depreciated
    (C) land is not depreciated
    (D) depreciation can be deferred and taken in a later year

49. In renting an apartment, a property manager may properly:

    (A) refuse to rent to persons suspected of having AIDS
    (B) check with prior landlords as to any previous problems
    (C) charge rent in excess of rent control maximum with the consent of the tenant
    (D) charge a higher security deposit to tenants having Seeing Eye dogs

50. Liquidation of a loan with equal payments is known as:

    (A) acceleration
    (B) compounding
    (C) amortization
    (D) ballooning

51. An investor had a paper loss on an investment because of depreciation taken. Nevertheless, the investor had $3,800 more in cash income than in total cash outlay, which:

    (A) is taxable as income
    (B) is known as *cash flow*
    (C) increases the investor's equity in the building by $3,800
    (D) results from the owner's using arbitrage

52. A requirement of every valid contract is that the:

    (A) contract be in writing.
    (B) signatures be notarized
    (C) parties be at least 21 years old
    (D) offer be accepted

53. A transfer of equitable title coupled with a retention of legal title describes a:

    (A) mortgage
    (B) land contract
    (C) trust deed
    (D) bill of sale

54. A deed restriction is best described as a(n):

    (A) general lien
    (B) specific lien
    (C) constructive lien
    (D) encumbrance

55. A facilitator or intermediary would be a:

    (A) buyer's agent
    (B) seller's agent
    (C) dual agent
    (D) neutral mediator.

56. The phrase that describes a broker's duty to keep a principal fully informed is:

    (A) ethical conduct
    (B) continuing responsibility
    (C) fiduciary obligation
    (D) informed consent

57. A minor discrepancy concerning a title would be:

    (A) the color of title
    (B) a cloud on the title
    (C) the chain of title
    (D) a broken title

58. The premium for title insurance is paid:

    (A) monthly with the mortgage payment
    (B) annually
    (C) on issuance of the title policy
    (D) by the original subdivider for all subsequent holders

59. An example of liquidated damages in a real property purchase contract would be:

    (A) damages paid to induce a party to contract
    (B) the forfeiture of a deposit
    (C) damages for willful action in excess of compensatory damages.
    (D) damages for a loss suffered because an owner diverted the flow of surface water

60. The annual percentage rate is:

    (A) the nominal rate
    (B) interest charges only
    (C) greater than the nominal rate
    (D) the nominal rate reduced by financing charges

61. Collateral for a real estate loan is the:

    (A) property
    (B) borrower
    (C) note
    (D) mortgage insurance

62. A clause in a mortgage that provides for the assignment of rents benefits the:

    (A) tenant
    (B) mortgagor
    (C) mortgagee
    (D) property manager

63. The *secondary mortgage market* refers to:

    (A) secondary financing
    (B) loans made by noninstitutional lenders
    (C) high-risk loans
    (D) the resale mortgage marketplace

64. Fannie Mae activities include:

    (A) insuring mortgages originated by financial institutions
    (B) guaranteeing mortgages originated by financial institutions
    (C) raising and lowering the discount rate to control the economy
    (D) purchasing mortgages originated by financial institutions

65. A straight 9 percent loan at 75 percent of a property's appraised value earned first-year's interest of $9,840. What was the property's valuation?

    (A) $82,000
    (B) $96,840
    (C) $109,333
    (D) $145,777

66. A property manager is an agent. How would the agency be commonly described?

    (A) The property manager is the agent of the owner.
    (B) The property manager is the agent of the tenant.
    (C) The property manager serves in a dual agency capacity representing owner and tenant.
    (D) The property manager is a transaction broker.

67. Which of the following is a lien?

    (A) An easement
    (B) A restrictive covenant
    (C) Delinquent taxes
    (D) A use in violation of zoning

68. A lease with a fixed rent that also has agreed-on rent increases at specified times is a(n):

    (A) net lease
    (B) step-up lease
    (C) index lease
    (D) variable annuity lease

69. The term *earnest money* refers to:

    (A) commissions
    (B) deposits given with purchase offers
    (C) funds in addition to the purchase price
    (D) the last month's rent given in advance by a tenant under a lease

70. The brokers in a community agreed that they would not cooperate with a large broker who offered lower rates of commissions and who wished to expand to their area. This agreement would be considered to be:

    (A) market allocation
    (B) price-fixing
    (C) a group boycott
    (D) redlining

71. Three brokers, who all had open listings on the same property, had contact with aparty who purchased directly from the owner. The broker who would be entitled to a commission is the:

    (A) first broker who had contact with the buyer
    (B) last broker to talk to the buyer prior to purchase
    (C) broker who had the most extensive contact with the buyer
    (D) broker who started an uninterrupted chain of events leading to the sale

72. A joint tenancy between two single persons would become a tenancy in common if one person:

    (A) dies without a will
    (B) sells his interest to the other
    (C) dies leaving the interest to another
    (D) sells his interest to a third party

73. A lender using an LTV ratio of 80 percent on a triplex appraised at $220,000 would make a maximum loan on the property of:

    (A) $160,000
    (B) $176,000
    (C) $200,000
    (D) 100 percent FHA

74. A requirement for an enforceable earnest money contract for the sale of real estate is that it be:

    (A) acknowledged before a notary public
    (B) properly recorded
    (C) in writing
    (D) accompanied by cash, a money order, or a cashier's certified check

75. The Real Estate Settlement Procedures Act applies to federally related purchase loans:

    (A) for all real estate transactions
    (B) only if there is secondary financing
    (C) of one to four residential units
    (D) for all types of residential property

76. A property manager may properly obey the principal's request to:

    (A) rent only to working families that can show an adequate income from their job
    (B) adopt tenant rules that will discourage families with children from renting
    (C) leave a unit vacant
    (D) put families with children in one building and adults in another building

77. An owner didn't want to sell or develop an undeveloped commercial lot but wanted additional income. This could be accomplished by a:

    (A) sale-leaseback
    (B) piggyback loan
    (C) ground lease
    (D) wraparound loan

78. The lower the loan-to-value ratio, the higher the:

    (A) lender risk
    (B) interest
    (C) loan amount
    (D) owner's equity

79. An example of a void contract would be a contract:

    (A) entered into because of misrepresentation by the seller
    (B) for an illegal purpose
    (C) entered into because of undue influence
    (D) with inadequate consideration

80. A 10,000-square-foot home was built between two similar large homes. The principle that explains the benefit of this placement is the principle of:

    (A) anticipation
    (B) conformity
    (C) contribution
    (D) competition

DIFFICULTY LEVEL I ANSWERS

1. (C) Inducing panic selling due to fear of entry of people of different race, color, religion, or national origin. (page 98)
2. (B) An estate for years is a lease for a definite period. (page 139)
3. (C) Renews unless notice given by lessor or lessee to terminate—generally 30 days. (page 139)
4. (B) The whole = the part ÷ rate; the part is $80,000 and the rate is 120% or 1.2 as a decimal. (page 158)
5. (C) It is the opposite of regression. (page 63)
6. (B) Receives purchase price plus removes mortgage from balance sheet. (page 140)
7. (C) Prohibited by Civil Rights Act of 1968. (page 98)
8. (A) The buyer must come up with this amount. It would be a credit to the seller. (page 129)
9. (A) With some limitations, interest is deductible as well as property taxes. (page 42)
10. (D) Federal requirement. (page 95)
11. (A) This is the only method currently authorized for real property. (page 44)
12. (D) It is a money charge (lien) as well as a charge or burden against the property. (page 26)
13. (B) Bait-and-switch advertising is a Truth-in-Lending violation. (page 125)
14. (C) The others are duties of attorney or accountant. (page 138)
15. (C) The appraiser must determine the interest to be appraised in what property and for what purpose. (page 71)
16. (D) Drug addicts are not a protected group. (page 99)
17. (B) With reasonable time to sell. The marketplace determines market value, appraisers only estimate it. (page 62)
18. (D) Commission must be subject to negotiation. It is an antitrust violation to set commission by broker or association agreement. (page 94)
19. (A) While not a requirement of purchase option agreements, it is a common provision. (page 141)
20. (A) Extended coverage policy goes beyond fire and lightning. (page 146)
21. (A) Tenancy would customarily be the length of rent-paying period. (page 143)
22. (B) This is built-in obsolescence. (pages 70–71)
23. (B) Rate = Part ÷ Whole or 21 ÷ 420. (page 157)
24. (A) Minors lack contractual authority so can't appoint agents to do what they cannot do themselves. (page 88)
25. (D) It would be grounds for disciplinary action. (page 92)
26. (D) 2,500 × $85 = $212,500 (building) + $75,000 for lot = $287,500. This equals sale price after 6% is taken out, or 94% of sale price. Whole = Part (287,500) ÷ percentage rate (.94). (pages 158–159)
27. (C) Appraiser would avoid distress sales, which would not be indicative of market value. (pages 65–66)
28. (A) 6% of $180,000 = $10,800 commission. 60% of $10,800 = $6,480 (.60 × 10,800): J gets 50% or $3,240. (page 159)
29. (B) It is a promise for a promise. The owner's promise is to pay a commission. (page 93)
30. (D) Must have an unambiguous description. Some states require a legal description. (page 48)
31. (A) The rate reflects risk, which affects quality of investments. (page 68)
32. (D) But the good-faith estimate is given within three business days of loan application (RESPA). (page 127)
33. (D) A forced or involuntary conveyance. (pages 46, 47)
34. (B) The vendee is the buyer and vendor is the seller. (page 112)
35. (C) Answer (A) is one person alone; (B) and (D) are only for married couples. (page 8)
36. (B) Answers (A) and (C) are for cost approach, and (D) is for sales comparison. (page 68)
37. (B) It compensates K for the amount of damages suffered. (page 86)
38. (C) It is only an estimate as of the date of the appraisal. (page 62)
39. (C) 80% of $90,000 = $72,000. Rate (points) = Part ($1,800) ÷ Whole ($72,000). (pages 117, 160)
40. (B) They are damages awarded to punish or make an example of a person for outrageous conduct. (page 86)
41. (C) However, for estimating value the appraiser would use an age-life table. (page 44)
42. (D) Difference between book value ($28,000) and sale price ($75,000). (page 43)
43. (D) External obsolescence deals with forces outside the property. (page 71)
44. (B) An alienation is a transfer. (page 46)

45. (D) Unless the contract calls for the contract to become a mortgage, the deed is not given until contract has been paid in full. (page 113)
46. (D) The beneficiary is the recipient of the payments, and the deed of trust is given for his or her benefit. (page 112)
47. (C) Need not be an attorney at law. (page 89)
48. (C) Only improvements have loss of value so they can be depreciated. They are considered to be wasting assets. (page 44)
49. (B) Credit, employer, and prior-landlord checks are proper. Others are prohibited. (page 99)
50. (C) A partially amortized loan would have a balloon payment before it is paid in full. (page 114)
51. (B) It is spendable cash and, in this case, would be sheltered from taxation. (page 33)
52. (D) Mutual consent is a necessary requirement of a contract. Only specified contracts need be in writing. (page 82)
53. (B) Vendor keeps legal title and gives vendee possession and equitable title. (page 112)
54. (D) It burdens the property but is not a monetary charge against the property (lien). (page 24)
55. (D) Allowed in some states. (page 88)
56. (C) A fiduciary duty is one of trust. Disclosure is a specific fiduciary duty. (page 91)
57. (B) Anything that casts doubt on the title. (page 53)
58. (C) It is a one-time charge that protects only insured and his or her heirs. (page 52)
59. (B) Purchase contracts usually provide for forfeiture of deposit as seller's sole remedy in event of buyer breach. (page 86)
60. (C) It would be adjusted upward based on loan costs from the rate in the note (nominal rate). (page 125)
61. (A) It is the security for the note that is the evidence of the debt. (page 124)
62. (C) The lender (mortgagee) has the right to collect the rents if the mortgagor is in default. (page 119)
63. (D) Fannie Mae, Freddie Mac, and Ginnie Mae are active in the secondary mortgage market. (page 119)
64. (D) It provides a secondary mortgage market so lenders can get cash if desired. (page 123)
65. (D) Whole = Part ÷ Percentage; Whole loan = Part ($9,840) ÷ Rate (9%) = $109,333 (loan). The loan is 75% of valuation so use the same formula again. Whole (value) = Part ($109,333) ÷ Rate (75% or .75). (page 158)
66. (A) In rare cases, tenants could have property managers who negotiate and oversee their leased property. (page 138)
67. (C) A lien is a money charge against a property. (page 26, 32)
68. (B) The increases are set forth in the lease. (page 139)
69. (B) Earnest money deposits are also given with lease applications. (page 95)
70. (C) A violation of the Sherman Act. (page 97)
71. (D) This would determine who is the procuring cause. (page 93)
72. (D) Answers (A) and (B) would result in a tenancy in severalty, and the interest cannot be passed by will. (page 8)
73. (B) 80% (.80) × $220,000. (page 159)
74. (C) Statute of frauds requires that every real estate sales contract be in writing. Earnest money is not essential to the contract, and between the parties, recording is not necessary. (page 83)
75. (C) FHA and VA loans or a federally insured lender or resale to a federally related buyer would make the loan federally related. (page 127)
76. (C) Other answers discriminate against families or violate the Equal Credit Opportunity Act. (page 138)
77. (C) The owner keeps title, gets rent and at the end of the lease gets the improvements. (page 140)
78. (D) Because a lower ratio would require a higher down payment (equity). (page 124)
79. (B) The others may be voidable. (pages 82, 83)
80. (B) Value is best maintained in an area of similar use. (page 63)

DIFFICULTY LEVEL II

1. What type of tax is the term *tax shelter* associated with?

   (A) Real property
   (B) Income
   (C) Sale
   (D) Personal property

2. A purchaser paid $138,000 for an investment property. He spent $24,000 on improvements, took $32,000 in depreciation and sold the property for $138,000. What is the taxable gain?

   (A) $ 0
   (B) $ 8,000
   (C) $24,000
   (D) $32,000

3. Which of the following tenancies is a freehold interest?

   (A) Life estate
   (B) Estate for years
   (C) Estate at will
   (D) Periodic tenancy

4. What would be the last action against a debtor?

   (A) Lis pendens
   (B) Attachment
   (C) Execution
   (D) Judgment

5. Accrued depreciation is important in the utilization of the:

   (A) gross multiplier
   (B) cost approach.
   (C) income approach
   (D) market comparison approach

6. FHA loans are made by:

   (A) HUD
   (B) the FHA
   (C) qualified lenders
   (D) the Federal Reserve

7. A person who is responsible to another only as to results would be a(n):

   (A) agent
   (B) servant
   (C) employee
   (D) independent contractor

8. What type of contract is an exclusive listing in a broker's inventory prior to sale?

   (A) Executed bilateral contract
   (B) Executory bilateral contract
   (C) Executed unilateral contract
   (D) Executory unilateral contract

9. An oil and gas lease would be classified as:

   (A) personal property
   (B) an emblement
   (C) a remainder interest
   (D) a reversionary interest

10. Lenders will often offer an introductory rate on an ARM less than the index plus the margin to:

    (A) allow for negative amortization
    (B) provide a cap rate
    (C) induce a borrower to agree to an ARM
    (D) provide for depreciation

11. A borrower keeps control of the loan collateral but gives the lender a lien. This would be known as:

    (A) a pledge
    (B) hypothecation
    (C) reconciliation
    (D) a collaterally secured loan

12. In renting apartments, a property manager may require that:

    (A) unmarried mothers have lease cosigners
    (B) the security deposit be $200 per person for each unit
    (C) all lessees provide three character references
    (D) families without children receive a $100 discount from scheduled rent

13. A landlord would have proper cause to evict a single person who:

(A) joined a tenant organization
(B) became pregnant
(C) complained to health authorities about the condition of the rental
(D) refused to pay the last month's rent when the security deposit was greater than the rent due

14. Homeowners insurance includes:

(A) mortgage life coverage
(B) flood insurance
(C) earthquake damage
(D) liability protection

15. A property is purchased based on fraudulent income statements prepared by the listing broker. Therefore, the sale contract would be:

(A) void
(B) voidable
(C) valid
(D) illegal

16. A real estate license is required by a:

(A) developer selling more than ten homes
(B) attorney-in-fact selling property for a principal
(C) trustee selling under court order
(D) attorney at law taking a listing

17. Broker *J* listed widow *K's* property for an 8 percent commission. After the sale, *K* discovered that *J* had been listing similar property at a 6 percent commission. Based on these facts:

(A) *J* has done nothing wrong
(B) *J* can lose her license
(C) *K* can recover from the state recovery fund
(D) *K* is entitled to a refund

18. *J* leased property to *K* for 20 years. One year later, *J* died intestate, leaving no heirs. The effect of *J's* death is that:

(A) the lease ended with the death of *J*
(B) *K* owns the property
(C) the state will acquire the property without the lease
(D) the state will acquire the property subject to the lease rights of *K*.

19. Owner *N* advertised a home for $300,000. Buyer *O* sent *N* a letter stating, "I hereby accept your offer to sell the home advertised at a price of $300,000." What are *O's* rights?

(A) *O* has a unilateral contract.
(B) *O* can obtain specific performance if *N* refuses to convey.
(C) *O* has the right to void the contract.
(D) *O* is an offeror.

20. The act that requires accessibility to places of public accommodation is:

(A) RESPA
(B) the Americans With Disabilities Act
(C) the 1988 Fair Housing Amendment Act
(D) the Civil Rights Act of 1968

21. *J* closed a sale and received a commission from the buyer and seller. The double payment of commission was proper if:

(A) the listing did not prohibit it
(B) both parties agreed to it
(C) the listing was nonexclusive
(D) separate services were performed for both parties

22. A property manager has a chance for a management contract for a large commercial building that has been vacant for 3 years. The manager should insist on a:

(A) holdover clause
(B) minimum fee
(C) percentage fee for repairs
(D) fee based on net income

23. When a new mall opened, rental income for the old mall was reduced by $4,600 per month. Assuming a 12½ percent capitalization rate, what was the loss in value for the old mall?

    (A) $ 36,800
    (B) $ 55,200
    (C) $441,600
    (D) $538,996

24. *J* agreed to buy *K's* farm, but the deed given by *K* had the wrong legal description, describing land that *K* did not own. *J*, who wants the land bargained for, would ask the court for the remedy of:

    (A) rescission
    (B) accord and satisfaction
    (C) novation
    (D) reformation

25. A tenant's five-year lease expired on June 1. On June 2, the tenant's continued occupancy would be a:

    (A) tenancy in common
    (B) periodic tenancy
    (C) tenancy at sufferance
    (D) license

26. With an assessed value of $149,500, an equalization factor of 118 percent and a tax rate of .018, the taxes would be:

    (A) $2,691
    (B) $2,791
    (C) $3,175
    (D) $3,764

27. Rental security deposits would be handled on a closing statement as:

    (A) credits to the buyer
    (B) credits to the seller
    (C) debits to the buyer
    (D) prorated items

28. A lender agrees to make an 80 percent loan on a $124,000 home purchase. The lender wants 1½ points to make the loan. The point charges will amount to:

    (A) $ 992
    (B) $1,488
    (C) $1,500
    (D) $1,860

29. A broker owns a separate mortgage company that rents space in the broker's office and competes for loans on the broker's sales. This activity would be considered to be:

    (A) tie-in sales
    (B) market allocation
    (C) a controlled business arrangement
    (D) a required provider

30. The four forces affecting value are:

    (A) land, labor, capital, and profit
    (B) physical, economic, political, and social
    (C) location, physical, political, and social
    (D) neighborhood, cost, appreciation, and contribution

31. The term quiet enjoyment refers to:

    (A) the neighborhood
    (B) the tenant's right of possession
    (C) the tenant's right to use without interference from owner or others claiming an interest
    (D) habitability

32. The last step in an appraisal would be to:

    (A) define the problem
    (B) report the value
    (C) determine highest and best use
    (D) determine land value

33. A broker who has a property listing receives two purchase offers on the same property from two different offices. How should the broker proceed with the presentation of the offers?

    (A) Only the highest priced offer need be submitted.
    (B) Both offers must be presented at the same time.
    (C) The broker should present the first offer received. Only if it is rejected should the second offer be presented.
    (D) The broker must return the second offer received to the offering broker and present a single offer to the owner.

34. The zoning of a parcel was changed from agricultural use to manufacturing. This is an example of:

    (A) downzoning
    (B) upzoning
    (C) conservation zoning
    (D) bulk zoning

35. In a sale transaction, a broker worked directly with a buyer and seller but represented neither party. The broker:

    (A) made a controlled business arrangement
    (B) served as a facilitator
    (C) was a designated agent
    (D) was involved in split agency

36. The capitalization method is used to:

    (A) forecast future income
    (B) determine the capitalization rate
    (C) determine the highest and best use
    (D) convert income into value

37. A new neighbor built a plain 1,100-square-foot home on the lot next to your 2,900-square-foot colonial home. You would be concerned with the principle of:

    (A) anticipation
    (B) regression
    (C) supply and demand
    (D) balance

38. Ingress and egress refer to:

    (A) assumability
    (B) leases
    (C) easements
    (D) transferability

39. *L*'s business activities consist of bringing prospective borrowers and lenders together for loans secured by the borrower's property. *L*'s activities are those of a:

    (A) mortgage banker
    (B) mortgage broker
    (C) mortgagee
    (D) mortgagor

40. With a capitalization rate of 5 percent, an appraiser would say that each additional dollar of expenses affects the value of income property by:

    (A) raising it $20
    (B) lowering it $5
    (C) lowering it $10
    (D) lowering it $20

41. A lender might prefer to make an FHA or a VA loan rather than a conventional loan because of the:

    (A) lower risk
    (B) higher interest
    (C) longer investment period
    (D) federal tax benefits

42. Loan-to-value ratio refers to the ratio of the loan to:

    (A) appraised value
    (B) assessed value
    (C) book value
    (D) utility value

43. Fidelity bonds protect a broker against:

    (A) employee turnover
    (B) employee theft
    (C) liability for injury
    (D) damage to property

44. What is an attorney-in-fact?

    (A) A properly licensed lawyer
    (B) An agent operating under a power of attorney
    (C) A court-appointed guardian
    (D) An agent authorized to act for both buyer and seller

45. What do owners under both joint tenancy and tenancy in common have in common?

    (A) Equal right of possession
    (B) Survivorship
    (C) Interests acquired at the same time
    (D) Equal interests

46. A valid deed requires:

    (A) recording
    (B) witnesses
    (C) acceptance
    (D) acknowledgment

47. A duplex that rents for $275 per unit is located in the same area as a slightly smaller duplex in similar condition that rents for $240 per unit and just sold for $67,200. Based on these data only, the larger duplex has a value of:

    (A) $67,200
    (B) $70,000
    (C) $77,000
    (D) $77,500

48. If Z's interest in land entitles her to impose restrictions on its future use, her interest is a(n):

    (A) life estate
    (B) nonfreehold interest
    (C) fee simple estate
    (D) estate for years

49. The ratio of rents to sale price would be of concern to an appraiser using the:

    (A) gross multiplier
    (B) cost approach
    (C) income approach
    (D) market comparison approach

50. Depreciation is calculated by an appraiser using the:

    (A) market comparison approach
    (B) cost approach
    (C) income approach
    (D) development method

51. A good-faith estimate of settlement costs must be provided to a borrower:

    (A) at the time of the loan application
    (B) within three business days of the loan application
    (C) within three business days of loan closing
    (D) at the loan closing

52. Purchasing subject to a loan means that the purchaser has what liability?

    (A) Primary
    (B) Secondary
    (C) Deficiency
    (D) No liability

53. The loan that would command the highest loan-to-value ratio would be for:

    (A) a single-family residence
    (B) agricultural land
    (C) a residential lot
    (D) commercial property

54. For tax purposes, nonresidential property is depreciated based on a life of:

    (A) 15 years
    (B) 27 ½ years
    (C) 31 years
    (D) 39 years

55. To determine monthly interest on a loan, the lender multiplied .006 by the loan principal owed. What was the interest rate of the loan?

    (A) .6
    (B) 6.
    (C) 7.2
    (D) 8.4

56. In the absence of a specified closing date, a real estate transaction must close:

    (A) immediately
    (B) within 3 days
    (C) within 30 days
    (D) within a reasonable period of time

57. The name of a firm ends with LLC, which indicates that the firm is:

    (A) licensed to conduct real estate activities
    (B) an S corporation
    (C) owned in severalty
    (D) taxed as a partnership

58. A property manager determined that the lessee on a commercial lease had been declared incompetent prior to entering into the lease. The lease is:

    (A) void
    (B) voidable at the option of the lessee
    (C) voidable at the option of the lessor
    (D) voidable at the pleasure of the court

59. A real estate salesperson, in selling listings of another broker, is directly responsible to:

    (A) his or her broker
    (B) the owner
    (C) the listing broker
    (D) the Multiple Listing Service

60. Exceptional landscaping and a hot spa that enhance the value of a residential property would be classified as:

    (A) personal property
    (B) chattels real
    (C) amenities
    (D) beneficial encumbrances

61. The seller agreed to pay 60 percent of the total closing related charges with the buyer paying 40 percent. Title insurance cost $438, miscellaneous fees and costs totaled $378.50. To the nearest dollar, how much more did the seller pay than the buyer?

    (A) $163
    (B) $327
    (C) $490
    (D) $817

62. Broker *N* earned a commission when owner *P* sold her home without the help of any agent. *N* had what type of listing?

    (A) Exclusive agency
    (B) Exclusive right to sell
    (C) Net
    (D) Open

63. Which is the first and which is the second mortgage can be determined by:

    (A) title of the instrument
    (B) date of the mortgages
    (C) time and date of recording
    (D) amount of the liens

64. An exculpatory clause in a lease:

    (A) provides for payment of needed repairs and maintenance
    (B) provides for forfeiture of lease rights should the tenant breach the lease
    (C) carries a warranty of habitability
    (D) holds the landlord harmless for loss or injury due to the condition of the premises

65. A partially amortized loan has a:

    (A) prepayment penalty
    (B) balloon payment
    (C) due-on-sale clause
    (D) subordination clause

66. It would be proper to include in an ad that a property:

    (A) has a 55-year age restriction
    (B) is across the street from a Catholic church
    (C) owner prefers married couples
    (D) is in the most desirable Chinese neighborhood

67. Freddie Mac mortgage activities are primarily involved in:

    (A) RESPA enforcement
    (B) the secondary mortgage market
    (C) enforcement of the Foreign Investment in Real Property Tax Act
    (D) direct loans for low-income homebuyers

68. An unmarried couple purchased their residence together for $382,000. Three years later they sold their residence for $750,000. They would have a tax liability on a gain of:

    (A) $ 0
    (B) $ 23,600
    (C) $ 73,600
    (D) $150,000

69. A person died intestate. The court would appoint a(n):

    (A) executor
    (B) administrator
    (C) devise
    (D) testator

70. A tenant vacated premises with nine months remaining on the lease. To mitigate damages, the owner should:

    (A) improve the premises and advertise at a higher rent
    (B) bring legal action as each month's rent becomes due
    (C) keep the premises vacant until the lease expires
    (D) immediately advertise the premises for rent

71. An example of voluntary alienation is:

    (A) a deed
    (B) escheat
    (C) eminent domain
    (D) police power

72. A policy of insurance a broker would consider that is similar to medical malpractice coverage is:

    (A) a fidelity bond
    (B) errors and omissions coverage
    (C) a liability policy
    (D) a homeowner policy

73. A contract would be void if it were entered into:

    (A) based on the fraud of one party
    (B) because of duress exercised by one party
    (C) because one party used undue influence against the other party
    (D) for an illegal purpose

74. By increasing the amortization period of a loan, the:

    (A) monthly payment would decrease
    (B) interest rate would decrease
    (C) total loan costs would decrease
    (D) lender risk would decrease

75. A deed transfers title when:

    (A) it is acknowledged
    (B) it is recorded
    (C) it is delivered
    (D possession is given

76. What does the term *procuring cause* relate to?

    (A) Entitlement to commission
    (B) Depreciation
    (C) Exercise of options
    (D) Mortgage insurance

77. An appraiser wishes to take into consideration the great amenity value that a property has. Which appraisal method would consider the value of the amenities?

    (A) Cost approach
    (B) Sales comparison approach
    (C) Income approach
    (D) Gross rent multiplier

78. The buyer on a fixed rate FHA loan was informed that monthly payments were to increase. The reason for the increase would be:

    (A) an increase in an index
    (B) increased taxes
    (C) an acceleration of the loan
    (D) adjustment to the margin

79. What is the nominal rate of interest?

    (A) The rate stated in the note
    (B) The true rate expressed as the APR
    (C) The minimum interest allowed by law
    (D) The usury rate

80. An irrevocable listing would be a sale listing:

    (A) for one to four residential units
    (B) where an advanced fee was paid
    (C) coupled with an interest
    (D) for one year or less

DIFFICULTY LEVEL II ANSWERS

1. (B) It shelters income from taxation. Depreciation is a tax shelter. (page 45)
2. (B) Cost $138,000 + improvements of $24,000 = $162,000 – depreciation of $32,000 = $130,00 cost basis. A sale at $138,000 means a taxable gain of $8,000. (page 43)
3. (A) Life estates and fee simple are freehold estates. Leasehold interests are nonfreehold estates. (page 6)
4. (C) Sheriff's seizure and sale of assets after judgment. (page 27)
5. (B) Because it is cost to replace less accrued depreciation plus land value. (page 66)
6. (C) Institutional lenders approved by FHA. They may be able to have direct endorsement because the lender decides if the loan can receive FHA insurance. (page 120)
7. (D) Differs from an employee who would be subject to supervision and control. (page 90)
8. (B) Executory because broker has not yet found a buyer and bilateral because there were mutual promises. (page 81)
9. (A) Lease interests are personal property (chattels real), but oil and gas rights would be real property. (page 140)
10. (C) Also to qualify borrowers who could not qualify for a fixed rate loan. (page 115)
11. (B) As in a mortgage or deed of trust. (page 111)
12. (C) Reasonable and nondiscriminatory—others discriminate as to familial status. (page 99)
13. (D) Prohibited by Uniform Residential Landlord and Tenant Act. (A) and (C) are a retaliatory eviction and (B) is prohibited by Fair Housing Law. (page 143)
14. (D) Others require separate policies. (page 147)
15. (B) At the option of the purchaser.(pages 83–84)
16. (D) The attorney isn't acting as an attorney but as a real estate broker. (page 88)
17. (A) Commissions are subject to negotiation. (page 94)
18. (D) Death of lessor does not terminate lease rights. (page 85)
19. (D) A newspaper ad is considered an invitation to negotiate and not an offer. *O's* acceptance was merely an offer that required acceptance to form a binding agreement. (page 84)
20. (B) Must be accessible if *readily achievable*. (page 100)
21. (B) Both parties must agree to both dual agency and receiving any commission from another party. Otherwise it could be a breach of fiduciary duty. (page 89)
22. (B) Because handling a vacant property is costly in both time and effort. (page 138)
23. (C) $4,600 per month × 12 = annual reduction of $55,200. To find value of this amount, divide by the cap rate of .125. (page 68)
24. (D) To have the deed read as the parties intended it to read. (page 87)
25. (C) A holdover tenant has a tenancy at sufferance. (page 139)
26. (C) Multiply assessed value of $149,500 × equalization factor of 1.18 which equals $176,410, which the tax rate applies to; $176,410 × .018 = taxes of $3,175. (page 32)
27. (A) They must be turned over to the buyer. They are debits to the seller. (page 129)
28. (B) .80 (80%) × $124,000 = $99,200 loan. 1½ points is 1½% or .015; .015 × $99,200 = $1,488. (page 117)
29. (C) Allowed under RESPA. (pages 127–128)
30. (B) While these four forces affect value, the four elements of value are utility, scarcity, demand, and transferability. (pages 64–65)
31. (C) It is an implied covenant in a lease. (page 140)
32. (B) Which is the appraisal report. (page 71)
33. (B) Otherwise it would be a breach of broker's fiduciary duty. (page 91)
34. (B) It is the opposite of downzoning. It is a change to a higher or more productive use. (page 23)
35. (B) The broker was not an agent, so he had the duty of fair dealing but not agency duties. (page 88)
36. (D) The value of the income is determined by use of the capitalization method. (pages 67–69)
37. (B) Loss in value due to proximity of lower cost property. (page 63)
38. (C) Entering and exiting. (page 28)
39. (B) *L* doesn't make loans but charges a fee to borrower for arranging the loan. (page 120)
40. (D) Divide $1 by capitalization rate of .05 (as a decimal). (pages 68–69)
41. (A) Because of FHA insurance or VA guarantee. (page 124)
42. (A) Lenders loan based on their appraisal. (page 120)
43. (B) Protection to broker and principal. (page 148)
44. (B) Not necessarily legally trained. (page 89)

45. (A) This is the only one of the four unities of joint tenancy also present in tenancy in common. (page 9)
46. (C) Although in some cases acceptance can be presumed. Between the parties recording is not required. (page 48)
47. (C) Unit that sold rented at $240 per unit or $480 per month. It sold for $67,200; $67,200 ÷ 480 = 140 which is the gross monthly rent multiplier; Apply the multiplier of 140 to the other duplex renting for $275 per unit or $550 per month; $550 ÷ 140 = $77,000. (page 69)
48. (C) Because fee simple ownership has no time limitation, the owner can impose restrictions as to future use. (page 6)
49. (A) The multiplier is applied to the gross to arrive at value. (page 69)
50. (B) Because it is cost less depreciation plus land. (page 66)
51. (B) A RESPA requirement. (page 127)
52. (D) But will be foreclosed if the payments are not made. (page 118)
53. (A) For some loans it can be 100% and seldom less than 80%. (page 123)
54. (D) Residential property is depreciated over 27½ years. (page 44)
55. (C) .006 (one month) × 12 = .072 or 7.2% per year. (page 160)
56. (D) A court would decide what is reasonable if conflict arises. (page 97)
57. (D) Limited liability company (LLC) is taxed as a partnership. (pages 12–13)
58. (A) A person declared incompetent cannot contract. (pages 82, 83)
59. (A) A salesperson answers to his or her broker. (page 140)
60. (C) These are features that make a property more desirable and would be considered when using the sales comparison approach as to the comparables. (page 65)
61. (A) Costs are $438 and $378 or a total of $816. 60% of 816 = $489.60. 40% of 816 = $326.40. The difference is $163. (page 159)
62. (B) This is only type of listing where commission is earned if the owner sells without an agent. (page 93)
63. (C) Known as the *race of the diligent*. Who records first gets first interest. (page 113)
64. (D) Not allowed in residential leases. (page 141)
65. (B) Payments are based on an amortization schedule, but the balloon payment comes before loan can be paid off. (page 115)
66. (A) Exception under the 1988 Fair Housing Amendment Act. (pages 98, 100)
67. (B) Freddie Mac buys mortgages and sells securities (participation certificates) backed by a pool of mortgages. (page 123)
68. (A) Because each has $250,000 (universal) exclusion. (page 42)
69. (B) Appointed by the court to act as a representative of the deceased. An executor is named in a will by the decedent. (page 53)
70. (D) Duty to keep damages low. (page 144)
71. (A) Others are involuntary transfers. (pages 46, 48)
72. (B) Covers negligence of agent but not willful act. (page 147)
73. (D) The others make the contract voidable. (page 83)
74. (A) But the total interest paid for the term of the loan would increase. (page 165)
75. (C) Title is transferred on delivery. (page 48)
76. (A) It determines entitlement to a commission on an open listing or exclusive-agency listing. Must have started an uninterrupted chain of events that led to sale. (page 93)
77. (B) Amenity value could be considered with comparables. (page 65)
78. (B) FHA loans have an impound account for taxes. (page 121)
79. (A) Which, because of loan fees, would be less than the APR. (page 125)
80. (C) Owner cannot revoke listing coupled with an agent's interest in the property. (page 92)

DIFFICULTY LEVEL III

1. A certificate of reasonable value is required for a(n):

   (A) certified appraisal
   (B) FHA loan
   (C) VA loan
   (D) loan with private mortgage insurance (PMI)

2. On a real estate closing statement, prepaid rent would always be a:

   (A) debit to the buyer
   (B) debit to the seller
   (C) credit to the seller
   (D) balance factor

3. Meridians are of concern to a(n):

   (A) appraiser
   (B) mortgage broker
   (C) surveyor
   (D) property manager

4. To be eligible for the homeowner capital gains exclusion:

   (A) the home must be the principal or secondary residence
   (B) the homeowner must not have previously taken the exclusion
   (C) 5-year ownership is required
   (D) 2-year occupancy is required

5. A grantor is a lessee in the case of a:

   (A) sandwich lease
   (B) sale-leaseback
   (C) gross lease
   (D) percentage lease

6. Subleasing could be described as being:

   (A) an assignment
   (B) greater than an assignment
   (C) a hypothecation
   (D) less than an assignment

7. Death of a party to an agreement voids the agreement when the agreement is a(n):

   (A) purchase contract
   (B) land contract
   (C) option to purchase
   (D) exclusive-right-to-sell listing

8. *L* took title to property under the name *ML*. When *L* sold the property, *L* signed the deed as *KL,* grantor. The buyer has:

   (A) a cloud on the title
   (B) color of title only
   (C) an exception on the deed
   (D) clean title

9. An $1,800 loan is repaid with $600 payments every six months plus 9 percent annual interest. What is the total interest paid?

   (A) $ 81
   (B) $162
   (C) $216
   (D) $243

10. To what loan type would obligatory advances apply?

    (A) Shared appreciation mortgage
    (B) Construction loan
    (C) Growing equity mortgage
    (D) Participation mortgage

11. When an appraiser refers to future benefits, the appraiser is discussing:

    (A) value
    (B) cost
    (C) depreciation
    (D) price

12. *J* received a property by descent. Therefore, *J* received the property by:

    (A) escheat
    (B) dedication
    (C) inheritance
    (D) adverse use

13. When parties own property as tenants in common, each owner:

    (A) must be mentioned in the same instrument (deed or will)
    (B) owns an individual divided share of the property
    (C) must have acquired rights simultaneously with the other owner(s)
    (D) has ownership of no specific part of the property

14. What effect would rising interest rates have on the value of a commercial property that is on a long-term lease at a fixed rent?

    (A) They would result in the use of a lower capitalization rate.
    (B) They would increase the gross multiplier.
    (C) They would lower the property's value.
    (D) They would require that the property be appraised using the cost approach to value.

15. The Real Estate Settlement Procedures Act applies to:

    (A) home equity loans
    (B) purchase loans on one to four residential units
    (C) loans for one to six residential units
    (D) residential, commercial, and industrial financing

16. A parcel of land sold for $328,000, which was 82 percent of its list price. What was it listed at?

    (A) $268,960
    (B) $387,040
    (C) $400,000
    (D) $437,000

17. A property is listed by broker N at $92,500 with $30,000 down. N brought in a full-price cash offer that the owner rejected. N is entitled to:

    (A) the full commission
    (B) half the commission
    (C) the commission split agreed on
    (D) nothing

18. A residential lease provided that the landlord would supply water. The water to the building was cut off because the landlord had not paid the water bill. The tenant can leave the premises with no further lease obligations based on:

    (A) condemnation
    (B) surrender
    (C) constructive eviction
    (D) sufferance

19. Under RESPA, a lender is required to provide the purchaser with a:

    (A) good-faith estimate of closing costs
    (B) home protection warranty
    (C) mortgage insurance policy
    (D) certified appraisal

20. A legal process used to clear a title is a(n):

    (A) quitclaim deed
    (B) action to quiet title
    (C) action in personam
    (D) writ of mandamus

21. A $7,000 investment in a straight mortgage earns $210 in 3 months. What is the annual percentage return on the investment?

    (A) 9%
    (B) 11%
    (C) 12%
    (D) 14%

22. The term *menace* would be associated with:

    (A) restrictive covenants
    (B) contracts
    (C) easements
    (D) financing

23. The cost basis of a residence is affected by:

    (A) repairs
    (B) interest paid
    (C) amortization of the loan
    (D) a room addition

24. Because *L* mistakenly measured from the wrong surveyor's stake, *L* built a fishing cabin on *M's* land. What are the rights of the parties?

    (A) *M* would take title to the cabin by accession.
    (B) *L* has the right to buy the land at its tax-appraised value.
    (C) *L* would be allowed to remove the improvements, provided any damage to the property is repaired.
    (D) *M* retains title to the land, but L is allowed to use the cabin.

25. A life estate holder purchased the interest of the remainderman. The life tenant now holds:

    (A) a fee simple
    (B) a life estate for two lives
    (C) a tenancy in common
    (D) two separate estates

26. A women's rights group established a nonprofit housing project that gave preference to single women with children. Its action is:

    (A) proper if the organization is also nonprofit
    (B) proper if there is no racial discrimination
    (C) improper under the Civil Rights Act of 1866
    (D) improper under the Civil Rights Act of 1968 as amended

27. The broker's authority under a listing includes:

    (A) everything necessary to conclude a sale
    (B) any act performed in the owner's best interest
    (C) the customary authority of a general agent
    (D) only the authority granted or implied

28. What law allows personal information about a neighbor to be available to a prospective purchaser?

    (A) Americans with Disabilities Act
    (B) Megan's Law
    (C) 1988 Fair Housing Amendment Act
    (D) Civil Rights Act of 1968

29. Oil and gas leases differ from mineral, oil, and gas rights in that:

    (A) mineral, oil, and gas rights are chattels real
    (B) mineral, oil, and gas rights require royalty payments
    (C) oil and gas leases are personal property
    (D) oil and gas rights may not be transferred

30. An example of functional obsolescence is a(n):

    (A) building that, because of wear and tear, is no longer suitable for its intended purpose
    (B) large commercial structure with inadequate on-site parking
    (C) encroaching use
    (D) political change that has reduced value

31. While a property had an annual gross income of $68,000, an appraiser used an income of $84,000 for the income approach. This higher income was used because the appraiser considered the principle of:

    (A) anticipation
    (B) conformity
    (C) integration and disintegration
    (D) regression

32. The maximum civil penalty for the first discriminatory act in violation of the Americans with Disabilities Act is:

    (A) $ 1,000
    (B) $10,000
    (C) $25,000
    (D) $50,000

33. All of the rights of ownership, including the rights to use, encumber, transfer, and exclude, are known as:

    (A) emblements of title
    (B) the bundle of rights
    (C) chattels real
    (D) fructus naturales

34. Because a property manager expects residential rental demand to exceed the rental supply within a short period of time, the manager wants new leases to:

    (A) reflect the CPI
    (B) be based on a percentage of the gross
    (C) be for relatively short terms
    (D) obligate the tenant to a long-term commitment

35. By calling in a loan, the lender:

    (A) gives a new loan
    (B) accelerates loan payments
    (C) shortens the loan term
    (D) changes the interest rate

36. A right of first refusal differs from an option in that the:

    (A) holder of the option right must exercise it
    (B) right of first refusal sets the exact price and terms
    (C) right of first refusal can be exercised only if the owner decides to sell or lease
    (D) right of first refusal is for leasing only, while the option is for purchase

37. *D* agreed in writing to make a gift of her home to her friend. The agreement could be described as what type of contract?

    (A) Valid
    (B) Void
    (C) Voidable
    (D) Implied

38. As part of a purchase agreement, the seller agreed to complete a roof repair prior to closing. The seller now refuses to complete the repair. What rights does the buyer have?

    (A) Reformation
    (B) Accord and satisfaction
    (C) Rescission
    (D) Novation

39. In determining net operating income, a cost deducted from the gross income would be:

    (A) interest expense
    (B) payments on loan principal
    (C) depreciation
    (D) operating expenses

40. A listing stated "14 acres MOL." What does MOL stand for?

    (A) Measurement of land
    (B) Measurement owner's liability
    (C) More or less
    (D) Measured on legal

41. A seller agrees to finance a buyer but will not allow the buyer to assume the existing below-market-rate mortgage. To keep this low-interest benefit, the seller would use what type of mortgage?

    (A) Shared appreciation
    (B) Participation
    (C) Blanket
    (D) Wraparound

42. An option does not become a binding contract on both parties until the:

    (A) consideration is paid
    (B) option is signed by both parties
    (C) option period expires
    (D) option is exercised

43. The Uniform Residential Landlord and Tenant Act requires that the landlord inform the tenant about:

    (A) the basis of any rent increase
    (B) any encumbrances against the property
    (C) the name and addresses where notices should be sent
    (D) any pending sale of the premises

44. Which of the following acts of a listing agent would be proper conduct?

    (A) Remaining silent about a plumbing problem when directed by the seller to not disclose the information to the buyer
    (B) Telling a prospective buyer about a recent violent death on the premises
    (C) Informing a prospective buyer to lower an offer because the seller would accept less
    (D) Volunteering information to prospective buyers about the racial composition of the area

45. The activities of Fannie Mae in the secondary mortgage market serve to:

    (A) create a market for existing home loans
    (B) encourage lenders to make commercial loans
    (C) insure or guarantee home loans
    (D) make construction standards uniform

46. Salesperson *L*, working for broker *M*, was able to complete a complex transaction that benefited both the buyer and seller. The parties wanted to show their appreciation by giving *L* additional compensation. *L* can receive this compensation from:

    (A) the seller
    (B) the buyer
    (C) the buyer and seller equally
    (D) broker *M*

47. What type of mortgage has compound interest?

    (A) Straight
    (B) Bimonthly
    (C) Reverse annuity
    (D) Amortized

48. Which of the following transactions will result in the greatest net for the seller?

	Sale Price	Commission	Closing Costs
(A)	$182,000	5%	$4,380
(B)	$190,000	6%	$1,250
(C)	$195,000	7½%	$2,850
(D)	$197,000	8%	$1,480

49. When title is conveyed to two persons not married to each other and no mention is made of how they are to take title, ownership is presumed to be as:

    (A) community property
    (B) tenants in common
    (C) joint tenants
    (D) tenants in the entirety

50. A political factor that influences value is:

    (A) location
    (B) rent control
    (C) inflation
    (D) change in family values

51. An offer is terminated by:

    (A) rejection by the offeror
    (B) rejection by the offeree
    (C) revocation by the offeree
    (D) request for an extension by the offeree

52. A company that acts as a liaison in bringing lenders and borrowers together is engaged in:

    (A) the secondary mortgage market
    (B) mortgage banking
    (C) mortgage brokerage
    (D) direct endorsement

53. The process of warehousing refers to:

    (A) loans being used as collateral for other loans
    (B) servicing mortgages for other owners
    (C) the process of assemblage
    (D) nonconforming loans

54. On a closing statement, seller financing would be shown as:

    (A) a prorated factor
    (B) a credit to the buyer and a debit to the seller
    (C) a debit to the buyer and a credit to the seller
    (D) It would not be shown

55. What advantage does trading property have over selling?

    (A) Avoidance of commission
    (B) Higher prices
    (C) Deferring taxes
    (D) Avoidance of the due-on-sale clause

56. A permanent loan that replaces a construction loan would be a:

    (A) take-out loan
    (B) purchase-money loan
    (C) packaged loan
    (D) participation loan

57. A property owner paid $112,000 for a lot and spent $720,000 building an apartment building. He has since fully depreciated the improvements. The property owner would have an adjusted cost basis of:

    (A) $ 112,000
    (B) $ 318,000
    (C) $ 430,500
    (D) $1,050,500

58. Instruments that could contain subordination clauses are:

    (A) deeds
    (B) mortgages
    (C) leases
    (D) options

59. Property of an owner was seized before a judgment was rendered. The seizure would be a(n):

    (A) execution of the judgment
    (B) sheriff's sale
    (C) attachment
    (D) lis pendens

60. A characteristic of fee simple ownership is that the ownership is:

    (A) by a single person
    (B) freely transferable
    (C) without any encumbrance
    (D) of a definite duration

61. Lowering interest rates would be expected to result in:

    (A) lower sale prices
    (B) more buyers entering the market
    (C) a reduction in sales activity
    (D) higher capitalization rates

62. A monthly amortized loan payment differs from the prior month's payment in that the prior month's payment:

    (A) was a greater amount
    (B) was a lesser amount
    (C) applied more money to principal
    (D) applied more money to interest

63. A new runway at an airport put a subdivision under the aircraft-landing pattern which resulted in a lowering of values. This would be considered:

    (A) functional obsolescence
    (B) external obsolescence
    (C) physical deterioration
    (D) inverse condemnation

64. A property manager leased a store for three years. The first year's rent was $1,000 per month and was to increase 10 percent each year thereafter. The broker received 7 percent commission for the first year, 5 percent for the second year, and 3 percent for the balance of the lease. Total commission earned was:

    (A) $ 840
    (B) $1,613
    (C) $1,936
    (D) $2,784.70

65. A loan that provides for future advances is a(n):

    (A) open-end loan
    (B) shared appreciation loan
    (C) growing equity mortgage
    (D) blanket mortgage

66. A broker made one of the salespeople the sole agent for an owner. That salesperson would be considered:

    (A) a facilitator
    (B) a dual agent
    (C) the designated agent
    (D) a cooperating agent

67. A tenant received permissive possession without a tenancy agreement. The tenant was a:

    (A) trespasser
    (B) month-to-month tenant
    (C) tenant at will
    (D) tenant for years

68. A conveyance from *J* to *K* for life and then to *L* if *L* is still alive gives *L* a:

    (A) reversionary interest
    (B) fee simple
    (C) contingent remainder interest
    (D) vested remainder interest

69. What is the hazardous substance associated with electrical equipment?

    (A) Asbestos
    (B) Radon
    (C) PCBs
    (D) Lead

70. What is a characteristic of both FHA and VA loans?

    (A) Absence of prepayment penalties
    (B) Absence of loan points
    (C) Requirement of mortgage insurance
    (D) Requirement of a certificate of reasonable value

71. A group of brokers agreed that none of them would advertise in a paper that had run articles critical of the activities of real estate brokers. This agreement would be considered:

    (A) a tie-in agreement
    (B) market allocation
    (C) price-fixing
    (D) a Sherman Antitrust Act violation

72. An owner could be required to make readily achievable modifications to premises because of:

    (A) RESPA
    (B) the Americans with Disabilities Act
    (C) the 1988 Fair Housing Amendment Act
    (D) the Civil Rights Act of 1968

73. An income property is valued at $800,000 by an appraiser who used a capitalization rate of 8 percent. If the appraiser had used a capitalization rate of 6½ percent, what would be the appraiser's estimate of property value?

    (A) $443,000
    (B) $470,000
    (C) $650,000
    (D) $984,615

74. An example of a stigmatized property would be a house:

    (A) condemned by the city as unfit for habitation
    (B) in an undesirable neighborhood
    (C) with numerous physical defects
    (D) regarded by the community as being unlucky

75. The terms *good, valuable,* and *legal* refer to:

    (A) income
    (B) consideration
    (C) commission
    (D) capacity

76. A 6-foot fence is to be built around all four sides of an 80′ × 120′ rectangular lot. The cost for the fence will be $2.50 per linear foot for labor plus $ .42 per square foot for material. What is the total cost of the fence?

    (A) $1,008
    (B) $1,168
    (C) $2,008
    (D) $2,168

77. A buyer paid one point to obtain a home loan. The point paid by the buyer:

    (A) is tax deductible by the buyer as interest
    (B) would be added to the buyer's cost basis
    (C) is taxable as income to the buyer
    (D) may be depreciated by the buyer

78. At closing, which of the following would be a debit to the seller?

    (A) Loan points
    (B) Broker's commission
    (C) Lender's extended coverage policy of title insurance
    (D) Prepaid property taxes

79. Before the expiration of an exclusive listing, the owner terminated the listing without cause. Based on the owner's action, the broker:

    (A) is entitled to specific performance
    (B) is entitled to damages
    (C) can still earn a commission if a buyer can be located prior to the expiration date on the listing
    (D) has no recourse against the owner because listings can be terminated at will

80. The principle that value is best maintained when there is a proper proportion of land, labor, capital, and management is the principle of:

    (A) competition
    (B) supply and demand
    (C) balance
    (D) conformity

DIFFICULTY LEVEL III ANSWERS

1. (C) The CRV is the VA appraisal valuation. (page 121)
2. (B) The seller has to turn over the unearned rent to the buyer. (page 128)
3. (C) Government survey lines. (page 3)
4. (D) And it can be taken every two years. (page 41)
5. (B) The grantor sells and becomes a tenant of the grantee. (page 140)
6. (D) The original lease remains with the sublessor. (page 144)
7. (D) Death of principal or agent terminates an agency. (page 92)
8. (A) It is an apparent discrepancy causing doubt as to title. Is *ML* the same person as *KL*? (page 53)
9. (B) 9% (.09) × $1,800 = $162 per year or $81 for 6 months. (page 161)
   9% (.09) × $1,200 = $108 per year or $54 for 6 months.
   9% (.09) × $600 = $54 per year or $27 for 6 months.
   $81 + $54 + $27 = $162.
10. (B) They are the advances the lender is obligated to make as work meets agreed-upon stages of construction. (page 116)
11. (A) Value is the present worth of future benefits. (page 62)
12. (C) Acquiring property by inheritance. (page 54)
13. (D) An undivided interest in the whole. (page 9)
14. (C) Rising interest rates would result in the investor's using higher capitalization rates that would result in lower value. (pages 68–69)
15. (B) That are federally related. (page 127)
16. (C) Whole = Part ($328,000) ÷ Percentage (.82). (page 157)
17. (D) The offer was not in accordance with terms specified in the listing. (page 93)
18. (C) Conduct that disturbs the tenant forcing the tenant to vacate. (page 142)
19. (A) Within three business days of loan application. (page 127)
20. (B) Court makes determination of title. (page 52)
21. (C) 210 × 4 = $840 per year. Rate = Part ÷ Whole. (page 160)
22. (B) Menace makes a contract voidable by the injured party. (page 83)
23. (D) It is an improvement, and cost basis of a residence is cost plus improvement. (page 41)
24. (C) *L* is an innocent improver, so *L* can remove improvement. (page 31)
25. (A) One party now has all ownership interests. (page 7)
26. (D) Both sexual and familial status discrimination. (pages 98–99)
27. (D) It is a special agency. (page 90)
28. (B) Buyer may be informed as to availability of data about sex offenders in the area. (page 95)
29. (C) Mineral, oil, and gas rights are real property. (page 140)
30. (B) Built-in obsolescence. (pages 70–71)
31. (A) Used the benefits (rents) that should result. (page 63)
32. (D) $100,000 for subsequent violations. (page 100)
33. (B) All beneficial rights of ownership. (page 1)
34. (C) So new leases can reflect the economic condition when leases expire. (page 139)
35. (B) Under an acceleration clause. (page 118)
36. (C) It is a chance to meet purchase or lease terms of another that the owner is willing to accept. (page 86)
37. (B) Because it lacks valuable consideration. While good consideration, love and affection is not valuable to support a promise. (page 83)
38. (C) Or the buyer could waive the seller's breach and insist on closing. (page 87)
39. (D) Net operating income (NOI) is gross less all operating expenses, an allowance for vacancy and collections as well as management costs. (page 68)
40. (C) Used when exact acreage is difficult to ascertain, as with a metes-and-bounds description. (page 3)
41. (D) The wraparound loan (all-inclusive loan) covers the first and second loan at one interest rate and is paid to the seller while the seller makes payments on the first loan. (page 116)
42. (D) When exercised, the optionee agrees to be bound. (page 86)
43. (C) A tenant contact person must be named. (page 143)
44. (B) Although state law might not require disclosure. (pages 91–92)
45. (A) By buying FHA, VA, and conventional loans made by direct lenders. (page 123)

46. (D) The only party that can compensate a salesperson is his or her own broker. (page 90)
47. (C) Because the interest accruing each month accrues on previously charged interest. (page 116)
48. (D) $197,000 – $15,760 (8%) – $1,480 = $179,760. (page 159)
49. (B) Joint tenancy must be stated or, in some states, be conveyed to the husband and wife. (A) and (D) require marriage. (page 9)
50. (B) An ordinance passed by local government. (A) is a physical, (C) is an economic, and (D) is a social factor. (page 65)
51. (B) The offeror can revoke but the offeree rejects. (page 85)
52. (C) Mortgage brokers arrange but do not make loans, while mortgage bankers make loans that they sell. (page 120)
53. (A) A mortgage banker would borrow on the inventory of loans. (page 117)
54. (B) It is credited to the buyers as part of what they have to pay and deducted (debited) from what the sellers will receive at closing. (pages 128–129)
55. (C) Provided it is like-for-like (business or investment property). (page 44)
56. (A) The take-out loan replaces (takes out) the construction loan. (page 116)
57. (A) Cost basis is cost less depreciation. Because only the $720,000 was depreciated, the cost basis would be the cost of the land. (page 43)
58. (B) It makes a loan secondary in priority to a later recorded loan. (page 119)
59. (C) Attachment is a prejudgment lien to make certain there will be something to go against after a judgment. (page 27)
60. (B) It can be encumbered and there is no time limitation. (page 6)
61. (B) Because more buyers could qualify for loans. (page 124)
62. (D) With an amortized loan each month's payment applies less to interest and more to principal than the prior month's payment. (page 114)
63. (B) Forces outside the property and usually incurable. (page 71)
64. (C) 7% of $12,000 = $840
     5% of $13,200 = $660
     3% of $14,520 = $436
     $1,936 (page 159)
65. (A) Up to an agreed-upon limit. Home equity loan approvals and home equity credit cards do the same thing. (page 116)
66. (C) Another salesperson could be the buyer's agent. Designated agency is an attempt to avoid the problems of dual agency. (page 89)
67. (C) Entered with permission, as when a buyer is given possession prior to closing. (page 139)
68. (C) Because title goes to a third party, it is a remainder interest contingent on *L*'s living longer than *K*. (page 7)
69. (C) A carcinogen used in electrical transformers. (page 146)
70. (A) Neither penalizes prepayment. (page 123)
71. (D) The agreement is a group boycott. (page 97)
72. (B) For handicap access. (page 100)
73. (D) To find the interest earned (part): .08 (interest rate) times $800,000 = $64,000; $64,000 is the net income. If we used 6½%, we would capitalize the $64,000 income, $64,000 ÷ .065, which equals $984,615. (pages 68, 159)
74. (D) Nonphysical perception of the property. (pages 91–92)
75. (B) Love and affection would be "good" consideration but not "valuable". (pages 49, 82)
76. (C) 80' × 120' lot has 400' perimeter; 400' × 2.50 = $1,000; 6' × 400 = 2,400 square feet; 2,400 × .42 = $1,008 + $1,000 = $2,008. (pages 159, 163, 164)
77. (A) In the year paid. (page 117)
78. (B) The others would be buyer debits. (page 128)
79. (B) While an owner can always terminate since agency requires consent, breach of agreement could expose party to damages if wrongful. (page 93)
80. (C) When agents of production are in balance, prices of construction should be relatively stable. (page 63)

DIFFICULTY LEVEL IV

1. If $1,925 is paid over a five-month period on a $30,000 straight mortgage, the interest rate is more than:

    (A) 8% but less than 10%
    (B) 10% but less than 12%
    (C) 12% but less than 14%
    (D) 14% but less than 16%

2. Liens to be assumed by the buyer would be shown in a settlement statement as:

    (A) buyer debits
    (B) seller debits
    (C) seller credits
    (D) balance factors

3. A nonconforming loan is a loan that:

    (A) is delinquent in payments
    (B) is secured by personal property rather than real estate
    (C) does not meet the purchase requirements of Fannie Mae
    (D) lacks government guarantee or insurance

4. The buyer under a sale-leaseback expects:

    (A) to free capital
    (B) an annuity type benefit
    (C) to trade on equity
    (D) to fully deduct rent payments

5. A life tenant committed waste. The life tenant:

    (A) kept the property vacant
    (B) failed to utilize the property for its highest and best use
    (C) damaged the property
    (D) depreciated the property

6. A veteran has made the last payment on a VA loan. The veteran is now entitled to:

    (A) the return of funding fees
    (B) restoration of loan benefits
    (C) proration of loan points
    (D) a policy of title insurance

7. To determine if a modification is readily achievable in accordance with the Americans with Disabilities Act, consideration is given to:

    (A) other similar properties being required to make similar modifications
    (B) the fact that a modification is physically possible
    (C) the cost to comply compared with the property value
    (D) whether the modification will increase the property value by the cost of the modifications

8. An owner gave false information to a prospective buyer in the presence of the owner's agent. The agent should:

    (A) keep silent
    (B) notify the owner that, in the future, the agent will answer all questions
    (C) correct the owner in private
    (D) immediately provide the correct information to the buyer

9. The person on a trust deed who is in the same position that a mortgagor is in on a mortgage is known as a:

    (A) trustee
    (B) vendee
    (C) beneficiary
    (D) trustor

10. The state wants to condemn a diagonal strip of land that bisects *O*'s farm. The farm value will decrease far more than the per-acre value offered for the land taken. *O* should ask for:

    (A) severance damages
    (B) exemplary damages
    (C) nominal damages
    (D) an injunction

11. The chain of title for a property is revealed in the:

    (A) preliminary title report
    (B) abstract
    (C) attorney's title opinion
    (D) standard policy of title insurance

12. A fee simple subject to a condition subsequent would:

    (A) automatically revert to the grantor on breach of the condition
    (B) require that the grantor exercise his or her right of reentry
    (C) not be lost by failure to exercise rights
    (D) have its duration spelled out in the deed

13. Debits on a seller's closing statement include:

    (A) seller financing
    (B) purchase price
    (C) fuel in tank
    (D) prepaid insurance

14. A mortgage banker borrows on an inventory of loans. This is known as:

    (A) a wraparound loan
    (B) mortgage warehousing
    (C) discounting mortgages
    (D) secondary financing

15. "The owner is legally entitled to fair market value" describes:

    (A) a management contract
    (B) a lease
    (C) eminent domain
    (D) purchase contract

16. The rescission provisions of the Truth-in-Lending Act apply to what type of loans?

    (A) Construction
    (B) Home equity
    (C) Business
    (D) Agricultural

17. A purchaser checks the county records and determines that the seller was the grantee on a deed of the property involved, but that there were no further recordings involving the grantee. The purchaser could reasonably assume that:

    (A) the seller has marketable title
    (B) there are no encumbrances against the property
    (C) taxes are current
    (D) the seller has not mortgaged the property

18. How much can a lender charge for preparing the disclosure of loan costs that is required by the Real Estate Settlement Procedures Act?

    (A) No charge is allowed.
    (B) Only actual preparation cost can be charged.
    (C) $50
    (D) $100

19. A feature of a VA loan is the:

    (A) use of pass-through certificates
    (B) application of the tandem plan
    (C) use of mortgage-backed certification
    (D) requirement of a funding fee

20. In preparing a settlement statement, a broker should understand that:

    (A) the party who receives a deed pays to draft it
    (B) the party giving a deed pays to record it
    (C) unless agreed otherwise, buyer loan costs are split between buyer and seller
    (D) title insurance costs would never be a credit on a closing statement

21. A topographical map has contour lines that are very close together in one area. It indicates:

    (A) a very high elevation
    (B) that the land is relatively flat
    (C) a low elevation
    (D) a steep slope

22. What type of conveyance would turn a freehold interest into a nonfreehold interest?

    (A) Sale of air rights
    (B) Sale of mineral rights
    (C) Sale leaseback
    (D) Thirty-year lease

23. At closing, the lender requests $680, which will be kept in a special fund. This money is:

    (A) a security deposit
    (B) for taxes and insurance
    (C) to ensure against default
    (D) to cover points

24. In the absence of permission to disclose, a listing broker may tell a prospective purchaser:

    (A) that the seller must conclude a sale
    (B) that the property is not desirable
    (C) what the owner actually will accept
    (D) what the owner originally paid

25. Under RESPA, what are the maximum advance tax reserves that a lender can require at the time of the loan?

    (A) Two months in advance
    (B) Three months in advance
    (C) Six months in advance
    (D) One year in advance

26. A broker's own interests would be in conflict with those of his or her principal if the broker took a(n):

    (A) open listing
    (B) net listing
    (C) exclusive-right-to-sell listing
    (D) buyer agency agreement

27. An owner adds a clause to a listing stating "Sale will be only to a white person." The broker must:

    (A) accept the listing if the owner refuses to remove it
    (B) agree to the clause only if the owner agrees to pay any damages and penalties
    (C) refuse to accept the listing
    (D) inform the owner that the advertising cannot reflect this agreement

28. *J* and *K* owned property together in joint tenancy. *J* owed numerous creditors, and several of them have obtained judgments. *J* died before the creditors were able to seize and partition the joint tenancy property. What are the rights of the creditors?

    (A) The judgment creditors become tenants in common with *K*.
    (B) All the creditors are equal in status and have the right to one-half of the property.
    (C) The probate court would take title to one-half of the property.
    (D) The creditors have no right to the property.

29. A valid contract could be unenforceable because of:

    (A) lack of contractual capacity
    (B) the statute of limitations
    (C) the absence of consideration
    (D) an illegal purpose

30. What type of property interest would be personal to the holder, revocable at will, and unassignable?

    (A) Easement in gross
    (B) License
    (C) Periodic tenancy
    (D) Life estate

31. *M* knows the owner is considering an offer. *M* asks the listing broker the amount of the offer so *M* can exceed it. The broker should:

    (A) disclose because it is in the owner's best interests
    (B) disclose because a broker must reveal to a buyer everything the broker knows about a property
    (C) notify the owner of the request
    (D) tell the prospective buyer that no other offers can be considered while an offer is pending

32. A piece of property is priced at $300,000, using a 6 percent capitalization rate. If the prospective investor wanted an 8 percent return, the value of the property to the investor would be:

    (A) $210,000
    (B) $225,000
    (C) $270,000
    (D) $290,000

33. Why would a large shopping center offer an anchor tenant a below-market-rate percentage lease?

    (A) Because they hope the volume will make up for the low percentage
    (B) Because of the effect on other tenants' leases and volume
    (C) Because of economics of scale
    (D) To reduce operational costs

34. A property has a net operating income of $27,600 per year, and 8½ percent is an appropriate capitalization rate. If the value of the land is $135,000, how much of the value is attributable to the building?

    (A) $179,600
    (B) $185,000
    (C) $189,705
    (D) $716,800

35. Which of the following restrictive covenants would be enforceable?

    (A) A property cannot be used for any commercial purpose that competes with the use of a neighboring parcel.
    (B) The parcel cannot be occupied by non-Christians.
    (C) The property must be kept in agricultural use.
    (D) The property can only be sold to blood relatives of the original grantor.

36. A determination of net income is necessary when utilizing the:

    (A) market comparison approach
    (B) gross multiplier
    (C) cost approach
    (D) income approach

37. Before closing, the seller and buyer agree to a rescission of their sales agreement, with the buyer asking the listing broker for the return of his deposit. The broker should:

    (A) return the deposit in full
    (B) deduct the commission due and return the balance
    (C) keep half of the commission due and return everything else
    (D) hold all monies for a court determination of the broker's rights

38. A disadvantage of ownership in a cooperative versus condominium ownership is the:

    (A) restriction on profit on resale
    (B) danger that other owners might be unable to pay their shares toward the mortgage and taxes
    (C) personal liability of owners should they default on their payments
    (D) higher tax assessment

39. A tenant on a long-term commercial lease wants to go out of business. Because the rent is worth much more than the tenant is paying, the tenant should consider:

    (A) assigning the lease
    (B) subletting the property
    (C) a novation
    (D) surrendering the premises

40. A loan impound account belongs to the:

    (A) lender
    (B) broker
    (C) borrower
    (D) closing agent

41. A lease used the terms *minimum rent* and *gross income*. What kind of lease was it?

    (A) Gross lease
    (B) Net lease
    (C) Percentage lease
    (D) Periodic tenancy

42. An 1,800-square-foot home has just been built next to a 3,800-square-foot home. The owner of the larger home would be concerned with the principle of:

    (A) integration and disintegration
    (B) balance
    (C) regression
    (D) conformity

43. A newspaper advertisement by a broker is considered to be a(n):

    (A) irrevocable offer
    (B) revocable offer
    (C) invitation to negotiate
    (D) firm offer

44. *J* sold his residence of 8 years for $400,000. He had paid $80,000 for the home and invested $30,000 in improvements. He remarried a year before the sale and his new wife was living in the house at the time of sale. Assuming *J* is in the 28 percent tax bracket, how much will *J* be taxed on the sale?

    (A) Nothing
    (B) $ 8,000
    (C) $56,000
    (D) $60,000

45. A broker violated the Sherman Antitrust Act when the broker:

    (A) refused to accept less than 6 percent as a listing commission
    (B) agreed with another broker to respect each other's designated territory
    (C) agreed with a group of brokers to cooperate on listings
    (D) agreed to abide by minimum ethical standards of a broker organization

46. A landlord was found to be guilty of retaliatory eviction because the landlord:

    (A) refused to renew a one-year residential lease after the tenant complained to health authorities about a rodent problem
    (B) made unnecessary and loud repairs to harass a tenant
    (C) used threats and profanity toward the tenant
    (D) refused to clean common areas

47. After street parking was made illegal, the rents of a small office building declined $1,000 per month. Assuming a capitalization rate of 9 percent, the building suffered loss in value of:

    (A) $ 9,000
    (B) $ 81,000
    (C) $120,000
    (D) $133,333

48. With the seller's knowledge, the buyer under an executory verbal purchase agreement made extensive improvements to a property. The seller later refused to honor the sale agreement. The buyer would likely assert:

    (A) the parol evidence rule
    (B) the statute of frauds
    (C) laches
    (D) the doctrine of estoppel

49. Who would have a less than freehold estate?

    (A) A sublessor
    (B) A lessor
    (C) A life tenant
    (D) An owner in fee simple

50. A unilateral contract that becomes bilateral upon being exercised is a(n):

    (A) exclusive listing
    (B) option
    (C) purchase contract
    (D) mortgage

51. A capital improvement to real estate would:

    (A) be written off as an expense in the year of the improvement
    (B) increase the book value by the cost of the improvement
    (C) decrease the book value by the cost of the improvement
    (D) increase the book value by the increase in appraised valuation

52. In preparing a competitive market analysis a broker would consider:

    (A) physical deterioration, functional obsolescence, and external obsolescence
    (B) the reproduction cost
    (C) the applicable capitalization rate
    (D) the replacement cost

53. Tenant obligations under a lease will cease with:

    (A) tenant eviction
    (B) the sale of the property
    (C) condemnation of the property
    (D) failure of the tenant to exercise a purchase option

54. A deed uses the description "728 N. Main Street." The description would be:

    (A) based on government survey
    (B) a lot and block description
    (C) a metes-and-bounds description
    (D) an informal description

55. A broker violated antitrust laws when the broker:

    (A) charged every seller a flat 6 percent commission
    (B) refused to show property listed at less than 6 percent commission
    (C) agreed with other brokers to refuse to cooperate with cut-rate offices
    (D) listed property at a price above market value

56. *J* offered to buy *K's* home for $150,000. *K* accepted the written offer with the notation, "Seller may remove the rosebushes by the patio." *K* received no further reply from *J*, so *K* sent *J* a signed memo: "I will leave the rosebushes." What are *J's* obligations as to the purchase?

    (A) *J* is bound to her offer because *K's* memo removed the condition.
    (B) *J's* offer was never accepted so *J* is not obligated.
    (C) Because the rosebushes are minor items, *K's* acceptance formed an agreement binding *J*.
    (D) The contract is voidable at the option of either *J* or *K*.

57. An ejectment action can be used against a(n):

    (A) tenant who has failed to pay the rent
    (B) owner who has committed waste
    (C) tenant at sufferance
    (D) trustor who is in default

58. A broker wants to advertise a property located in an African American neighborhood in a newspaper aimed at African American readership. To do so, the broker needs to:

    (A) indicate compliance with the fair housing laws
    (B) also advertise properties in white neighborhoods in the same paper
    (C) include the Equal Housing Opportunity logo in the ad
    (D) identify the exact location in the ad

59. Responsibility for disclosure under RESPA rests with the:

    (A) seller
    (B) broker
    (C) lender
    (D) title company

60. *L*, a seller, lied to *M* about the zoning to induce *M* to buy a ten-acre parcel. Before completion of the sale, *M* learns of the deception. What are the contractual rights of *L* and *M*?

    (A) The sale is void as to both *L* and *M*.
    (B) *L* can be held to the sales agreement by *M*.
    (C) Either *L* or *M* can void the agreement.
    (D) The agreement is binding on both *L* and *M*, although *M* may be entitled to damages after the closing.

61. Which law requires that a good-faith estimate of settlement costs be given by a lender to a borrower within three days of a loan application?

    (A) Real Estate Settlement Procedures Act
    (B) Fair Credit Reporting Act
    (C) Equal Credit Opportunity Act
    (D) Truth-in-Lending Act

62. *C* gave a deed to *E* with an oral agreement that the deed was not to be recorded until after *C* died. The deed was:

    (A) valid
    (B) void
    (C) voidable
    (D) illegal

63. A handicapped tenant intends to make extensive modifications to the interior of an apartment to meet particular needs relating to the handicap. The tenant should realize that the landlord:

    (A) can condition approval to the modification on an agreement to restore the premises at the end of the tenancy
    (B) can insist on an additional security deposit to guarantee restoration
    (C) is obligated to pay reasonable modification costs
    (D) can refuse to allow the modification

64. The lender under a construction loan would provide the builder with the final payment on:

    (A) receipt of the deed
    (B) receipt of the occupancy permit
    (C) notice of completion
    (D) expiration of the mechanic's lien period

65. *J* owns a lot free and clear valued at $30,000, on which he plans to construct a commercial building and lease it at an annual rent of $65,000. Total expenses are estimated at $11,000 per year. If an 8 percent net return is expected on the total investment, what will be the cost of the improvements?

    (A) $435,750
    (B) $595,000
    (C) $645,000
    (D) $675,000

66. Under a lease a landlord:

    (A) subrogates his or her rights
    (B) subordinates his or her rights
    (C) assigns his or her rights
    (D) hypothecates his or her rights

67. A lease clause provides that if the lease is not extended or renewed, the rents shall increase 50 percent should the tenant fail to vacate. What type of clause is it?

    (A) Defeasance
    (B) Alienation
    (C) Holdover
    (D) Subordination

68. Losing a right due to the failure to assert it in a timely manner is called:

    (A) laches
    (B) dereliction
    (C) satisfaction
    (D) surrender

69. A rectangular lot has an apartment structure on it worth $193,600. This value is the equivalent of $4.40 per square foot for the lot. If one lot dimension is 200′, what is the other dimension?

    (A) 110′
    (B) 220′
    (C) 400′
    (D) 880′

70. The Truth-in-Lending Act is also known as:

    (A) the Credit Insurance Act of 1968
    (B) Regulation Z
    (C) the Federal Usury Law
    (D) the Fair Housing Act

71. Monthly rent on a warehouse was set at $1 per cubic yard. Assuming the warehouse was 36′ × 200′ and it was 12′ high, what would be the annual rent?

    (A) $ 3,200
    (B) $28,800
    (C) $38,400
    (D) $86,400

72. Mr. *X*'s home recently was appraised at $105,000. Based on the appraisal, it has depreciated 30 percent in the three years since it was purchased. What was the original cost?

    (A) $ 80,769
    (B) $136,500
    (C) $139,650
    (D) $150,000

73. A standard policy of title insurance provides an owner protection against:

    (A) problems that would be discovered by survey
    (B) unrecorded interests of a party in possession
    (C) unrecorded liens not known to the policyholder
    (D) defects apparent from public records

74. Functional obsolescence can be created by:

    (A) forces outside the property
    (B) an overimprovement
    (C) zoning change
    (D) termite infestation

75. A seller's agent lied to the buyer to induce the buyer to purchase a property. Who could be held liable if the buyer suffers a loss because of the agent's fraud?

    (A) Agent only
    (B) Agent and owner
    (C) Owner only
    (D) No one, based on caveat emptor

76. What principle should an apartment owner consider when deciding if an apartment should add a fitness center for the tenants?

    (A) Principle of completion
    (B) Principle of contribution
    (C) Principle of integration and disintegration
    (D) Principle of substitution

77. Both FHA and VA loans may be obtained to purchase:

    (A) rental and owner-occupied housing
    (B) business and home loans
    (C) farm and business loans
    (D) a four-family apartment

78. Under a sale-leaseback the:

    (A) lessee is the seller
    (B) lessee retains the tax benefits of ownership
    (C) lessor has the tax deduction of rent
    (D) seller is the lessor

79. How would you eliminate a restrictive covenant from a property?

    (A) By quiet title action
    (B) By appealing to the zoning commission
    (C) By transferring title without reference to the restriction
    (D) By an agreement with all others subject to the restriction

80. An attorney in fact violated fiduciary duty in:

    (A) purchasing the principal's property
    (B) leasing the principal's property to a 3rd party
    (C) selling the principal's property
    (D) placing a lien on the principal's property

DIFFICULTY LEVEL IV ANSWERS

1. (D) $1,925 ÷ 5 = $385 (1 month's interest). $385 × 12 = $4,620 (1 year's interest). Rate = Part ($4,620) ÷ Whole ($30,000) = .154 or 15.4%. (page 157)
2. (B) They were owed by seller so seller debits and buyer credits. (page 128)
3. (C) Such as a jumbo loan above limits for purchase. (page 124)
4. (B) The seller would free capital and be able to deduct rent as an expense (business). (page 140)
5. (C) Abused the property or failed to maintain it. (page 6)
6. (B) So another VA loan would be possible. (page 122)
7. (C) As well as financial ability of owner. (page 100)
8. (D) Duty of fairness to buyer. (page 91)
9. (D) Trustor and mortgagor are borrowers on a note. (pages 111, 112)
10. (A) For the loss in value of the remaining land. (page 48)
11. (B) It shows all recorded documents from the original government conveyance (patent). (page 52)
12. (B) But a fee simple determinable automatically ends the estate. (page 6)
13. (A) It would be deducted from cash seller is entitled to at closing. (page 128)
14. (B) Mortgage bankers often borrow on loans. The loans are said to be *collaterally secured.* (page 117)
15. (C) If owner is not satisfied with sum offered, can have court determine fair market value. (page 47)
16. (B) Others are exempt. (page 125)
17. (D) Because a mortgage would have to be recorded to take priority over a purchaser. (pages 50–52, 113)
18. (A) No charge allowed for RESPA disclosures. (page 127)
19. (D) Which varies, based on down payment. (page 122)
20. (D) They are debited (paid) by either one or both parties. (pages 128, 129)
21. (D) When they are far apart, land is relatively flat. (page 5)
22. (C) The grantor now would have a leasehold interest. (pages 7, 140)
23. (B) This would be an impound account. (page 119)
24. (B) Broker has duty to convey known negative information to the buyer. (page 91)
25. (A) Plus prorated amount to time of closing, to be placed in impound account. (page 127)
26. (B) It would be in broker's best interest to get as high a price as possible and in the owner's best interest for as quick a sale as possible. (page 94)
27. (C) Listing would be in violation of fair housing laws. (pages 97–98)
28. (D) *K* owns property in severalty clear of creditor's rights. (page 9)
29. (B) Delay in enforcing rights where enforcement is barred. (page 87)
30. (B) A license is permissive use. (page 31)
31. (C) Fiduciary duty to disclose all pertinent information. (page 91)
32. (B) Part = Rate (.06, as decimal) × Whole ($300,000) or $18,000. If net is $18,000, use of 8% rate would be $18,000 ÷ .08 = $225,000. (pages 68, 159)
33. (B) Anchor tenant (major store) would increase traffic and increase volume for other tenants. (page 140)
34. (C) Capitalize income: $27,600 ÷ .085 = $324,706. $324,705 – $135,000 (land value) = $189,705 attributable to building. (pages 68, 70)
35. (C) If reasonable, it would be enforceable. The others are restraint on trade, restraint on alienation, or fair housing violation. (page 25)
36. (D) We capitalize the net income to determine value. (pages 67–68)
37. (A) It is buyer's money, and commission is owed by seller. Broker may have separate claim against seller for commission. (pages 93, 96)
38. (B) Which could lead to foreclosure of entire property. (page 14)
39. (B) At a higher rent, thus keeping the difference. (page 144)
40. (C) It is kept by the lender to make certain funds will be available to pay taxes. (page 119, 128)
41. (C) Percentage leases are based on gross income but usually have a minimum rent. (page 140)
42. (C) Lower cost home could reduce the value of the larger home. (page 63)
43. (C) It is not regarded as an offer that can be accepted. (page 84)
44. (B) *J*'s cost basis is $80,000 (cost) + $30,000 (improvements), or $110,000. A sale at $400,000 means a gain of $290,000. *J* has $250,000 exclusion, but *J*'s wife does not qualify for the exclusion (2-year occupancy). Therefore, $40,000 is taxable at 20% capital gain rate. (pages 41–42, 43)
45. (B) This would be market allocation. (page 97)

46. (A) The others could constitute constructive eviction. (page 144)
47. (D) Capitalize annual loss of $12,000 using the 9% rate. (page 68)
48. (D) The seller, by allowing the buyer to act to his or her detriment, is barred (estopped) from raising the defense of the statute of frauds. (page 83)
49. (A) A sublessor is a lessee on another lease. A leasehold interest is a nonfreehold interest. (pages 6, 144)
50. (B) Prior to exercise of an option the optionee is not bound.(page 86)
51. (B) Book value is cost plus improvements less depreciation. (pages 41, 43)
52. (A) All would affect adjustments to comparables. (page 66)
53. (C) The others do not end contractual obligations. (page 142)
54. (D) It is not a legal description. Some states require legal descriptions on deeds. (page 2)
55. (C) This would be a group boycott. (page 97)
56. (B) The change was a counteroffer that rejected J's offer. It cannot now be accepted. (page 85)
57. (C) Or a trespasser. Ejectment action is used against someone not legally in possession. (page 139)
58. (B) Otherwise it would be steering. (page 98)
59. (C) It is a lender disclosure law. (page 127)
60. (B) Or *M* can void the agreement if he or she wishes. Voidable at the option of the injured party. (pages 83–84)
61. (A) Three business days. (page 127)
62. (A) Between the parties recording is not necessary. The deed was delivered. (pages 48–49)
63. (A) 1988 Amendment to Civil Rights Act of 1968. (page 99)
64. (D) Or lien waivers are provided. (page 116)
65. (C) Gross income ($65,000) – expenses ($11,000) = $54,000 net income. Capitalize the net using the 8% rate: $54,000 ÷ .08 = $675,000. Deducting the land value of $30,000 leaves $645,000 for the building. (page 68)
66. (B) Gives up right of occupancy to a tenant. (page 139)
67. (C) Purpose is to induce tenant to either agree to new lease or vacate premises. (page 141)
68. (A) Undue delay that adversely affects the other party. (page 25)
69. (B) $193,600 ÷ $4.40 = 44,000 sq. ft. Divide known area (44,000) by known dimension (200′) = 220′ (other dimension). (page 165)
70. (B) Part of Consumer Credit Protection Act of 1968. (page 124)
71. (C) To find cubic feet multiply length × width × depth or 36′ × 200′ × 12′ = 86,400 cubic feet. Because a cubic yard has 27 cubic feet, divide 86,400 by 27 = 3,200 cubic yards or $3,200 per month. $3,200 × 12 = $38,400 annual rent. (page 164)
72. (D) $105,000 is 70% of original cost (depreciated 30%). Whole = $105,000 (Part) ÷ .70 (percentage as decimal), or $150,000 original cost. (page 158)
73. (D) Others are covered by extended coverage policy. (pages 52–53)
74. (B) It is built-in obsolescence. (pages 70–71)
75. (B) The principal is liable for the acts of the agent, and the agent is liable for wrongful acts. (pages 88, 92)
76. (B) What it will add to value. (page 62)
77. (D) Both allow one to four residential units. VA loans require owner occupancy, and FHA loans are for housing only. (page 123)
78. (A) Who gives up ownership for a position as a tenant. (page 140)
79. (D) Persons subject to restrictions can agree to end them. (page 25)
80 (A) By acting as a principal and selling to himself or herself, the agent would create a conflict of interest and this would be a breach of fiduciary duty. (page 91)

DIFFICULTY LEVEL V

1. A broker's trust account ledger had the following entries:

   Credits

Money in account	$ 8,000
Money due from other agents	6,000
	$14,000

   Debits

Buyer deposits	$ 8,100
Rentals received and due owners	1,300
	$9,400

   The account indicates a:

   (A) surplus of $1,400
   (B) surplus of $4,600
   (C) shortage of $1,400
   (D) shortage of $4,600

2. *L* sold a furnace to *M*. *L* recorded a financing statement. *M* installed the furnace in a home encumbered by a mortgage from lender *K*. As to the furnace:

   (A) *K* has a priority lien because it has become a fixture
   (B) *L* has the equivalent of a second mortgage
   (C) *L's* right to the furnace is superior to the right of *K* should *M* default
   (D) it does not become a fixture

3. A broker is instructed not to show a property while the owner, who is white, is away. While the owner is out of town, an African American couple request to be shown the property. The broker should:

   (A) show the property
   (B) refuse to show the property
   (C) ask HUD for an exception to the Fair Housing Act
   (D) inform the prospects that the home is no longer available to buy

4. A home was sold on September 30. Taxes are based on a fiscal year ending June 30. Taxes have not been paid for the current fiscal year. If the seller is responsible for the day of closing, which of the following statements is true regarding the charges on the closing statement?

   (A) The buyer owes the seller for three months' taxes.
   (B) The buyer owes the seller for four months' taxes.
   (C) The seller owes the buyer for three months' taxes.
   (D) The seller owes the buyer for four months' taxes.

5. In determining the cost to build various structures on a vacant lot and the value the property would have with the improvements, an appraiser uses the:

   (A) cost approach
   (B) development method
   (C) land residual method
   (C) observed condition method

6. State licensed or certified appraisers are required by:

   (A) FIRREA
   (B) CERCLA
   (C) FIRPTA
   (D) GNMA

7. Using a capitalization rate of 8 percent, what would be the value of a property having a gross monthly scheduled income of $1,200, a 10 percent vacancy and collection loss factor, and monthly operating expenses of $280?

   (A) $ 10,000
   (B) $100,000
   (C) $120,000
   (D) $144,000

8. Which loan transaction is exempt from Truth-in-Lending disclosure requirements?

 (A) Agricultural loans
 (B) Secondary financing
 (C) Home improvement loans
 (D) Home purchase loans

9. *L* deeded property to *M*; however, the owner of the property was *N*. *N* later deeded the property to *L*. *M* would have a title problem if *L's* deed to *M* were a:

 (A) grant deed
 (B) quitclaim deed
 (C) special warranty deed
 (D) general warranty deed

10. A subordination clause in a deed of trust benefits the:

 (A) trustor
 (B) trustee
 (C) beneficiary
 (D) vendee

11. A valid tax-deferred exchange requires that:

 (A) the properties be of equal value
 (B) the exchange be immediate on closing
 (C) boot be received
 (D) properties be held for income or investment

12. *G* derives 90 percent of income from activities involving the sale of real estate. *G* is not a licensed real estate salesperson or broker, yet *G's* activities are entirely proper if:

 (A) *G* is an employee of a licensed broker
 (B) *G's* activities are restricted to nonresidential real property agency sales
 (C) *G* sells her own property
 (D) *G* is paid on a contract fee rather than a commission basis

13. A home sale included a garden tractor. Ownership of the garden tractor would be conveyed by a:

 (A) packaged deed
 (B) bill of sale
 (C) special warranty deed
 (D) bargain and sale deed

14. *L* leased a commercial building for $3,200 per month. Assuming annual expenses of taxes at $4,700, utilities at $3,100, maintenance at $4,480, and management costs at $1,920, what would be the value of the structure using a capitalization rate of 8 percent?

 (A) $302,500
 (B) $320,800
 (C) $384,000
 (D) $480,000

15. An offer is accepted one day after the offer period expires. The offeror can treat the late acceptance by the offeree as valid because of the principle of:

 (A) waiver
 (B) novation
 (C) accord and satisfaction
 (D) rescission

16. An optionee properly notified the optionor that the optionee was exercising the option. The option now is a(n):

 (A) voidable contract
 (B) bilateral contract
 (C) implied contract
 (D) unilateral contract

17. An accountant would have the greatest interest in:

 (A) book value
 (B) appraisal value
 (C) market value
 (D) assessed value

18. Which determination would be first in appraising unimproved property?

    (A) Highest and best use
    (B) Net income
    (C) Accrued depreciation
    (D) Loan value

19. You are negotiating a very complex sales agreement as the agent of a sophisticated seller. During the negotiation, it becomes obvious that the buyer, who is not represented by an agent and who is a first-time buyer, does not understand the legal and tax consequences of the agreement proposed by your principal. You should:

    (A) suggest the buyer seek professional advice
    (B) refuse to negotiate any further with the buyer
    (C) not concern yourself with the buyer's ignorance
    (D) analyze the buyer's situation and change your principal's proposal to help the buyer

20. An appraiser used the term *adjusted selling price* for comparable property. What is the appraiser referring to?

    (A) Net price to the seller after deducting selling expense.
    (B) Sales price in constant dollars adjusted for inflation
    (C) Sales price of the comparable adjusted for features of the property being appraised
    (D) Selling price adjusted for state and federal taxes

21. How does an S corporation differ from other corporations?

    (A) Investors are personally liable for corporate debt.
    (B) Profits are taxed like a partnership.
    (C) S corporations may hold title as joint tenants.
    (D) The investor's interests are not transferable.

22. *P* sells Greenacres to *Q*, who does not take possession or record. *P* then borrows against the property, giving a recorded mortgage to *R*. *P* later transfers title to *S*, without any consideration for the transfer, and *S* records the deed. What are the rights of the parties?

    (A) *P* retains title because *Q* did not record and *S* did not pay consideration.
    (B) *Q* has title subject to the mortgage to R.
    (C) *Q* has title clear of the mortgage.
    (D) *S* has title with a mortgage to *R*.

23. A property manager, in deciding about rents, would consider the:

    (A) capitalization approach
    (B) market comparison approach
    (C) cost approach
    (D) residual approach

24. A seller's agent breached a fiduciary duty. The agent:

    (A) refused to follow illegal instructions of the principal
    (B) cannot remember what became of the $10,000 cash deposit the agent received
    (C) presented an offer to the owners for less than the list price, although the owners had indicated that they did not want to see such an offer
    (D) refused to tell a buyer why the seller was selling

25. As a condition of selling a lot to a builder, a broker required that the builder list the house to be constructed with the broker. This is an example of:

    (A) a boycott
    (B) price-fixing
    (C) a tie-in sale
    (D) market allocation

26. *L* wishes to build a rectangular structure 30' wide, 160' deep, and 24' high with a flat roof. *M* offers to build the structure for $8.50 per square foot. *P* offers to build the structure for $.375 per cubic foot. Whose offer is lower and by how much?

    (A) *M's* by $2,400
    (B) *M's* by $4.75 per square foot
    (C) *P's* by $2,400
    (D) *P's* by $1.62 per square foot

27. A broker is involved in a controlled business arrangement when the broker:

    (A) personally owns the building and rents space to his real estate firm
    (B) owns a mortgage company that rents space within the real estate sales office and works with the broker's buyers
    (C) acts as a dual agent
    (D) represents only one buyer

28. As used by lenders, qualifying ratios refer to:

    (A) collateral
    (B) capacity
    (C) character
    (D) points

29. A property on a long-term flat lease has a property tax increase. The value of the property:

    (A) increases by the amount of the tax increase
    (B) increases by an amount greater than the tax increase
    (C) decreases by the amount of the tax increase
    (D) decreases by an amount greater than the tax increase

30. In a real estate transaction, who is the seller's agent?

    (A) The salesperson who obtained the listing
    (B) The broker of the salesperson who obtained the listing
    (C) The cooperating broker who obtained the offer to purchase
    (D) The MLS

31. The lead paint disclosure applies to residential property built prior to:

    (A) 1988
    (B) 1968
    (C) 1978
    (D) 1998

32. A property manager of a mall is worried that a prospective tenant will not be able to generate the gross that the manager expects, even though the tenant has agreed to the percentage lease and minimum rent. To protect the owner in this situation, the property manager would include which clause in the lease?

    (A) Exculpatory
    (B) Holdover
    (C) Recapture
    (D) Right of first refusal

33. A buyer entered into a contract to purchase a home through a broker. Before closing, the buyer asked the broker if he could enter the residence and paint as well as make minor repairs. The broker should:

    (A) refuse the request
    (B) allow the buyer to enter if the buyer agrees to prorate settlement to date of possession
    (C) relay the request to the owner
    (D) allow buyer to enter only if a licensed contractor is used

34. A lender's requirement for a loan that the borrower retain a minimum balance would result in a:

    (A) collaterally secured loan
    (B) compensating balance
    (C) discount loan
    (D) construction loan

35. Broker *K* has an exclusive-right-to-sell listing for owner *L*'s home. Buyer *M* gives *K* an offer to purchase *L*'s home. Buyer *M*, who knows that *K* is *L*'s agent and has no buyer agency duty, mentions that if the offer is not accepted, they will be willing to increase the offer by $10,000. Broker *K*:

    (A) must convey this information to *L*
    (B) must ask *M* to deal through a buyer agent
    (C) need not convey the information received to *L*
    (D) must withdraw from the transaction

36. A lease has been executed. The lease:

    (A) has been terminated
    (B) conveys an ownership interest
    (C) requires recordation to be binding
    (D) has been honored by the parties

37. A property manager would prefer shorter term residential leases when:

    (A) there is a high vacancy factor
    (B) interest rates and inflation are increasing
    (C) the property is subject to rent control
    (D) overbuilding is likely

38. A commercial lot was 200 feet deep before it lost 50 feet of its rear depth because of eminent domain. If the value of the lot before the taking was $600,000, using the 4-3-2-1 approach, what was the lot value after the taking?

    (A) $450,000
    (B) $500,000
    (C) $540,000
    (D) $560,000

39. Hazardous substances were released on a property years before the property was purchased by the present owner. The owner, who had no knowledge of the release or use of hazardous substances on the property, could be held liable for cleanup costs in accordance with:

    (A) FIRREA
    (B) FIRPTA
    (C) CERCLA
    (D) FNMA

40. Mortgage loan brokers differ from mortgage bankers in that mortgage loan brokers:

    (A) service the loans they sell
    (B) use their own money to make loans
    (C) sell the loans they make
    (D) are not principals to their loans

41. A 240-foot-deep commercial lot lost the rear 10 feet of depth because of an eminent domain action. The result was that the:

    (A) value per front foot increased
    (B) value per square foot increased
    (C) front foot value remained constant
    (D) value per square foot decreased

42. What type of agency could be created by inaction of the principal?

    (A) Express agency
    (B) Agency by estoppel
    (C) Agency by ratification
    (D) Designated agency

43. The variance in the VA funding fee is based on the:

    (A) down payment
    (B) amount of the loan
    (C) amount of the VA guarantee
    (D) veteran's credit rating

44. "Passive investors having no management control" describes a:

    (A) joint venture
    (B) security
    (C) common interest subdivision
    (D) planned unit development

45. A note was given with a mortgage. The purpose of the note was to:

    (A) be security for the mortgage
    (B) evidence the debt
    (C) provide a lien on the property
    (D) create a real property interest

46. A fee-simple determinable differs from a fee simple on condition subsequent in that for a fee simple determinable:

    (A) the duration may be determined from the deed
    (B) the grantor must physically retake the premises
    (C) failure to assert rights will result in the loss of the rights
    (D) it can only involve personal property

47. An advantage of seller financing to the seller would be:

    (A) a government guarantee
    (B) that profit is taxed in the year received
    (C) the avoidance of capital gains tax
    (D) no tax on interest received

48. After notice to neighboring owners, a public hearing would be held prior to granting:

    (A) a building permit
    (B) a zoning variance
    (C) title insurance coverage
    (D) a tax shelter

49. A recorded deed would adversely affect a person who has rights in a property based on:

    (A) an existing easement
    (B) a prior recorded judgment against the grantor
    (C) work performed prior to recording
    (D) a prior unrecorded deed if the party had failed to take possession

50. A broker listed a home for $105,000 with an exclusive-right-to-sell listing that specified a 6 percent commission. While the listing was in effect, the broker received a verbal offer of $100,000. The broker relayed the offer to the owner, who signed a written acceptance. The broker transmitted the acceptance to the buyer but was informed that the buyer had found another property and would not complete this purchase. The broker is entitled to:

    (A) $6,000 commission from the buyer
    (B) $6,000 commission from the seller
    (C) specific performance from the buyer
    (D) nothing

51. A lot has three possible uses. As a gas station, an investment of $342,000 would provide a net income of $27,832; as a fast-food location, an investment of $620,000 would yield a net income of $52,800; and leased as a parking lot, the site with improvements of $45,000 would yield $12,000 net income. Assuming a capitalization rate of 8 percent for all three investments, which use would result in the highest and best use of the land?

    (A) Gas station
    (B) Fast-foods
    (C) Parking lot
    (D) Leaving property undeveloped

52. A lessor wished to end a tenancy. The lessee would be best protected if the lessee had a:

    (A) tenancy at will
    (B) tenancy at sufferance
    (C) month-to-month tenancy
    (D) tenancy for years

53. J's activities consists of originating loans secured by real property using J's own funds and then selling the loans to lending institutions and investors while retaining loan-servicing responsibilities. J's activity is that of a:

    (A) mortgage broker
    (B) mortgage banker
    (C) mortgage loan correspondent
    (D) mortgagor

54. A lender must inform the borrower that:

    (A) paying more than required reduces total interest costs
    (B) the loan and the servicing of the loan may be assigned
    (C) a longer loan term means more interest paid
    (D) a greater down payment would mean lower monthly payments

55. A disadvantage of a lender's accepting a deed in lieu of foreclosure as an alternative to mortgage foreclosure would be:

    (A) cost
    (B) time
    (C) intervening liens
    (D) redemption rights

56. Tearing down a profitable commercial garage to build an office building would be the result of applying the principle of:

    (A) highest and best use
    (B) conformity
    (C) progression
    (D) substitution

57. Participation certificates refer to:

    (A) partnerships
    (B) securities
    (C) cooperatives
    (D) limited partnerships

58. IRS Code Section 1031 deals with:

    (A) imputed interest
    (B) exchanges
    (C) the $250,000-$500,000 exclusion
    (D) installment sales

59. "To have and to hold" is included in a(n):

    (A) habendum clause
    (B) alienation clause
    (C) mortgage
    (D) legal description

60. There are four units in a common interest development. The bylaws of the homeowners' association provide for the apportionment of shared common area costs in proportion to the original purchase price of the units. The original sale prices were $87,500, $75,800, $62,900, and $58,500. If the common area annual costs come to $17,800, what is the share for the most expensive unit?

    (A) $3,560
    (B) $4,760
    (C) $4,870
    (D) $5,470

61. In accordance with the Americans With Disabilities Act, a place of *public accommodation* would include:

    (A) one to four residential units
    (B) all residential units
    (C) a retail store
    (D) only property built after 1988

62. To perfect a lien against personal property, a creditor would record a(n):

    (A) financing statement
    (B) attachment
    (C) bill of sale
    (D) personal property mortgage

63. A lease clause in which a mortgagee agrees to honor a lease should the mortgagee foreclose is a(n):

    (A) nondisturbance clause
    (B) attachment
    (C) subrogation
    (D) subordination

64. What is a government lot?

    (A) A property acquired directly from the government
    (B) A lot after land was taken for streets by eminent domain
    (C) A parcel by government survey less than 160 acres
    (D) An area zoned for civic purposes only

65. To accommodate a handicap, a tenant had handrails installed in the public hallways leading to the tenant's apartment. As to the installation of the handrails, the:

(A) landlord must reimburse the tenant's costs
(B) tenant must remove them when the tenancy ends
(C) tenant must post a bond for removal costs
(D) tenant has acted within the law

66. An example of statutory dedication is:

(A) a deed containing a reservation
(B) recording an approved subdivision map showing areas dedicated to public use
(C) eminent domain
(D) deeding property to a government entity

67. RESPA requirements include:

(A) a limitation on brokerage fees
(B) a prohibition of a broker affiliation with a provider of services for a real estate closing
(C) the prohibition of a broker's receiving a referral fee from a lender
(D) maximum allowable interest

68. Required seller disclosures include:

(A) flood hazard areas and prior flood disaster assistance
(B) the reason for the sale
(C) the amount of commission the seller is required to pay
(D) former residents who had AIDS

69. The W½ of the NW¼ of the NW¼ of the SE¼ of the SW¼ of a section is to be paved for parking at a cost of 38 cents per square foot. The total paving cost will be:

(A) $5,173
(B) $10,345
(C) $20,691
(D) $41,382

70. What type of deed has the most covenants?

(A) Grant deed
(B) Warranty deed
(C) Quitclaim deed
(D) Bargain and sale deed

71. Which of the following would be considered to be the equivalent of an annuity by an owner?

(A) Productive farmland
(B) A paid-for residence
(C) A long-term ground lease
(D) Vacant land in the path of progress

72. An earnest-money deposit is given with an offer to purchase to:

(A) validate the contract for recording
(B) compensate the broker if the offer is not accepted
(C) indicate good faith of purchaser
(D) cover settlement costs

73. Without the owner's permission, a seller's agent told a buyer that the seller was desperate and would lose the property to foreclosure unless it could be quickly sold. Which fiduciary duty did the agent break?

(A) Care
(B) Loyalty
(C) Disclosure
(D) Obedience

74. *L* verbally agrees to lease *M*'s store for six months starting next month. A week before she is to take occupancy, *L* notifies *M* that she is revoking the agreement because she has found a better location at a lower rent. What are the rights of the parties?

(A) The lease is valid and *M* can hold *L* to the agreement
(B) *L* is liable for three weeks' rent because she failed to give a 30-day notice
(C) The lease was void because it was verbal
(D) The lease was voidable because it was verbal

75. *Q* deeds property to *R*. After the conveyance the parties agree to rescind the transaction. How can they accomplish this?

    (A) By writing "canceled" on the deed and both signing it
    (B) By *R's* returning the deed to *Q*
    (C) By *R's* giving a new deed to *Q*
    (D) By destroying the deed

76. A mortgagee will benefit by a blanket mortgage because of:

    (A) shorter foreclosure time
    (B) personal liability
    (C) the guarantee
    (D) greater security

77. The lender must provide the borrower with a booklet prepared by the Federal Reserve when financing involves:

    (A) more than one lender
    (B) balloon payments
    (C) an adjustable rate loan
    (D) other than federally related financing

78. When listing a property for sale, owner *M* tells Broker *N* not to take an offer from *O*, whom owner *M* has had problems with. Broker *M* receives an offer from *O* for *M's* property. Broker *O* must:

    (A) return the offer to *O* with no explanation
    (B) return the offer to *O*, giving the reason
    (C) accept but not present the offer from *O*
    (D) present the offer to *M*

79. Taxes are paid on a calendar year. Taxes of $1,788.50 were paid by the seller for the year. The closing was on February 25 with the seller responsible for the date of closing. The closing statement would reflect a:

    (A) seller credit of $274
    (B) seller credit of $1,514
    (C) Seller credit of $1,606
    (D) buyer debit of $274

80. A lender discovered that a home was two feet from a lot line and a neighbor's easement for ingress ran right through a borrower's home. How did the lender make these discoveries?

    (A) By checking the spot survey
    (B) By checking the abstract
    (C) By checking the title opinion
    (D) By checking the standard policy of title insurance

DIFFICULTY LEVEL V ANSWERS

1. (C)   There is only $8,000 in the account, and there should be $9,400. (pages 125–127)
2. (C)   By recording the financing statement, *L* has a priority interest in the furnace. (page 116)
3. (B)   This refusal is based on obeying the principal's instructions that were reasonable and did not discriminate. (page 91)
4. (C)   Because the seller had possession during this period. The actual days the seller is responsible for would be 92 (31 days for July, 31 days for August, and 30 days for September). (pages 162–163)
5. (B)   Determine the cost to build for each use and deduct the cost from the value the property would have if built, which gives the value of the land for that use. It would indicate the highest and best use. (page 69)
6. (A)   Federal Financial Institutions Reform, Recovery and Enforcement Act. (page 72)
7. (C) $1,200 (monthly gross) minus $120 (10% monthly vacancy and collection loss) minus $280 for monthly operating expenses = $800 monthly net. $800 × 12 = $9,600 (annual net). To find value divide $9,600 (net) by .08 (cap rate), which equals $120,000. (page 68)
8. (A)   As are business loans. (page 125)
9. (B)   The other deeds would convey after-acquired title. (page 50)
10. (A)   As the trustor on a deed of trust could borrow on the property, giving the lender greater security. The trustor would be using the equity of the beneficiary as security for the loan. (page 119)
11. (D)   Properties must be like-for-like. A tax-free exchange is not possible with a personal residence. (page 44)
12. (C)   A person need not be licensed to sell his or her own property. Not acting as an agent for others. (page 88)
13. (B)   Used to transfer title to personal property. (pages 48, 127)
14. (A) $3,200 rent × 12 = $38,400 per year. (page 68)

Taxes	$4,700
Utilities	3,100
Maintenance	4,480
Management	1,920
	$14,200

$38,400 – $14,200 = $24,200 net. $24,200 ÷ .08 = $302,500.

15. (A)   A person can waive any provision that is for his or her sole benefit. (page 87)
16. (B)   When the optionor is notified of exercise of option, both parties are bound. (page 86)
17. (A)   Other values are of little interest to an accountant. (page 62)
18. (A)   The use that would result in greatest benefit from property. (page 63)
19. (A)   Duty of fair dealing with buyer. (page 91)
20. (C)   If the comparable has a better feature, the comparable's sales price is adjusted downward. If it lacks a feature of the property being appraised, its sales price would be adjusted upward. (page 66)
21. (B)   Corporation benefits but avoids double taxation. (page 12)
22. (B)   Because *R* had no notice, *R* has a prior lien. A person receiving title by gift does not take priority over an unrecorded deed for value. (pages 50–52)
23. (B)   Market rents would be considered for comparable property. (page 63)
24. (B)   This would be a breach of the duty of care (obvious negligence). (page 91)
25. (C)   Prohibited by Sherman Antitrust Act. (page 97)
26. (A)   30′ × 24′ × 160′ = 115,200 cubic feet; 115,200 × $.375 = $43,200. 30′ × 160′ = 4,800 sq. ft.; 4,800 × $8.50 = $40,800; $43,200 – $40,800 = $2,400. (page 163)
27. (B)   Broker controls service provider. (pages 127–128)
28. (B)   To determine if buyer qualifies for a loan. (page 124)
29. (D)   Because net is decreased, and net is capitalized to determine value. (pages 68–69)
30. (B)   The broker, not the salesperson, is the agent. (page 88)
31. (C)   Federal disclosure requirement. (page 95)
32. (C)   If the tenant is a poor operator and is unable to reach required gross, the lease can be terminated. (page 141)
33. (C)   This is not the agent's decision. Agent has a duty to relay request to owner. (page 91)
34. (B)   The result is to increase the effective rate of interest because the borrower does not receive full amount of the loan but pays interest on it. (page 117)
35. (A)   Fiduciary disclosure duty to principal. (page 91)

36. (D) An executed contract is one fully performed. To execute can also mean to sign and be bound by an agreement. (page 81)
37. (B) As renewals will likely be for higher rents. (page 139)
38. (C) The 4-3-2-1 approach to depth valuation is that 40% of the value is in the irst 25% of the depth, 30% in the next 25% of depth, 20% of value in the next 25% of depth, and 10% of value in the rear 25% of depth. The lot lost the rear 25% of the lot or 10% of its $600,000 value. (page 70)
39. (C) Comprehensive Environmental Response, Compensation and Liability Act. Owner could have avoided liability by having an environmental study of property. (page 145)
40. (D) Mortgage brokers arrange loans and are not a party to the loans. Other answers describe mortgage bankers. (page 120)
41. (B) The lowest-value portion of the lot was taken away. However, total value and front foot value would decline. (page 70)
42. (B) Owner could be barred from denying an agency if the owner failed to notify a party whom the owner knew believed an agency existed. (page 91)
43. (A) The lower the down payment the higher the funding fee. (page 122)
44. (B) As an example, shares in a Real Estate Investment Trust. (page 13)
45. (B) A note is the primary evidence of the debt, and the lien (mortgage or trust deed) is given to secure the note. (page 111)
46. (A) Answers (B) and (C) deal with a fee simple on a condition subsequent. (page 6)
47. (B) Can spread capital gain over a number of years. (page 43)
48. (B) As well as conditional use permit and rezoning. (page 23)
49. (D) There was no constructive notice of a property interest. (pages 51–52)
50. (D) A verbal offer for real estate, when accepted, does not result in a contract. (page 83)
51. (C) This is development method. Determine value of developed property and deduce development cost to find land value for the use. Gas station: $ 27,832 ÷ .08 = $347,900 value – $342,000 (development cost) = $5,900 attributable to land. Fast-food: $52,800 ÷ .08 = $660,000 – $620,00 = $40,000 attributable to land. Parking lot: $12,000 ÷ .08 = $150,000 – $45,000 = $105,000 attributable to land. (pages 68–69)
52. (D) Tenant knows fixed period of tenancy. (page 139)
53. (B) Unlike a mortgage broker, the mortgage banker or mortgage company uses its own funds to fund loans. (page 120)
54. (B) Required by RESPA. (page 127)
55. (C) While foreclosure would wipe out junior liens. (page 114)
56. (A) For greater profit. (page 63)
57. (B) Issued by Freddie Mac and backed by a pool of mortgages. (page 123)
58. (B) Tax-deferred exchanges of like-for-like business or investment property. (page 44)
59. (A) Sets forth the estate being conveyed. (page 48)
60. (D) Total purchase price. $284,700. To find percentage, divide the part by the whole. $87,500 ÷ 284,700 = .3073 or 30.73%. Multiply shared cost ($17,800) by .3073 = $5,470. (page 157)
61. (C) Nonresidential affecting commerce. (page 100)
62. (A) To establish the personal property lien of the security agreement. (page 116)
63. (A) Without the clause, the foreclosure of a prior mortgage or trust deed would terminate the lease. (page 118)
64. (C) Caused by lakes and rivers, so the parcel is less than 160 acres. (page 4)
65. (D) 1988 amendment allows tenant modification. Modification to public areas need not be restored. (page 99)
66. (B) The recording indicating dedicated area is considered to be dedication. (page 46)
67. (C) Prohibits kickbacks. (page 127)
68. (A) Federal requirement. (page 95)
69. (C) Going backward the parcel will be found to contain 1.25 acres. 43,560 × 1.25 = 54,450 sq. ft. × .38 = $20,691. (pages 4–5)
70. (B) Five covenants. (page 49)
71. (C) No maintenance, usually a regular long-term fixed income. (page 140)
72. (C) Not required for a valid contract. (pages 95–96)
73. (B) Had a duty to keep information confidential, and telling about the owner breaches owner loyalty. (page 91)
74. (A) The lease could be completed within one year so need not be in writing. (page 83)

75. (C) A deed is used only once. Once delivered, title is passed. To return title requires a new deed. (page 48)
76. (D) Blanket mortgage covers more than one property. (page 116)
77. (C) Entitled to a "Consumer Handbook on Adjustable Rate Mortgages." (page 128)
78. (D) Every offer must be presented to the owner unless it is clearly frivolous. (page 91)
79. (B) Seller is responsible for 31 days in January and 25 days in February, a total of 56 days. Daily tax proration would be $1,788.50 ÷ 365 = $4.90 per day. $4.90 × 56 = $274.40. Seller paid $1,788.50 and used $274.40 so is entitled to a credit of $1,514. Buyer would be debited this amount. (page 162)
80. (A) A spot survey shows location of buildings, easements, and encroachments. (page 52)

Appendix A

While not included in the ASI Content Outline, construction related questions are often included in the state portion of examinations. We have included Appendix A as an aid for the state portion of your real estate examination.

Construction Diagram

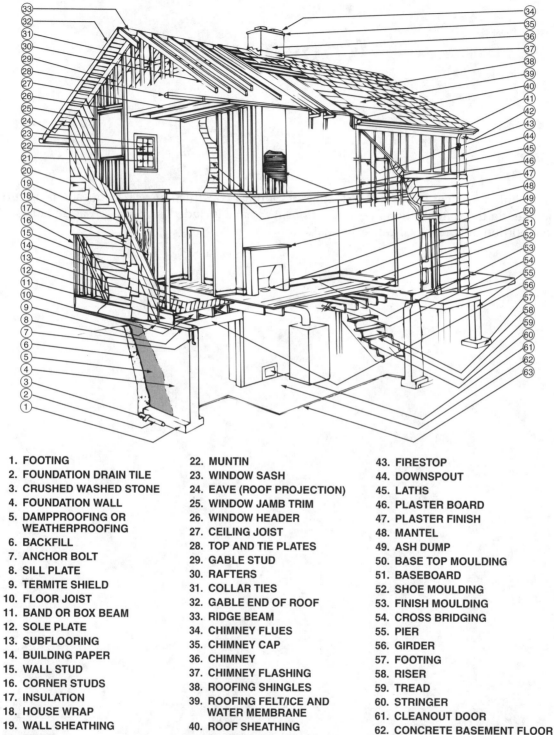

1. FOOTING
2. FOUNDATION DRAIN TILE
3. CRUSHED WASHED STONE
4. FOUNDATION WALL
5. DAMPPROOFING OR WEATHERPROOFING
6. BACKFILL
7. ANCHOR BOLT
8. SILL PLATE
9. TERMITE SHIELD
10. FLOOR JOIST
11. BAND OR BOX BEAM
12. SOLE PLATE
13. SUBFLOORING
14. BUILDING PAPER
15. WALL STUD
16. CORNER STUDS
17. INSULATION
18. HOUSE WRAP
19. WALL SHEATHING
20. SIDING
21. MULLION

22. MUNTIN
23. WINDOW SASH
24. EAVE (ROOF PROJECTION)
25. WINDOW JAMB TRIM
26. WINDOW HEADER
27. CEILING JOIST
28. TOP AND TIE PLATES
29. GABLE STUD
30. RAFTERS
31. COLLAR TIES
32. GABLE END OF ROOF
33. RIDGE BEAM
34. CHIMNEY FLUES
35. CHIMNEY CAP
36. CHIMNEY
37. CHIMNEY FLASHING
38. ROOFING SHINGLES
39. ROOFING FELT/ICE AND WATER MEMBRANE
40. ROOF SHEATHING
41. EVE TROUGH OR GUTTER
42. FRIEZE BOARD

43. FIRESTOP
44. DOWNSPOUT
45. LATHS
46. PLASTER BOARD
47. PLASTER FINISH
48. MANTEL
49. ASH DUMP
50. BASE TOP MOULDING
51. BASEBOARD
52. SHOE MOULDING
53. FINISH MOULDING
54. CROSS BRIDGING
55. PIER
56. GIRDER
57. FOOTING
58. RISER
59. TREAD
60. STRINGER
61. CLEANOUT DOOR
62. CONCRETE BASEMENT FLOOR
63. CRUSHED WASHED STONE

Glossary

This glossary has been designed as a quick reference to help students understand the language of the real estate profession. A complete vocabulary review before your state examination also will serve to bring together the many different facets of real estate that you have been studying. Some of the terms included may not apply to your state, as they may be regional in nature. Terms that you are less likely to encounter may not be in the text material but have been included in this glossary, both to aid your general understanding and to allow the glossary to serve as a resource tool.

As a quick aid, remember that words ending in "-or" are givers: donor, grantor and optionor. Words ending in "-ee" are receivers: donee, grantee, and optionee.

abatement A legal action to stop a nuisance. Also can be a reduction of a property tax assessment.

absorption rate The rate at which new or vacant space (such as office space) will become occupied.

abstract A history of every recorded document dealing with a property. It is examined to determine whether there is marketable title.

abstractive method A means of obtaining land value by deducting the value of improvements from the total property value.

abstract of judgment A condensation of a court judgment. When recorded, the judgment becomes a general lien on the property of the debtor within the county where recorded.

accelerated depreciation Any method of depreciation for tax purposes that gives greater initial depreciation than the straight-line method.

acceleration clause A provision in a note making all payments due on the happening of a certain event (such as missing a payment or selling the property).

acceptance An act or agreement that forms a contract.

accession Obtaining title as a result of attaching or joining property to other property.

accommodation party A third person (cosigner) who signs a negotiable instrument agreeing to be liable personally to the payee.

accord and satisfaction The act of accepting a different consideration than agreed; for example, if there is a dispute as to performance and one party accepts less than bargained for originally.

accretion A gradual buildup of soil by action of water or wind.

accrued depreciation Depreciation to date; measured by the difference between the replacement cost new and the present value.

acknowledgment A declaration customarily made before a notary, certifying that the signing of an instrument is the signer's own free act.

acre A measure of land equal to 43,560 square feet.

action in personam A legal action against a person. When recorded, a judgment from such an action is a general lien against all of a debtor's property in the county where recorded.

action in rem A legal action against property. When recorded, a judgment from such an action is a specific lien against the particular property involved in the action.

actual notice Personal knowledge of an interest or instrument.

ademption Disposal of property by a testator prior to death. It defeats the rights of a specific beneficiary under the will. (The beneficiary is not entitled to the sale proceeds or value.)

adjustable-rate mortgage (ARM) A mortgage bearing a rate of interest subject to change (based on a particular index, such as the T-bill rate) during the term of the loan. ARMs generally have caps on the interest that can be charged.

adjusted basis Acquisition cost less depreciation plus cost of improvements. The adjusted basis is deducted from the sales price to determine gain or loss.

adjusted gross income Gross income adjusted for a vacancy factor and collection loss.

adjusted market price The adjustment of a comparable property's sales price to account for differences in features and amenities of a property under appraisal (using the market comparison approach).

administrator A man appointed by a probate court to administer the estate of a deceased; a woman appointee is an administratrix.

ad valorem A tax according to value; real property taxes are considered to be ad valorem taxes.

advance commitment A lender agreement to provide permanent financing upon completion of a construction project.

advance fees Fees paid in advance of services rendered.

adverse possession A means of obtaining title from another by open, hostile, and continuous use for a statutory period of time. In some states, adverse possession also requires payment of taxes.

affidavit A statement sworn to under oath or by affirmation before a notary.

affirmation A formal declaration as to the truthfulness of a statement; made by a person whose religious beliefs prohibit swearing under oath.

affirmative easement An easement that allows the easement holder a right of use over the land of another.

after-acquired interest An interest acquired by a grantor after he or she has conveyed property. Under some deeds, after-acquired interest is said to pass to the grantee.

age-life tables Appraisal tables that indicate the economic life for various types of structures.

agency A contractual relationship in which one person (an agent) represents another (a principal).

agency by estoppel An agency created when the principal's words or conduct led another to believe in the agency and thereby act to the other's detriment.

agency by ratification An agency created by a principal approving an unauthorized act of another.

agency coupled with an interest An irrevocable agency under which the agent has an interest in the subject matter of the agency.

agent A person representing another, acting in his or her behalf.

air lot A described air space over a property that is subject to being transferred.

air rights The rights of a property owner to the reasonable use of the airspace over his or her property. Air rights are considered to be real property and can be separately leased or conveyed.

ALC (Accredited Land Consultant) A professional designation of the REALTORS® Land Institute.

alienation A transfer of property or property rights.

alienation clause *See* due-on-sale clause.

all-inclusive mortgage *See* wraparound loan.

allodial system Ownership by individuals rather than the government. The United States follows the allodial system of ownership.

alluvion Soil added gradually to land by action of water or wind (accretion). The soil belongs to the land it is added to by this accretion process.

ALTA (American Land Title Association) Also a type of title insurance policy providing extended coverage to the lender. The same extended coverage also may be available for the buyer.

alteration Modification of a contract or note by one party without the consent of the other.

amend escrow instructions A change in the escrow instructions after they have been signed. The signatures of both buyer and seller are required to amend the instructions.

amenities Features of a property that enhance the satisfaction and use of the property; for example, an extra bath, a flower garden, mature shade trees.

AMO (Accredited Management Organization) A management company that meets the standards of the Institute of Real Estate Management (IREM).

amortized loan A loan that is liquidated by equal payments.

anchor bolt A bolt that ties the mudsill (the lowest board in a house) to the foundation.

anchor tenant A major tenant, usually located at one end (or both ends) of a shopping center. Lesser shops benefit by being between or close to anchor tenants.

ancillary probate A probate for real property located in a state other than the domicile of the deceased.

annexation Adding to something, as when a city annexes outlying land.

annual percentage rate (APR) An interest rate expressed in simple interest considering all finance charges.

anticipatory breach An action or a statement of a party prior to the performance due date that indicates the party will breach the contract. The other party can bring suit upon anticipatory breach without waiting for an actual breach.

antimerger clause A clause in a mortgage that prevents loss of lien priority should the lienholder receive a deed. Otherwise, a deed in lieu of foreclosure would convey title subject to later liens.

appraisal An estimate of market value.

Appraisal Foundation Organization responsible for the Uniform Standards of Professional Appraisal Practice.

appurtenances Rights, benefits and attachments that transfer with real property; for example, buildings, easement rights, water rights, and the like.

appurtenant easement A beneficial easement that transfers with the land.

arbitrage Taking advantage of the interest rate differential by buying at one interest rate and selling at a higher interest rate by either land contract or the use of a wraparound loan.

arbitration A nonjudicial process for resolution of disputes whereby the parties agree to abide by a decision made by a third person.

ARELLO (Association of Real Estate License Law Officials) An organization of real estate commissioners from each state.

ARM (Accredited Residential Manager) A designation awarded to on-site managers by the Institute of Real Estate Management (IREM). *See also* adjustable-rate mortgage.

arm's-length transaction A bargain freely entered into without duress, undue influence, or collusion (deceit).

artificial monument A surveyor point for metes-and-bounds descriptions that is manmade, such as an iron stake, a fence, or a canal.

asbestos A mineral that was formerly used for insulation and in housing products. Asbestos dust is a hazardous material.

ASI (Assessment Systems, Inc.) An independent testing organization that prepares the Real Estate Assessment for Licensure (REAL) examination.

as is A phrase intended to mean that the seller does not warrant a property's condition. Such phrase, however, does not protect the seller in cases of concealment or fraud. Some courts hold that it applies only to readily observable defects, not to known but undisclosed latent defects.

assemblage The act of bringing adjacent parcels of land under one ownership; the opposite of subdividing. Assemblage usually results in an increase in value. *See also* plottage.

assessed value Value placed by a tax assessor.

assessment The process of valuing a property for taxation purposes.

assets Property owned by or owed to a business or person.

assignee (assigns) One who receives an assignment.

assignment The complete transfer of one person's rights to another. The assignee takes over the rights and duties of the assignor.

assignment of rents A mortgage clause that allows the mortgagee to collect rents during the foreclosure period. Could also be a transfer of rents to a third party.

assignor One who makes an assignment.

assumption The act of taking over the responsibilities for an obligation and agreeing to be liable personally for the obligation. A deficiency judgment might be possible against an assuming party.

attachment The legal seizure of property under court order prior to a judgment when there is belief that the property will not be available after judgment.

attestation The act of witnessing; to attest is to bear witness. Formal wills require witnesses.

attorney-in-fact A person operating as an agent (not an attorney at law) under a power of attorney.

attornment An agreement between owner and sublessee that the owner will recognize the sublease and the sublessee will pay the owner should the sublessor's interests be foreclosed.

attractive nuisance A doctrine holding the owner of land liable for injury to children due to the unsafe condition of property where property is likely to attract children as trespassers.

avulsion The sudden tearing away or loss of real property by action of water, such as a river's changing course.

axial growth City growth along transportation routes from the city center (resembles the spokes of a wheel).

back-end ratio The ratio of gross income to loan payments (PITI) plus long-term installment debt payments. (Used to qualify buyers.)

bailment Giving possession of personal property to another but retaining title; for example, storing goods in a warehouse, renting a trailer, giving existing mortgages to a lender as security for a loan.

balance sheet A financial statement showing assets and liabilities. The balance sheet shows net worth.

balloon payment A final installment of an unamortized loan that exceeds the previous payments.

band of investment method A procedure to determine the capitalization rate to be used for a particular property under the income approach.

banker's interest Interest based on a 30-day month and a 360-day year.

bankruptcy A legal procedure to eliminate unsecured debts. To eliminate secured debts, the security must be surrendered.

bargain and sale deed A deed for consideration that uses the terms *bargain* and *sale*. It contains no warranties other than an implied interest by the grantor.

baseboard A molding placed against the wall on the floor around a room.

base lines The principal east and west surveyor lines established by government survey.

basis (cost basis) Cost plus improvements less depreciation. Used to determine profit for tax purposes on sale.

batten Wood strips used to cover joints; used in board-and-batten siding.

beam A horizontal structural member giving support to a structure.

bearer paper A negotiable instrument made out to cash or bearer that can be transferred without endorsement.

bearing wall A wall with a footing under it that bears the load of the structure.

bench mark A marker placed by a government surveyor showing elevation above sea level and used by surveyors as a reference point.

beneficiary The person receiving payments under a deed of trust; similar to a mortgagee.

beneficiary statement A statement of a lender of the balance due on a loan.

bequeath To give personal property by will.

bequest Personal property that is given by will.

betterment An actual improvement (not a repair) to real estate.

bilateral contract A mutual exchange of promises whereby each promise is consideration for the other promise.

bill of sale A written agreement transferring title to personal property.

binder Insurance coverage given by an agent prior to the issuance of a policy or payment of a premium.

blanket mortgage A mortgage covering more than one property.

blended mortgage rate A refinance rate that is less than the current market rate but more than the old rate.

blind advertising An advertisement that fails to indicate that the advertiser is a real estate agent.

blind pool A syndicate in which the property to be purchased will be selected after the money has been raised.

blockbusting The act of inducing panic selling for gain by exploiting the fear of loss in value due to minority members moving into an area. Blockbusting is illegal under the Civil Rights Act of 1968.

blue-sky laws Security registration requirements to protect consumers against investments in fraudulent schemes.

board foot A unit of lumber measurement equal to 144 cubic inches (1'×1'×1").

book value Cost plus improvements less depreciation taken; the value assigned an asset for bookkeeping purposes.

boot Money, personal property, or debt relief given to even off a trade. Boot is taxable to the person receiving it.

bracketing The process of selecting a value that lies between selling prices of comparable properties having more and fewer amenities; used in the market comparison method of appraisal.

breach The breaking of a law or contract.

bridge loan See gap loan.

broker A licensed agent employed by a principal for real estate transactions. Only a broker can employ a salesperson.

broker's net income An income figure that does not consider a vacancy factor, collection costs, or management expenses.

BTU (British thermal unit) The unit of heat needed to raise one pound of water one degree Fahrenheit. The BTU is used to rate the capacity of heating and air-conditioning units.

budget mortgage A loan by which the borrower pays one-twelfth of the estimated property tax and insurance payment with each monthly payment.

buffer zone An area separating different land uses, often a green area.

building line The setback from the lot line.

building permit Construction permit issued by local building inspector office.

built-up method A process for arriving at a capitalization rate by rating a risk-free, management-free investment and then adding for risk and management problems.

bulk sales act A part of the Uniform Commercial Code; requires recording and publication of sales not in the course of normal business. It applies to the sale of stock in trade when a business is sold. If the act is not complied with, the sale is void as to the vendor's creditors, who can then treat the stock as if the vendor still owned it.

bulk zoning Zoning for density with height, setback, and open space requirements.

bundle of rights All rights incidental to ownership, such as rights to lease, use, encumber, sell, exclude, and so forth.

business opportunity A business including stock, fixtures, and goodwill.

buydown A financing technique in which a seller makes a property more attractive by paying a lender points to lower the effective interest rate on a mortgage.

buyer agency Agency where agent is the buyer's representative rather than the seller's agent.

buyer's agent An agent representing the buyer rather than the seller.

buyers' market A market condition characterized by more sellers than buyers, so buyers have a more commanding position.

bylaws The rules of how a corporation shall be governed; sets forth the authority of its officers.

cap A limit, usually on the interest rate or rate increases, on an adjustable-rate mortgage (ARM).

capital asset A physical asset such as land, a building, and equipment, usually for a business or trade. Capital assets other than land may be depreciated.

capital gain Profit from the sale of a business or an investment property. Under the Taxpayer Relief Act of 1997, capital gains held over one year are treated favorably for income tax purposes.

capitalization method An appraisal approach whereby the net income of an investment property is capitalized to determine its value (the net income is divided by a capitalization rate).

capitalization rate A desired rate of return for an investment that is divided into the net income to determine a property's value.

capital loss Loss from a sale of a capital asset or other real property. (For tax purposes, there is no deductible loss from the sale of a residence, although a gain is taxable.)

cash flow The net spendable cash remaining after all cash outlays are subtracted from the gross income.

caveat emptor "Let the buyer beware." This old rule has been modified by consumer rights laws.

CCIM (Certified Commercial Investment Member) A professional designation of the Commercial Investment Real Estate Institute (CIREI).

CC&Rs *See* restrictive covenants.

certificate of eligibility Obtained by the veteran to be eligible for a VA loan. The veteran must submit discharge information.

certificate of occupancy Frequently required before a new structure can be occupied; usually provided by the building inspector.

certificate of reasonable value (CRV) An appraisal required for VA loans.

certificate of title Evidence of title issued by a registrar under the Torrens title system.

chain A surveyor measurement of 66 feet.

chain of title The history of a property showing all conveyances from the original government conveyance (called the *patent*).

chattel An item of personal property.

chattel mortgage A mortgage of personal property; generally has been replaced by financing statements under the Uniform Commercial Code.

chattel real A personal property interest in real property, such as a lease, mortgage, trust deed, land contract, or share in a real estate syndicate.

check A 24-mile-by-24-mile area formed by guide meridians and parallels under government survey that correct for the curvature of the earth.

Civil Rights Act of 1866 Law that prohibits race discrimination in housing.

Civil Rights Act of 1964 Law that prohibits discrimination in government-related housing.

Civil Rights Act of 1968 Title VIII of this act is known as the federal Fair Housing Act. It prohibits discrimination.

closing statement The final accounting showing all debits and credits in the sale of real property or a business; also known as a *settlement statement.*

cloud on title A claim, document, or discrepancy that casts doubt on the marketability of a title.

cluster zoning Zoning allowing units to be placed close together but with green areas so the density is maintained.

codicil An amendment to a will that requires the same formalities as the will itself.

coinsurance A requirement that a property carry a minimum coverage (usually 80 percent of replacement cost) in order to collect 100 percent of the loss. If a person carries a lesser percentage of the amount required, that person receives only that percentage of the loss suffered.

collateral Property that secures a loan.

collaterally secured Secured by other loans.

color of title Because of a defect, having only the appearance of title instead of true title; for example, a title under a forged deed.

commercial acre The amount left in an acre after deducting land for streets and walks; less than 43,560 square feet.

commingling The act of mixing personal funds and a principal's funds; considered grounds for disciplinary action.

commission An agent's fee or percentage for successfully completing a sale or lease.

common elements Areas in a common interest subdivision owned in common with other owners and used by all of the owners.

common law The unwritten law of England established by court precedent. English common law is the basis for U.S. statutory real estate law.

community property Property acquired during marriage that is considered equally owned by both spouses. Presently, community property states are Arizona, California, Idaho, Louisiana, Nevada, New Mexico, Texas, Washington, Wisconsin, and Hawaii.

compaction The compressing of soil so that it will support a structure.

company dollar The broker's share of the gross commission earned before expenses.

comparables Properties used to estimate the value of a property using the sales comparison method.

comparative market analysis An estimated sale price prepared by an agent using recent comparable sales to indicate the likely sales price of a property.

comparative unit method An appraisal method to determine replacement cost. In general, the method is based on current price per square foot or cubic foot of similar construction.

compensating balance The requirement of a lender that a borrower keep a specified balance on deposit with the lender.

compensatory damages Money damages awarded to indemnify the injured party for a loss because of another's wrongful act.

complete escrow An escrow for which everything necessary to be done has been accomplished.

competitive market analysis An appraisal prepared by an agent using recent comparable sales to indicate the likely sales price of a property.

compound interest Interest that compounds on interest as well as principal. Because interest is paid monthly on standard real estate loans, it is simple, not compound, interest.

Comprehensive Environmental Response, Compensation, and Liability Act (CERCLA) Federal law that sets forth responsibility for environmental cleanup of hazardous sites.

comps *See* comparables.

computerized loan origination (CLO) Requires disclosure of any fees and that fees can be saved by applying direct to lenders. Loan application through the Internet.

concentric circle growth City growth in rings from the city center.

concurrent estates More than one estate in the same real property at the same time (one person could have a fee simple interest and another, a leasehold estate).

condemnation (1) The legal action to take property for public use by eminent domain. (2) The process of declaring property unfit for use.

conditional loan commitment A promise to make a loan on a property to a buyer yet unknown, so long as the buyer otherwise qualifies for the loan.

conditional sales contract A security sales agreement for the sale of personal property where title remains with the vendor (the vendee has possession). Title is transferred only when goods are paid for (has generally been replaced by financing statements).

conditional use permit Special permission for a use not otherwise allowable under the zoning but considered under special criteria in the zoning.

condition precedent A condition that must happen prior to the vesting of title in another. Until the condition occurs, title remains with the grantor.

condition subsequent A transfer of title with the requirement that a specified condition be met. If the condition is breached, the grantor must declare a forfeiture and retake the property within a reasonable period of time.

condominium A vertical subdivision with common ownership of land and common areas and individual ownership of the units.

conforming loan A loan that meets the purchase requirements of Fannie Mae or Freddie Mac.

conservation easement Negative easement requiring that land be kept in a natural or agricultural state.

conservator A person appointed by the probate court to manage and protect the assets of one who is unable to handle his or her own affairs.

consideration Something of value given or promised in exchange for a promise, an act, or property of another. A promise made without consideration is deemed void and unenforceable. Love and affection, although deemed good consideration, are not regarded as valuable consideration to support a promise or an act of another.

constructive eviction An act of a property owner that interferes with a tenant's quiet possession, thus allowing the tenant to consider the lease at an end and to be free from further obligations.

constructive notice The notice given by occupancy or recording to subsequent purchasers or lienholders of a prior interest in the property.

contingent remainder A remainder interest in property that will vest only if some specified contingency is met, such as the holder outliving a life tenant.

continuation statement A statement filed with the secretary of state that extends a financing statement (personal property) for five years.

contour lines Topographical lines on a map that follow elevations. Lines close together indicate a slope, and lines far apart indicate a relatively level area.

contract An agreement, enforceable by law, between two or more competent parties for consideration to perform or not to perform a legal act.

contract of adhesion A one-sided take-it-or-leave-it contract. Courts will refuse to enforce oppressive provisions.

controlled business arrangement (CBA) A company that offers a variety of services such as title insurance, property insurance, mortgage banking, home inspection, etc. (one-stop shopping), through firms where the broker has an ownership interest.

conventional loan A loan made by a conventional lender without government guarantee or insurance.

conversion Taking property entrusted to you and converting it to your own use; a form of larceny.

cooperating broker A sale broker selling the listing of another.

cooperative An apartment structure owned by a corporation wherein each shareholder occupies a specific unit under a proprietary lease.

corner influence An increase in value of commercial property because of the additional traffic and exposure of being located on two streets.

corporation A separate legal entity whose shareholders are not liable personally for corporate debts.

corporeal property Tangible property (real or personal).

correction lines Surveyor corrections to compensate for curvature of the earth.

correlation Interpreting value by combining two or more methods of appraisal; also known as *reconciliation*.

cost approach A method of appraisal whereby the cost to replace the structure is calculated. Accrued depreciation is determined and deducted from the replacement cost; the land value is then added to determine property value.

counteroffer An offer from the offeree that rejects the original offer and makes the original offeree an offeror.

covenant A promise that runs with the land.

CPI (consumer price index) An index that reflects by its changes the changes in the purchasing power of the dollar; widely used as a measurement of inflation.

CPM (Certified Property Manager) A designation of the Institute of Real Estate Management (IREM, an affiliate of NAR).

crawlspace The space between the ground and the floor on a house not built of a slab or with a basement.

CRB (Certified Residential Broker) A National Association of REALTORS® designation.

CRE (Counselor of Real Estate) A member of the American Society of Real Estate Counselors.

credit A plus factor on a buyer's or seller's closing statement.

creditor One to whom something is owed.

cripple Vertical piece of 2″ × 4″ framing above or below an opening (window or door).

CRS (Certified Residential Specialist) A designation of the Residential Sales Council of the National Association of REALTORS®.

cubage The number of cubic feet in a structure.

cul-de-sac A dead-end street having a rounded end. It is desirable for housing because there is no through traffic.

cumulative zoning Zoning that allows the designated category of use as well as less restrictive uses.

curable depreciation Depreciation that can be economically corrected.

curtail schedule A payment schedule that indicates principal reduction of a loan for each payment.

curtesy A common-law right of a husband in the estate of his deceased wife. Some states have made this a statutory right to a life estate in the wife's property, whereas other states grant undivided fee simple interest in a portion of the wife's estate.

datum plane A surveyor's plane from which elevations and depths are measured.

dealer A person who makes a regular part of his or her income by buying and selling property.

debt capital Money raised by a business by borrowing through bonds or other debentures.

debit A minus factor on a buyer's or seller's closing statement.

debtor One who owes money to a creditor.

decedent A person who has died.

declaration of homestead A formal procedure of recording a homestead declaration. It protects the homestead from unsecured creditors up to a statutory amount.

declaration of restrictions A declaration of the restrictive covenants recorded by the subdivider. In each deed, the subdivider usually incorporates the restrictions by referencing the recording of the document.

declining balance depreciation An accelerated method of depreciation used for tax purposes whereby a percentage of the straight-line depreciation is taken from a constantly declining balance.

dedication The gift of real property to a governmental unit, usually by a subdivider, in order to gain approval. If the dedication is given for a particular purpose and that purpose is later abandoned, the land dedicated may revert to the grantor.

deed A document that conveys title to real property from a grantor to a grantee.

deed in lieu of foreclosure A deed from owner to lienholder. Unlike foreclosure, it may not wipe out junior encumbrances.

deed of reconveyance A deed given by the trustee to the trustor when the trustor has paid the beneficiary in full. It is used for trust deeds to remove the lien in the same manner as a satisfaction is used to remove a mortgage.

default The breach of a promise or an agreement.

default clause A mortgage provision that allows a junior lienholder to cure any default of a prior lien (and then foreclose on his or her own lien).

defeasance clause A mortgage provision that defeats (or cancels) the mortgage on the full payment as agreed.

defeasible estate An estate that can be lost should a certain event take place.

deferred maintenance Maintenance that has been postponed.

deficiency judgment A judgment obtained when a foreclosure sale does not satisfy a debt. Deficiency judgments are difficult to obtain in many states because of restrictions on them. In some states, they are not allowed at all.

degree A measurement for angles, used in metes-and-bounds descriptions. One degree (1°) is 1/360 of a circle.

delivery The actual transfer of an interest; requires the intent to make an irrevocable transfer.

demise The transfer of a leasehold interest.

Department of Veterans Affairs (VA) The new name for the Veterans Administration.

depreciation A loss in property value from any cause.

depth table An appraiser's table that determines additional value attributable to additional depth.

dereliction Land that is created by the recession of water. It belongs to the adjacent landowners. Also called *reliction.*

descent Hereditary succession by act of law when property does not pass by will.

designated agency (split agency) An agency where one salesperson in the listing broker's office is designated the agent of the owner. If the property is sold by the listing office, the selling salesperson would be the agent of the buyer.

designated broker The licensed broker who has the direct responsibility for the real estate activities of a firm.

desk cost The office overhead cost per desk. It is determined by dividing overhead by number of salespeople in an office.

determinable fee An estate that would end on the happening of an event that may or may not happen.

development method An appraisal method to determine land value where cost of development is deducted from estimated value after development.

devise The passing of real property by will.

devisee The person receiving real property by will.

devisor The testator or testatrix who transfers real property by will upon his or her death.

direct endorsement A lender authorized to make FHA-insured loans without FHA approval.

discounting a loan Selling a loan for less than its face value (common with second mortgages or loans bearing low interest rates).

disintermediation The sudden withdrawal of savings from lending institutions, resulting in a tight money market.

distribution The apportionment and division of an estate in probate after debts and costs have been paid.

documentary transfer tax Formerly a federal tax on real property conveyances that, when abandoned by the federal government, was adopted in many states; also known as *revenue stamps.*

domiciliary probate Probate in the deceased's state of residence.

dominant tenement An estate using the land of another under an easement. The easement is an appurtenance to the dominant tenement.

donee The person who receives a gift.

donor The person who gives a gift.

double escrow The use of one escrow to purchase and resell a property.

dower A wife's common-law right in the estate of her husband should she survive him. In some states, it is a statutory right, such as one-third interest.

downzoning A change in zoning resulting in a lower-density use or lesser use.

dragnet clause A provision extending a mortgage to cover future obligations that may arise between the parties; used in an open-end mortgage.

dual agency An agency created when an agent acts for the buyer as well as the seller in a transaction.

due-on-sale clause A type of acceleration clause in a note that makes all future payments due when a property is sold. It prevents an assumption of the loan. Also called *alienation clause.*

duress The use of force or threat to make a person act; makes a contract voidable.

earnest money A good-faith deposit made by an offeror with an offer.

easement The right of a person to use another's land.

easement by estoppel An easement created when one person's words or actions lead another to believe in the existence of an easement, causing the second person to act to his or her own detriment. The person who made the assertion will be estopped by court action from denying the existence of the easement.

easement by necessity An easement sometimes granted when there is no other possible access to a property.

easement by prescription An easement created by open, notorious, and hostile use of property for a prescribed period of time.

easement in gross A personal easement to use land of another where there is no dominant tenement being benefited.

ECOA *See* Equal Credit Opportunity Act.

economic life That period for which improvements give a return attributable to the improvements alone.

economic rent The rental value of a property in the marketplace.

economics of scale The savings possible by increasing production.

effective age An age placed on property for appraisal purposes based on the condition of the property. The effective age may be more or less than the chronological age.

effective gross income The gross income less the vacancy factor and an allowance for collection loss.

egress A way to exit a property.

ejectment A legal action to oust an encroacher or a trespasser.

elevations (1) Views of a structure from various directions on a builder's plans. (2) Height above sea level.

emancipated minor A minor who, under state law, may contract as an adult.

emblements Cultivated annual crops; considered to be personal property.

eminent domain The government right to take private property (title or easement) for public use. It is not under the police power, for the owner is paid for the property taken.

employee A person who works under the direction and supervision of an employer.

enabling act A legislative act that confers power on local governments that they would not have otherwise. Zoning and planning powers were given under enabling acts.

encapsulation Sealing off hazardous substances, such as painting over lead paint.

encroachment A trespass by placing an improvement on or over the land of another.

encumbrance Anything that affects title or limits use, such as liens, easements, or restrictions.

endorsement The signature of a holder on the back of a negotiable instrument.

entitlement That portion of the loan the VA guarantees.

environmental impact report (EIR) A report required for projects that may have a significant effect on the environment.

Environmental Protection Agency (EPA) An agency that enforces federal environmental standards.

Equal Credit Opportunity Act (ECOA) A federal act that prohibits credit discrimination based on age, sex, race, or marital status.

equal dignities rule If an act must be in writing, the agency agreement appointing someone to perform the act must also be in writing.

equilibrium point The price that results in a number of buyers equal to the goods available.

equalization factor A factor to bring into line low assessed valuations in some areas. The value is multiplied by the factor to determine the value that the tax rate will be applied to.

equitable title An interest in property prior to receipt of legal title. Examples would be a trustor under a trust deed, or a buyer under a sales contract (land contract).

equity (1) The difference between the value of a property and the liens against it. (2) That which is right or just.

equity capital Money raised by a business through selling shares in the business.

equity of redemption The right of a mortgagor to redeem during and after foreclosure; governed by state statute.

erosion The wearing away of soil by acts of wind and/or water.

errors and omissions insurance Malpractice insurance carried by brokers and salespeople.

escalator clause A contract or lease provision allowing for payments to rise or fall.

escape clause Lets a party out of contract responsibilities in the event of stated situations.

escheat The reversion of property to the state when a person dies intestate and without known heirs.

escrow A neutral depository that handles real estate closings as agent for the buyer and the seller.

escrow account *See* impound account.

estate An interest in property.

estate at will A leasehold estate for an undetermined time period; may be terminated at any time by the lessor or lessee. Most states require a statutory notice period.

estate for life A freehold interest whereby a person has property for his or her life or the life of another named person. The life tenant cannot encumber the property beyond his or her interest. At the end of the estate, the interest either reverts back to the grantor or passes as a remainder interest to a third party.

estate for years A lease for a definite period of time, the result of an express agreement.

estate of inheritance An estate that can be inherited, such as a fee simple estate.

estate on a condition subsequent An estate given based on a specific condition. Upon breach of the condition, the grantor can declare a breach and regain the property.

estoppel A doctrine whereby a party is barred from raising a defense when that person's acts or words induced another party to act to his or her detriment.

estoppel certificate Statement by borrower as to amount owed and loan terms and that he or she has no defense or offsets against lender (obtained when loan is to be sold).

estover Necessity that the law allows, such as the right of a tenant to use timber for fuel and repair needs.

et al. "And others."

et ux. "And wife."

eviction A dispossession by process of law.

exception in a deed An exclusion in a deed; deeding only part of a property.

excess land Land that does not contribute economically to use and/or value.

exchange value The value a property has as to other goods.

exclusionary clause *See* exception in a deed.

exclusionary zoning Zoning that excludes a stated use.

exclusive-agency listing A listing whereby the broker is the exclusive agent of the owner and is entitled to a commission if the broker or any other agent sells the property. If the owner sells the property without an agent, the broker is not entitled to a commission.

exclusive-right-to-sell listing A listing whereby the agent is entitled to a commission if the property is sold during the listing term by anyone, including the owner.

exculpatory clause A contract provision excusing a party for injuries to another; frequently used by lessors in leases. Exculpatory clauses do not affect the rights of third parties who may be injured on the premises.

execute To sign a document.

executed contract A contract where all performance has been completed.

execution of judgment The action of the sheriff in seizing and selling property of the debtor to satisfy a judgment.

executor A man appointed by a will to administer the estate of a deceased; a woman is an executrix.

executor's deed A deed during probate containing the warranty that the executor(trix) has not encumbered the property.

executory contract A contract that has yet to be performed.

exemplary damages Punitive damages awarded in excess of compensatory damages when an action was performed with willful intent.

express contract A contract that is stated verbally or in writing, as opposed to an implied contract, which is understood but not stated.

extended coverage policy Extends basic fire policy (fire, lightning, and smoke) to cover additional perils, such as windstorm, hail, and riot.

extension of a lease Continued occupancy under the terms of an existing lease. (A lease renewal is a new lease.)

facilitator (intermediary) A person working as a liaison betwen buyer and seller but without agency duties.

Fair Credit Reporting Act Allows a person to know what is in his or her credit file and to have explanations inserted and information investigated and removed if wrong.

Fair Housing Act *See* Civil Rights Act of 1968.

fair market value *See* market value.

Fannie Mae A private corporation that provides a secondary marketplace for mortgages.

FDIC (Federal Deposit Insurance Corporation) Insures bank and savings and loan deposits. The maximum federal insurance is $100,000 for an account.

feasibility study A study of the economic practicality of an investment.

Federal Land Bank A farm credit administrative agency that provides financing for farm purchases.

Federal Reserve System A federal agency that regulates the money supply, interest rates, and reserve requirements of member banks.

fee An estate of inheritance.

fee appraiser An appraiser who works either as an independent contractor or for an independent appraisal firm.

fee simple The highest ownership possible; has no time limit and can be transferred or inherited. (The word *fee* means an inheritable estate.) Also known as *fee simple absolute*.

fee simple determinable A grant that automatically ends should a property no longer be used for a designated purpose.

fee tail An estate in which conveyance is limited to the descendants of the grantee.

FHA (Federal Housing Administration) A federal agency that insures mortgage loans.

FHLB (Federal Home Loan Bank) Provides a credit system for savings and loan associations to borrow from.

fictitious name A name that does not include the surname of every principal in a business. To use a fictitious name, the fictitious name publication and recording statutes must be complied with.

fidelity bond Bond for employee covering employee honesty.

fiduciary The duty of trust and honesty of an agent to the principal.

filtering down The process in which housing passes down to lower economic groups.

financing statement An instrument filed by a lender on a personal property loan to give public notice that the goods are security for the loan (under the Uniform Commercial Code).

finder's fee A fee paid to a nonlicensee for an introduction only; legal in some states.

fire block A horizontal block between studs to prevent a fire from rising through a wall.

fire wall A wall built of fireproof material to limit or contain a fire.

firm commitment A loan commitment made for a particular borrower and property.

FIRPTA (Foreign Investment in Real Property Tax Act) Requires buyer withholding of taxes when the seller is a foreign national, except for exempt sales.

FIRREA (Financial Institutions Reform, Recovery, and Enforcement Act) Requires state licensing and certification of appraisers.

first right of refusal *See* right of first refusal.

fixture A former item of personal property that has become so connected to the realty that it has become part of the real property.

flat lease A level-payment lease with no escalation clause; also known as a *gross lease*.

floodplain Level areas along waterways subject to inundation.

floodwater The water overflowing a defined channel.

floor space The interior square footage measured from the inside walls.

FmHA (Farmers Home Administration) Now known as Rural Economic and Community Development Administration (RECD); insures, subsidizes, and makes loans in rural areas. Preference is given to veterans.

Fannie Mae A private corporation that sets the market in FHA and conventional loans by buying and selling loans.

footing The concrete poured in the ground on which the foundation rests. The footing distributes the building load to the soil.

foreclosure The legal procedure whereby the lender forces the sale of property to pay indebtedness in the event of default.

foundation The masonry substructure on which the building rests. The foundation rests on the footing.

franchise A right to distribute goods and services under a marketing plan established by a franchisor.

fraud An intentional act or omission to deceive another to the detriment of that party.

Freddie Mac A private corporation that serves as a secondary mortgage market and sells participation certificates.

freehold A higher-interest category of estates (fee simple and life estates), as opposed to nonfreehold estates, which are leasehold interests.

front-end ratio The ratio of gross income to total loan payments (PITI); used to qualify buyers.

front foot A linear measurement of land based on the number of feet fronting on a road (could also refer to water frontage).

functional obsolescence Obsolescence that is built in by design or by construction.

funding fee A fee paid by a veteran for a VA loan.

gable roof A roof in which the two opposite planes slope down from a ridge line.

gambrel roof A roof with a steep lower slope and a flatter upper slope; found on some barns and on Dutch colonials.

gap loan A temporary loan, usually at a higher interest rate, where the borrower intends to obtain better financing; also known as a *bridge loan* or *swing loan*.

GEM (growing equity mortgage) A mortgage with increasing payments, causing the principal to be rapidly decreased.

general agent An agent having all necessary authority to conduct a business or trade.

general lien A lien against all property of a debtor (for example, judgment liens and federal tax liens).

general partner A partner who is active in management and liable for the debts and actions of the partnership.

general power of attorney A broad power given by a principal to an agent that enables the agent to act for the principal. (A specific power of attorney allows the agent to act only in the manner and area specified.)

general warranty deed A deed where the grantor warrants title as to the claims of all others.

gift deed A deed given for love and affection. Creditors of the donor can reach the property if it can be shown that the gift was made while the donor was insolvent in an effort to evade creditors. A recorded gift deed does not take precedence over a prior unrecorded deed by the grantor for value.

gift tax A federal tax on gifts. Donor exemption of $10,000 annually per donee.

Ginnie Mae A federal corporation that provides assistance for federally aided housing projects that are at below-market interest rates. Funds are raised through the sale of government-backed securities.

good consideration Love and affection are considered good consideration for a completed gift transfer; however, they are not considered valuable consideration to enforce a promise to make a transfer.

good funds Closing funds where the checks have cleared; cashier's checks or certified checks.

government lot A portion of land less than a quarter section because of physical features such as lakes that limit the size of the lot. Established by government survey.

government survey The survey system used for most of the nation whereby land is measured from principal base lines and meridians and laid out in townships and sections.

grace period A period allowed for late payments without penalty.

graduated lease A step lease with payments that increase as of agreed-on dates.

graduated payment mortgage (GPM) A loan where early payments are lower and increase during the term of the loan, making it easier for young people, whose incomes are likely to increase, to purchase property.

grandfather clause A regulation that permits existing conditions or uses to continue despite new laws against them; applies to prior-use zoning.

grant A transfer of title.

grant deed A deed used in some states in conjunction with title insurance whereby the seller warrants that title has not been con-veyed previously and that there is nothing against the property that the seller knows of that has not been disclosed to the buyer.

grantee The person who receives the grant from the grantor.

granting clause A deed provision indicating that title is passing.

grantor The person who makes the grant to the grantee.

grantor/grantee index A recorder's index system by grantor/grantee name that makes it easy to research a title.

GRI (Graduate REALTORS® Institute) A professional designation that requires seminar attendance and courses of study.

gross income The total income before any expenses or deductions.

gross lease *See* flat lease.

gross profit Gross sales less cost of the merchandise. To obtain net profit, all other expenses also must be deducted.

gross rent multiplier method An appraisal variation to get an approximate idea of value where gross income is multiplied by a gross rent multiplier. It does not take into account unusual expenses.

ground lease A lease of land only; tenant puts in the improvements.

ground rent The portion of the rent attributable to land rather than to improvements.

ground water Underground nonflowing water.

group boycotting An agreement to refuse cooperation with another business to reduce competition.

guardian A person lawfully charged with managing the property of another who is legally incapable.

guide meridians North-south survey lines running east and west of a principal meridians. They are 24 miles apart.

habendum The "to have and to hold" clause in a deed indicating the extent of ownership being transferred (such as fee simple or life estate).

habitability Reasonably fit for human habitation.

hard-money loan A cash loan rather than seller financing.

header A beam over a window or door.

head lease A master lease under which the lessee subleases portions of the premises.

hereditament Any item capable of being inherited.

highest and best use That use which results in the greatest value for a property.

hip roof A roof where all sides slope to the eaves.

holder in due course A person who, in the course of commerce, takes a negotiable instrument good on its face for value prior to the due date, without notice of any defense of the maker.

hold-harmless clause One party agrees to indemnify the other for any loss suffered because of the contract or lease.

holdover clause A lease condition that provides for a very high rent should the tenant fail to vacate at the end of the lease, discouraging a holdover situation.

holdover tenant A tenant retaining possession after expiration of the lease. See tenancy at sufferance.

holographic will A handwritten, signed, and dated will. No witnesses are needed.

homeowners policy A comprehensive insurance policy covering fire, vandalism, theft, liability and other hazards.

homestead A home on which a declaration of homestead has been filed to protect the home from unsecured creditors up to a statutory amount.

HUD Federal Department of Housing and Urban Development.

hypothecate To give something as security without giving up possession.

illegal In violation of an existing law.

illiquidity An asset that is not readily convertible to cash. Real estate is considered to be illiquid.

illusory contract An agreement that appears to be binding but in which one party actually is not bound; not enforceable.

implied agent An agent not expressly appointed but implied by actions of the parties.

implied contract An agreement not expressly stated but implied by actions of the parties.

implied easement An easement implied when the grantor conveys property that is landlocked by other property of the grantor or where the grantor created the use, then sold the parcels separately.

impound account A reserve for taxes and insurance kept by the lender to which the borrower pays, along with regular principal and interest payments; also called an *escrow account.*

improvement An addition to property, such as a room or air-conditioning. Unlike repairs, improvements increase the cost basis of the property.

imputed interest An interest rate that will be implied for tax purposes when a note shows a rate of interest less than a statutory minimum (a person will be taxed as if the minimum acceptable rate was received).

incentive zoning Encourages particular improvements; for example, zoning that allows greater height if a public plaza is included.

inchoate right A right not yet perfected, such as a mechanic's right to file a lien or a wife's dower rights that won't come into being until the death of her husband.

incompetent A person who, because of age or mental capacity, lacks the legal ability to enter into valid contracts.

incorporeal property Intangible property.

incorporeal rights Nonpossessor rights in real estate arising out of ownership, such as the right to rents.

increment Any increase in value.

incurable depreciation Depreciation where the cost of correction is prohibitive.

indefeasible Cannot be voided.

independent contractor A contractor employed to complete a task who is not under the supervision or control of the employer.

index lease A lease tied to an index such as the consumer price index.

index method A method of determining cost of replacement by taking the actual costs when built and applying the increases in the construction cost index since that date.

informal description A description of property that is not a legal description, such as by street address or name of owner.

ingress A means of entering.

injunction A court action to cease and desist from a course of action.

interest rate The percentage of a loan balance charged by the lender for the use of money.

interim loan A short-term or gap loan.

intermediate theory (mortgage) A security theory where title remains with the mortgagor but automatically transfers to the mortgagee in the event of default.

internal rate of return (IRR) A method of measuring returns on investment that considers tax consequences.

interpleader action An action requested by a party to determine rights when two or more people claim to have an interest in property, such as an action brought by a broker where the buyer and seller each claim rights to a deposit.

Interstate Land Sales Act A federal disclosure act for projects of 25 or more unimproved lots to be sold in interstate commerce.

intestate Dying without a will. Property passes to the heirs according to state statute governing intestate succession.

inverse condemnation An action by an owner to force a government unit to take property when, by its action, the government has wrongfully restricted use.

investment contract A security in which the investor invests money with the expectation of profits from the efforts of another.

involuntary lien A lien imposed without the consent of the landowner, such as a tax lien. A mortgage is a voluntary lien.

joint and several The agreement to be liable together as well as separately.

joint liability The agreement that each party will be equally liable for an obligation.

joint tenancy An undivided interest with the right of survivorship. Owners must take title at the same time, by the same instrument, with equal interests, and with equal rights of possession.

joint venture A partnership for a particular undertaking only. It differs from a standard partnership in that a sole joint venture partner cannot obligate the other joint venture partners.

joist A horizontal board that supports a floor or ceiling.

judgment The final order of a court as to money owed. When recorded, the judgment becomes a general lien on the property of the debtor.

junior lien A subordinate lien as determined by the time of recording or the nature of the lien.

key lot A lot having a number of other lots abutting a side line (undesirable for residential use).

key money A payment made to the lessor to obtain a lease.

laches The doctrine that upholds the loss of the right to enforce an agreement or a restriction because the delay in bringing action worked to the detriment of the other party.

land contract A contract under which the seller keeps title while the buyer gets possession. Title passes when the property has been fully paid for. Also known as a *contract for sale*.

landlocked Property that has no access because of surrounding property and the absence of any easement.

land residual method A means to determine land value by deducting the value of the income attributable to the improvements alone from the value of the income of the property.

late charge A charge imposed by a lender for late payments. Late charges are regulated by state law.

latent defect A defect not apparent from a reasonable visual inspection.

lateral support The support a landowner has a duty to provide to the land of adjacent property owners.

lease A tenancy agreement between landlord (lessor) and tenant (lessee).

leased fee The leasehold estate of the lessor.

leasehold A lease estate in realty; a nonfreehold or possessory interest only.

legacy A bequest of money by will.

legal description A description of real property by government survey; metes and bounds; or reference to a recorded lot, block, and tract.

lessee A tenant under a lease.

lessor A landlord who has given a lease.

leverage The use of other people's money to make money. Purchasing real property with a minimum down payment is a use of leverage.

license A revocable privilege to use the land of another.

lien A monetary encumbrance that is secured by real estate.

lien theory The theory in a majority of states that a mortgage is a lien and not a transfer of title. *See* title theory.

life estate An estate in property for the life of a person that may not be inherited.

like for like An exchange of similar property that qualifies for a tax-deferred exchange; for example, real property for real property.

limited common elements Areas in a common interest subdivision owned in common with other owners but designated for the exclusive use of particular owners, such as parking spaces or storage lockers.

limited liability company (LLC) A business entity with limited liability that is taxed like a partnership. It avoids the restrictions of S corporations or limited partnerships.

limited partnership A partnership in which one or more partners have liability limited only to the extent of their investments. Limited partners cannot be active in the business management.

link A surveyor's measure equal to 7.92 inches.

liquid Cash or assets readily convertible to cash.

liquidated damages Advance agreement as to the amount of damages for nonperformance when exact damages may be difficult to ascertain. If so unreasonable that the court considers them a penalty, they will not be enforced.

liquidity Ability to turn assets into cash.

lis pendens A recorded notice of a pending lawsuit concerning a property. Though not a lien, lis pendens provides constructive notice that an action is pending against the property.

listing An agency agreement between owner and broker wherein the owner authorizes the broker to attempt to find a buyer and to agrees to pay a certain commission should the broker succeed.

littoral property Property located on the shore of a lake or an ocean.

littoral rights Rights of a property owner to reasonable use of lake, pond, or ocean water bordering the property. *See* riparian rights.

livable floor space The space measured by the interior of each room, excluding interior walls and closets.

lock-in clause A provision that allows prepayment provided full interest is paid as if the loan had gone to maturity; the borrower is "locked in" as to interest.

longitude and latitude Longitude is measured in terms of north-south meridians; latitude is referenced by lines parallel to the equator. Both are measured in degrees (°), minutes (') and seconds (").

lot, block, and tract system Legal description based on reference to a recorded subdivision map.

LTG (Leadership Training Graduate) A professional designation of the National Association of REALTORS®.

LTV (loan-to-value) ratio The percentage of the value (or ratio) that a lender will lend against a property.

MAI (Member, Appraisal Institute) A professional membership designation of the Appraisal Institute.

maker The person who signs a negotiable instrument.

mansard roof A French-style roof with a steep lower slope and a very gentle upper slope.

margin The different between the index rate and the rate of interest charged on an adjustable rate mortgage.

margin of security The lender's security that is the difference between the mortgage amount and the value of the property.

marketable title A title that is clear of objectionable liens and encumbrances; a merchantable title.

market comparison approach An appraisal method wherein value is based on sales of comparable properties.

market price The price actually paid.

market value The price a willing, informed buyer would pay to a willing, informed seller, allowing a reasonable sale time.

markup The percentage added to cost to determine selling price.

master lease The original lease between lessor and lessee when the lessee later subleases.

master plan Comprehensive land use plan.

mechanic's lien A specific lien by a contractor, subcontractor, materialman, or laborer for work performed or material supplied for a property but not paid for.

mediation A nonjudicial process to resolve disputes where a third party acts as a facilitator to aid the parties in reaching an agreement.

megalopolis An urban sprawl.

menace A threat of force that makes a contract voidable.

merger The joining of a lesser right with a superior right so as to extinguish the lesser one; for example, a tenant having an estate for years buys the property in fee simple, in which case the lease is extinguished because the owner and tenant now are one and the same.

meridians Government surveyors' north-south lines that intersect base lines. Land is measured from the intersection of these lines.

metes and bounds Land description by measurements and boundaries.

MGIC (Mortgage Guaranty Insurance Corporation) A private mortgage insurance (PMI) carrier.

mile A linear measure of 5,280 feet.

mill One-tenth of a cent, or 1/1000 of a dollar, written as $.001. Property taxes often are expressed in mills.

mineral, oil, and gas lease Lease rights to extract minerals, oil and gas for the lease period (a personal property interest).

mineral, oil, and gas rights The absolute right to extract minerals, oil, and gas (a real property interest).

minor Any person younger than contractual age.

MIP (mortgage insurance premium) FHA insurance.

misrepresentation A false statement to induce another to act. It makes a contract voidable at the option of the injured party. Unlike fraud, misrepresentation does not require intent to deceive.

mitigation of damages The duty of an injured party to use reasonable efforts to keep the damages as low as possible when the other party breaches a contract.

monument A fixed surveyor's marker for a metes-and-bounds description; can be natural (such as a rock or tree) or artificial (such as an iron stake).

mortgage A security device for real estate. In lien theory states, the mortgagor retains title and gives the mortgagee a lien. In title theory states, the borrower retains possession but gives the lender or trustee title as security.

mortgage banker Mortgage company that originates loans that are then sold in secondary mortgage market.

mortgage broker Broker who arranges loan between borrower and lender.

mortgagee One who receives the mortgage; a lender or a seller (under a purchase-money mortgage).

mortgage loan correspondent A firm that arranges the sale of existing loans in the secondary mortgage market.

mortgage note The note that reflects the promise to pay the mortgage debt. The mortgage is security for the note.

mortgage warehousing *See* warehousing.

mortgagor The owner or buyer of property who gives the mortgage.

mudsill The lowest board on a house that rests on the foundation. It is often of redwood to resist rot. Also called a *sill*.

multiple listing A listing, usually an exclusive-right-to-sell listing, given out to a group of cooperating brokers who are members of a multiple-listing service.

muniment of title Deeds.

mutual consent The meeting of minds required for a binding contract.

mutual mistake The mistake of both parties to an agreement. A mutual mistake as to fact allows a mistaken party to void the agreement.

mutual mortgage insurance FHA insurance that protects the lender against buyer default.

mutual savings bank A bank owned by its depositors and paying dividends, not interest, to the depositors. Located in several northeastern states, such a bank can make real estate loans anywhere in the nation.

naked title Legal title only, without another right of ownership; for example, a trustee under a deed of trust.

NAR National Association of REALTORS®.

narrative report An appraisal written in a narrative form; the most comprehensive form of appraisal report.

National Association of REALTORS® *See* NAR.

National Environmental Policy Act (NEPA) Requires an environmental impact statement

(EIS) on federal projects that can significantly affect the environment.

National Flood Insurance Act Legislation that makes flood insurance available in communities that have developed a flood-protection plan.

natural monument A surveying point for metes-and-bounds descriptions that is natural, as opposed to manmade; for example, a tree, rock, river bank.

negative amortization A loan whose monthly installments are not sufficient to pay the interest, so the principal increases.

negative cash flow An investment or a business that requires a regular infusion of cash because the cash outlay exceeds the cash receipts.

negative covenant A promise not to do something; for example, a restrictive covenant that prohibits detached garages.

negative declaration A statement that a development will not have a significant adverse effect on the environment.

negative easement An easement right that prohibits an owner from a use.

negative fraud Fraud resulting from failure to disclose rather than from an affirmative act.

negotiable instrument A written unconditional promise or order to pay a certain sum in money now or at a definite time in the future.

neighborhood An area of social conformity.

net lease A lease under which the tenant pays all operational and maintenance expenses, and gives the lessor a net amount as rent.

net listing A listing whereby the broker receives as a commission that portion of the sales price that exceeds the listing price. In some states, net listings are illegal.

net operating income (NOI) Gross annual income less operational costs (does not deduct for debt service or depreciation).

net profit The profit after all expenses (excludes payment on the principal of loans and taxes on the profit).

net spendable See cash flow.

net worth The difference between total assets and total liabilities.

nominal (1) The rate stated in the instrument. (2) A minimum quantity.

nominal damages A token amount awarded by a court when no actual damages result from a wrongful act.

nominee A new person designated to perform under a contract in the place of another. Unlike an assignment, where the original party maintains some secondary liability, the original person is relieved totally of his or her obligations by the designation of a nominee.

nonconforming loan A loan that fails to meet the purchase requirements of Fannie Mae or Freddie Mac; usually held by the lender as a portfolio loan.

nonconforming use A use existing prior to zoning that does not conform with the zoning.

noncumulative zoning Zoning that allows only a specified category of use (not less restrictive uses).

nondisturbance clause A mortgage condition by which the mortgagee agrees not to terminate the lease (if the lessee is in compliance with lease terms) in the event of mortgage foreclosure.

nonfreehold estate A leasehold interest.

noninstitutional lender A lender other than a bank, a savings and loan association, or an insurance company; for example, a pension fund or a private individual.

nonjudicial foreclosure Foreclosure under the power of sale provision of a mortgage or trust deed.

nonrecourse loan A loan for which the borrower is not personally liable (no deficiency judgment is possible).

note A signed instrument that acknowledges a debt and agrees to pay it either on demand or at a set date in the future. The mortgage or trust deed secures the note in real estate transactions.

notice of completion A notice filed by an owner that starts a statutory period in which mechanics' liens must be filed.

notice of default A notice given under a trust deed that sets the statutory period for the trustor to pay his or her obligations.

notice of nonresponsibility A notice filed by an owner to protect the property from liens for work authorized by another person; for example, a tenant.

notice to quit A statutory notice given by a landlord to a tenant to vacate the premises.

not-to-compete clause A clause in an employment or a sales contract that prohibits competition by former employees or sellers within a reasonable distance and for a reasonable time period. (If a court determines that the restrictions are unreasonable, such a clause will not be enforceable.)

novation The substitution of one agreement for another, or the substitution of parties to the agreement.

nuisance A use of property that interferes with the quiet enjoyment by others of their properties. An abatement action can be taken to stop (abate) the nuisance.

nuncupative will An oral deathbed will for personal property of low value. It must be reduced to writing by the witnesses. It is not valid in all states.

objective value Market value as opposed to subjective value, which is use value.

obligatory advances Loan advances required by a lender under an agreement as construction progresses.

observed condition method The method of determining the effective age of a property by its condition.

obsolescence Loss in value due to reduced desirability because of built-in design (functional obsolescence) or forces outside the property itself (economic obsolescence).

occupancy permit Permit issued by building inspector when a new structure has been completed in accordance with codes.

offset statement A statement by a lender as to the current status of a loan (balance due). *See* beneficiary statement.

100 percent location The best retail location within a community.

one-stop shopping A brokerage firm that handles financing and closing functions. *See* controlled business arrangement.

open-end mortgage A mortgage that can be increased in the future up to an agreed-on maximum amount. *See* dragnet clause.

open listing A nonexclusive agency whereby the owner agrees to a fee only if the broker is the first to procure a buyer under the exact terms of the listing or any other terms to which the owner agrees.

open mortgage (1) A loan that can be prepaid without penalty. (2) A mortgage in default prior to the foreclosure sale.

opportunity cost The loss of other opportunities by making an investment; for example, a long-term, low-yield investment could result in illiquidity whereby the investor would have to forgo a later, more attractive investment opportunity.

option A noncancelable right given by an owner to another to buy or lease a property at an agreed-on price within a stated period of time. To be valid, consideration must have been given to keep the offer open.

optionee The party who purchased the option and has the right to exercise it.

optionor The owner who gives the option.

order paper A note payable to a named person or order that allows it to be negotiated by endorsement.

orientation The way a structure is placed on a site.

origination fee The points paid to obtain a loan.

"or more" clause A provision that allows prepayment without penalty.

ostensible agency An agency that is implied by the actions of the parties.

overimprovement An improvement that cannot be recaptured by increased income or sale value.

package mortgage A mortgage that includes personal property as well as real property.

parol evidence rule The rule that bars verbal (parol) evidence from being used to show that a contract means other than what it says. Parol evidence can be used to clarify ambiguities or to show fraud.

partially amortized loan A loan whose payments over the loan term leave a balance (a balloon payment).

participation loan A loan agreement under which the lender receives a share of the revenue or profits in addition to the interest. The lender takes an equity share as a limited partner or shareholder as partial consideration for the loan.

partition A legal action to break a joint ownership.

partition in kind The splitting of property into separate parcels to dissolve a joint tenancy or tenancy in common.

partnership An agreement between two or more persons to unite for business purposes and to share profits.

party wall A common wall on the property line maintained by both owners.

passive loss A paper loss from depreciation.

pass-through certificate A certificate sold to investors backed by a pool of GNMA-insured mortgages. The principal and interest paid by borrowers is passed through to the certificate owners.

patent The original conveyance of land from the government.

patent defect A defect that would be obvious from a visual inspection.

payback period The time it will take for the income generated by a property to return the investment (down payment).

penny A measure for nails shown as the letter *d*. The larger the penny value, the larger the nail.

percentage lease A lease in which the rent is a percentage of the gross income.

percolation The ability of soil to absorb water. Percolation tests are required in many areas before a permit is issued for a structure requiring a septic system.

perfect escrow An escrow in which all signed documents and funds have been deposited with the escrow and the transaction is ready for closing.

periodic tenancy A rental from period to period that renews itself automatically unless notice is given by the lessor or lessee.

personal property Property that is not classified as real property.

Personal Responsibility and Work Opportunity Act An act that prohibits public benefits, including professional licensing, to illegal aliens.

per stirpes An inheritance by right of representation. Children share equally in the share their deceased parent would have received. This is different from per capita distribution, where all heirs obtain the same amount.

physical deterioration Depreciation caused by age and use.

pitch The slope of a roof; usually expressed in inches per foot. A 5-12 pitch drops five inches in each horizontal foot. Generally, roofs with steeper pitch have longer lives than more gently sloped roofs.

PITI Denotes that a payment includes principal, interest, taxes, and insurance.

planned unit development A development with individual lot ownership and shared ownership of common areas such as recreational areas; also called a *planned development project.*

planning commission A group of appointed officials responsible for planning and zoning.

plat A map or plan of a subdivision showing individual lots.

plate A horizontal board (2″ × 4″) to which studs are nailed. There is both a top plate and a bottom plate, called a *sole plate.*

pledge The depositing of personal property as security for a debt with another while retaining title.

plot plan The layout of a lot showing placement of the structure in relationship to lot lines.

plottage The increase in value from the process of assemblage (joining several adjacent parcels to form a larger parcel).

PMI (private mortgage insurance) Insures conventional loans.

POB The point of beginning in a metes-and-bounds description.

pocket listing A verbal listing not made available to other agents.

points A fee charged by the lender that amounts to advance interest, making up for an interest rate the lender considers too low. Each point paid is 1 percent of the loan amount. Each point received increases the lender's yield by ⅛th percent.

police power The power of the state to adopt and enforce laws to promote order, safety, health, morals, and general welfare. No compensation is given for financial losses resulting from the exercise of police power. It cannot be delegated to a nongovernmental body. Examples include zoning, health code, and building code enforcement.

portfolio income The passive income received from investments rather than from a salary or business.

portfolio loan A loan held by the lender as an investment rather than one made for resale on the secondary mortgage market.

power of attorney A written agency agreement given by a principal to an attorney-in-fact to act on his or her behalf.

PRE (Professional Real Estate Executive) A professional designation of the National Association of REALTORS® earned by corporate real estate executives.

preliminary title report A report indicating the present condition of the title and indicating the conditions upon which title insurance will be issued.

prepayment penalty A penalty for prepaying a loan prior to the payment schedule of the note.

prescription Obtaining an easement by open, hostile, and continuous use for a statutory period of time.

price-fixing Illegal practice of conspiring to set fixed prices for goods or services.

primary financing First mortgages and trust deeds.

primary mortgage market Characterizes the actual granting of loans from the lender to the borrower.

principal (1) One who engages an agent to act on his or her behalf. (2) A party to a contract. (3) A sum of money.

principle of anticipation Value changes based on anticipated future use and income.

principle of balance The highest value is created and maintained by a proper mix of land use resulting in the highest and best use for a site.

principle of change Real estate values do not remain constant.

principle of competition When extraordinary profits are being made, competition will enter the area and profits will drop.

principle of conformity A property will have its maximum value when it is located in an area of similar properties.

principle of contribution Improvements should not be made to a property unless the value of the property or rent is increased enough to justify the improvements.

principle of dependency The value of a parcel changes based on changes in the use of surrounding parcels.

principle of diminishing returns As demand is met, new units will result in a lower return.

principle of integration and disintegration Property goes through three phases of development: integration, equilibrium, and disintegration (growth, stability, and decline).

principle of substitution A person will not pay more for a property than the price of a property of equal utility and desirability.

principle of supply and demand The greater the supply, the lower the value; the less the supply, the higher the value. The greater the demand, the greater the value; the less the demand, the less the value.

principle of surplus productivity The net income remaining after allowing for costs of labor, management, and capital is imputed to the land.

prior appropriation A theory used in some western states that the first user of water has priority rights over later users of water from the same source.

private offering A real estate security offering that is exempt from state or federal registration. (Intrastate offerings are also exempt from federal registration.)

privity The relationship of parties to a contract.

probate The legal proceedings to pay debts and distribute assets of a deceased.

procuring cause The cause originating a chain of events that, without a break in continuity, resulted in the object of an agent's employment (sale or lease).

profit and loss statement A financial operating statement showing profit or loss for a designated period.

profit a prendre The right to take crops, soil, or profit from the land of another.

pro forma financial statement An estimated operating statement based on anticipated returns and expenses. It is used where no actual data are available.

progression The increase in value of a less expensive home resulting from more expensive homes being built around it.

proprietary lease A lease by a cooperative to a shareholder providing a right to occupy a unit.

proration To apportion based on actual time to the date of closing, as with taxes, insurance, and rents.

PUD See planned unit development.

puffing A statement of opinion given in a sale; not a warranty.

punitive damages Exemplary damages beyond actual damages awarded for a wrongful, willful act for the purpose of punishing the wrongdoer.

pur autre vie A life estate for the life of a person other than the life tenant.

purchase-money mortgage (1) A mortgage given by the buyer to the seller to finance the purchase. The seller is financing the buyer. Actual cash does not change hands. (2) A loan given to a buyer to finance a property purchase.

purchase saleback or purchase leaseback The investor buys property and sells or leases it to the original owner. Normally, a leaseback is used by an owner to free capital for operational purposes. A purchase saleback is sometimes used in place of a mortgage to provide greater security for the lender.

pyramiding Refinancing or selling property that has increased in value to buy additional or larger property.

qualified endorsement An endorsement of a negotiable instrument "without recourse." The endorser is not liable if the instrument is not honored by the maker.

quantity survey A detailed method to determine replacement cost by pricing out all the elements of a structure in the same manner as a builder would estimate costs.

quiet enjoyment The right of an owner or a tenant to use the property without interference.

quiet title A court action to determine ownership rights.

quitclaim deed A deed conveying whatever interest the grantor may have without making any claims as to ownership.

radon A colorless and odorless naturally occurring gas resulting from decomposition of radioactive minerals.

rafter A diagonal roof beam running from the eaves to the ridge of the roof.

RAM (reverse annuity mortgage) A mortgage in which the mortgagee makes monthly payments to the mortgagor. The loan is paid back when the property is sold or the mortgagor dies.

range A vertical row of townships, measured east and west from the meridian.

ratification The approval of an act of the agent by the principal when the agent exceeded his or her authority. By taking the benefits of the act, the principal also accepts its obligations.

real estate board An organization of brokers and associates (salespeople).

real estate investment trust (REIT) An unincorporated group of 100 or more investors who have limited liability. Under federal law, REITs are taxed on retained earnings only.

Real Estate Settlement Procedures Act (RESPA) A federal disclosure act requiring that a borrower be given an estimate of settlement costs and an information booklet. RESPA is administered by HUD.

real property Land and all that goes with the land (appurtenances).

Realtist A real estate broker who is a member of the National Association of Real Estate Brokers.

REALTOR® A member of the National Association of REALTORS®.

recapture clause A provision in a percentage lease that gives the lessor the right to terminate the lease if a specified volume of sales is not reached.

reconciliation The process whereby an appraiser assigns various weights to value determined by different appraisal methods (correlation).

reconveyance deed The deed from the trustee returning title to the trustor when the trustor has satisfied the debt to the beneficiary.

recordation The act of recording with the county recorder so as to give constructive notice to all of the instruments recorded.

recorded lot, block, and tract system A legal description based on recorded subdivision description.

recovery fund A fund maintained by many state real estate departments to repay persons who suffer losses because of wrongful acts of licensees. Recovery is up to a statutory limit and usually requires an uncollected judgment against the licensee.

redemption right The right of the mortgagor to redeem the property after a foreclosure sale.

(Prior to a sale, it generally would be a reinstatement right.)

red flag Anything that should alert an agent as to a property problem.

redlining Refusing to make loans within designated areas; considered to violate the Civil Rights Act of 1968.

reformation A court action to rectify a mistake in a deed or contract so it reads as it was intended to read.

regression A loss in value because a home was placed in an area of less expensive homes.

Regulation Z That portion of the Consumer Protection Act of 1968 known as the Truth-in-Lending Act.

rehabilitation Repair without changing.

release clause A provision in a blanket encumbrance allowing separate releases from the encumbrance by paying a stated sum of money.

reliction *See* dereliction.

remainder depreciation The depreciation that an owner has left to take.

remainder interest An interest that a third person has in property after the death of a life tenant.

renewal of lease An extension of a lease that continues the old lease.

REO (real estate owned) Refers to property that is lender owned as the result of a foreclosure.

replacement cost The cost of replacing a structure of the same desirability and utility values using modern methods and materials.

reproduction cost The cost to reproduce a structure exactly with the same design and materials.

rescission of contract Setting aside the contract and placing the parties back in the conditions they were in prior to the contract (as opposed to a waiver, which leaves them as they are).

reservation The retention of a right, such as an easement, when property is conveyed. (An exception retains part of the property.)

reserve for replacement A reserve fund established to replace an asset.

Residential Sales Council A division of the National Association of REALTORS®.

respondeat superior The doctrine that a master is liable for the acts of his or her servants. It applies to employees as well as agents.

restoration Returning to an original condition.

restricted license A probationary license granted by some states after a license has been revoked, suspended, or denied.

restrictive covenant A private beneficial restriction whereby an owner is limited as to the use of his or her property; for example, minimum size, setback, and height limitations. Also known as *CC&Rs (covenants, conditions and restrictions).*

restrictive endorsement An endorsement on a negotiable instrument that restricts any further endorsement; for example, "for deposit only."

revenue stamps *See* documentary stamps.

reversionary interest An interest whereby a property goes back to the original grantor on the occurrence of an event such as the death of a life tenant.

reverse mortgage A loan where the borrower receives annuity-like payments from the lender but the loan is not repaid until the property is sold or the borrower(s) dies.

rezoning Change of zoning, as opposed to a variance, which is an exception to zoning.

R factor The resistance factor used to measure insulation.

ridge board The highest board in a house, located between the tops of the opposing rafters.

right of correlative user The right of a land-owner to the reasonable use of underground percolating water (the water table).

right of first refusal A right sometimes given to a tenant to meet the price and terms at which the owner will sell or lease the property to another party. The owner must offer it to the holder of the right before a sale or lease can be made to another. In this case, the owner is not required to sell or lease, as he or she is with an option.

right-of-way The right to pass over another's land, as in an easement.

riparian rights Rights of a landowner to reasonable use of the flowing water located on, under, or adjacent to his or her property.

RLI (REALTORS® Land Institute) A land brokerage organization that is part of the National Association of REALTORS®.

RNMI (REALTORS® National Marketing Institute) A National Association of REALTORS® organization that promotes professional competence.

rollover mortgage *See* RRM (renegotiable-rate mortgage).

RRM (renegotiable-rate mortgage) A short-term mortgage where the lender will rewrite the loan, when due, at the current interest rate (rollover mortgage).

rule against perpetuities Requires that a private trust be restricted to a statutory life limit. (The deceased or grantor is limited as to how long he or she can continue to exercise control over property after death.)

safety clause A listing provision that grants the broker a commission for a sale made within a specified period of time after a listing expires, if the broker submits the name of the buyer to the owner within a stated period of time as a party with whom the broker had negotiated prior to expiration of the listing.

sale-leaseback A sale in which the grantor becomes the tenant of the grantee.

sales comparison approach *See* market comparison approach.

SAM (shared appreciation mortgage) A mortgage under which the mortgagee shares in the appreciated value of the property.

sandwich lease *See* sublease.

sans French for "without."

satisfaction of mortgage Given by the mortgagee to the mortgagor when the mortgage has been satisfied. Recording the satisfaction removes the lien.

scheduled gross income Gross income based on 100 percent occupancy and scheduled rents.

S corporation A small, closely held corporation that has elected to be taxed as a partnership.

seal An impression or a stamp to authenticate the signature on a document, which is required in some states on formal documents. Generally, "(seal)" or the letters "L.S." are sufficient. (L.S., *locus sigilli*, is Latin for "place of the seal.")

seasoned loan A loan with a payment history. Such a loan is desirable on the secondary mortgage market.

secondary financing Second mortgages or trust deeds.

secondary mortgage market Describes the buying and selling of existing mortgages.

secret profit An undisclosed profit of the agent, regardless of the amount.

section A parcel of land one mile square containing 640 acres, formed by government survey.

security An investment where the investor invests money but has no control or management over the investment.

security agreement A security interest that a creditor retains in personal property of a debtor (under the Uniform Commercial Code).

seisin Possession by one who claims rightful ownership.

sellers' market A market condition characterized by more buyers than sellers, so sellers have a more commanding position.

send-out slip An agreement that if a broker discloses a property to a prospective buyer, the buyer will negotiate for that property only through that broker.

separate property Property owned individually by a spouse in which the other spouse has no interest.

servicing a loan The business of loan collection, maintaining impound accounts and record-keeping.

servient tenement An estate that is used by another under an easement.

setback The building line distance from the lot line.

severalty ownership Ownership by one person or entity alone.

sheathing A covering over studs and rafters, which may be plywood, board, or composition board, over which the siding or roofing is placed.

sheriff's deed A deed given by the sheriff when property is sold for execution of a judgment or sheriff's foreclosure sale.

Sherman Antitrust Act Federal law that makes price-fixing, market allocation agreements, and other actions to reduce competition illegal.

short rate refund A less-than-prorated refund received by an insured who cancels an insurance policy.

short sale A sale where the lender agrees to accept sales proceeds for the debt because sale price is less than the amount owed. (Where mortgage exceeds value it is known as an *upside-down-sale*.)

SIOR (Society of Industrial and Office REALTORS®) A National Association of REALTORS® subsidiary organization. The SIOR designation is earned by the members.

situs The preference of buyers for particular areas.

soil pipe The sewage pipe carrying waste from a building to the sewer or septic system.

solar easement Easement of light.

Soldiers and Sailors Civil Relief Act A law that restricts foreclosure on a person in military service.

special agent An agency in which the agent is authorized to perform only designated acts (specific agency).

special assessment A charge against a property for a specific improvement such as a street or sewer; usually assessed on a front-foot basis.

special warranty deed A deed in which the seller warrants title only as to defects arising during the grantor's ownership.

specific lien A lien against a particular property only, as opposed to a general lien, which applies to all property of the debtor.

specific performance The legal remedy of requiring a party to perform as agreed; ordinarily granted when money damages are inadequate.

spite fence A fence that exceeds statutory height; considered a nuisance.

split rate The use of separate capitalization rates for land and improvements.

spot survey A survey that shows the location and outline of improvements, easements, and encroachments.

spot zoning Small areas of zoning use that do not fit with the general use of the area (frequently resulting from political influence).

square footage The measurement arrived at by taking exterior dimensions, excluding the garage.

SRA (Senior Residential Appraiser) A designation of the Appraisal Institute.

stagflation Inflation without economic growth.

standard parallels East-west survey lines that run north and south of the baseline. They are 24 miles apart.

stare decisis The legal principle stating that previous decisions (precedent) should be considered by the courts.

Starker exchange A delayed exchange where the exchange property must be designated within 45 days of closing on the first property, and the exchange must be completed within 180 days of the closing on the first property.

statute of frauds Legislation requiring that certain contracts, including those dealing with real estate, be in writing to be enforceable.

statute of limitations Sets forth the time limit within which legal action must be taken or rights will lapse.

statutory dedication Dedication that results from the recording of a subdivision map that indicates land dedicated to public use.

steering The illegal practice of directing buyers to certain areas, based on race or national origin.

step lease A lease with graduated increases.

stigmatized property Nonphysical factors that effect desirability of a property.

stock cooperative project A cooperative in which each owner owns stock in the project and has the right to occupy a unit.

straight-line depreciation A method of depreciation whereby an equal amount is deducted each year over the life of the asset.

straight note A note on which interest only is paid, with the entire principal payable on the due date (a term loan).

straw man A substitute used to conceal the identity of an actual purchaser.

strict foreclosure Foreclosure by peaceful entry of the mortgagor without a sale (allowable in several states).

studs Vertical 2″ × 4″ boards in a wall; usually 16 inches on center (from the center of one to the center of the next stud).

subagent A person whose agency status was conferred by an agent, not the principal.

subdivision Land division in accordance with state subdivision laws.

subjacent support Support of the surface by the underlying ground.

subjective value The use value to the owner.

"subject to" mortgage An agreement that allows the buying of real estate without agreeing to pay an encumbrance. Buyer is not personally liable on the loan, so a deficiency judgment is not possible. Buyer must make payments, however, or lienholder will foreclose.

sublease A lease given by the original lessee, who becomes a sublessor. The sublessee is the tenant of the sublessor, not of the original lessor. Also known as a *sandwich lease.*

subordinate An agreement that a loan will be secondary to another encumbrance.

subrogation The substitution of one party for another as to his or her interests.

sum of the years An accelerated depreciation method; also called the *sum of the digits.*

supplemental tax bill A tax bill given when property is reassessed on sale to cover the increased tax for the increased assessment.

surface water Water not in a defined channel.

surrender The mutual agreement of the parties to end a lease. All further obligations of the parties are terminated.

survey A location or verification of property lines by a surveyor.

survivorship On the death of a joint tenant, the tenant's interest ceases to exist, and all interests remain undivided with the survivors.

sweat equity Equity earned through an owner's construction or improvements.

swing loan *See* gap loan.

syndicate Two or more persons who have joined together for investment purposes. A descriptive term for multiple ownership, syndicates may be general partnerships, limited partnerships, corporations, or REITs, although most syndicates are limited partnerships.

tacking on Adding a previous owner's use to satisfy the statutory period of use for an easement by prescription or a title by adverse possession.

take-out loan Permanent financing that replaces (takes out) a construction loan.

tandem program A program under which Fannie Mae buys below-market-interest mortgages at par value and resells them to encourage low-interest housing loans. Ginnie Mae makes up the loss between market value and par value.

tax base An assessed value of all taxable property within a tax region (Tax Rate = Needed Revenue ÷ Tax Base).

tax collector Collects property tax and conducts tax sales.

tax deed The deed given at a tax sale.

tax-deferred exchange (1031 exchange) An exchange of like-for-like property held for income or investment. Only boot received is taxed.

tax shelter A way of excluding income from taxes by such means as depreciation, which is a paper expense and can offset other income.

tenancy A mode of holding ownership or interest in property.

tenancy at sufferance A situation arising when a tenant holds over (continues occupancy) after expiration of a lease. Tenant is subject to an ejectment or an unlawful detainer action.

tenancy at will A tenancy for an indeterminate period.

tenancy by the entirety A form of joint tenancy for husbands and wives. Neither spouse can separately convey to break the tenancy.

tenancy in common Ownership by two or more persons, each of whom has an undivided interest without the right of survivorship.

tender An unconditional offer to perform (*legal tender* is money).

tenement Right that transfers with the real property.

termination statement A statement filed to remove a personal property lien from a financing statement.

term loan *See* straight note.

testate To die with a will.

testator A person who has a will.

tie-in agreement A requirement that a buyer of goods or services agree to purchase other goods or services as a condition of the original agreement.

tie-in sale A requirement that a buyer be obligated for further business (generally illegal).

tier A horizontal row of townships, measured north or south from the base line.

time is of the essence A statement that makes prompt performance mandatory.

time-share An interval ownership plan used for vacation property.

title Ownership. Title is passed by deed.

title insurance An insurance policy that agrees to indemnify the owner for defects in title caused by specified risks.

title theory The theory that a mortgage is a transfer of title to secure a loan and not just a lien (used in a minority of states).

Title I loan FHA home improvement loan.

Title II loan FHA home purchase loan for one to four residential units.

topographical line Line on a map indicating the contour of the land.

topography The surface elevations of a property.

Torrens title A system of registering ownership in which the court keeps the record of title and issues certificates of title.

town house Row housing having common walls with adjoining housing.

township An area established by U.S. government survey that is six miles square and contains 36 sections.

trade fixture Personal property installed by a tenant to carry on a trade or business; remains personal property and can be removed by the tenant any time prior to the lease expiration.

trading on equity Borrowing money on equity in property *in order* to invest it at a higher rate of return.

trespass A wrongful intrusion on the land of another.

triple net lease A net lease where the tenant pays taxes and insurance in addition to all maintenance and operational expenses.

trust deed The transfer of title from the trustor (borrower) to a trustee (third party) as security for a note to a beneficiary (lender).

trustee The third party who holds the trust deed.

trustor The debtor who gives title to the trustee as security for the loan.

Truth-in-Lending Part of the Consumer Credit Protection Act; also known as Regulation Z. It is a disclosure act requiring the lender to show the interest as an annual percentage rate (APR).

turnkey project Completed project from building permit to occupancy permit.

turnover The number of times an inventory is sold in one year.

ultra vires An act outside the authority of the person acting. That person is responsible personally for his or her actions.

unconscionable contract A contract that is so unfair or harsh that the courts will refuse to enforce it.

underimprovement An improvement that, because of a deficiency in size or cost, fails to achieve the highest and best use for the property.

undivided interest An unspecified interest in the whole rather than a separate interest in a particular portion of a property.

undue influence Taking advantage of another because of a unique position of trust, such as a doctor-patient or an attorney-client relationship.

unearned increment An increase in value that is not due to any effort of the owner.

Uniform Commercial Code A group of standardized commercial laws adopted in whole or part by most states. They cover negotiable instruments, as well as liens on personal property (financing statements).

Uniform Residential Appraisal Report (URAR) A form used for VA, FNMA, HUD, FHLMC and FmHA loans.

Uniform Residential Landlord and Tenant Act An act adopted in whole or in part by a number of states and designed to provide uniformity as to rights and obligations of residential tenants and landlords.

Uniform Standards of Professional Appraisal Practice (USPAP) Standards developed by the Appraisal Foundation with which appraisers for federally related transactions must comply.

unilateral contract A promise in exchange for an act; accepted by the offeree's performance.

unit-in-place method An appraisal method whereby cost is priced per unit, such as price per square foot.

universal agent An agent appointed to perform all acts that the principal can delegate lawfully to another.

unlawful detainer A legal eviction procedure.

upset price The minimum bid at an auction.

upzoning Rezoning to a more intensive use.

usury An unlawful rate of interest.

VA Acronym for the Department of Veterans Affairs (formerly known as the Veterans Administration).

valid escrow Escrow in which an agreement has been reached and there has been conditional delivery of transfer agreements (deeds) to escrow. Delivery is conditioned upon escrow receiving all required funds and/or liens.

valley An internal angle in a roof. Metalwork often is used in a valley to prevent leaks.

variance An exception to zoning.

vendee The buyer.

vendor The seller.

verification A sworn statement before an officer of the court as to the correctness of the contents of an instrument.

vested A present or sure interest that cannot be revoked.

vested remainder A remainder interest that cannot be defeated, such as a remainder interest to a life estate. The remainder holder or heirs are bound to get the property.

void Having no legal effect.

voidable Capable of being voided by one party only; valid until voided.

voluntary lien A lien, such as a mortgage, placed by an owner.

wainscoting The treatment of the lower portion of a wall in a different manner than the rest of the wall; half paneling.

waive To give up or relinquish a right.

waiver Accepting something less than contracted for. A waiver leaves the parties as they are. Rescission places them back as they were.

walk-through Buyer's final inspection of property prior to closing of a sale.

warehousing The practice of mortgage companies of accumulating a stock of mortgages and borrowing on them until they can be sold.

warranty deed A deed under which the grantor warrants the marketability of the title. *See* general warranty deed, special warranty deed.

waste Destruction or damage to a property (usually by a tenant).

wetlands Marsh or swampland where the water table is close to or at the surface. They are protected from development by federal and state conservation regulations.

WCR (Women's Council of Relators®) A subsidiary organization of the National Association of Realtors®.

wild document A recorded deed or lien on a property outside the chain of title (placed by one not having a recorded interest in the property).

will Testamentary statement.

wraparound loan A loan written for the amount of both junior and senior liens. The borrower makes the entire payment to the lienholder, who then makes the payment on the senior encumbrance. Also called an *all-inclusive mortgage*.

zero interest loan A loan in which the seller buys down the interest rate to zero; usually a short-term loan.

zero lot line A building can be erected to the edge of the property.

zoning City or county regulation on land use; considered to be an exercise of police power

INDEX